The Bible Believer's Guide To

DISPENSATIONALISM

The Bible Believer's Guide To

DISPENSATIONALISM

David E. Walker Th.D.

PO Box 464 Miamitown, Ohio 45041

COPYRIGHT © 2005
DAVID E. WALKER

All rights reserved. No part of this book may be transmitted in any form or by any means, electronic or mechanical, including photocopying, recording, or by any information storage and retrieval system, without written permission from the author.

ISBN 978-1-890120-35-1

Library of Congress Control Number
2005932695

Books By David E. Walker

The Bible Believer's Study Course
Basic Bible Doctrine – Volume One
Basic Bible Doctrine – Volume Two

The Bible Believer's Guide to Dispensationalism

In Memory of:

Dr. James A. Lince

Founder of
Blue Ridge Bible Institute
Valdese, North Carolina

Without his ministry and influence,
this book would not have been written.

CONTENTS

PREFACE i

PART ONE: *Introductory*
LAYING THE GROUND RULES

CHAPTER: **PAGE:**

1   DEFINITION, DESCRIPTION, AND DISTINCTION 2
    Why the Background 2
    Dispensationalism 3
    Covenant Theology 5
    "Dispensation" 6
    "Covenant" 11
    Dispensational Camps 12
    "Age" 14
    "Age" vs. "World" 16
    Eschatology 18
    Eschatological Views 18
    Incorrect Concepts 21
    Eschatological Schools of Thought 21
    Premillennialism 23
    What is Premillennialism 23
    The Tenets of Premillennialism 24
    The Characteristics of Premillennialism 24
    Amillennialism 27
    Blunders of Amillennialism 29
    Postmillennialism 30
    Cliques of Postmillennialism 31

2   BIBLICAL INTERPRETATION 32
    Private Interpretation 32
    Two Schools of Interpretation 34
    Allegorical Method 34
    Roots of the Allegorical Method 35
    Roots of Literal Interpretation 36
    Darkness Sets In 36
    Revival of Biblical Interpretation 38
    Literal Interpretation is Biblical 40
    Prerequisites for Proper Understanding 40
    Grammatical Principals 41
    Allegories and Parables 44
    Historical Principals 44
    Other "Basics" 48
    Three Applications 50
    Three Applications Demonstrated 52

3   HISTORY OF DISPENSATIONAL THOUGHT 54
    A False Indictment 54
    Summary of Anti-dispensational Rhetoric 56
    Dispensationalism, When and Where? 57
    Early Christian Writings 57

Dispensationalism before Darby ... 58
Progressive Revelation ... 59
Pre-trib Rapture in 3rd Century ... 60
Pre-Darby Dispensationalism ... 62
John Nelson Darby ... 63
Cyrus Ingerson Scofield ... 65
The Scofield Reference Bible ... 68
Clarence Larkin ... 70
Larkin's Greatest Book ... 71
Post-Scofield Contributors ... 72
Development of Hyper-dispensationalism ... 74
Ethelebert William Bullinger ... 75
American Hypers ... 75

PART TWO: *Polemic*
DISPENSATIONAL TRUTH

CHAPTER: **PAGE:**

4 SOME BASIC DIVISIONS ... 78
Dispensational Approach – A Must ... 78
Books of Old and New Testaments ... 80
Variations Between the two ... 82
Other Differences ... 83
Jew, Gentile, and Church ... 85
Kingdoms of God and Heaven ... 88
Numerous "Kingdoms" in Scripture ... 89
Kingdom of God defined ... 91
Kingdom of Heaven defined ... 92
Different Kingdoms ... 93
Harmonizing Kingdoms ... 96
Distinction within the Kingdom of God ... 97
Jesus Reigning Now? ... 100
Rejecting Literal Interpretation ... 102
The First and Second Advents ... 102
Contrasts Between the Two ... 104
Jesus Taught it ... 105
Both Advents In One View ... 106
Rapture and Revelation ... 109
Misapplication ... 110
Knowing the Day and Hour ... 111
Not Simultaneously ... 112
Summary ... 114

5 DISPENSATIONAL SALVATION ... 116
Old Testament vs. the New ... 116
Unscriptural Clichés ... 117
"Save," "Saved" ... 118
NSRB Correcting Scofield ... 119
Noah's Preaching ... 123
Scared of the Truth ... 123
Old Testament Faith ... 128
Israel and the Old Testament Law ... 129
Galatians "Catch All" ... 130
Romans Two ... 131
The Definitive "Works" Chapter: Ezekiel 18 ... 132
Luke 16 with Ezekiel 18 ... 133
More Evidence ... 133

Salvation in the Tribulation 147
What's The Big Deal? 147
Tribulation Salvation in Revelation 148
The Big Three 162
Tribulation Salvation in Hebrews 168
Bible Interpretation of Hebrews Six 184
Tribulation Salvation in Matthew 191
Salvation in the Millennial Kingdom 195
Transition Periods 197
Three Major Transitions 198
From Old to New Testaments 198
Salvation in the Transitions 201
Progression of Revelation in Matt.-Luke 203
Transitions in the Book of Acts 203
Why the Differences? 208
The Transition Books 210

PART THREE: *Expository*
COVENANTS AND DISPENSATIONS

CHAPTER: PAGE:

6   A BEGINNING SUMMARY 213
      Covenant Examination 213
      How Many Dispensations? 214
      Nine Dispensations 214
      A Brief Overview 216

7   BEFORE EDEN 219
      Too Much! 219
      Gap Theory or Fact? 220
      Gap Proofs 222
      Why "Replenish" 231
      An Argument 234
      The Original Plan and Purpose 242

8   EDENIC AND ADAMIC COVENANTS 246
      Why Eden? 246
      The Nature of the Covenant 247
      The Gospel of Eden 247
      The Adamic Covenant 249
      Covenant Overlaps 251
      Corrupted Seed 251
      The Sons of God 254
      Other Notes of Interest 258
      The Flood 260

9   NOHAIC AND ABRAHAMIC COVENANTS 261
      Starting Over Again 261
      Noah's Salvation 262
      The Legs of Peleg and the Tower of Babel 263
      The Abrahamic Covenant 267
      Circumcision – The Sign 268
      Abraham's Salvation 269

10 MOSAIC AND DAVIDIC COVENANTS 271
   A Nation With Laws 271
   What is "The Law?" 271
   The Captivities and Dispersion 275
   The Davidic Covenant 275
   Corruption 276
   Incentive For Virgin Birth 277
   David's Salvation 278

11 THE NEW COVENANT AND BEYOND 279
   "Line Upon Line" 279
   Two Applications 280
   To the Jew First 280
   For the Church Also 281
   The Church is Not Israel 283
   The Pretribulation Rapture 287
   2 Thess. 2 and the Imminent Return 288
   Why "Day of Christ?" 296
   Who is "he?" 296
   The Tribulation Period 298
   Chronology of the Tribulation 298
   Other Considerations 301
   Revelation 12 – The Man Child 301
   Rapture of Tribulation Saints 302
   Differences Between the Two Raptures 306
   The Millennial Age 307
   People in the Millennium 310
   The Eternal Covenant 311

PART FOUR: *Apologetic*
ANSWERING ERRORS

CHAPTER: PAGE:

12 HYPER-DISPENSATIONALISM 316
   Their Founding Fathers 316
   "Ultra," or "Hyper" 316
   What is "Paul's gospel?" 317
   The "issue" 318
   "In the Body, or Out of the Body?" 320
   "One Baptism" 325
   Hung Up to Dry 326
   Confession of Sin 329
   Fruits of Hyper-dispensationalism 341

13 ANSWERS FOR THE CRITICS 342
   Melodramatic Nonsense 343
   Pre-Trib before 1830 344
   1 Thessalonians 5 346
   2 Peter 3 – "Looking" 347
   Old Testament Saints "Born Again?" 348
   Preterists Psychosis 349
   Olivet Discourse Fulfillment 349
   "Day of the Lord" = 70 A.D.? 351
   The 2nd Coming of Elijah 352
   The "Last Days" are Gone 353

Amillennial Absurdity 355
In a Nut Shell 355
Promises to Israel, David and Abraham 356
Romans Chapter 11 359
The Amillennial "Millennium" 360
Tribulation and Millennium Together? 362
Two Questions Answered 362

EPILOGUE 367
BIBLIOGRAPHY 369
SUBJECT INDEX 375
NAME INDEX 383
VERSE INDEX 387

LIST OF ILLUSTRATIONS AND CHARTS

TITLE:	PAGE:
The Physical World and the "Ages"	20
Premillennial and Postmillennial Views	27
Dispensational Systems before Darby	62
The Underworld	84
Jew, Gentile, and Church	85
Kingdoms of God and Heaven	88
Trail of the Kingdom	95
Both Kingdoms "At Hand"	99
First and Second Advents Contrasted	104
Old and New Testament Compared	145,146
Dividing Books into Dispensations	199
Matthew-Luke Compared to John	200
References to "Darkness"	229
Local Church and Body of Christ	284
Four Accounts of the Tribulation	299
Post-trib rapture of Tribulation Saints	306

THE BIBLE BELIEVER'S GUIDE TO
DISPENSATIONALISM

Preface

The Bible is unlike any other book on earth. It is the book *of* God, and the book *from* God. It is a Holy book, and a living book (1 Peter 1:23). It is a book that *reads you* while you read it (Heb. 4:12,13).

It is also unlike any other book because it is the only book that people seem more interested in what it *means* or is *presumed* to teach than what it actually says! Enter the so-called "problem of interpretation."

Some think interpreting the Bible is relative and dependent upon *personal preference*. Others insist that various systems of study are necessary to find the right interpretation. Still yet, some go as far to claim that their church or organization has the only key to unlocking the Bible's meaning.

All of these views err tremendously. Joseph acknowledged the only one who can "interpret" when he said: "**Do not interpretations belong to God?**" (Gen. 40:8). Furthermore, Simon Peter declared "**that no prophecy of the scripture is of any private interpretation**" (2 Peter 1:20).

So, if "interpretations belong to God," and we are not to "privately interpret" the scriptures, how are we to *understand* what we read (Acts 8:30)?

The answer to that question brings us to the premise of this work. Namely, that God has given us a book without error, inconsistency or contradiction, and He has laid out a *method* that guarantees correct interpretation every time. This biblical method is actually God's system of validating His own word, and is known as "**rightly dividing the word of truth**" (2 Tim. 2:15). When one traces this biblical practice throughout church history he finds its most common name: dispensationalism.

A Christian employs this full-proof God-given process by "searching the scriptures" (John 5:39), and obeying the mandate for Christian stewardship found in 2 Timothy 2:15: **Study to shew thyself approved unto God, a workman that needeth not to be ashamed, rightly dividing the word of truth.**

The Bible Believer's Guide To Dispensationalism is divided into four parts. It begins by laying a foundation of definitions and descriptions. This is helpful to the beginner, and establishes a basis for further learning. Biblical interpretation is also presented along with the contrary views, so the student can weigh the evidence for himself.

Tracing biblical dispensationalism through the ages, part one also acknowledges the men in history that have "contended for the faith" (Jude 3) as well as those who have "corrupted the word of God" (2 Cor. 2:17).

Part two is the polemic section, where a few debatable topics are resolved. Here some of the basic divisions are listed as well a discussion about the controversial topic of "dispensational salvation."

In part three, a concise analytical breakdown of the covenants and dispensations are given, along with the vital events and teachings of each covenant. This section differs some because it probes into the "meat" (Heb. 5:12,14) of the word.

The last segment of the book is the apologetic portion. Here the opposing views of dispensationalism are refuted as well as heretical deviations of so-called dispensational groups.

A work of this sort is distinct and unique in that it is ideologically pro-King James. The author claims irrevocable authority for the Authorized Version, believing it to be "**the holy scriptures**" (2 Tim. 3:15). As such, it is the book God has entrusted us to rightly divide, and is indeed "**the word of truth**," and "**given by inspiration of God**" (2 Tim. 3:16).

May the Lord Jesus Christ do for the readers of this work, what He did for the disciples on the road to Emmaus:

> "Then opened he their understanding, that they might understand the scriptures"
> Luke 24:45

DISPENSATIONALISM

Part One:
INTRODUCTORY

LAYING THE GROUND RULES

CHAPTER 1

Definition
Description
&
Distinction

WHY THE BACKGROUND?

Before the Bible student can equitably plunge into a study of dispensational truth, there are some preparatory ground rules and guidelines that need to be established.

Just as some background notes on evolution, the new age, and different religions are helpful to the soul winner, so it is with a study of dispensationalism. To write a treatise on dispensationalism without reference to church history, what major authors have said about it, and what the majority of people are being taught about it, would not be considered thorough. Laboring through history and quotations establish the whole picture. To omit that would do you a great injustice. Furthermore, it would fail to give the background material needed to defend the truth. The view of truth is more certainly distinguished when all error is exposed and wiped off the lens.

Knowing that Satan is the great counterfeiter, the student of the word of God must be aware that Bible truths are often *perverted*. This is readily seen with definitions of Bible words, and additions of extra-canonical words. The former can be demonstrated with the word "dispensation," and the later with the word "sovereign." "Dispensation" has been altered to mean, "a period of time,"[1] and the word "sovereign" is NOT a part of the "authorized canon!" Satan also *counterfeits* his counterfeits. For example, some would say that since the words "trinity" and "rapture" are not found in the Bible, what they describe and teach is not true. This is ridiculous. If an extra-canonical word (like "trinity," and "rapture") explains a *true biblical concept* there is no harm in using it.

Since Satan did more damage with his tongue (Gen.3), utilizing *words*, (even *positive words!*) it is essential for the child of God to be "**sober**," and "**vigilant**" (1 Peter 5:8) regarding definitions, implications, and systems of Bible study. It is pertinent that definitions and descriptions are made clear from the beginning, so the student does not get lost in the high weeds of tradesman terminology.

DISPENSATIONALISM

Dispensationalism (except where it teaches that "men are saved the same in the Old Testament as they are in the New") is simply "**rightly dividing the word of truth**" (2 Tim. 2:15). Adherence to this type of Bible study:

> is the interpretive key that unlocks the pages of Scripture, opens the door for our understanding of prophecy, and orients our thinking about God's blueprint for human history.[2]

---

[1] Scofield Reference Bible (New York: Oxford, 1909) 5.
[2] "Dispensations," *Tim LaHaye Prophecy Study Bible*, (AMG Publishers) 10.

Dispensationalism as a system of theology has been defined various ways. One Reformed author defines it "as that system of theology which sees a fundamental distinction between Israel and the church."[3] That is true, but leaves much wanting. A true dispensationalist while "**rightly dividing the word of truth**" understands that there is also a distinction between the "**Gentiles**" (1 Cor. 10:32), as well as Israel and the Church.

1 Cor 10:32 **Give none offence, neither to the Jews, nor to the Gentiles, nor to the church of God:**

Ryrie summarizes:

> Dispensationalism views the world as a household run by God. In His household-world God is dispensing or administering its affairs according to his own will and in various stages of revelation in the passage of time. These various stages mark off the distinguishably different economies in the outworking of His total purpose, and these different economies constitute the dispensations. The understanding of God's differing economies is essential to a proper interpretation of His revelation within those various economies.[4]

The key word in understanding dispensationalism is the negative word "divide." Dr. Ruckman:

> In the second clause in this verse ("**rightly dividing the word of truth**"), is found the METHOD of Bible study, if it is going to be a scriptural method of study. This method is negative; you are to "divide" something. You are not to "integrate" anything, you are not to try to get anything (or anyone) "together," and you are not to "join together" what "God hath sundered." You are to

---

[3] Mathison, Keith A., *Dispensationalism* (New Jersey: P&R Publishing, 1995) 8.
[4] Ryrie, Charles C., *Dispensationalism* (Chicago: Moody Press, 1995) 29.

DIVIDE, you are to SEPARATE, you are to "put asunder" what God "hath not joined."[5]

Remember, *division* was behind Israel's crossing of the Red Sea; Gideon's three hundred; the cities of refuge, and the choosing of the disciples. Do not forget that the Lord Jesus Himself *prompted* division (see Luke 12:51; John 7:43; 9:16; 10:19). Dividing and separating is not *all* pessimistic and bad. It can be healthy and purifying!

While anti-dispensationalists attribute all Bible division to *men* (like Poythress: ". . . they divide the course of history into a number of distinct epochs"[6]), God Himself is the most ardent dispensationalist. In Genesis alone, we read of Him DIVIDING light (Gen. 1:4), waters (Gen. 1:7), the earth (Gen. 10:5), and the nations (Gen. 10:25).

Dispensationalism then, encompasses the complete system of Bible study known by the biblical phrase, **"rightly dividing the word of truth."**

COVENANT THEOLOGY

The contrary theological position to dispensational thought is covenant theology, which Poythress terms the "principal rival"[7] of dispensationalism. Dr. Vance summarizes:

> Covenant theology, like Calvinism, is a Reformed doctrine, not to be confused with sound Bible doctrine. In this system, two covenants, works and grace, govern the whole of Scripture. Some Reformed theologians have added a third covenant: the "covenant of redemption,"

---

[5] Ruckman, Peter S., *How to teach Dispensational Truth* (Pensacola: Bible Believers Press, 1992) iii.
[6] Poythress, *Understanding Dispensationalists*, 9.
[7] Poythress, Vern S., *Understanding Dispensationalists* (New Jersey: P&R Publishing, 1987) 7.

made in eternity between God the Father and God the Son.[8]

The "covenant of works" relates to Adam before the fall, and the "covenant of grace" relates to all men *after* the fall. It is based on the death of Christ. Covenant theologians, as most dispensationalists, teach that all men *after* Adam are saved by "**grace through faith**" in the finished work of Christ. We will later substantiate the fallacy and misconceptions of that claim.

Although the name "covenant theology" sounds appealing and biblical, it is tremendously deficient as a system of study. Pentecost aptly clarifies: "Covenant theology is woefully inadequate to explain the Scriptures eschatologically, for it ignores the great field of the biblical covenants which determine the whole eschatological program."[9] What good is a "covenant" system of study that overlooks and neglects *all* of the biblical covenants? Covenant theology fails to "**declare. . . all the counsel of God**" (Acts 20:27), and abandons the orders to "**rightly divide the word of truth**" (2 Tim. 2:15).

"DISPENSATION"

The word dispensation has been incorrectly defined by many, to mean "a period of time." Note:

> A dispensation is a <u>period of time</u> during which man is tested in respect of obedience to some specific revelation of the will of God.[10]

> <u>A period of time</u> under which mankind is answerable to God for how it has obeyed the revelation of God which it has received.[11]

---

[8] Vance, Laurence M., *The Other Side of Calvinism* (Pensacola: Vance Publications, 1991) 85.
[9] Pentecost, J. Dwight, *Things to Come* (Grand Rapids: Zondervan, 1958) 66.
[10] *Scofield Reference Bible*, 5.
[11] "Dispensation," *Nelson's Illustrated Bible Dictionary*, (Thomas Nelson Publishers; PC

Definition, Description, and Distinction 7

A dispensation is an <u>era of time</u> during which man is tested in respect to obedience to some definite revelation of God's will.[12]

It means the last dispensation; or, <u>that period</u> and mode of the divine administration under which the affairs of the world would be wound up. There would be no mode of administration beyond that of the gospel. But it by no means denotes necessarily that the continuance of this period called "<u>the last times</u>," and "the ends of the world" would be brief, or that the apostle believed that the world would soon come to an end. It might be the <u>last period</u>, and yet be longer than any one <u>previous period</u>, or than all the <u>previous periods</u> put together.[13]

A dispensation then is a <u>period of time</u> in which God is dealing with men in some way in which he has not dealt with them before.[14]

. . . a "DISPENSATION" stands for a "moral" or probationary" <u>period</u> in the world's history.[15]

The word "dispensation" is used in the Bible four times. In every case, it is obvious from the context that God is referring to a <u>period of time</u>.[16]

The authors quoted above made reference to "a period of time" because dispensations always occur *during* "a period of time." McGee states: "A dispensation *may* fit into a certain period of time, but it actually means the way God runs something at a particular time; it is the way God does things."[17] The fact of the matter is that most Bible teachers, and authors

---

Study Bible)
[12] "Dispensation," *The New Unger's Bible Dictionary,* (Moody Press, PC Study Bible)
[13] Barnes, Albert, *Notes on the Old Testament* (Electronic Database: Biblesoft)
[14] Ironside, H.A., *Wrongly Dividing the Word of Truth* (New York: Loizeaux Brothers, 1938) 6.
[15] Larkin, Clarence, *Dispensational Truth* (Glenside: Rev. Clarence Larkin Est., 1920) 21.
[16] Modlish, James, *Mystery of the Ages* (Port Orchard: Local Church Publishing, 1997) 7.
[17] McGee, J. Vernon, *Thru the Bible with J. Vernon McGee Vol. V* (Pasadena: thru the Bible Radio, 1983) 223.

(even if they *know* the word "dispensation" is not a "period of time") refer to it as such, and have for about three hundred years now. Nothing is going to change that. Ryrie makes a suitable point stating that "it is perfectly valid to take a biblical word and use it in a theological sense *as long as the theological use is not unbiblical.*"[18] Maybe so, and maybe not. Take the "theological use" of the Bible word "election." It is obvious that it has been perverted to teach Calvin's nonsense for hundreds of years now, insomuch as Bible believers seldom mention the biblical word in their preaching or teaching. Will the Bible word "dispensation" have the same fate as other Bible words like "perseverance," "tongues," "chosen," and "elect?"

There is no possible way you could force the definition of "dispensation" as "a period of time," unless you fail to examine the English text where the word appears (see 1 Cor. 9:17; Eph. 1:10; Eph. 3:2; and Col. 1:25). If you still insist it means "a period of time," you would create a "period of time" called "God!"

Col 1:25 **Whereof I am made a minister, according to the <u>dispensation of God</u> which is given to me for you, to fulfil the word of God;**

The breakdown of the word "dispensation" is as follows:

1. To distribute. Note the origin of the word:

> Dispense comes ultimately from Latin dispender "weigh out" (partial source of English spend) . . . It had a derivative, dispensare, denoting repeated action; hence

---

[18] Ryrie, *Dispensationalism*, 27.

"pay out, distribute," senses which passed into English via Old French dispenser.[19]

2. The English definition is:
    a. the act or an instance of dispensing; distribution.
    b. something that is distributed or given out.
    c. a specified order, system, or arrangement; administration or management.[20]

3. The Greek word "οικονομια" (oikonomia) comes from the verb that means to manage, regulate, administer, and plan. The word itself is a compound whose parts mean literally 'to divide, apportion, administer or manage the affairs of an inhabited house.'[21]

4. It is from this Greek word that we derive our English word, "ecumenical," and "economy."

Dispensations are closely related to "ages" but, as Ryrie states,

> the words are not exactly interchangeable. For instance, Paul declares that the revelation of the present dispensation was hidden "for ages," meaning simply a long period of time (Eph. 3:9). The same thing is said in Colossians 1:26. However, since a dispensation operates within a time period, the concepts are related.[22]

Dispensations then, are NOT "time periods," and they are not "ages." This is glaringly true when one considers the so-called "dispensation of the Grace of God." The burden of proof as to whether or not such a "period of time" exists is

---

[19] Ayto, John *Dictionary of Word Origins* (New York: Arcade Publishing, 1990) 176
[20] "Dispensation," *The Random House College Dictionary*: 382.
[21] "Dispensation," *Dictionary of Premillennial Theology*: 93.
[22] Ryrie, *Dispensationalism*, 27.

propounded by this question: Since when, was there *not* a "period of time" when God's grace was *not* manifested in some way or another? Grace was exhibited in the lives of Noah, Samson, David, and countless other Old Testament saints who lived **"under the curse"** (Gal. 3:10). If it was not manifested, there would be no children of Israel, no Gentiles, and no people! Old Testament characters were given grace dozens of times, even though they were NOT saved **"by grace through faith"** (Eph 2:8,9). [They could not have been saved by faith in the testament of Jesus Christ, because the **"where a testament is, there must also of necessity be the death of the testator. For a testament is of force after men are dead: otherwise it is of no strength at all while the testator liveth"** (Heb 9:16-17). How could Jesus be **"dead"** when he had not been born yet? To respond by saying Jesus was **"slain from the foundation of the world"** (Rev. 13:8) is to confuse the omniscience of God with the appropriation of the sacrifice to the sinner.]

Now, we understand what is meant by "the dispensation of the Grace of God." What is meant, is that the **"gospel of the grace of God"** (Acts 20:24) was NOT preached until after the death, burial and resurrection of Christ. But since the Bible does not assume people understand what is *meant*, neither should we.

One can also discern that dispensations are not "time periods," by the multiple *overlaps* contained within the different dispensations. For example, under the dispensation of Conscience, details concerning the curse of the earth, childbirth, and headship of the man (although that one seems to be on the way out!!) remain doctrinally true through the next *five* dispensations. Under the dispensation of Human Government, administrative rules (or truth) regarding capitol punishment remain in effect through the Law, to the Church Age. Even though certain aspects of dispensational truth have

Definition, Description, and Distinction **11**

occurred at specific points in time and history (such as the fall of man, the flood, the giving of the law, and the cross), many of them extend beyond "periods of time," and some (like the Law - Rev. 12:14), skip over past the Church Age and return again in the Tribulation or Millennium.

Dispensations are administrations of truth (methods or systems) that God has dispensed *during* a period of time. To say that "a dispensation can be used to reference a period of time"[23] (as Dr. Stauffer does) can be misleading.

"COVENANT"

The English word "covenant" in the singular form appears 292 times in the AV, three times as "covenants," and four times as "covenanted." A covenant is a binding agreement between two parties. The Hebrew word for "covenant" בְּרִית ("beryith") comes from the word בָּרָא ("bara") meaning "to cut, to cut out, to carve, to form by cutting or carving."[24] Hence, the Abrahamic Covenant is marked with a "cutting" or a "**dividing**" (Gen. 15:9,10) of the sacrifices, and the New Covenant with the "piercing" or "cutting" in the Saviour's side. All the unnecessary discussion from LaHaye and Ice ("the royal grant treaty . . .the suzerain-vassal treaty . . .and the parity treaty"[25]) to describe the difference between a *conditional* covenant and an *unconditional* covenant is unnecessary. There are basically two types of covenants: conditional and unconditional.

Some insert a "Palestinian covenant"[26] after Mosaic, and do

---

[23] Stauffer, Douglas D., *One Book Rightly Divided* (Millbrok: McCowen Mills Publishers, 1999) 237.
[24] Gesenius, William, *A Hebrew and English Lexicon of the Old Testament* (Boston: The Riverside Press, Cambridge, 1880) 155.
[25] LaHaye, Tim, Ice, Thomas, *Charting the End Times* (Eugene, Oregon: Harvest House Publishers, 2001) 78.
[26] *Scofield Reference Bible*, 250.

not list the "Eternal Covenant," still arriving at eight. The "conditions under which Israel entered the land of promise"[27] (called the "Palestinian Covenant") is technically included under the Mosaic Covenant (see Deut. 28-30).

The eight well-defined covenants in scripture are:
1. An Edenic Covenant (Gen. 2-3).
2. An Adamic Covenant (Gen. 3).
3. A Noahic Covenant (Gen. 8,9).
4. An Abrahamic Covenant (Gen. 12, 15, 17, 22).
5. A Mosaic Covenant (Ex. 19-34).
6. A Davidic Covenant (2 Sam. 7).
7. A New Covenant (Matt. 26).
8. An Eternal Covenant (Rev. 21, 22).

A thorough examination of the covenants will yield more insight into locating the various dispensations, than merely a study of the dispensations. The dispensations occur within the set covenants, and are limited to the "dispensing of truth," or the "order of arrangement." The Kingdom Age (or Millennial Age) can be categorized under the Davidic Covenant, and the Abrahamic Covenant *plus* the New Covenant (Heb. 8). There are different dispensations under each of those covenants however.

DISPENSATIONAL CAMPS

A dispensationalist is one who follows and obeys 2 Tim. 2:15, thus allowing the Holy Spirit to be the "interpreter" (Gen. 40:8; Dan. 5:16; 2 Peter 1:20) of scripture. To some degree, everyone who divides the Old and New Testaments is a dispensationalist. But just as Baptists must be classified and

---

[27] *Ibid.*, 250.

sorted (i.e. Primitive, Hard-shell, Independent, American, General, Southern ect.) so it is with dispensationalists. The assorted dispensational "camps" are as follows:

1. <u>Normative</u> - those who follow Scofield, Chafer, Ironside, Walvoord, Pentecost, and Ryrie.

2. <u>Ultra</u> - broken up into two groups:
    a. the *extreme* -Bullinger and Welch (of London).
    b. the *moderate* -C.R. Stam, O'Hair, and Baker (of America).

Hyper-dispensationalists pervert the scriptures by "wrongly dividing" the word. They eliminate water baptism for this age, misrepresent prayer and confession of sin, and eventually revert to Calvinism.

3. <u>Progressive</u> - a modern trend in dispensational circles moving ever closer to the adversary of Covenant Reformed theology:

> We can see how close Progressive Dispensationalism has come to Covenant theology in the very way it defines a dispensation.[28]

Progressive dispensationalists call the church "the new Israel" and state that part of the promises of the Abrahamic Covenant belong to the church. They also teach that Christ is reigning now as king on the Davidic throne in heaven, even though they still believe that He will reign in the future Millennial kingdom. "Progressives do not see the church as

---

[28] Henzel Ronald M., *Darby, Dualism and the Decline of Dispensationalism* (Tucson, Arizona: Fenestra Books, 2003.) 197.

completely distinct from Israel as normative dispensationalists have maintained."[29]

Some see five groups; making a difference between "pre Scofieldian dispensationalism," (some calling this "classic dispensationalism") "Scofieldian dispensationalism," "moderate," "ultra," and "progressive."

4. King James Bible believing – this is the category upon which this author will fall.

While considered "moderate" or "normative" up to a point, this group cannot be considered "ultra," or "hyper." They hold to water baptism and the Lord's supper for this age, and apply portions of Matthew, Acts, and Hebrews through Revelation to the Church Age. They do affirm that salvation has *not* always been by "**grace through faith**" (Eph. 2:8,9), and that no one in the Old Testament was saved by "looking forward to the cross."

The most prolific author in this "camp" is Dr. Peter S. Ruckman. Others who have addressed dispensationalism in this light would include: Dr. James Modlish, Dr. Samuel Gipp, Dr. Ken Blue, and Dr. Douglas Stauffer. The out-standing characteristic of this camp is their complete adherence to the AV text as the absolute and final authority.

"AGE"

Most dispensationalist use the terms "age" and "dispensation" interchangeably although technically (as Ryrie's quote stated) the dispensation operates *within* the "age."

---

[29] Ryrie, *Dispensationalism*, 174.

The English word "age" never appears in the sense of a "period of time" with regard to the dispensations of history. We only find reference to the "age" of individuals. The plural form "ages" occurs four times and is undoubtedly "periods of time" connected with different dispensations:

> *Eph 2:7* **That in the ages to come he might shew the exceeding riches of his grace in his kindness toward us through Christ Jesus.**
>
> *Eph 3:5* **Which in other ages was not made known unto the sons of men, as it is now revealed unto his holy apostles and prophets by the Spirit;**
>
> *Eph 3:21* **Unto him be glory in the church by Christ Jesus throughout all ages, world without end. Amen.**
>
> *Col 1:26* **Even the mystery which hath been hid from ages and from generations, but now is made manifest to his saints:**

Larkin makes a formidable distinction between "age" and "dispensation" even fastidiously demarcating an "age" as "a period between two great physical changes in the earth's surface."[30] He then lists the "Ages" as:

> 1. The Ante-Diluvian Age.
> 2. The Present Age.
> 3. The Age of Ages composed of the Millennial Age and the Perfect Age.[31]

---

[30] Larkin, Clarence, *Rightly Dividing the Word of Truth,* (Glenside: Rev. Clarence Larkin Est., 1920) 7.
[31] *Ibid.*, 7.

"AGE" vs. "WORLD"

Much unnecessary ruckus is made against the AV translation of "world," for the Greek word "αιων." The *Old Scofield Reference Bible* supplied a definition in the margin, either by "i.e. earth," or "i.e. age" theoretically *helping* the reader out. Redefining and "rewriting" (not to mention "retranslating") only confuses matters, and is anti-biblical in approach to Bible study. The Bible method of learning the meaning and "interpretation" or words, is by contrast and association (see Acts 8:31-35).

Though the editorial committee of the 1967 *New Scofield Reference Bible,* claimed their work was "not a new translation of the Hebrew and Greek texts,"[32] they still re-translated "world" (where it was translated from "aion") with "age" (except in 1 Cor. 8:13, and Eph. 3:21). These changes are completely unnecessary (as are thousands in the 1967 *New Scofield*), and reveal the misleading nature of modern scholarship. [By the way, how could C.I. Scofield be the "editor" of the *New Scofield Reference Bible* when he had been dead forty-six years? The title page claims he is the editor! Did the editorial committee (E. Schuyler English, Frank E. Gaebelein, William Culbertson, Charles L. Feinberg, Allan A. MacRae, Clarence E. Mason, Alva J. McClain, Wilbur M. Smith, and John F. Walvoord) believe in necromancy? Would not an editor's job be to approve or disapprove changes? Did Scofield endorse the changes *within* the AV text? He did not, and probably never would have. When he was alive he flatly rejected the RV and the ASV (of 1901) stating the King James to be "accurate," and "superior," possessing "unrivalled preeminence."[33] It is interesting to note that in 1998 a new edition

---

[32] *New Scofield Reference Bible* (New York: Oxford, 1967) vi.
[33] *Scofield Reference Bible* (New York: Oxford, 1909) iii., iv.

of the *New Scofield Study Bible* was published which placed the Authorized Version back in the text.]

Below are the facts substantiating *why* the AV translators were correct in their utilization of "world:"

1. The modern "world" (point proven) has no trouble differentiating between *two meanings* of the word "world." People often speak of New York City as being "*another world*," but at no time are they referring to another planet. The previous sentence just proved "world" can be used to designate an "age" or "period of time" (i.e. modern world vs. ancient world).

2. The dictionary gives one definition (among nineteen) as: "this or some specified other existence: *this world; the world to come.*"[34]

3. "World" is the best translation of "aion" in some cases (like Matt. 12:32) because "The 'world to come' has literal cities (Luke 19), with literal rulers (Matt. 19), and literal transformations in nature (Isa. 11, Rom. 8)."[35]

4. The word "age" expresses an idea but does not provide tangible substance and literalness like "world" does. Changing "world" to "age" deletes the connection between the physical "world" to the different "ages." The physical world WAS affected under some of the various "ages." In fact, there are *nine* earth *transformations* that coincide with the beginning and/or end of a specific "age" (see chart – *The Physical World and the "Ages"* page 20).

---

[34] "World," *The Random House College Dictionary*: 1517.
[35] Ruckman, Peter S., *Matthew* (Pensacola: Bible Believers Press, 1970) 212.

Let us never doubt the English AV text where "world" (instead of "age") occurs, discerning its proper application with reference to the located "periods of time."

ESCHATOLOGY

Eschatology (from the Greek word: εσχατος) is the study of "last things" and concerns particularly the prophecies of the second coming of Jesus Christ.

One cannot study dispensationalism without making reference to eschatology. Most of the prophetic authors (Lindsey, LaHaye, Walvoord, Grant, Pentecost, et. al) are dispensationalists because eschatology and dispensationalism compliment one another. Dispensational theology encompasses God's overall plan for the ages, which includes not only the past ages, and the current age (Church Age), but the future ages: Tribulation, Millennium, and Angelic Age, or Eternal State.

ESCHATOLOGICAL VIEWS

The prophetic interpretations of the second coming of Jesus Christ and the unveiling events found in Revelation and Daniel can be summarized as:

1. **Symbolic** - the prophetic events are not actual events, but merely symbols of truth, not real occurrences. "Christ is viewed as coming within the individual's own experience."[36]

2. **Preterist** - from the Latin "preter" which means past. "Thus, a preterist interpretation of a given prophecy would

---

[36] "Eschatology" *Dictionary of Premillennial Theology:* 107.

attempt to explain it as an event that has already taken place."[37] Preterist believe that the prophetic events were current with the writer of scripture or fulfilled soon after.

There are basically two *contemporary* schools of preterism: moderate (or *partial*) and extreme (*radical* or *full*). Partial preterists (like R.C. Sproul) believe the coming of Christ was fulfilled in A.D. 70 *but* with a "future consummation of Christ"[38] later; while full preterists "see virtually the entire New Testament eschatology as having been realized already."[39] Radical preterist believe in NO *future* second coming at all, and NO *future* rapture or resurrection:

> Full preterism does not see a prophesied end of history. In fact, full preterists say we are not merely in the millennium, but we are now living in what we would call the eternal state or the new heavens and new earth of Revelation 21-22.[40]

3. **Historical** - prophetic events were future from the standpoint of when they were written, but they are all now in the past. They contend that the book of Revelation presents the entire course of church history from the first century to the end of time.

4. **Futuristic** - prophetic events are all in the future. All Bible believing dispensationalists are futurists, and hold to a literal interpretation of prophetic scriptures.

---

[37] "What is Preterism," *The End Times Controversy* (Oregon: Harvest House, 2003) 18.
[38] Sproul, R.C., *The Last Days According to Jesus* (Grand Rapids: Baker Books, 1998) 68.
[39] *Ibid.*, 68.
[40] "What is Preterism," *The End Times Controversy* (Oregon: Harvest House, 2003) 23.

THE PHYSICAL "WORLD" AND THE "AGES"

Original Earth — Gen. 1:1
LUCIFER AND THE SONS OF GOD.
EZEKIEL 28:14
JOB 16, 2:1

Voidless Earth — Gen. 1:2
"without form and void" = judgment and catastrophe.
Jer 4:23
Psa 89:39
Nah 2:10

JUDGMENT
Satan falls: Sin enters universe

Restored Earth
SATAN AND THE "gods" (GEN 3:5) IN THE GARDEN OF EDEN WITH "MAN." THE NEW "SON OF GOD" (LUKE 3:38).
ADAM TOLD TO "REPLENISH THE EARTH" (GEN 1:28)

MAN FALLS: SIN ENTERS WORLD

Flooded Earth
All breathing life destroyed, including the sons of God and their offspring (Gen 6:1-4)

JUDGMENT
Noah and his family sole survivors.

Present Earth
NOAH TOLD TO "REPLENISH" (GEN. 9:28)
"AGES" OF HUMAN GOV., PROMISE, LAW AND CHURCH

Distressed Earth — 666
Son of Perdition's revelation (2 Thess. 2)
Earthquakes (Mt 24:7),
Tidal waves (Lk. 21:25).

JUDGMENT
Water pollution, (Rev. 8:8), global forest fires (Rev 8:7), hailstorms (Rev. 11:19) and plagues

Regenerated Earth
SATAN IS BOUND (REV. 20:1,2)
NO EVIL SPIRITS (ZECH 13:2)
GOD'S "SEED" IS RULING ON DAVID'S THRONE (EZK. 48:35)

KINGDOM AGE 1000 YEARS EARTH RESTORED TO STATE BEFORE THE FLOOD

Burned Earth
Under leadership of Satan the world rebels against the King of Kings.

JUDGMENT
Called the "day of God" (2 Peter 3:12)

New Earth
SATAN AND ALL UNSAVED MAN BANISHED TO THE LAKE OF FIRE FOR ETERNITY
No SIN, SORROW OR DEATH

GOD'S ORIGINAL PLAN AND PURPOSE FULFILLED THROUGH JESUS CHRIST

Eph 3:21 Unto him be glory in the church by Christ Jesus throughout **all ages**, world without end. Amen.

Thus chart chronicles the **nine** distinct "phases" of the physical world in relation to the different "ages."
The correlations are as follows:
1 Original Earth with New Earth
2 Voidless Earth with Burned Earth
3 Restored Earth with Regenerated Earth
4 Flood Earth with Distressed Earth
5 Present Earth by itself —encompassing the greatest time frame under the most covenants and the dispensations

Timeline .... ???? .... 4004 B.C. .... 2350 B.C. .... A.D. 2000? .... A.D. 3000?

COPYRIGHT © 2004
DAVID E. WALKER

INCORRECT CONCEPTS

There are several incorrect notions (matching the symbolic, preterist, and historical views) about the second coming of Jesus Christ. Larkin lists the following:

1. The coming of the Holy Spirit at Pentecost.
2. Salvation.
3. Death.
4. Destruction of Jerusalem.
5. Spread of Christianity.[41]

The Bible plainly teaches that the coming of Jesus Christ will be literal, personal, visible, and bodily. The above ideas will not "jive" with scripture.

> *Acts 1:11* **Which also said, Ye men of Galilee, why stand ye gazing up into heaven? this same Jesus, which is taken up from you into heaven, shall so come in like manner as ye have seen him go into heaven.**

Other references are: Dan. 7:13-14; Matt. 24:30; Matt. 25:31; Mark 13:26; Luke 21:27; Rev. 1:7.

ESCHATOLOGICAL SCHOOLS OF THOUGHT

There are three prevailing positions of thought with regard to the study of the end times, particularly relating to the Millennial Kingdom.

---

[41] Larkin, *Dispensational Truth*, 9-10.

1. **Premillennialism** – Jesus Christ will return back to this earth *before* the Millennial Kingdom, *after* the Church Age. Among those who hold to the premillennial view are:
    - **a.** *Pre-tribulationists* - believe the church will be raptured *before* the Tribulation.
    - **b.** *Mid-tribulationists* – believe the church will be raptured during the *middle* of the Tribulation.
    - **c.** *Post-tribulationists* – believe the church will be raptured *after* the Tribulation.

Premillennialism believes in the future restoration of Israel, and the promises relating to them as "**his people**" (Rom. 11:2).

2. **Amillennialism** – There will be no literal period of one-thousand year reign of Jesus Christ. Many amillennialists see the "millennial prophecies as being fulfilled in eternity."[42]

There is no rapture with the amillennial system, and the promises made to the nation of Israel are misapplied to the church.

3. **Postmillennialism** – The Millennial Kingdom is interpreted as the Church Age. Only after the church converts the world will Jesus return and "announce that His kingdom has been realized."[43]

Postmillennialism adheres to no rapture, is anti-Israel, and pro-Catholic in polity.

---

[42] "Eschatology" *Dictionary of Premillennial Theology:* 107.
[43] *Ibid.*

PREMILLENNIALISM

Dispensationalism and premillennialism are virtually inseparable. It could be said that a dispensational approach would lead to a premillennial view, and a premillennial view would lead to a dispensational approach. Gerstner attempts to make "historic premillennialism" different than "dispensational premillennialism"[44] in order to establish an historical argument, namely, that "dispensationalism . . .diverges from orthodox Christianity."[45]

WHAT IS PREMILLENNIALISM?

Premillennialism is the belief that Jesus Christ will return to the earth literally, and bodily, to reign as King *before* the Millennial Age ensues. The premillennial teaching is based upon the *literal, grammatical-historical* method of interpretation, rather than the *allegorical* method promoted and developed by the apostate Origen.[46] [It is interesting to note that most dispensational authors (like Walvoord, Pentecost, LaHaye, Crutchfield, Ryrie, et. al) attack Origen and his doctrine, calling him an "Alexandrian theologian"[47] while simultaneously promoting the "Alexandrian type" of manuscripts behind the new Bible versions. Modern dispensational authors, although they may be adequate Bible *teachers*, are NOT Bible *believers*.]

"Of the three views concerning the Millennium, the premillennial view is the oldest"[48] because it is the biblical view. The fact that the early church believed in the literal,

---

[44] Gerstner, John H., *Wrongly Dividing the Word of Truth,* (Morgan: Soli Deo Gloria Publications, 2000) 70-75.
[45] *Ibid.,* 74.
[46] Pentecost, J. Dwight, *Things to Come* (Grand Rapids: Zondervan, 1958) 22.
[47] "Origen,"*Dictionary of Premillennial Theology:* 289.
[48] "Premillennialism," *Dictionary of Premillennial Theology:* 310.

visible return of Jesus Christ to this earth before the Millennium is not disputed.[49] What *is* disputed are the tenets of premillennialism. [For detailed proof of the premillennial view in the early church see *Things to Come* by Pentecost, pages 370-380.]

THE TENETS OF PREMILLENNIALISM

1. Jesus Christ will return to this earth literally and bodily.

2. He will establish the kingdom thus fulfilling the promises of hundreds of Old Testament prophecies.

3. The kingdom will fulfill the promises of the covenants to the nation of *Israel* literally.

4. This kingdom will continue for a thousand years "after which the kingdom will be given by the Son to the Father when it will merge with His eternal kingdom."[50]

Premillennialism is not only the oldest view (although Gerstner differentiates between "older premillennialism and "modern dispensationalism"[51]) it is the biblically correct view.

THE CHARACTERISTICS OF PREMILLENNIALISM

Premillennialism takes the Bible at "face value." In other words, "God means what He says, and says what He means." Reformed Calvinists may say: "What about parables and symbols given in scripture?" Jesus Christ (the true manifestation of the "word" – i.e. "Word") expounds the case

---
[49] Pentecost, *Things to Come*, 373-376.
[50] *Ibid.*, 372.
[51] Gerstner, *Wrongly Dividing the Word of Truth*, 15.

in point time and time again. For example, when Jesus wanted to use a symbolic meaning He made it clear by using "like:"

> *Matt 13:33* **Another parable spake he unto them; The kingdom of heaven <u>is like</u> unto leaven, which a woman took, and hid in three measures of meal, till the whole was leavened.**

Sometimes He would give the "similitude" (Hos. 12:10) and then *explain* it:

> *John 6:57* <u>As</u> **the living Father hath sent me, and I live by the Father: so he that eateth me, even he shall live by me.**

> *John 6:63* **It is the spirit that quickeneth; the flesh profiteth nothing: the words that I speak unto you, they are spirit, and they are life.**

When Jesus wanted the symbol or figure explained He made it clear:

> *Matt 13:25* **But while men slept, his enemy came and sowed tares among the wheat, and went his way.**

> *Matt 13:38* **The field is the world; the good seed are the children of the kingdom; but the tares are the children of the wicked one;**

Notice the definition and interpretation of the "fire" in the parable:

Matt 13:30 **Let both grow together until the harvest: and in the time of harvest I will say to the reapers, Gather ye together first the tares, and bind them in bundles <u>to burn them</u>: but gather the wheat into my barn.**

Matt 13:40 **As therefore the tares are gathered and <u>burned in the fire</u>; so shall it be in the end of this world.**

Matt 13:42 **And shall cast them into <u>a furnace of fire</u>: there shall be wailing and gnashing of teeth.**

The logical "face value" understanding can easily be seen. "Fire" *is* "fire." How can that type of reasoning be hard, or considered fallacious? It is only unreasonable to those who have been educated out of their belief in the Bible (whether by secular or seminary measures). [It is significant that the unwarranted "educated" rejection of the word of God can be manufactured after only six to eight grades of public school instruction. What once germinated in the minds of atheistic professors, has now sprung up in the minds of unsaved teenagers and street kids! Juvenile delinquents will dispute a literal hell, argue about Cain's wife and endorse Darwinism as articulately as some college students do. If you do not believe me, open the floor for questions at a Youth Detention Center!]

Premillennialism is also a position that endeavors to guard, maintain, and **"contend for the faith"** (Jude 3). It avows the integrity of scripture over personal prejudices. If the Bible is to be taken "at face value," the true biblical eschatological system must be premillennial. Premillennialism allows the scriptures to harmonize, correspond, and synchronize, by accepting the veracity of Old Testament prophecies instead of pretending God *meant* something He did not *say*! The very people who accuse dispensationalists and premillennialists of "divid[ing] the Bible into sections which share little or no unity,"[52] create a system of interpretation that generates contradictions, inconsistencies, ambiguity and doubt! "**Rightly dividing the word of truth**" (2 Tim. 2:15) is a command that not only properly instructs, but unifies and bonds the scriptures together as a whole. Notice the contradiction of the postmillennial system with the following verse in mind:

2 Tim 3:13 **But evil men and seducers shall wax worse and worse, deceiving, and being deceived.**

PREMILLENNIAL VIEW NO CONTRADICTION	POSTMILLENNIAL VIEW CONTRADICTION
APOSTASY PREVALENT BEFORE JESUS RETURNS	THINGS GET BETTER BEFORE JESUS RETURNS

The premillennial system gives the prevailing glory to Jesus Christ alone. It is the premillennial system (and Bible teaching) that identifies ALL "betterment of societal ills" to Jesus Christ *alone*, APART from any organization, church, or alliance. Premillennialsim teaches that this world will NEVER be a peaceful "habitation for humanity" until, and ONLY until, Jesus Christ [the armies follow him, not lead him - Rev. 19:14] returns bodily to this earth so as to humiliate, defeat, and dethrone the "**god of this world**" (2 Cor. 4:4) and take back the "**throne of his father David**" (Luke 1:32).

AMILLENNIALISM

"Amillenarians believe that the millennium is a present reality (Christ's heavenly reign), not a future hope (Christ's

---
[52] *Ibid.*, 109.

rule on earth after his return)."[53] Amillennialism, as Walvoord states, "is basically non-millennial. It denies there will be a millennium."[54]

> The amillennial view holds that the kingdom promises in the Old Testament are fulfilled spiritually rather than literally in the New Testament church. Those who hold this view believe that Christ will literally return, but they do not believe in His thousand-year reign on the earth. According to the amillennial view, the kingdom of God is present in the church age, and at the end of the church age the second coming of Christ inaugurates the eternal state. The book of Revelation is interpreted as a description of those events that take place during the church age.[55]

What two great personages do we have to blame for this undue perversion of millennial truth? Origen and Augustine:

> With the contribution of Augustine to theological thinking amillennialism came into prominence. While Origen laid the foundation in establishing the non-literal method of interpretation, it was Augustine who systematized the non-literal view of the millennium into what is now known as amillennialism.[56]

Augustine (354-430 A.D.), followed Origen's allegorizing of scripture, and thus engendered the amillennial philosophy.

> Augustine abandoned the premillennial position for the superficial reason that some millenarians had envisioned a kingdom age of unparalleled fruitfulness featuring banquet tables set with excessive amounts of food and drink (city of God 20.7).[57]

---

[53] Riddlebarger, Kim, *A Case for Amillennialism* (Grand Rapids: Baker, 2003) 11.
[54] Walvoord, John F., *The Final Drama* (Grand Rapids: Kregel, 1993) 139.
[55] "Amillennialism," *Dictionary of Premillennial Theology:* 37.
[56] Pentecost, *Things to Come*, 381.
[57] "Augustine," *Dictionary of Premillennial Theology:* 59.

Once "Augustine set forth the idea that the church visible was the Kingdom of God on earth,"[58] no literal fulfillment of the promises to Israel were even considered, and since the millennium was the "inter-advent period,"[59] Jesus was now reigning (notice the removal of "**now**" in the RSV in John 18:36) on a throne instead of sitting on the right hand of the Father awaiting the future kingdom!

Heb 1:13 **But to which of the angels said he at any time, <u>Sit on my right hand</u>, until I make thine enemies thy footstool?**

[Hebrews 1:13 reminds me of a father telling his son as they gaze at the beautiful sunset: "Look son, what a lovely sunset God has painted for us. Isn't it pretty?" "It sure is dad," answered the son, "and God painted it with His left hand." The father replied, "Son, how do you know that God painted it with His left hand?" "Because," said the son, "The Bible says that Jesus is sitting on His right hand!"]

Adherents to amillennialism include Reformed theologians, Roman Catholics, Lutherns, Episcopalians, Protestant Reformers, Southern Baptist liberals, some Presbyterian churches, and Hardshell Primitive Baptists.

BLUNDERS OF AMILLENNIALISM

1. Amillennialism fosters no literal interpretation of scripture, even though Old Testament verses quoted in the New Testament were taken literally by New Testament authors, and Jesus Christ Himself.

---

[58] Pentecost, *Things to Come*, 382.
[59] *Ibid.*, 382.

2. Amillennialism equates the Kingdom of God, the Kingdom of Heaven and the church. This permits misapplication of doctrinal passages. For example, if the Kingdom of Heaven is synonymous with the church, then it would be possible for a saved person to be "**cast out into outer darkness**" (Matt. 8:12).

3. Amillennialism teaches that the current age *is* the Millennial age. But the characteristics of the Millennium (Satan bound, no curse, no devils, absolute peace, longevity of life, ect.) are *not* in effect today.

4. Amillennialism also alleges that the first resurrection is a spiritual resurrection, like Eph. 2:1,2. Once the literal, bodily resurrection is done away with, who is to say that Jesus Christ rose bodily? [See the readings in the NWT and NASB that deny the bodily ascension of Jesus Christ in Luke 24:51,52.]

POSTMILLENNIALISM

Postmillennialism teaches that Jesus Christ will return at the end of the Millennium. Daniel Whitby (1638-1725) is attributed with propelling this ideology into a systematic form. Reworking the amillennial perspective, "Whitby popularized the concept that the world would grow progressively better until it climaxed in a golden age of one thousand years during which the Gospel would be triumphant."[60]

In Walvoord's book *The Final Drama*, he uses a question to explain the viewpoint of postmillennialism:

> Will the world get better and better and more Christianized through preaching the Gospel until it

---
[60] Walvoord, *The Final Drama*, 17.

reaches a thousand years of a golden age, with Christ coming at the end of the period?[61]

The postmillennial heresy was augmented with textual criticism, and the propaganda of evolution. All three teach "upward progression," ("a better age," "a better rendering," "a better ape"), and have damned millions of souls to hell.

After WWI however, the postmillennial divergence took a fall that did not recover until the sixties. Currently the postmillennial position is held by liberal theologians (whether they are Presbyterian, Methodist, or Baptist) who "tend to deny judgment on the wicked and reject the literal resurrection of the body and the actual second coming of Christ."[62]

CLIQUES OF POSTMILLENNIALISM

Orthodox - believe the Millennium will be brought in through preaching of the gospel.

Liberal - believe that the Millennium will be brought in by humanism and socialism.

Theonomist (Christian Reconstructionist) – believe the Millennium is realized by the establishing of the Old Testament Law.

> This new and growing movement emphasizes the covenant theology and postmillennialism of Reformed theology but with an added twist; phonemic ethics; meaning: we are still under the Old Testament law, the book of Galatians notwithstanding.[63]

---

[61] *Ibid.*, 2.
[62] *Ibid.*, 18.
[63] Vance, *The Other Side of Calvinism*, 56.

CHAPTER 2

Biblical Interpretation

PRIVATE INTERPRETATION?

2 Peter 1:20-21
**20 Knowing this first, that no prophecy of the scripture is of any private interpretation.
21 For the prophecy came not in old time by the will of man: but holy men of God spake as they were moved by the Holy Ghost.**

Probably one of the most used alibis by lost people in order to evade **"the truth of the gospel"** (Col. 1:5), relates to interpretation. It normally goes something like this: "Well, there are just so many *interpretations* of the Bible. How are you to know which one is right?" Or, "You have *your interpretation* and I have mine." Some might even say, "Nobody can claim to have the *right interpretation.*"

Responses like this are as old as Satan himself (see Gen. 3), and are the impetuous reflections of the old Adamic nature. Just as the "theory" (religion) of evolution makes sense to the "**fool**" (Ps. 14:1), this "interpretation line" seems reasonable to the unsaved. For it provides them with an ostensibly shrewd and insightful answer to the terrifying question: "**What shall I do then with Jesus which is called Christ?**" (Matt 27:22). If interpretation becomes the final authority, one can easily evade pointed, direct references to hell, the judgment, and salvation by grace without works.

But the Bible teaches emphatically that "**interpretations belong to God**" (Gen. 40:8), with absolutely NO "**private interpretation**" (2 Peter 1:21) involved. The problem with the unsaved sinner, as well as the "learned" (Isa. 29:11) theologian is not a "hermeneutical" one. [Hermeneutics is another tradesman term for "interpretation," from the Greek, derived from "Hermes" - the "messenger of the gods."] The problem has, and always will be the "**evil heart of unbelief**" (Heb. 3:12). Isaiah did not ask: "Who hath properly interpreted the exegetical premise," he said: "**Who hath BELIEVED our report**" (Isa. 53:1).

The fact that there are two major schemes of interpretation (literal and allegorical), are irrelevant to the Bible believer, because the Bible must first be established as the definitive authority, NOT the system! Theologians and scholars have put "the cart before the horse" and have consequently "**trodden under foot**" (Heb. 10:29) the word of God with their hermeneutical classifications.

[Note William Grady's comment on scholars: " . . . the dictionary would limit a scholar to 'one who has mastered his subject,' the pretentious office of '*Bible* scholar' is invalidated on the grounds of being a misnomer."[1]]

---

[1] Stauffer, *One Book Rightly Divided*, xii.

So, when we deal with Bible hermeneutics in regard to dispensationalism, we will put the BOOK first, and the system second.

[The Bible can ruin *any* system, and *any* "interpretive process." Take for example the ideology that the body of Christ is missing from the Tribulation (which I believe and teach). What does one do with: **Rev 14:13** - *And I heard a voice from heaven saying unto me, Write, Blessed are the dead which die* **in the Lord** *from henceforth* . . . There is someone in the Tribulation that is said to be "**in the Lord**." Are there *two* bodies of Christ (sounds like a "hyper") in the book of Acts?]

TWO SCHOOLS OF INTERPRETATION

Biblical interpretation could essentially be identified as "biblical approach," and has previously been defined in the general sense as "belief." As mentioned beforehand, there are basically two schools of interpretation: allegorical and literal. The literal school of interpretation (called the grammatical - historical) is more biblical, except where it attempts to correct the King James text in an etymological "resultant meaning"[2] fashion. Since dispensationalism is heavily dependent upon the literal method instead of the allegorical, it is pertinent for us to appraise each of these views.

THE ALLEGORICAL METHOD

The allegorical method rejects the plain (Prov. 8:8,9), literal meaning of scripture and seeks for a deeper, spiritual lesson. It interprets the supernatural events recorded in scripture to be the result of natural causes. The motive behind the allegorical

---

[2] Ryrie, *Dispensationalism*, 82.

method is antithesis of the grammatical-historical method of interpretation.

Those who allegorize scripture, do so because of agnosticism, and skepticism toward the word of God. [This, by the way, was the motive for Origen's Hexapla.] They simply do NOT believe that **"miracles"** (Num. 14:22) and **"wonders"** (Ex. 11:10) could have occurred (see the RSV reading of Isa. 7:14). The other basis for **"corrupt[ing] the word of God"** (2 Cor. 2:17) by allegorizing scripture is anti-Semitism. All postmillennialists and amillennialists reject Gen. 12:1-4 without blinking an eye. They do so without regard to Romans 11, and with the intent of ecclesiastical expansion.

ROOTS OF ALLEGORICAL METHOD

Alexandria, Egypt (go figure) was the boiling pot for this allegorizing pottage. Clement of Alexandria, (the founder of the school of Alexandria) adopted the allegorical method of the apostate Jew, Philo. Later, Origen (a heretic of the worst sort) established this system of allegorical interpretation, thus opposing the premillennial teaching of the time. "Origen was the first church leader of stature to challenge the premillennial orthodoxy of the early church."[3] It is fitting then, that most "church leaders" of today follow either his method of interpretation or his "revisions" of the received text. Sadly, many dispensationalists (Ryrie, Walvoord, Paul Tan, Lightner, Crutchfield, Thomas Ice, et. al) who would never succumb to the concepts of Origen's allegorical method consistently slurp his blend of leaven found in the "LXX" – which appeared in Origen's Hexapla.

---

[3] "Origen," *Dictionary of Premillennial Theology*: 289.

ROOTS OF LITERAL INTERPRETATION

On the other hand, the literal method of interpretation has its roots in Antioch of Syria, where the believers were first called Christians (Acts 11:26), and where the true biblical line of scripture was preserved.

> Antioch of Syria founded a school in the third and fourth centuries whose curriculum emphasized normal-literal interpretation and was self-consciously opposed to the method taught by the school of Alexandria.[4]

DARKNESS SETS IN

After the Nestorian controversy (a debate about the humanity and divinity of Christ), the school of Antioch lost influence, and by the Dark Ages (NOT "Middle Ages"), the Alexandrian school was powerfully promoting the allegorical method, and did so until the Reformation. It does not take a historian to see the fruits of the allegorical method: ecclesiastical bloodshed. Once the literal promises were taken from the literal Jew and given to the church; "preachers" (a New Testament office) faded into "priest" (an Old Testament office), "ordinances" (New Testament) were transformed into "sacraments" (see 1967 *New Scofield* page 1174), "justification by faith" (New Testament) became "salvation by works," the "holy city" (Old Testament - Jerusalem - Neh. 11:1) became Rome, and the lights that were shinning (Matt. 5:16) went OUT!

The hermeneutical approach of Erasmus, along with his publication of a Greek and Latin Bible began to dismantle the authority of the bloody Roman Catholic Church (revealing the gross errors of the Latin Vulgate), and "paved the way for the

---

[4] "Hermeneutics, Antiochian School," *Dictionary of Premillennial Theology*: 145.

exegetical and hermeneutical revolution of Luther. According to a popular sixteenth century saying, "Erasmus laid the egg and Luther hatched it."[5]

When Luther came along he blasted Origen (and rightly so) stating:

> Allegories are empty speculations and as it were the scum of Holy Scripture. Origen's allegories are not worth so much dirt. To allegorize is to juggle the Scripture. Allegorizing may degenerate into a mere monkey game. Allegories are awkward, absurd, inventive, obsolete, loose rags.[6]

The foundation of the Reformation rested upon the principle of literal interpretation *without* the aid of outside interpreters (popes and priests). The dogma "sola scriptura" (scripture alone) flattened the stranglehold of church tradition, and unbolted the door of the Dark Ages to let the "**light of the world**" (John 8:12) shine again.

As all good things must come to an end (although we understand that the true Bible believing churches - Waldensians, Paulicians, ect. were still *persevering*) the Reformation was replaced with rationalism: German rationalism. Hobbes, Des-cartes, Locke and Spinoza blew out the fires of much literal interpretive thought, and Johann A. Bengel (1687-1753) along with Wettstein led textual criticism (with Alexandrian manuscripts - Codex Alexandrinus surfaced in 1628),[7] by utilizing human reasoning in study of the Bible and manuscript evidence. Coupled with textual criticism and rationalism, was the scientific (much of which was "**falsely so called**") discoveries of Copernicus, Bruno, Kepler, and Galileo. This caused many to "swerve," and "turn aside" (1

---

[5] "Hermeneutics, Reformation," *Dictionary of Premillennial Theology*: 163.
[6] *Ibid.*, 164.
[7] Hermeneutics, Post-Reformation," *Dictionary of Premillennial Theology*: 158

Tim. 1:6). When David Hume (Scottish philosopher, 1711-1776) and Immanuel Kant (German philosopher, 1724-1804) arrived on the scene, "sola scriptura" was not even an option. Since Hume denounced all miracles, and Kant arrived at truth based on personal observations, the allegorical method of interpretation had resilient support.

REVIVAL OF BIBLICAL INTERPRETATION

Once Europe had rejected the God honored text of 1611, the Holy Spirit (moving East to West) began using men like Darby, Scofield, and Larkin, to teach the principals of biblical interpretation. The stimulus that the *Scofield Reference Bible* had on pastors and Bible teachers cannot be underestimated. Dr. Ruckman explains:

> This Scofield Reference Bible became the means of keeping nearly half the Baptist ministers in America teaching Premillennialism when the schools they attended and graduated from were teaching Amillennialism . . .
> J. Frank Norris kept the Baptists straight on modernism and separation and Scofield kept them straight on the Second Coming.[8]

Larkin (1850-1924), with his seminal work, *Dispensational Truth*, taught more Bible in about 400 regular pages, than any of the major seminaries, or "preacher boy schools" of the past or present. Larkin taught that true biblical interpretation was dependent upon avoiding three things: "the misinterpretation of scripture, the misapplication of scripture, and the dislocation of scripture."[9] Larkin hit the nail, and the "scholars" on the head:

---

[8] Ruckman, Peter S. *The History of the New Testament Church, Vol. 2* (Pensacola: Bible Believers Press, 1984) 114.
[9] Larkin, *Dispensational Truth*, 2.

> [T]he trouble is men are not willing to let the Scriptures say what they want to say. This is largely due to their training, environment, prejudice, or desire to make the Scriptures teach some favorite doctrine.[10]

He taught that the "futurist school" of interpretation was correct because it took the Bible literally, and he stated that "the second and premillennial coming of Christ is the 'key' to the Scriptures."[11]

Several principles of true biblical interpretation were preserved through assorted dispensationalists and dispensational schools (like Chafer and Dallas Theological Seminary), but since the King James text has been ousted, the nucleus of biblical interpretation has been completely lost to the mainstream Christian (and dispensational) community. If the book from which come the principles of interpretation cannot be trusted, neither can the rules that govern the interpretation. If, as Ryrie asserts, "the area of linguistics has contributed to an understanding concerning language . . . that has aided biblical interpretation"[12] then interpretation is "relative" and "resultant" with absolutely NO final authority. Once allowance is given for "improvements" to the Bible "linguistically" (a cover up for "**chang[ing] the truth of God into a lie**" - Rom. 1:25), all solid interpretive rules are shot! If the word, or phrase you are interpreting literally can be *changed* (like "**do his commandments**" to " wash their robes" - Rev. 22:14), your literal interpretation is ineffective and useless. This is where dispensational biblical interpretation has consummated.

Be thankful to God, that at the present time (2005), on the precipice of the one world unifying religion of the Antichrist, there is a remnant of Bible believing dispensationalists who

---
[10] *Ibid.*, 2.
[11] *Ibid.*, 5.
[12] Ryrie, *Dispensationalism*, 79.

still believe THE book from which dispensational theology is derived. While not "recognized" by the leaders of contemporary dispensationalism, this vestige of true Bible believers declares "**all the counsel of God**" (Acts 20:27), even where it is not popular or conventional.

LITERAL INTERPRETATION IS BIBLICAL

Literal interpretation (as opposed to allegorical) is biblical because it allows the Bible the preeminent place. The "golden rule of interpretation" by Dr. David Cooper summarizes the heart of the literal view:

> When the plain sense of Scripture makes common sense, seek no other sense; therefore, take every word at its primary, ordinary, usual, literal meaning unless the facts of the immediate context, studied in the light of related passages and axiomatic and fundamental truths, indicate clearly otherwise.[13]

PREREQUISITES FOR PROPER UNDERSTANDING

Just taking the Bible in a literal sense does not necessarily yield the accurate view. There are some prerequisites that lead to the proper understanding.

Salvation - If a person is not saved, he will *never* be able to properly understand scripture.

> *1 Cor 2:14* **But the natural man receiveth not the things of the Spirit of God: for they are foolishness unto him: neither can he know them, because they are spiritually discerned.**

---

[13] Cooper, David L., *The God of Israel* (Los Angeles: Biblical Research Society, 1945) iii.

The soul-winner is well acquainted with people saying, "Well, I've read the Bible and I just cannot understand it." The reason they cannot understand it is because they have not been born again by the Spirit of God. Since the Bible is a spiritual book, a person *must* be "spiritual" to understand it.

Belief - A person must *believe* that the words are *in fact* the *very* words of the living God. Belief in the "verbally inspired original autographs" has never been a biblical approach to literal interpretation! In fact, when the word "scripture" appears in the canon, it never *only* refers to the originals, but also to the *inspired copies!*

1 Thess 2:13 **For this cause also thank we God without ceasing, because, when ye received the word of God which ye heard of us, ye received it not as the word of men, but as it is in truth, the word of God, which effectually worketh also in you that believe.**

Reverence - A person must have respect and reverence for the Bible.

Isa 66:2 **For all those things hath mine hand made, and those things have been, saith the LORD: but to this man will I look, even to him that is poor and of a contrite spirit, and trembleth at my word.**

GRAMMATICAL PRINCIPALS

The literal approach of Bible interpretation is often referred to as the "grammatical - historical" view.

The grammatical principles deal with the language, such as:

1. The meaning of words.

Countless hours of study could be dissolved if believers would simply allow the scriptures to define themselves. Riplinger has proven in *Language of the King James Bible*, and in the book *In Awe of Thy Word* that the AV contains its own "built in dictionary."

2. The literary style of the author.

It is important to remember that the Bible was written by both human and divine instrumentality. The style of the author sometimes plays an important role in our understanding. This is readily seen with the writings of the apostle to the Gentiles (Paul), where he *never* refers to the Lord Jesus as "son of man," but, rather, the "son of God." This particular style reveals the Jewish nature of "son of man," and verifies the truth of seemingly complex passages where "son of man" is used instead of "son of God."

3. The context of the passage of scripture.

Noting the context (as in the golden rule of interpretation) is essential to properly understanding a verse. Most heresies spring up from taking a verse out of its *context*. You can make the Bible teach *anything* if you neglect the context of the verse! For example, I could say that the Bible teaches suicide, by removing two verses out of context and placing them together: "**And he cast down the pieces of silver in the temple, and departed, and went and hanged himself . . . Go, and do thou likewise.**" (Matt 27:5 and Luke 10:37) That is the procedure of all Charismatics, Mormons, Jehovah's Witnesses and other cultic groups. Just because someone quotes a verse out of the

Bible does not mean anything! What is the *context* of the verse, and did the person quote the verse *in* its context?

4. The use of idioms.

Idioms are phrases and expressions that, many times take on their own meaning. For instance the idiom **"day of the LORD,"** is not just a phrase denoting that a day belongs to the LORD, rather, it is an expression that spans over a period of at least 1000 years. The phrase **"many days"** refers to a distinct period of 3 ½ years (see: 1 Kings 17:15; 18:1; James 5:17).

5. Figures of speech.

The *Companion Bible* elaborates:

> 'Figure of speech' relates to the form in which the words are used. It consists in the fact that a word or words are used out of their ordinary sense, or place, or manner, for the purpose of attracting our attention to what is thus said. A Figure of speech is a designed and legitimate departure from their laws of language, in order to emphasize what is said. Hence in such Figures we have the Holy Spirit's own marking, so to speak, of His own words . . . Figures are never used but for the sake of emphasis. Ignorance of Figures of speech has led to the grossest errors, which have been caused either from taking literally what is figurative, or from taking figurative what is literal. [14]

A good example of a figure of speech would be Gen. 3:15 where "bruising the heel must stand figuratively as meaning the least damage that one man could do to another . . ."[15] even though it is clear that **"bruise thy head"** is literal (Rom 16:20; 1 John 3:8; Ps. 68:21; 110:6; Hab. 3:13; Mark 12:4).

---

[14] "Appendix 6," *Companion Bible*: Grand Rapids: Kregel, 1990) 8.
[15] Ruckman, Peter S., *Genesis* (Pensacola: Bible Believers Press, 1969) 102.

ALLEGORIES AND PARABLES

There are several kinds of figures of speech in scripture. Bullinger gave 217 separate classifications with over 8,000 illustrations. The allegorical type falls under figures of speech. An allegory (not to be confused with the erroneous "allegorical method of interpretation") is a comparison by representation and implication. A good example would be Gen. 49:9 where Judah (the son of Jacob) is compared to a "**lions whelp.**" A parable is another figure of speech, and was used many times by the Lord Jesus. It is a continued simile, and compares by continued resemblance.

HISTORICAL PRINCIPALS

The historical principles relate to history, and testify to the genuineness of scripture:

1. The *historical author* of scripture, or who is making the address.

This is extremely important in the book of Ecclesiastes, where the author is a man "**under the sun**" (Eccl. 1:3,9,14 ect.) and is written from that viewpoint. The words of Satan are also *recorded* in scripture, and as such are "**given by inspiration of God**" (2 Tim. 3:16), although you would be a fool to follow them as instructions. Just because a word or phrase is *contained* in scripture, does not validate it to be *true*. I heard a Bible believer using the words of an unsaved Jew (Gamaliel) to defend a decision he made that later turned out to be detrimental. If the words of a lost Pharisee, "**if it be of God, ye cannot overthrow it**" (Acts 5:39) are true, then the Roman Catholic Church must be of God. It has not been overthrown in over 1400 years! Conversely are we to assume that the lives of the apostles were not "**of God**" since they died martyrs deaths, and were "overthrown." Though the phrase is *catchy* (like the words of a harlot - Prov. 7:13) and *seems* truthful, much damage can be done if it is followed and trusted. If the historical rule is adhered to, and the author of the passage is considered, this incorrect counsel can be avoided.

2. The *historical receiver* of scripture, or to whom the scripture is addressed.

This is particularly helpful while reading Acts 2, where a distinctly Jewish message is preached to a Jewish audience. This is helpful, since the "plan of salvation" included water baptism! [Read Acts 2:38!]

If the historical principle is followed, the student of the word of God will be aware that Acts 2:38 is NOT addressed to any Gentile (OR JEW) *after* Acts 15! The segment of scripture is related to the Jews who crucified the Messiah and *not* the Gentiles of then or today (see "**you**," "**house of Israel**," see verses 5, 14, 22, 23, 36, and 37; also "**we**," verse 39)! The Charismatic and Campbellite will point to verse 39 attempting to endorse verse 38 for us today, refusing to notice that the quotation is from Daniel 9:7 and deals with the Jewish people who were dispersed, *not* Gentiles! The early church was *so Jewish*, that the Lord had to convince Peter with a heavenly vision that it was okay to even preach to Gentiles. And even then, Jewish believers (including Peter) refused to fellowship with Gentile believers, and had to be rebuked by the "**apostle of the Gentiles**" (Rom. 11:13) in Galatians 2.

3. The *historical purpose* of the passage.

This would concern passages dealing with historical events such as the destruction of Jerusalem by Titus in 70 A.D. found in the gospel of Luke (Luke 21:20-24). Many Old Testament passages that concern the downfall of kings and rulers would fall under this category. The book of Daniel (although prophetic) contains much historical data. Scofield lists the "historical books" as Joshua to Esther, twelve in number.[16]

It is also imperative, that the student of the word of God bear in mind that each passage of scripture contains a historical meaning. For example, the 23rd Psalm *does* have historical significance in the life of David. He composed it (under the inspiration of the Holy Ghost) with application to *himself*, and did not automatically know that it would be the words of the Messiah. Devotionally, the verse could be applicable to *any* person who feels like God has forsaken them since the Lord does "**hide**" Himself sometimes (see Ps. 13:1; 27:9; 30:7; 10:1). Keep in mind that the historical worth of the passage should never be lost in the devotional or doctrinal meanings.

4. The *historical culture* connected to the passage.

This principle would apply to things in the scripture such as "foot washings," and "holy kisses." The next time you attend a Baptist church (normally Primitive Baptist) where they want you to "unloose" and you feel uncomfortable, just tell them to "pucker up." The very idea of attributing a Jewish custom of the day to the local New Testament church as an ordinance! It simply demonstrates the dearth of the word of God (Amos 8:11) among our Baptist brethren. I can hear the "foot washer" say, "Jesus commanded it in John 13:15 for us to follow his example." First of all, He did not command *us*, he commanded His Jewish disciples. Also, He told His disciples to "**observe and do**" everything the Pharisees were observing and doing that concerned following righteousness and the Old Testament

---

[16] *Scofield Reference Bible*, 257.

law (Matt. 23:3). When have you heard of a Baptist "foot washer" that wore "**phylacteries**?" They do not even know what they are. [That is one of the words people do not know how to pronounce, much less what it means!] The "**holy kiss**" is equally as biblical as "foot washing" yet refused as a practice by most Baptists. The insistent "foot washer" seeking for an emotional thrill in church fellowship (maybe because he is lacking fellowship with the Lord, and the word of God), will be adamant that he is "following Christ" by applying this cultural segment of scripture to the church. He is resolute that we are to take John 13:15 literally, but when it comes to the "**example**" of Christ in 1 Peter 2:21 he is not looking for a literal cross to die on. Obviously there are some cultural boundaries in place with scripture that we are to "rightly divide" from doctrinal necessities.

[I was in a meeting where the evangelist mentioned "foot washing" during his sermon, and toward the end of the message a visiting preacher said, "Bring me a pitcher of water. I am going to wash somebody's feet." Upon which I (seated at the piano ready to play the invitation hymn), resiliently sounded the first few notes of the song while the pastor attempted to quiet things down. Needless to say it ruined the invitation.]

5. The *historical geography* of the scripture passage.

This procedure of study is beneficial with apologetics (i.e. defending the Bible, or "**contend[ing] for the faith**" Jude 3). If the Bible believer is somewhat familiar with biblical geography he can refute the infidels who use their education to tear down the Bible. When the scripture says that the "**earth was divided**" (Gen. 10:32,35; 1 Chron. 1:19) an immediate explanation is given for the "continental drift theory." Also, if the student of scripture knows that Jerusalem is "up" geographically, there is NO contradiction in passages that mention going "up" to Jerusalem from a northern point.

Archaeological finds such as the weld prisom, the Adam and Eve seal, and the Babylonian creation tables give more solid evidence to the validity and veracity of scripture. Geographical, archaeological, and scientific substantiation for the Bible supplements the accuracy and literalness of scripture, and should not be ignored but researched and used for **"edification, and not to destruction"** (2 Cor. 13:10).

6. The *historical significance secular history* at the time of the writing.

The significance of this cannot be underestimated, especially in the sphere of chronology. If the prophecies of Isaiah, for instance, were not recorded *prior* to their fulfillment, then they are a hoax. LaHaye says that at least fifty-nine percent of Isaiah is prophetic: "no less than 754 verses out of 1,292 in Isaiah . . .are prophetic."[17] The time frame of events in scripture can be compared, many times, with the reign of secular kings, (like in Luke 3:1,2), or events (the flood of Noah was recorded in Egyptian, Indian, Chinese, Greek, British, American Indian, and Babylonian traditions) and verifies its astounding precision.

OTHER "BASICS"

There are some other hermeneutical dogmas that are equally important to the literal view as the grammatical and historical ones. They are:

1. The law of first mention.

---

[17] "Isaiah," *Tim LaHaye Prophecy Study Bible*, (AMG Publishers) 689.

Biblical Interpretation **49**

A good example of this is where "love" is first used in the Bible between a father and his son Gen. 22).

2. The law of full mention.

Never base a doctrine upon incomplete information about the subject. This law has been violated by all "Full Gospel" and Charismatic groups.
[It is funny how the T.V. preachers can only get the money they pray for by advertising their prayer to millions. Why can't they pray in secret for the money?]

3. Bible numerics.

The numerical principles must be adhered to if one is to follow the grammatical - historical method. Numbers have meanings in the text of scripture, and also in the numbering of the chapter and verse divisions.
[Now, we realize scholarship will reject the last part of that statement, because they believe only "the originals" were inspired (which contained no numerical chapter and verse divisions). But since "**all scripture is given by inspiration of God**" (2 Tim. 3:16), and the KJV is "**scripture**," we had better pay attention to the chapter and verse numberings.]

4. Bible typology.

Discerning the use of typology will also aid the literal view of scripture. Types are different than allegories in that a type is based upon an actual historical figure or event, whereas an allegory is a fictitious narrative. For example, Joseph is a type of Christ in 142 particulars, but Joseph was *first* a historical character. Typology expounds truths already apparent in scripture. The truth of the second coming of Jesus Christ is plainly taught in the New Testament but is intricately developed in many Old Testament types (such as Joshua and Solomon).

5. Association and Contrast.

The imperative of the literal interpretation of scripture cannot be realized without an acknowledging of associations and contrasts. The "sun" is associated with the "son" in Malachi 4 and Psalm 19, and the disparity of capitol punishment *before* the flood (Gen. 4:11-13) and *after* the flood (Gen. 9:5) is noticeably perceptible if one can READ.

[If some people obeyed traffic signs and lights like they do the laws of association and contrast, they would be locked up for reckless driving.] The old adage, "things different are not the same," sums up this rule perfectly.

6. Scripture with scripture.

This remains the foremost method of discerning a proper literal viewpoint (see 1 Cor. 2:13; Gen. 40:8; and John 16). Parallel passages (such as the Gospels, Kings and Chronicles) and supplemental passages (even comparing seemingly minute phrases such as Matt. 16:18 with John 1:42) provide the believer with the entire representation of the text in question.

THREE APPLICATIONS

Proper biblical interpretation also *discriminates* between applications a verse has. The three applications are: historical, doctrinal (mostly prophetic), and devotional (or spiritual).

HISTORICAL - The verse has a place in a specific time frame in history. The Bible is a record of *history* detailing what God wanted to pass on to future generations.

DOCTRINAL - Every verse in the Bible is aimed at a *specific* group of people in order to teach truth or truths that are precisely for *them*. Improper placement of verses *doctrinally* lead to heresy and false teachings. Be careful not to discount whole portions of scripture (like hypers) thinking, "They don't apply to me." Remember, 2 Timothy 3:16 proclaims that "**all scripture . . . is profitable for doctrine**," not just "parts of scripture." There is plenty of doctrinal material for the New Testament Christian in the Old Testament. While it may not relate to salvation, or "justification by faith," Old Testament "**doctrine which is according to godliness**" (1 Tim. 6:4) should be followed and heeded.

DEVOTIONAL or INSPIRATIONAL - Every verse has a spiritual application which can be used for instructional purposes although it may not be aimed at that person historically, or doctrinally.

> *2 Tim. 3:16* **All scripture is given by inspiration of God, and is profitable for doctrine, for reproof, for correction, for instruction in righteousness:**

A person begins teaching heresy when he abandons the *doctrinal* meaning of a verse. Some will incorrectly apply James 5:14 ("**anointing him with oil**") to the Church Age, even though the book is NOT written to the body of Christ (James 1:1). This is done to invent another "ceremony" (akin to "foot washing") that provides emotional appeal. The context of James 5:14,15 demands that the person WILL BE HEALED (as in Mark. 16:18), and thus terminates *any* present day application. Asserting this "**anointing,**" as a doctrinal truth for this age, is analogous to some Charismatics who put Crisco over the doors of their houses to ward off demons.

THREE APPLICATIONS DEMONSTRATED

A good verse to exhibit the three applications is Psalm 22:1:

> *Ps 22:1* **My God, my God, why hast thou forsaken me? why art thou so far from helping me, and from the words of my roaring?**

1. *HISTORICAL* - The author of the Psalm, David, feels that God has forsaken him.

2. *DOCTRINAL* - A prophecy of the words of Jesus Christ while hanging on the cross. Shows the propitiatory offering of Christ in relation to the Father.

3. *DEVOTIONAL* - Most people feel at one time or other that God has forsaken them.

Weak, enervated Bible teaching (like you hear on most Christian radio stations) emphasizes the devotional application because it appeals to the "persona," instead of the doctrinal application (which accentuates *truth* and *facts*). Solid preaching must be balanced. If you stress *only* the doctrinal meaning, you are left with *no practical application*. What good is a sermon if it does not apply to someone personally? But, as we stressed, if constant devotional application is emphasized, the Biblical *truth* or *doctrine* is often left up for grabs.

Note the following verses that point out the importance of *doctrine*:

Acts 2:42 **And they continued stedfastly in the apostles'** <u>doctrine and fellowship</u> **. . .**

Rom 16:17 **Now I beseech you, brethren, mark them which cause divisions and offences** <u>contrary to the doctrine</u> **which ye have learned; and avoid them.**

Eph 4:14 **That we henceforth be no more children, tossed to and fro, and carried about with** <u>every wind of doctrine</u>**, by the sleight of men, and cunning craftiness, whereby they lie in wait to deceive;**

1 Tim 1:3 **. . . that thou mightest charge some that they** <u>teach no other doctrine,</u>

1 Tim 1:10 **. . . and if there be any other thing that is contrary to** <u>sound doctrine</u>**;**

1 Tim 4:6 **. . . nourished up in the words of faith and of** <u>good doctrine</u> **. . .**

1 Tim 4:13 **. . . give attendance to reading, to exhortation, to** <u>doctrine</u>**.**

1 Tim 4:16 **Take heed unto thyself, and unto the** <u>doctrine</u>**. . .**

2 Tim 4:2 **Preach the word . . .with all longsuffering and** <u>doctrine</u>**.**

CHAPTER 3

History of Dispensational Thought

A False Indictment

Those who reject "**sound doctrine**" (2 Tim. 4:3), and refuse to "rightly divide" (2 Tim. 2:15) the Bible, often indict dispensationalism as being a novelty of the nineteenth-century Plymouth Brethren movement:

> Dispensationalism <u>arose in the early nineteenth century</u> in Great Britain within the Brethren movement, which was led by men such as John Nelson Darby, Samuel P. Tregelles, and Charles Henry Mackintosh. They and other Brethren leaders produced volumes of expositional works, which influenced many prominent Christians in the United States, including D.L. Moody, James H. Brookes, and C.I. Scofield. . . .The essential doctrine of

dispensationalism cannot be found prior to the nineteenth century.[1] *[emphasis added]*

Dispensationalism, as we know it today, had its beginning with the Brethren movement, which became prominent around 1830. This group came to be known as "Plymouth Brethren," because their publications centered in Plymouth, England. Ever since the days of John Nelson Darby, dispensationalists have been prolific writers, and their works are in abundance today.[2] *[emphasis added]*

Thus Darby is important, not merely as a founder of dispensationalism, but as a representative of some of the elements that continue to be strong concerns of dispensationalists to this day.[3] *[emphasis added]*

By the end of the 20th century--less than two centuries after he created it--John Nelson Darby's Dispensationalism had accomplished what few (if any) other theological movements had. . . . John Nelson Darby founded this unique theological perspective and his non-Plymouth Brethren followers eventually assumed the leadership of Dispensationalism as a movement during the late 19th and the early 20th centuries. These leaders included James Hall Brookes, C.I. Scofield, and Lewis Sperry Chafer. They were in turn succeeded by John F. Walvoord, J. Dwight Pentecost, Charles C. Ryrie and others. . . . traditional Dispensationalism . . . consists of a series of footnotes to Darby.[4] *[emphasis added]*

. . . dispensationalism, as a system of theological interpretation, dates from the nineteenth century . . . it was not known before in the history of Christian thought . . .as

---

[1] Mathison, Keith A., *Dispensationalism* (New Jersey: P&R Publishing, 1995) 10, 13.
[2] Cox, William E. *An Examination of Dispensationalism* (New Jersey: P&R Publishing, 1980) 1.
[3] Poythress, Vern S., *Understanding Dispensationalists* (New Jersey: P&R Publishing, 1987) 14.
[4] Henzel Ronald M. *Darby, Dualism and the Decline of Dispensationalism* (Tucson, Arizona: Fenestra Books, 2003.) 2, 48.

a system of thought dispensationalism can be traced to the theology and practice of John Nelson Darby . . . [5]

The Plymouth Brethren movement, from which modern Dispensationalism arose, began in the second decade of the nineteenth century.[6]

The implications, and allegations from the above statements are an attempt to sway the student away from dispensational thought. They want the student to think dispensationalism is some new unorthodox fad invented by men, instead of the biblical method of studying God's word.

SUMMARY OF ANTI-DISPENSATIONAL RHETORIC

1. Dispensationalism is man-made.

2. None of the "pre-Darby" dispensationalists (even though they taught different dispensations) can be considered dispensationalists, because their systems do not conform 100% to those of Darby, Scofield and Chafer. Therefore, dispensationalism can only be traced to the Plymouth Brethren movement.

3. "Since dispensationalism is recent, it is therefore unorthodox."[7] [Note: it is only "recent" by name, not theory or layout.]

4. "The idea came from Darby through Scofield and Chafer, and certainly not from the Bible."[8]

---

[5] Bass, Clarence B. *Backgrounds to Dispensationalism* (Grand Rapids: Baker Book House, 1960) 7.
[6] Gerstner, John H., *Wrongly Dividing the Word of Truth,* (Morgan: Soli Deo Gloria Publications, 2000) 17.
[7] Ryrie, Charles C., *Dispensationalism* (Chicago: Moody Press, 1995) 61.
[8] *Ibid.*

DISPENSATIONALISM: WHEN AND WHERE?

There are several things wrong with the above statements and their implications. First of all, if a teaching or system of thought is a Bible teaching, it is entirely immaterial (as to the veracity of it) *when* it surfaced in Christian publication circles. For example, since we have no records of the gospel being preached in America prior to the 1500's, does that mean there was *no gospel*? Of course not! If the Bible is the final authority, it matters little what human authors have said about it, and *when* they said it.

EARLY "CHRISTIAN" WRITINGS

Scholars, not soul-winners, are the ones concerned with the early traditions of church fathers and what *they* said. Real Bible students should be interested in "**what saith the scripture**" (Rom. 4:3). In all actuality it matters little if a "church father" (early or late) propagated dispensationalism. Real "thimkers" understand that early Christians were too busy obeying Matthew 28:19,20 to write voluminous essays on the "hermeneutical *approach* to the scriptures." Also, the common Christian of that day did not possess the financial backing and endorsement necessary to let their theological voice be heard! The "fathers" who were influential enough for their writings to pass down through time (like Origen) were so often corrupt you would be "hard pressed" to even validate their conversion! Should we adhere to *their* methodology of studying the Bible? Reformed Calvinistic "scholars" do, *real* Bible students do not.

The problem with anti-dispensationalists is their *rejection* of the Authorized King James Version, along with their acceptance of the *thoughts of men* (namely "church fathers").

A consideration of Church history will acquit dispensationalism from these frivolous accusations, demonstrating the *fact* of progressive revelation. Dispensational thought was NOT stimulated during the Dark Ages under Roman Catholic totalitarianism, nor shortly thereafter during the Protestant Reformation, when authors were ironing out the wrinkles of the doctrines of salvation. [This is not to say that dispensational thought was not present.] The *written world*, at that time, did not need a book on "dispensational truth," it needed books on Romans and Galatians teaching "justification by faith." Church history unfolds the reality that the body of Christ gained greater scriptural insight after, *and only after*, the publication of the King James text, and the revivals in America. Those *facts* can be ignored, but not disputed.

DISPENSATIONALISM BEFORE DARBY?

It is the game of classification and terminology (along with the subject of "progressive revelation"), that decides whether or not dispensational thought was around prior to Darby. Anti-dispensationalists will not allow a "pre-Darby" premillennialist to be called a dispensationalist, even if he used the word "dispensation" and made division between the "ages." For them, the term "dispensationalist" *must* refer to someone who strongly divided the Church and Israel, which many premillennial Bible believers did not. Once the weak Bible student is convinced that "the essential doctrine of dispensationalism cannot be found prior to the nineteenth century,"[9] he is ready to accept the corrupt Reformed paradigm.

Is this "historical argument" really valid? Church history proves an element of dispensationalism *preceding* Darby by at least two-hundred fifty years! And (as we have overtly stated), it makes little difference if there were *no* records of

---

[9] Mathison, *Dispensationalism*, 10, 13.

dispensational thought before Darby, since it is a biblical system of study!

PROGRESSIVE REVELATION

The fact of "progressive revelation" is apparent not only with dispensationalism, but with *every* other major doctrine or biblical ideology. A good Bible example is found in the book of Acts, where (although it was in effect), the truth of the gospel was revealed in stages. Peter was not preaching the substitutionary blood atonement of Christ for sinners in Acts 2. He was preaching the death of the promised Messiah! The death of Christ *as a sinless substitute for sinners* (Jew *and* Gentile) was first preached (minus all the *types*) in the book of Acts by Phillip in chapter *eight*. God chooses to reveal His word in phases to "**babes**" while purposely *hiding it* from the "**wise and prudent**" (Luke 10:21). He does not depend on "church fathers" to verify the truth.

To deny "progressive revelation" is to disavow *history*, for history chronicles the *enhancement* of biblically sound truths. LaHaye highlights the fact that prophecy developed with the availability of the Bible to the common people, which had been censored during the Dark Ages, and finally made accessible after 1,700 years.[10] If believers do not have Bibles, how can they learn, teach, and expound upon its precepts? Dispensationalism, or the pretribulation rapture, may not have enjoyed the discussion of subjects like the trinity, during the first three centuries of church history, but that does not cancel out its legitimacy.

---

[10] LaHaye, Tim, *The Rapture* (Eugene, Oregon: Harvest House Publishers, 2002) 42.

PRE-TRIB RAPTURE IN THIRD CENTURY

The suggestion that Scofield (through Darby's teachings) invented the pretribulation rapture is fallacious propaganda! [There is no recorded information that Scofield ever personally met Darby, though he studied under Brookes, an acquaintance of Darby.] The pretribulation rapture is discussed in a book by a Baptist pastor named Morgan Edwards called *Millennium, Last Days Novelities*, written in 1788.[11] And if that were not enough corroboration, there is a Latin manuscript named Ephraem Syrus, dated at 306-374 that states:

> For all the saints and the Elect of God are gathered prior to the Tribulation that is to come; they are taken to the Lord lest they see the confusion that is to overwhelm the world because of our sins.[12]

The fact of the matter is that God chose to reveal certain truths, and clarify them *through time* with specific men of God. [The modern colloquialism would be "tweak."] These men of God always acquired these *truths* from the "received text" of the Authorized Version (*before* or after 1611). Note, Dr. Ruckman:

> The truth of Progressive Revelation is that God the Holy Spirit continues to reveal new truths from the canonical Scriptures century after century, and these truths never contradict the canonical Scriptures. When we speak of "advanced revelations" coming from the Authorized Version, which obviously cannot be found in other translations (or any copies of Greek or Hebrew manuscripts), we are always speaking of the Holy Spirit's own choosing to work through an English text which

---

[11] *Ibid.*
[12] Ruckman, Peter S., *22 years of the Bible Believer's Bulletin* (Pensacola: Bible Baptist Bookstore, 2000) 442.

contains the canonical Scriptures. We have never added one word to the accepted canon.[13]

Ryrie designates the implications against dispensationalism as "straw men."[14] He points out the error of declining a doctrine simply because it was not developed fully in post-apostolic times (first or second centuries) stating:

> The fact that something was taught in the first century does not make it right (unless taught in the canonical Scriptures), and the fact that something was not taught until the nineteenth century does not make it wrong, unless, of course, it is unscriptural... the ultimate question is not, Is dispensationalism - or any other teaching historic? But, Is it scriptural.[15]

You see, the issue is, and always will be FINAL AUTHORITY. If men place their authority in "the fathers" (apostolic, ante-Nicene, post-Nicene, ect.), instead of the canon of scripture (i.e. rule or accepted text - the KJV *is* a "Textus Receptus") their "orientation" becomes *relative* to men instead of God! God the Holy Spirit bore witness to the text of the AV and made it the rule and standard canon. Being such, it continues to give "revelation" to those who uphold, honor and magnify it (NOT THE ORIGINALS) "**above**" the name of God Himself!

Ps 138:2 **I will worship toward thy holy temple, and praise thy name for thy lovingkindness and for thy truth: for thou hast magnified thy word above all thy name.**

---

[13] Ruckman, Peter S., *The Two Raptures* (Pensacola: Bible Baptist Bookstore, 1996) 2.
[14] Ryrie, Charles C., *Dispensationalism* (Chicago: Moody Press, 1995) 62.
[15] *Ibid.*

PRE-DARBY DISPENSATIONALISM

The evidence confirms that dispensational ideology ("certain features"[16]) was well established before Darby was even born (1800). This is because the tenets of dispensationalism are biblical. The following men produced

DISPENSATIONAL SYSTEMS *BEFORE* DARBY:[17]

WILLIAM GOUGE (1575-1653)	**PIERRE POIRET (1646-1719)**
ISAAC WATTS (1674-1748)	**JOHN FLECHIERE (1729-1785)**
JOHN TAYLOR OF NORWICH (1694-1751)	**JOHN PRIESTLY (1733-1804)**
DAVID BOGUE (1750-1825)	**GEORGE FABER (1773-1843)**
ADAM CLARKE (1762-1832)	**DAVID RUSSELL (1779-1848)**

Ryrie says that "evidence is available and shows that dispensational concepts were held early and throughout the history of the church,"[18] and lists Justin Martyr (110-165), Irenaeus (130-200), Clement of Alexandria (150-220), and even Augustine (354-430).[19] The idea that Darby "created" [20]

---
[16] *Ibid.*
[17] Ruckman, Peter S., *How to teach Dispensational Truth* (Pensacola: Bible Believers Press, 1992) 5.
[18] Ryrie, *Dispensationalism*, 63.
[19] *Ibid.*, 63, 64.
[20] Henzel, *Darby, Dualism and the Decline of Dispensationalism*, 2.

dispensationalism is absurd. Simply because he emphasized some Bible truths does not mean he invented them. That type of reasoning is akin to the hyper-dispensationalist who presupposes that since Paul was revealed the truth of the mystery of the body of Christ, it must have begun with him. *Knowing* something is not contingent on the thing being created, only *revealed*. Additionally, note comments by Timothy Rose:

> Darby is often referred to as "the father of modern dispensational theology." It is equivalent to William Cary being the "father of modern missions." Cary did not invent missions. Jesus Christ did. Carey was not the first missionary sent out of a local Church. Paul and Barnabas were. So it is with Darby. He did not invent Dispensational Thought. He propagated it on a universal level[21]

JOHN NELSON DARBY (1800-1882)

Darby did; however, play an important role in the history of dispensational thought and his contribution cannot go unnoticed.

Darby was born in London of wealthy Irish parents and was well educated at Trinity College in Dublin. He chose law as a career (like Scofield), which he forsook after a year to enter the ministry. After his conversion in 1825 he was ordained as a deacon and a priest in the Church of England, but grew discontent with the state-church, and began fellowship with believers outside of the "recognized church." He eventually left this apostate church system in 1831.

Joining the Plymouth Brethren movement, Darby found a soundboard which to broadcast his biblical ideas through the Powerscourt Conferences (1831-1833), and began writing

---

[21] Rose, Timothy P., *Bible Believing Dispensationalism* (Auckland: PRAE Books, 2004) 54.

profusely. He even translated the Bible into English, French, and German. "John Darby claimed he got the inspiration for the pre-tribulation rapture of the church in 1828 after he saw the distinction between Israel and the church in his study of the book of Ephesians."[22] But, as we noted before, he was certainly not the first to make this distinction.

Darby sparked an expectancy of the Lord's return teaching the imminency of the rapture, and his return prior to Daniel's Seventieth Week:

> At times Darby spoke of this seven-year period as entirely future, but at other times as only three and one-half years remaining for the future (the first three and one-half years being the earthly ministry of Christ).[23]

[Larkin obliterates this idea that the first part of Daniel's Seventieth Week took place during the earthly life of Christ:

> the bloody sacrifices of the temple did not cease at the crucifixion, nor were they put away by Christ. They did not cease until the destruction of the Temple by the Romans 40 years later.[24]

Dan. 9:27 states that the sacrifices will "**cease**" after the first 3½ years.]

Darby taught that a dispensation included:

> governmental administration, responsibility, and revelation to fulfill both . . . Darby did not think that any dispensations existed in the first world . . . only from Noah through the millennium could dispensations be distinguished. . . . Darby traced eight dispensations as

---

[22] LaHaye, *The Rapture*, 43.
[23] "John Nelson Darby," *Dictionary of Premillennial Theology:* 84.
[24] Larkin, Clarence, *The Book of Daniel* (Glenside, Pa: Rev. Clarence Larkin Est., 1929) 196.

follows: (1) Noah, (2) Abraham, (3) Israel under law (prophet), (4) Israel under the priesthood, (5) Israel under the kings, (6) Gentiles (from Nebuchadnezzar to the Antichrist,) (7) church or Christian (although he hesitates to call the church in its heavenly perspective a dispensation), and (8) Millennium or kingdom.[25]

Darby led the Brethren movement and influenced men like Moody, Brookes, and George Muller (although Darby and Muller parted fellowship). Through his voluminous writings he wrote "the 'Preface' for Scofield,"[26] who would later publish the greatest contribution to dispensational theology: the Scofield Reference Bible.

CYRUS INGERSON SCOFIELD (1843-1921)

C.I. Scofield, known mostly for the publication of the *Scofield Reference Bible*, was born in Michigan in 1843. His mother, unable to recover at his birth died, and Scofield was reared by his father and stepmother until he moved to Tennessee with his sister Laura and her husband. When the Civil War broke out (i.e. the War of Northern Aggression), he lied about his age in order to fight for the south. "He fought under Robert E. Lee and under fire in eighteen battles and minor engagements, he was awarded the Cross of Honor for bravery at Antietam."[27]

After the war he moved to St. Louis and married Leontine Cerre (a wealthy Roman Catholic), and then later moved to Kansas where he served as a District Attorney. "He was the

---

[25] *Ibid.*, 84.
[26] Ruckman, *How to teach Dispensational Truth*, 6.
[27] Reese, Ed., *The Life and Ministry of C.I. Scofield* (Lansing, IL: Reese Publications) 1.

youngest U.S. attorney in the country at that time."[28] With his marriage dissolving (Leontine was granted a legal separation in 1877), and the pressure from traveling back and forth from Kansas to St. Louis (where he had established a law practice in 1879), he began to drink heavily, becoming a drunkard.

Scofield was led to the Lord by a friend, Tom McPheeters (about his own age – 36) whom he had met in his law practice. McPheeters was a YMCA worker and a member of James Hall Brookes's Walnut Street Presbyterian Church. Brookes took Scofield under his wing and soon Scofield was assisting in the campaign of D.L. Moody in St. Louis, (1879-1880) and joined the Pilgrim Congregational Church.[29] He "became acting super-intendent of the local YMCA and was licensed to work in the Hyde Park Congregational Church (1880-82). He also worked with railroad men in East St. Louis."[30] In 1882 Scofield became the pastor of a small church (one man and eleven women) in Dallas: the First Congregational Church. He was ordained in 1883.

Although his small church grew better (up to four-hundred), his marriage did not, and the divorce was finalized Dec. 8, 1883. This was after many attempts by Scofield to reconcile. The church did not kick him out of the pastorate, nor did the "brethren" say that he did not "meet the scriptural qualifications for a Christian minister."[31] The preachers of the day even gave him a recommendation to REMARRY (after he wrote some 100 evangelical leaders for their opinion"[32]). This he did in 1884.

[The modern teaching that "**the husband of one wife**" (1 Tim. 3:2) refers to "one marriage license" is really stretching

---

[28] *Ibid.*, 2.
[29] "C.I. Scofield," *Dictionary of Premillennial Theology:* 390.
[30] Reese, *The Life and Ministry of C.I. Scofield*, 4.
[31] Custer, Stewart, *The Truth About the King James Only Controversy* (Greenville: Bob Jones University Press: 1981) 35.
[32] Reese, *The Life and Ministry of C.I. Scofield*, 5.

scripture. Everyone knows that polygamy was being practiced in apostolic times, and it was not considered unlawful. Note the comment by Barnes:

> . . . At a time when polygamy was not uncommon, to say that a man should "have but one wife" would be naturally understood as prohibiting polygamy.[33]

Since the tense of the verse is in the *present:* "**A bishop then must be**" (1 Tim. 3:2) how could it refer to *past* marriages? Some brethren teach that a man cannot pastor even if he was divorced and remarried *prior* to his conversion.

This "only one marriage license" doctrine suppresses some true God called preachers, and (to some extent) grants full control of the pastor's ministry to the WIFE. For, if she sins (not the preacher), and leaves, HE MUST quit preaching. The question then arises: What is he willing to compromise in order to keep her, and, consequently, the ministry? Thank God, Scofield was allowed to continue his ministry *after* his wife left him!]

Scofield had a vision for missions that was hardly surpassed by any contemporary pastor of his day. He and some laymen from his church founded a mission board for the work in Central America, and "soon the church was giving more to missions than to the home budget."[34] He also formulated a correspondence course that taught dispensational truth which was eventually sold to the Moody Bible Institute in 1915. This course is still available today.

D.L. Moody asked Scofield to become the pastor the Trinitarian Congregational Church of Northfield, and this opened up numerous doors for the talented Bible teacher. He began a traveling ministry of teaching in the Northfield

---

[33] Barnes, Albert, *Notes on the New Testament* (Electronic Database: Biblesoft)
[34] Reese, *The Life and Ministry of C.I. Scofield*, 5.

conferences, and was a featured speaker at the Niagara conferences, which focused primarily on dispensational truth and prophecy. He also became the president of the Northfield Bible Training School that Moody had established. With the termination of the Niagara conferences (because of a split between post and pretribulationalism), he began (along with Arno C. Gaebelein, John T. Pirie and Alwyn Ball) contemplating the production of a reference Bible from a premillennial, dispensational, pretribulational viewpoint.

In 1902 he returned to his Dallas pastorate and began assimilating the material for the monumental task of engendering a reference Bible. From 1902-1909, he devoted most of his time to the reference Bible making several trips to England (Oxford libraries) and finally he "finished the initial draft of the notes in Montreux, Switzerland, in 1907, and edited them at his summer home in New Hampshire and in New York City in 1908."[35] The Oxford University Press published it in 1909, with a revision in 1917.

THE SCOFIELD REFERENCE BIBLE

The impact of the Scofield Reference Bible on dispensational propagation cannot be overvalued. Dr. Ruckman:

> If any Southern Baptists showed up between 1910 and 1970 that were soul-winning, orthodox men . . . somewhere on them (or under their books in their offices) would be found TWO BOOKS. Clarence Larkin's Dispensational Truth and the Old Scofield Reference Bible of 1909.[36]

---

[35] "C.I. Scofield," *Dictionary of Premillennial Theology:* 391.
[36] Ruckman, Peter S. *New Testament Church, Vol. 2* (Pensacola: Bible Believers Press, 1984) 114.

Scofield chose to print the King James text even though the RV and ASV were the alleged "best translations" of the day. He explained in the Introduction to the 1909 edition:

> After mature reflection it was determined to use the Authorized Version. None of the many Revisions have commended themselves to the people at large. The Revised Version, which has now been before the public for twenty-seven years gives no indication of becoming in any general sense the people's Bible of the English-speaking world.[37]

It is true that there are *many* places where the margin "corrects," or "emends" (see Scofield's Introduction) the King James text, but at least he regarded the AV as the Bible for the English speaking world. [It would be interesting to know what kind of stand many of the old timers (like Scofield, Moody, Wesley, ect.) would take *today* with over 200 English perversions on the market. The King James issue is definitely a modern debate, that has taken precedence with the Laodicean Church Age.]

> The notes in the Old Scofield Bible teach that the Antichrist is a MAN, that hell is literal burning fire, that the security of the believer is eternal, that the Rapture is before the Tribulation, that the Millennial reign of Christ is a literal, bodily reign at the literal city of Jerusalem, and that the key to understanding the Bible is God's dealing with the Jews - the nation of Israel. With the King James text, the Scofield Bible was ANTI-CATHOLIC.[38]

Scofield was beyond doubt the most prominent influence of dispensational thought. He published not only a reference Bible teaching the principles of right division, but numerous

---

[37] Scofield Reference Bible (New York: Oxford, 1909) iv.
[38] Ruckman, *New Testament Church, Vol. 2*, 114.

articles, pamphlets, and books such as *Rightly Dividing the Word of Truth*, which is still published today.

Scofield also was,

> centrally prominent in the creation of several schools, beginning with the Southwestern School of the Bible during his first Dallas pastorate, then presiding over the Northfield Bible Training School, founding the New York School of the Bible, and, finally, establishing the Philadelphia School of the Bible (now Philadelphia College of Bible). In the field of missionary endeavor, he founded the Central American Mission and presided over its direction for nearly thirty years.[39]

CLARENCE LARKIN (1820-1924)

Clarence Larkin (best known for his monumental work *Dispensational Truth*, 1918), was converted at the age of nineteen and confirmed in the Episcopal church. He graduated with a degree in mechanical engineering, and became "a supervisor and instructor at the Pennsylvania Institution for the Blind where he served three years before entering private business. During this time he felt led into the ministry."[40]

Larkin, at thirty-two years of age, joined the Baptist Church, where he was ordained two years later and became a premillennialist. "He pastored first in Kennett Square, Pennsylvania; and later in Fox Chase, Pennsylvania, where he remained for twenty years."[41] It was during his pastorate that he began developing large charts on prophecy for use in his pulpit ministry. These charts became so popular that he

---

[39] "C.I. Scofield," *Dictionary of Premillennial Theology:* 393.
[40] "Larkin, Clarence," *Dictionary of Premillennial Theology:* 239.
[41] *Ibid.*

assimilated them and distributed them all over the nation. With the nation and the world at war, Larkin became the "man of the hour" with scriptural answers:

> At the beginning of World War I in 1914, Larkin gave an address, War and Prophecy, and soon after began working on a number of charts accompanied with descriptive texts.[42]

LARKIN'S GREATEST BOOK

He later published *Dispensational Truth or God's Plan and Purpose in the Ages* in 1918, and enlarged it in 1920. This work is by far the *definitive standard* and "granddaddy" of all dispensational works. There can be little improvement on the book. It is masterfully designed with charts and descriptions and, although he quotes the Revised Version twelve times (pages 22, 44, 56, 56, 98, 100 113, 118, 122, 135, 135, 136), the light and illumination is from the text of the King James Bible. Larkin does not rely on the Greek, Hebrew, or any corrupt editions from the Alexandrian line of manuscripts. It is decidedly anti-Catholic naming the "whore" of Revelation 17 the "papal church." He also accepts the "gap theory," as a "gap fact."

Larkin, never was a member of the "scholars union" (like Scofield, Chafer, and Ironside), and consequently in no way received the credit he deserved for the promotion and development of dispensationalism. In fact, because of his views on the gap, "the sons of God," and his teachings about the great pyramids in Egypt, he is often derided as too sensational:

---

[42] *Ibid.*, 239.

> Though frequently ridiculed by critics today as too intricate or sensational (and also for his presentations on Egypt's Great Pyramid and on the Gap Theory . . . .[43] Critics of dispensationalism have always found it easier to identify the simplistic approaches of Scofield, to criticize the excesses of Lewis Sperry Chafer, and to poke fun at the charts of Clarence Larkin . . . [44]

Even though "scholars" reject the simplistic style of Larkin, with his vivid charts, he (according to Ruckman) "was the man that taught every prophetic teacher in America from 1930-1983, everything they knew about the basics of prophecy and rightly dividing the word of truth."[45] Where Scofield dropped the ball (i.e. Gen. 6 - "**sons of God**") Larkin caught it and completed the play. Larkin's other published books include: *Revelation, Daniel, The Second Coming, Rightly Dividing the Word, The Spirit World, Why I am a Baptist,* and *A Medicine Chest For Christian Practitioners*. These books are a *must* for the dispensationalists' library.

POST-SCOFIELD CONTRIBUTORS

As stated earlier, no modern *recognized* dispensationalist (outside of the King James only crowd) will get any "deeper" than Scofield or Larkin. The Bereans (following Bullinger and Stam) go too far to the right and off the highway, while "normative" dispensationalists cannot get out of first gear.

Lewis Sperry Chafer (1871-1952) tried to wear the mantle of C.I. Scofield after training and traveling with him as a Bible teacher. In 1922 (after Scofield's death) he moved to Dallas to pastor the church that Scofield had founded: the First Congregational Church (renamed the Scofield Memorial

---

[43] *Ibid.*, 240.
[44] Blaising and Bock, *Dispensationalism, Israel and the Church*, 12.
[45] Ruckman, *New Testament Church, Vol. 2*, 197.

Church in 1923). The mantle (2 Kings 2:13,14) did not fit. Chafer was destined to be a scholar, which Scofield was not. Scofield was, first of all a man (Confederate Veteran), and after that a Bible teacher with a burden for *missions*. The old guard was dying out, and it would be another twenty-seven years until God would save a man (born the year Scofield died - 1921) who would pick up where Scofield and Larkin left off.

Chafer founded the Dallas Theological Seminary (originally called the Evangelical Theological College) in 1924. Chafer (though Calvinistic) promoted dispensationalism throughout his classic work *Systematic Theology* (eight volumes). It has been called "the first major attempt to set forth the teaching of dispensational premillennialism within the rubric of traditional systematics."[46] Dallas Theological Seminary still promotes dispensationalism although many of their faculty have wavered into what is known as "progressive dispensationalism."

Henry Allan Ironside (1876-1951) also furthered dispensational thought by his publication of over sixty books and pamphlets. Although he was not formally educated, he traveled and taught the Bible for over fifty years. He pastored the Moody Memorial Church in Chicago (1930-1948), and through his publications promoted dispensationalism. He influenced many pastors and teachers with a premillennial, dispensational approach.

Some *recognized* contemporary authors that supplemented the dispensational cause would include John F. Walvoord, Charles C. Ryrie, J. Dwight Pentecost, and Tim LaHaye. Most of them are associated with Dallas Theological Seminary, and fall short when discussing "dispensational salvation."

The greatest contributor of dispensationalism *after* Scofield and Larkin came from the King James Bible believing camp. This Bible teacher (though never accepted in the "scholars

---

[46] "Chafer, Lewis Sperry," *Dictionary of Premillennial Theology:* 70.

union") was born the year Scofield died (1921), and remains critical scholarships worst enemy. He is Peter Sturges Ruckman.

Although known for his ardent defense of the Authorized Version, Ruckman analytically picked up where "classic dispensationalism" fell short. While they hinted about various plans of salvation under different covenants (Scofield's note in John 1:17, and Bullinger's *Companion Bible* in Deut. 6:25), Ruckman documented it and proved it.

Being a prolific author, Ruckman has expounded on dispensational topics in books such as: *The Sure Word of Prophecy, How to Teach Dispensational Truth,* and *The Mark of the Beast.* His commentary series (covering every *major* Book in the Bible) called *The Bible Believer's Commentary Series* is his most outstanding endowment to the dispensational cause.

DEVELOPMENT OF HYPER-DISPENSATIONALISM

A survey of the history of dispensationalism cannot be divulged without mention of the ultra-dispensational movement. Keep in mind however that the label "ultra," or "hyper" has been applied by covenant theologians to *any* dispensationalist. Likewise fundamentalists brand someone a "hyper dispensationalist" if they believe salvation is different in the Old and New Testaments.

While the theological and eschatological errors of hyper-dispensationalism will be appraised later, note Ruckman's summary:

> Ultra-dispensationalism, or hyper-dispensationalism is characterized, mainly, by the elimination of water baptism, following the conversion of a sinner to Christ, and over-emphasis on 2 Corinthians 5:19-21 and the 'Pauline message,' a lack of emphasis on the local New

Testament church, and an ultra-GRACE format, that eventually leads to Hyper-Calvinism and 'Hard Shell' predestination.[47]

ETHELBERT WILLIAM BULLINGER (1837-1913)

Hyper-dispensationalism has it roots with Ethelbert William Bullinger, (1837-1913) "a direct descendent of Johann Heinrich Bullinger, a covenant theologian who succeeded Zwingli, in Zurich, in December of 1531."[48] His ideas were known as "Bullingerism," and were "spread through the notes of the *Companion Bible*, a work partly edited by Dr. Bullinger, though he died before it was completed."[49]

Bullinger taught soul sleep, and that the body of Christ did not begin until Acts 28. He eliminated water baptism and the Lord's supper. Many of his followers in England became annihilationists.[50] The cultic group founded by Armstrong (The Worldwide Church of God, *The Plain Truth* magazine) utilizes Bullinger's *Companion Bible* to defend their heretical tendencies. [A man I worked with used the *Companion Bible* to prove everything from Jesus dying on a "stake"[51] to the story of the rich man and Lazarus being a Talmudic tradition in Luke 16.]

AMERICAN HYPERS

In America, the most common group of ultra-dispensationalists are those associated with Cornelius R. Stam, J.C. O'Hair, and Charles F. Baker. The Berean Bible Society

---

[47] Ruckman, *How to teach Dispensational Truth*, 7.
[48] "Bullinger, E.W.," *Dictionary of Premillennial Theology:* 65,66.
[49] Ironside, H.A., *Wrongly Dividing the Word of Truth*, 8.
[50] Ryrie, *Dispensationalism*, 198.
[51] "The Cross and Crucifixion," *The Companion Bible*: 186.

publishes the hyper's magazine, *The Berean Searchlight*, which propagates this "wrongly divided truth."

Hyper-dispensationalists only consider Paul's prison epistles Christian doctrine. They teach that the books of Hebrews through Revelation are not applicable for the New Testament child of God. Some of them advocate that the believer does not need to confess his sins (1 John 1). They claim also that the gospel of John falls under the category of the Old Testament even though it was written *after* Paul's epistles. They are enamored with persuading people to forsake Baptism, and err in their dating of when the body of Christ began.

DISPENSATIONALISM

Part Two:
POLEMIC

DISPENSATIONAL TRUTH

CHAPTER 4

Some Basic Divisions

DISPENSATIONAL APPROACH – A MUST!

For the Bible believer to be a student of the word of God, it is absolutely imperative that he adopt the dispensational approach. Failure to implement the biblical principles of dispensationalism (termed in scripture as "**rightly dividing**" - 2 Tim. 2:15), will escort the student into Bible mayhem. It will give rise to doubt, disorder, and disagreement. Furthermore, a rejection of dispensationalism, yields to Bible incongruity and plain contradictions. Any *sensible* person can detect this. While the opposing view (Covenant theology) forces *unity* in scripture (i.e. one people of God, one plan of salvation ect.) it really manufactures *divisions of paradox* "**chaning[ing] the truth of God into a lie**" (Rom. 1:25).

To some degree, every preacher and theologian is a dispensationalist. This is apparent when you hear any modern day preacher (in ANY denomination) pray. Preachers in this present dispensation do NOT pray (or live for that matter) as people under the dispensation of the Law, or under the Davidic Covenant. If they did, they would be praying for God to kill and destroy their *personal enemies.* David did just that, and God blessed and honored his request. See: Psalm 5:10; 18:40: 118:11; and 143:12. The very fact that Jesus said "**bless them that curse you**" (Matt. 5:44) demonstrates that the old bottle was on the way out for the new (see Matt. 9:17).

Another glaring fact that proves the word of God should be "**rightly divided**" is found in Matthew 19:17 where Jesus tells a man to "**keep the commandments**" in order to have eternal life. How do you reconcile this with the Pauline epistles? Paul said (under the inspiration of the Holy Ghost): "**a man is not justified by the works of the law**" (Gal. 2:16). The epistles of Paul teach that eternal life is "**not of works**" but a "**gift of God**" (Eph. 2:8,9; Rom. 6:23). Who was right, Jesus or Paul, or both? [Some think Jesus told the rich man to keep the commandments in order for him to see that it was impossible to do so. This is in error. Under the Old Testament, men were commanded to keep the law and many of them kept it. Read: Deut 7:9; Ex. 34:7; Josh. 22:2; Judg. 2:17; 1 Kings 11:34; 2 Kings 8:6; 1 Kings 3:3; 2 Chron. 34:2. Keeping the law was *never* equated with sinlessness, but was the order (or *economy*) that determined a man's personal righteousness (Deut. 6:25).]

If you ever dispute with a Jehovah's Witness over Matthew 24:13, or a Campbellite over Acts 2:38 and Mark 16:16, or a Charismatic over Hebrews 6:4-6, you will see the importance of *rightly dividing.* Matthew 24:13 teaches enduring works for salvation; Acts 2:38 and Mark 16:16 *say* a man MUST be baptized; and Hebrews 6:4-6 *says* a man can LOSE his salvation and go to hell! That is what the verses *say* and *teach!*

But, you cannot apply them to a Church Age saint! Those verses are NOT *dispensationally applicable* TODAY! Acts 2 and Mark 16 are directed toward the early apostolic age, during which the sign gifts were present, and Matthew 24, and Hebrews 6 are pointed at someone in the Tribulation period.

[We know in Acts 2:38 everyone goes to the Greek to prove "εις" should have been translated "because of." Who needs "the Greek" when any *English* dictionary would have given you the same information? There is still a problem after you find out what "for" means. The prelude to those Jews in the passage receiving the Holy Ghost still hinged upon their water baptism! That is what the scripture *says*. The two words **shall receive** are FUTURE. So what if they repented and believed. They did not have the gift of the Holy Ghost until they were baptized!]

Simply because some well-named preacher, respected commentator, or favored theologian refuses to acknowledge the *differences* in scripture does not exclude their legitimacy.

While all dispensationalists concede that there are some dissimilarities between the Old and New Testaments, most "jump ship" when it comes to **"dividing the word of truth,"** in the New Testament. [Especially: Matthew, Acts, James and Hebrews.] As the Bible believer takes his journey searching the scriptures (John 5:39), he should adopt the preamble found in Rom. 3:4; Ps. 119:160; Ps. 33:4; and 2 Tim. 3:16, while at the same time purposely ignoring and disregarding systems of man's private interpretation.

Scofield properly summarizes:

> The Word of truth, then, has right divisions, and it must be evident that, as one cannot be "a workman that needeth not to be ashamed" without observing them, so any study

of that Word which ignores those divisions must be in large measure profitless and confusing.[1]

THE BOOKS OF THE OLD AND NEW TESTAMENTS

When any person picks up a Bible he will notice a definite break, or *division* between the first thirty-nine books and the last twenty-seven books. The first section is the Old Testament, and the latter is termed the New Testament. A gap of nearly four hundred years separates the two. The first section was written in Hebrew (with small portions in Aramaic) while the latter section was written in Greek. So, from the start we notice that the two sections are different with regard to *time*, and *language*. But that is not all.

The Old Testament was written and preserved through the priesthood of the Levitical tribe of Israel (see 2 Chron. 35:3; Ezra 7:10; 2 Chron. 15:3; 17:7; 30:22; Mal. 2:7; Deut. 17:11; Lev. 10:11; Jer. 18:18; Hag. 2:11,12), while the New Testament was preserved through the approval of the body of Christ by the doctrine of the priesthood of believers (see 1 Pet. 2:5,9; 1 Thess. 2:13; Acts 13:44,46). [It is interesting to notice in the book of Acts how the words of the apostles become the very word of God: Acts 4:29,31; 6:2,7; 8:14; 11:1; 12:24; Acts 17:13 (with 1 Thess. 2:13); 18:11; 19:20; 1 Thess 2:2.] The only thing similar regarding the preservation of the two canons (from the Greek word: κανον meaning rod, or measuring rule; hence "the rule") is their **"inspiration by God"** (2 Tim. 3:16).

The bulk of the Old Testament record (what is written, not the chronological data) concerns God's dealings with the nation of Israel, while the greater part (though not quite all) of the New Testament is relative to the church (which is neither Jew nor Gentile - 1 Cor. 10:32). The idea that God deals with

---

[1] Scofield, C.I., *Rightly Dividing the Word of Truth* (New Jersey: Loizeaux Brothers, 1896) 5.

people the same in the books of the Old and New Testaments is like saying two letters, written by the same person yet addressed to different people, is guaranteed to match! To whom scripture is addressed should be one of the chief observations of the Bible believer, and the fact that the Old and New Testaments are written primarily to *different* groups, is crucial to understanding the Bible.

VARIATIONS BETWEEN THE TWO

Now, since the Old Testament primarily addresses the nation of Israel, while the New Testament contains books (mostly letters called "epistles") for the church, would a believer be a "right workman" (2 Tim. 2:15) if he confounded the *messages* in the two? For instance, the Old Testament commands "believers" (New Testament lingo) to worship on Saturday. Does that mean you are breaking the command, **"Remember the sabbath day, to keep it holy"** (Ex. 20:8), if you attend church on Sunday instead of Saturday? Seventh-Day Adventists' think so. The problem is resolved with the principles of right division (dispensationalism). Some variation between the Old and New Testaments are as follows:

1. The Old Testament message is *primarily* for the nation of Israel.

2. The sabbath was created for the Jews: Ex. 31:16,17; Ezek. 20:12.

3. No one went to church in the Old Testament anyway, they went to the temple.

4. Their worship is not comparable to ours, since theirs included killing animals, while ours is **"in spirit and in**

truth" (John 4:24). [No Christian should go to church *only* to "worship God!" He should go to church to be fed the word of God, pray with other believers *and* worship God. He should *always* worship God, while he should not *always* be at the church building.]

5. New Testament Christians are to assemble on the first day of the week. Jesus rose from the dead on the first day of the week. The disciples met on the first day of the week. And the only time you find the apostles going to "worship" on the sabbath, they were going into synagogues (not churches) to preach to Jews (not the church)! See: Matt. 28:1; John 20:19; Acts 20:7; 1 Cor. 16:2. ["**We all have knowledge**" (2 Cor. 8:1) about the Catholics stealing the pagan SUNday from the gods of Babylon, but that does not change the scripture, nor does it change church history!]

OTHER DIFFERENCES

Other noticeable ordinances and observations in the Old Testament that are considered void in the New Testament would be feast days, animal sacrifices, dietary ordinances, temple worship, and obedience to the law for righteousness. Three major differences would be the work of the Holy Spirit, the content of message, and where the soul went after death. The latter difference being the most outstanding. How could anyone claim that the two testaments are indistinguishable when believers from both eras go to *different places* when they die? Old Testament saints went to Abraham's bosom (Luke 16), while New Testament believers go directly to the third heaven (2 Cor. 5:6; Phil. 1:21).

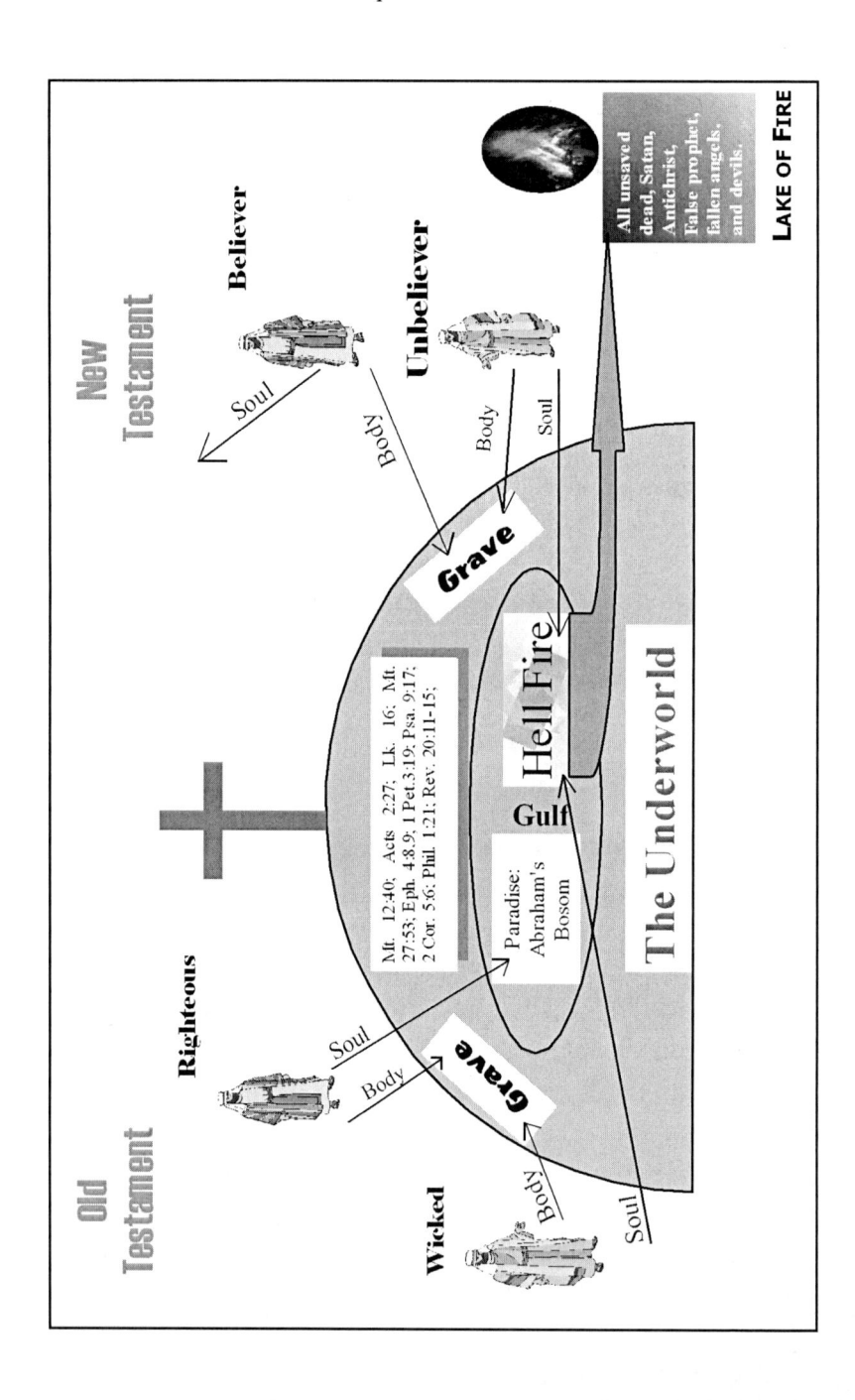

84   *Dispensationalism*

JEW, GENTILE, AND CHURCH OF GOD

1 Cor 10:32 **Give none offence, neither to the Jews, nor to the Gentiles, nor to the church of God:**

JEW	GENTILE	CHURCH
Descendants of Abraham, Isaac, and Jacob	Any NON-Jew	Any believer in Jesus Christ

Anti-dispensationalists correctly state that one of the major tenets of dispensationalism is the distinction between Israel and the church (see *any* anti-dispensational work). They fail to see; however, that it is the Bible, not dispensationalism, that draws the line between the nation of Israel, Gentiles and the church.

Every verse in scripture has *three* applications: doctrinal, historical, devotional (see *Three Applications* pages 50-53). These three applications are also aimed at one of three respective groups: Jew, Gentiles, or the church (i.e. body of Christ). Most heretical deviations (such as postmillennialism and amillennialism) are conceived by the misapplication of a verse to the incorrect corporate group. It is also important to remember that verses are written sometimes to individuals and sometimes to groups *only*. A good rule to remember is: *The whole Bible is written FOR you, but the whole Bible is not written TO you.*

Scofield suitably stated that,

> whoever reads the Bible with any attention cannot fail to perceive that more than half of its contents relate to one nation: the Israelites.[2]

---

[2] *Ibid.*, 6.

The Bible facts as to the Jewish nation are as follows:

1. God specifically called out a people from Abram (Gen. 12) to be separated unto Himself.

2. He gave them national status with certain physical and spiritual blessings.

3. He gave them His law and special revelation through "signs and wonders" (Ex. 7:3; Deut. 4:34; Dan. 6:27; John 4:48; Acts 2:22; 4:30; Rom. 15:19).

4. God even chose to bless the entire earth through this one group. He even chose to send His seed through this pedigree, by which He would redeem the world.

Gen 12:3 **And I will bless them that bless thee, and curse him that curseth thee: and in thee shall all families of the earth be blessed.**

John 4:9 **Then saith the woman of Samaria unto him, How is it that thou, being a Jew . . .**

Larkin explains:

> The history of the Jewish race is without a parallel in human history. Though oppressed, downtrodden, carried captive to other lands and scattered through the nations, the Jew has outlived all his conquerors and walks unscathed amid the nations. Any other race would have been swallowed up and its identity and national characteristics lost. The preservation of the Jewish race is

the "MIRACLE OF HISTORY." Their "Emblem" is a "BUSH BURNING AND UNCONSUMED."[3]

In the Old Testament God promised an unconditional land grant to Abraham and his posterity (Isaac and Jacob - Israel). God promised that He would "**never break**" His covenant with them (Judg. 2:1). This allotment of land was never completely given to the Jews, but will be in the future (see: Gen. 13:15, 16; 15:5-18; 17:7-12). The postmillennialists will spiritualize the literal, physical promises to Abraham and apply them to the church. This kind of Bible exposition is what produced a totalitarian church state (Roman Catholic) that demanded (and will demand) conversion at sword point, and in the future - at *mark of the beast* point.

If the Bible believer is to "rightly divide the word," then he cannot blend the physical promises to the Israelites with the spiritual promises (Eph.1:3) to the church. He also cannot confuse the kingdom of heaven (a literal, physical, visible kingdom) with the kingdom of God (a spiritual kingdom entered by the new birth). The church, therefore is NOT Israel, and Israel is not identical to the church, nor are the Gentile nations synonymous with the two. Below are some examples substantiating the differences:

1. Jews were told to be separated from the Gentiles in the Old Testament: Ezra 9:12; 10:2-44; Neh. 10:30.

2. Gentiles (often termed "nations," and "heathen" in scripture) were to follow their conscience in Old Testament times (Rom. 2), as that *was* their law instead of the ten commandments. [See Gen. 20:2-5 where a Gentile *knows* the sin of adultery *without* the law.]

---

[3] Larkin, Clarence, *Rightly Dividing the Word of Truth* (Glenside: Rev. Clarence Larkin Est., 1920) 29,31.

3. The church is composed of Jews and Gentiles (Rom. 10:12; 1 Cor. 12:13; Gal. 3:28; Eph 2:19) and consists of a spiritual body of believers "in Christ" by faith. This is not to be confused with the *visible local congregation* called a church.

4. As Pentecost points out, "natural Israel and the Gentiles are contrasted in the New Testament (Acts 3:12; 4:8; 21:28; Rom. 10:1),"[4] as well as Israel and the church (Rom. 11:1-25; 1 Cor. 10:32). They are NOT the same, and applying verses to one group that are explicitly intended for another, shows contempt for the word of God.

KINGDOMS OF GOD AND HEAVEN

In his magnificent book, *The Sure Word of Prophecy,* Dr. Ruckman proves conclusively that the theme of scripture is "the kingdom," and "who" has control of the kingdom. Whereas, most *contemporary* Christians immediately *assume* the Bible's theme is John 3:16, that is highly inaccurate.

The theme of scripture is, nonetheless, the kingdom. The word "kings" appears 334 times, "kingdom," 342 times; "kingdoms," 57 times, "crown," 66 times; "throne," 176 times; "thrones," 9 times; and there are

Kingdom of Heaven	= A literal physical, visible kingdom located on the earth: Matt. 13:3; 8:12; 5:10; 19:14 ect. . .
Kingdom of God	= A spiritual kingdom entered by the new birth: John. 3:3-5; Rom. 14:17. Both "at hand" when the King is on the earth: Matt. 5:3 with Luke 6:20.

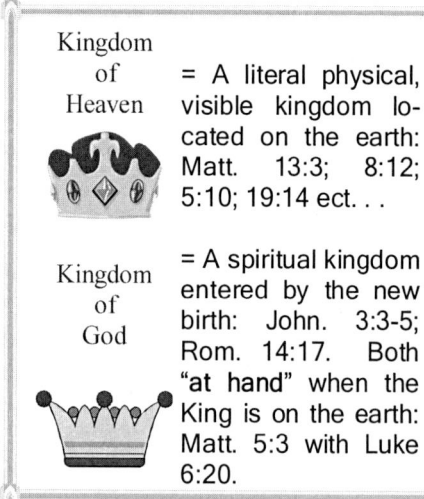

[4] Pentecost, J. Dwight, *Things to Come* (Grand Rapids: Zondervan, 1958) 88.

FOUR books in the Bible called THE BOOK OF THE KINGS totaling 93,729 words, not counting 1 and 2 Chronicles!

To keep this in perspective, the word "salvation," occurs 164 times, "saved," 104 times, and "born again," only 3 times. This is not to say that being "born again," and "saved" are not important. To believers, the death, burial and resurrection of Christ is of utmost importance, but to God (who sees the whole picture from beginning to end), His kingdom plan with Jesus Christ as KING OF KINGS is predominant. You know this to be true, because there are five times as many verses in the Bible concerning the second advent of Christ reigning as KING, than there are about the first advent. When Jesus was crucified, He was declared King to all, by the three languages, to the three races of people (Hebrew - Shem, Greek -Japheth, Latin - Ham); and when He returns He will have "**KING OF KINGS, AND LORD OF LORDS**" (Rev. 19:16) written on His vesture, and Jesus will finally reign on "**the throne of his father David**" (Luke 1:32).

NUMEROUS "KINGDOMS" IN SCRIPTURE

1. Satan's kingdom: Matt. 12:26.

2. Israel's kingdom: 1 Sam. 15:28; 24:20; 1 Kings 21:7.

3. The "kingdoms of this world:" Rev. 11:15; Isa. 19:2; Jer. 18:7; 27:8; Dan. 4:17 ("kingdom of men.")

4. Kingdom of Cyrus: Ezra 1:1.

5. Kingdom of Ahasuerus: Est. 1:2.

6. Four Gentile kingdoms of Daniel 2.

7. God's universal kingdom. This a reference to God's universal rule at all times, although many of these references very well could refer to the millennial reign of Christ: Dan. 4:3,25; Ps. 103:19-22; 9:7; 11:4; 47:2; Isa. 66:1; Eph. 1:21-22; 1 Pet. 3:22; Matt. 28:18; Lam. 5:19; 2 Ki. 19:15; 2 Pet. 1:11; Rev. 12:10.

8. The kingdoms of Belshazzar and Darius (Dan. 5-7).

9. The four kingdoms of Daniel 7.

10. The kingdom out of which ten kings arise (Dan. 7:24; Rev. 17:12,17).

11. The kingdom of Alexander the Great (Dan. 11:4).

12. The kingdom of Herod (Mark 6:23).

13. The kingdom of the beast (Rev. 16:10).

14. The kingdom of heaven (kingdom of our father David - Mark 11:10).

15. The kingdom of God (kingdom of Christ and of God - Eph. 5:5; kingdom of his dear Son - Col. 1:13; heavenly kingdom - 2 Tim. 4:18).

The fact that the "kingdom of God" (appearing 69 times) and the "kingdom of heaven" (appearing 32 times, only in the book of Matthew) are *atypical* is of paramount consequence. If you make these two kingdoms the same, you wind up with a postmillennial, contradictory, devotional application of the kingdom every time. [The Bible is the only book, where, when someone reads it they immediately attempt to tell you what it *means* instead of what it *says!* People refuse to hear what it SAYS, so they seek an *explanation* to cover up the *true* meaning - what it *says*.]

Adherents to "progressive dispensationalism" (a defecting faction of dispensationalism) like Kenneth Barker assume Paul was preaching the same kingdom that was heralded in the gospels.[5] This grave mistake contributes to dispensational anarchy and sways toward Covenant Reformed theology. Even more orthodox dispensationalists (like Mal Couch, editor of *The Dictionary of Premillennial Theology*), argue that the two (Kingdom of God and Kingdom of Heaven) are the same. He says, "though some dispensationalists may disagree, it appears by all the evidence that the two expressions are used synonymously, but with a certain emphasis."[6]

KINGDOM OF GOD DEFINED

The kingdom of God can be defined several ways etymologically. How to use "of" is the big question.

1. The kingdom FROM God. This designates *origin*.

2. The kingdom BY God. This designates *identity*.

3. The kingdom FILLED WITH God. This indicates material components or *content*; i.e. a dress of silk; a throne of gold; a distance of five miles.

4. The kingdom BELONGING TO, or PERTAINING to God. To indicate *ownership*.

---

[5] Blaising and Bock, *Dispensationalism, Israel and the Church* (Grand Rapids, MI: Zondervan, 1992) 314.
[6] "Kingdom of God, of Heaven," *Dictionary of Premillennial Theology:* 230.

Utilizing the Bible method of comparing scripture with scripture, we find that the kingdom of God *IS literal*, but NOT *physical*. Rather, it is a *spiritual* kingdom. Note the following verses:

> Luke 17:21 **Neither shall they say, Lo here! or, lo there! for, behold, the kingdom of God is within you.**
>
> *Rom 14:17* **For the kingdom of God is not meat and drink; but righteousness, and peace, and joy in the Holy Ghost.**
>
> *1 Cor 15:50* **Now this I say, brethren, that flesh and blood cannot inherit the kingdom of God; neither doth corruption inherit incorruption.**
>
> *2 Cor 10:4* **(For the weapons of our warfare are not carnal, but mighty through God to the pulling down of strong holds;)**
>
> *Eph 6:12* **For we wrestle not against flesh and blood, but against principalities, against powers, against the rulers of the darkness of this world, against spiritual wickedness in high places.**

KINGDOM OF HEAVEN DEFINED

Following our dictionary we can similarly define the kingdom of heaven as:

1. The kingdom FROM heaven.

2. The kingdom BY heaven.

3. The kingdom FILLED WITH heaven.

4. The kingdom BELONGING TO, or PERTAINING TO heaven.

Dan 2:44 **And in the days of these kings shall the God of heaven set up a kingdom, which shall never be destroyed: and the kingdom shall not be left to other people, but it shall break in pieces and consume all these kingdoms, and it shall stand for ever.**

The phrase "kingdom of heaven" only occurs in the gospel of Matthew: Matt. 3:2; 4:17; 5:3; 5:10; 5:19 (twice); 5:20; 7:21; 8:11; 10:7; 11:11; 11:12; 13:11; 13:24; 13:31; 13:33; 13:44; 13:45; 13:47; 13:52; 16:19; 18:1; 18:3; 18:4; 18:23; 19:14; 19:23; 20:1; 22:2; 23:13; 25:1; 25:14.

DIFFERENT KINGDOMS

The context of the passages indicate that the kingdom of heaven (*contrary* to the kingdom of God) is a physical, literal, visible, messianic kingdom. Scofield distinguishes the kingdom of God and the kingdom of heaven:

> **1.** The kingdom of God is universal (including angels, ect...), while the kingdom of heaven is messianic, and Davidic.
> **2.** The kingdom of God is entered only by the new birth, while there are unbelievers in the kingdom of heaven (Matt. 13:3; 8:12). The parables of the wheat and the tares, and of the net (Matt. 13:24-30, 36-43, 47-50) are not spoken of the kingdom of God.
> **3.** The kingdom of God "comes not with outward show" (Luke 17:20), but is chiefly that which is inward

and spiritual (Rom. 14:17); while the kingdom of heaven is organic, and is to be manifested in glory on the earth.

4. The kingdom of heaven merges into the kingdom of God when Christ, having "put all enemies under His feet," "shall have delivered up the kingdom to God, even the Father" (1 Cor. 15:24-28).[7]

Modern Americans are so familiar with using the word "heaven" in the sense of the "third heaven" (2 Cor. 12:2). They forget that the solar system contains our planet, which is "in the heavens." The earth is located in these heavens (see Gen. 1,2) and one day Jesus Christ will establish a kingdom of heaven ON THIS EARTH.

Basic language skills, plus common sense should give it away that the kingdom of God and the kingdom of heaven are different.

In Dr. Peter Ruckman's book *The Sure Word of Prophecy*, he lists twelve reasons why the words "God," and "heaven" are not identical terms:

1. Birds fly in heaven, they do not fly in God.
2. There are clouds in heaven; there are no clouds in God or God's "kingdom."
3. God created the heavens; they did not create him.
4. God was in the beginning; the heavens were not.
5. The heavens are material; you can SEE them.
6. God is a Spirit, and cannot be seen.
7. God has a moral nature, the universe is a-moral.
8. God controls the heavens' they do not control Him.
9. The heavens declare the glory of God; not the other way around.
10. The heavens contain darkness, and in God there is no darkness.

---

[7] *Scofield Reference Bible*, 1003.

Some Basic Divisions 95

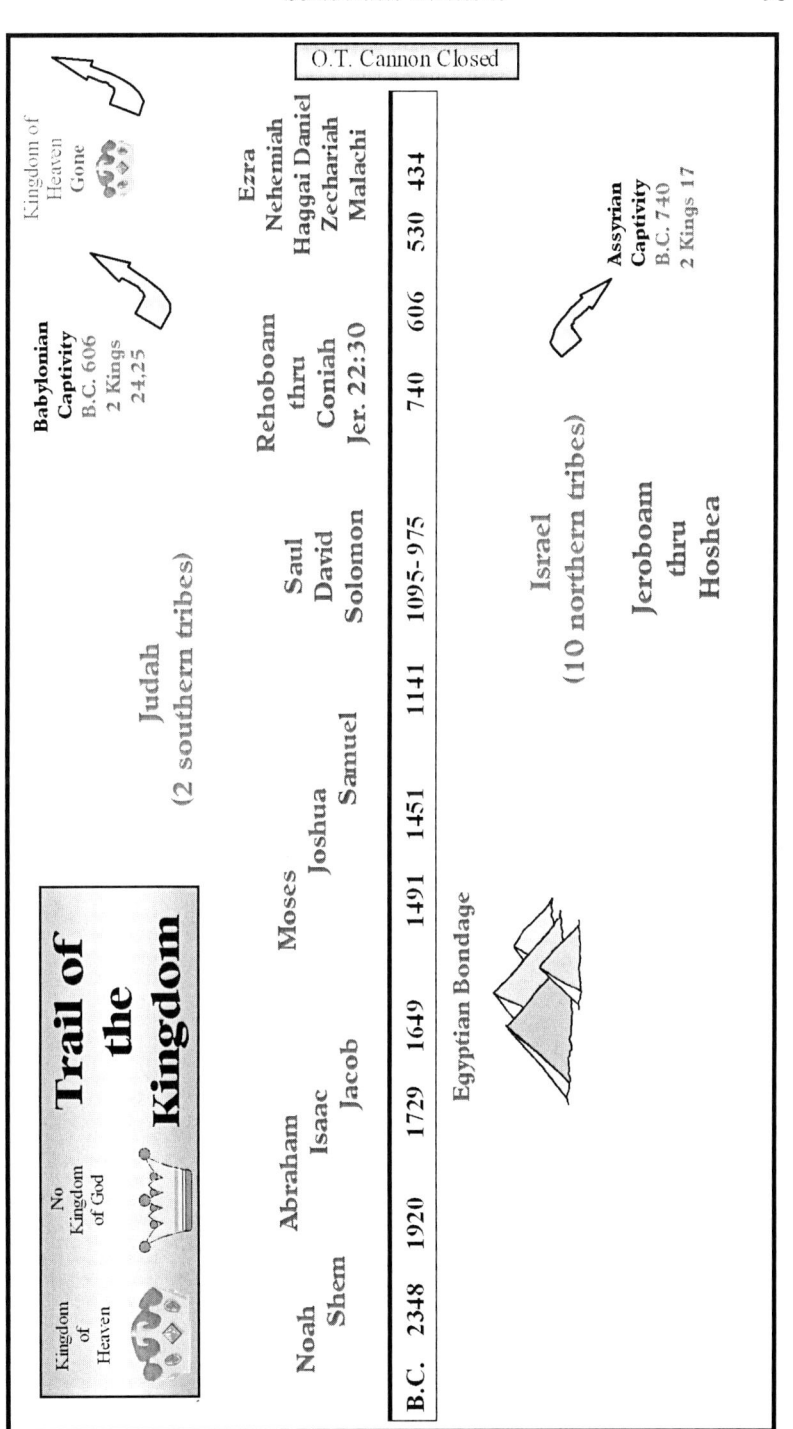

Trail of the Kingdom

Kingdom of Heaven

No Kingdom of God

Kingdom of Heaven Gone

O.T. Cannon Closed

| Noah Shem | Abraham Isaac Jacob | Moses Joshua Samuel | Saul David Solomon | Rehoboam thru Coniah Jer. 22:30 | **Babylonian Captivity** B.C. 606 2 Kings 24,25 | Ezra Nehemiah Haggai Daniel Zechariah Malachi |

Judah
(2 southern tribes)

| B.C. | 2348 | 1920 | 1729 | 1649 | 1491 | 1451 | 1141 | 1095-975 | 740 | 606 | 530 | 434 |

Egyptian Bondage

Israel
(10 northern tribes)

Jeroboam thru Hoshea

Assyrian Captivity
B.C. 740
2 Kings 17

11. The heavens can be populated; God cannot.
   12. The words God and heaven are spelled with different letters.[8]

HARMONIZING KINGDOMS

There are thirteen (go figure!) places in the gospels where the kingdom of God matches the kingdom of heaven. In other words, places where Matthew will say "kingdom of heaven," and Mark and Luke will assert "kingdom of God." John uses the "kingdom of God," and never coincides with Matthew's "kingdom of heaven." Below are the counterparts:

1. Matt. 19:23,24 (a unique place where "kingdom of heaven," and "kingdom of God" are used almost side by side) with Mark 10:23; Luke 18:24.

2. Matt. 4:17 with Mark 1:14.

3. Matt. 3:2 with Mark 1:15.

4. Matt. 5:3 with Luke 6:20.

5. Matt. 8:11 with Luke 13:28 and Luke 13:29.

6. Matt. 10:7 with Mark 1:15 and Luke 10:9.

7. Matt. 11:1 with Luke 7:28.

8. Matt. 18:3 with Mark 10:14,15 and Luke 18:16-17.

9. Matt. 13:31 with Mark 4:30 and Luke 13:18.

---
[8] Ruckman, Peter S., *The Sure Word of Prophecy* (Pensacola: Bible Believers Press, 1969) 57,58.

10. Matt. 13:33 with Luke 13:20,21.

11. Matt. 19:14 with Mark 10:14.

12. Matt. 11:11 with Luke 7:28.

13. Matt. 11:12 with Luke 16:16.

The understandable reason that BOTH kingdoms would be mentioned interchangeably in some cases, although they are "not synonymous,"[9] would be the fact that the King of both the physical and spiritual kingdoms, was present in the person of the Lord Jesus Christ.

DISTINCTION WITHIN THE KINGDOM OF GOD

There also needs to be a distinction made between the "kingdom of God" in Galatians 5:21 with regard to that in Romans 14:7. The "kingdom of God" referred to in Gal. 5:21; Rom. 8:17; 2 Tim. 2:11-13; Col. 3:23,24; Eph. 5:5 and Acts 20:32 is connected with an *inheritance* and *rewards* for the believer IN the kingdom of God, and not simply the fact of the believers entrance (John 3:3,5) and his "translation" (Col. 1:13) into this kingdom. We know this is true, because it is said to be entered through *service* (Col. 3:24), and not simply by belief as in John 3:3.

The fact that the spiritual kingdom of God existed prior to the fall of man is apparent when we read about Adam's "one on one" fellowship with God. Adam was a **"son of God"** – Luke 3:38) and **"God is a spirit"** (John 4:24). This kingdom however, vanished with the fall of man, and was not offered to man again until the **"only begotten son of God"** died and was

---

[9] Pentecost, *Things to Come*, 144.

resurrected. Once the "**corn of wheat**" died (John 12:24) and was buried (John 12:24) it could be reproduced in others and multiply.

> *John 1:12* **But as many as received him, to them gave he power to become the sons of God, even to them that believe on his name:**

> *Rom 7:4* **Wherefore, my brethren, ye also are become dead to the law by the body of Christ; that ye should be married to another, even to him who is raised from the dead, that we should bring forth fruit unto God.**

> *1 Peter 1:23* **Being born again, not of corruptible seed, but of incorruptible, by the word of God, which liveth and abideth for ever.**

"**The kingdom of God is at hand**" (Mark 14:42) during the earthly ministry of Christ, and the Lord Jesus even gives instructions to Nicodemus on how to enter this kingdom.

[It is noteworthy that John records the new birth instead of Matthew, Mark, or Luke. John wrote his epistle at least thirty-nine years *after* Paul recorded the mystery of the body of Christ. When John wrote, he was supernaturally *reminded* (John 14:26 - "**bring all things to your remembrance**") of Christ's words commenting on the Church Age. John 3 then, IS Church Age material, as well as John 14,15,16. The theme of John's writings is belief in the Son of God, and matches perfectly the "Pauline revelation" that hyper-dispensationalists are so obsessed with.]

Some Basic Divisions 99

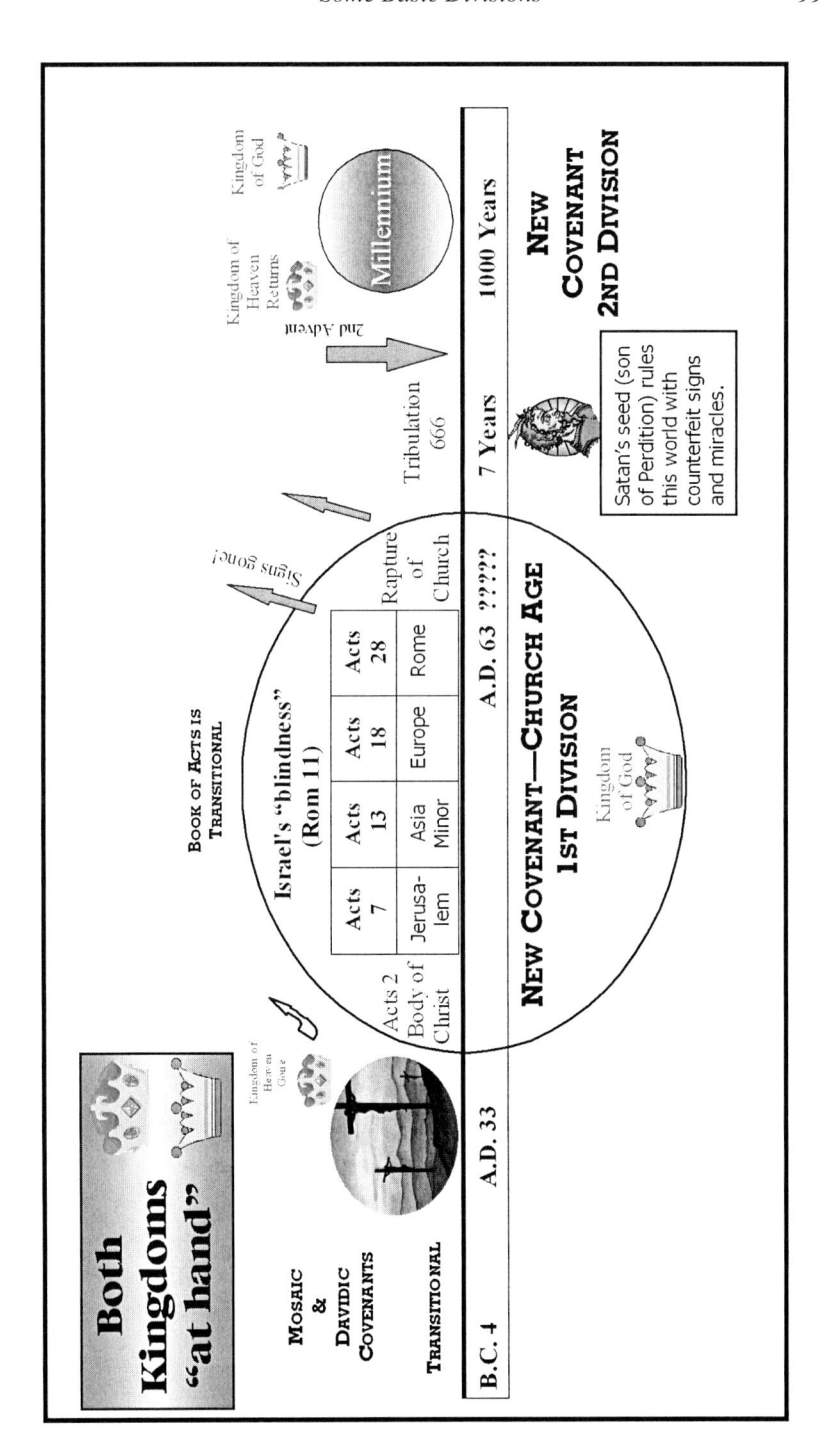

This "kingdom" will continue throughout the Church Age, and will be realized in full when the two kingdoms *merge* during the millennial reign of Christ. The modern new age movement, and the charismatic movement, are working on what the eastern religions have been attempting for years - to join the physical and spiritual realms. These two worlds were separated with Adam's tragedy, and only interrupted a few times in Bible history (Gen. 6, Matt. 1), but will be consummated with the return of the second Adam, who has already redeemed seventy-five percent (soul and spirit) of the believer, and will ultimately restore the "**image of God**" (Gen. 1:26,27; 5:3; Rom. 8:29) to those who become His "**brethren**" (Heb. 2:11), and "**sons of God**" (John 1:12) by the new birth.

"**The kingdom of heaven is at hand**" when Jesus Christ is on earth because He is the promised King, the Messiah that is to rule the nation of Israel, and the world in a literal kingdom. This kingdom is NOT "**at hand**" again until the "**time of Jacob's trouble**" (Jer. 30:7), when the Messiah comes to her the "**second time**" (Gen. 41:5; 43:10; Isa. 11:11; Acts 7:13 especially!) to rescue believing Israel and fulfill the promises she thought was the program for His first coming. Stauffer calls this time the "Age of Readiness"[10] based on Matthew 24:44.

> *Matt 24:44* **Therefore be ye also ready: for in such an hour as ye think not the Son of man cometh.**

Jesus Reigning Now?

No matter what you call it (we will get into that later), the fact of the matter remains, that we are NOT currently living during the literal, physical, reign of Jesus Christ, nor awaiting a

---

[10] Stauffer, Douglas D., *One Book Rightly Divided* (Millbrok: McCowen Mills Publishers, 1999) 240.

physical appearance of Christ to set up the kingdom. We are awaiting a "catching up," or a "seizing," or a "rapture," by Jesus Christ in the clouds, not a physical landing on the earth!

"Progressive dispensationalists" (as their *future* brothers – Reformed Calvinists) insist that Jesus is reigning on the throne of David *now*. Note the words of the Dallas Theological Professor, Darrel L. Bock:

> What is crucial is that David's awareness of this covenant promise is immediately linked to his understanding of the resurrection promise in Psalm 16, which in turn is immediately tied to the resurrection proof text of Psalm 119 (vv. 31-35). Being seated on David's throne is linked to being seated at God's right hand. In other words, Jesus' resurrection-ascension to God's right hand is put forward by Peter as a fulfillment of the Davidic covenant...[11]

Bock does not see that the Davidic throne is a literal, physical, earthly throne located in a literal, physical place in the kingdom of heaven. He, as all progressive dispensationalists (and other s*cholars* - see Mal. 2:12), only *uses* the Bible to give weight to his theological ideas. He rejected the comment of the Holy Spirit in 1 Ki. 2:12,24; Ps. 132:11,12; Isa. 9:7; Jer. 13:13; 17:25, and Luke 1:32. Instead, he insists that "throne is a pictorial description for rule, and that the allusion to Jesus' sitting next to God is an allusion to the promise of Psalm 110, a Davidic promise."[12] Do you see how it is done? He takes a literal word with a literal, physical, visible meaning, and *changes* the word of God (hello Eve - Gen. 3:3), to an ambiguous *idea*: "a pictorial description for rule."

Notice one of three main warnings not to change or add to the word of God:

---

[11] Blaising and Bock, *Dispensationalism, Israel and the Church*, 49.
[12] *Ibid.*, 51.

Prov 30:5-6
5 Every word of God is pure: he is a shield unto them that put their trust in him.
6 Add thou not unto his words, lest he reprove thee, and thou be found a liar.

REJECTING LITERAL INTREPRETATION

In effect, tampering with the word of God is akin to rejection of the literal, grammatical-historical interpretation of scripture. When a man declines the literal meaning of literal words, *anything goes*. The literal return of Jesus Christ can *mean* "Jesus reigning in your heart." A saved person being "**conformed to the image of his son**" (Rom. 8:29) could *mean*, "the spiritual journey a Christian has in attempting to be like Christ." That is how all Southern Baptists (and most Independent Baptists) teach Rom. 8:29 is it not? When the BOOK OF BOOKS is allowed to be tampered and meandered with, the kingdom of heaven becomes a spiritual kingdom coequal with the kingdom of God. This error has produced more bloodshed than any terrorist will ever hope to see.

THE FIRST AND SECOND ADVENTS

Since the true test of scripture is prophecy (not tradition, or church authority, or the verification of church fathers), it behooves the dispensational student of scripture, to rightly divide "seemingly contradictory lines of prediction concerning the coming Messiah."[13] In the Old Testament, Jesus Christ is foreseen as a ruler, judge, and a reigning king; while at the same time anticipated as a man "**despised and rejected of**

---

[13] Scofield, *Rightly Dividing the Word of Truth*, 17.

men; a man of sorrows, and acquainted with grief" (Isa. 53:3).

It is obvious that the prophecies concerning the birth, death, burial, and resurrection of Christ were fulfilled, but why was there a division between the *suffering* of the Saviour and the *splendor* of the Saviour and His kingdom?

First of all, notice that the Old Testament prophet, along with the disciples, did not understand the paradox of the Messiah suffering and yet exalted:

> *1 Peter 1:10-11*
> **10 Of which salvation the prophets have inquired and searched diligently, who prophesied of the grace that should come unto you:**
> **11 Searching what, or what manner of time the Spirit of Christ which was in them did signify, when it testified beforehand the sufferings of Christ, and the glory that should follow.**
>
> *Mark 9:31-32*
> **31 For he taught his disciples, and said unto them, The Son of man is delivered into the hands of men, and they shall kill him; and after that he is killed, he shall rise the third day.**
> **32 But they understood not that saying, and were afraid to ask him.**

From the above verses you can see that it is almost fanatical for someone to claim that the disciples and those in the Old Testament were saved by grace through faith in the death, burial and resurrection of Jesus Christ! The disciples (excluding John) did not even think He could rise from the dead! See: Luke 24:11.

They could not understand that before a crown could be worn, a cross would be borne. Jesus Christ himself proclaimed that He was preparing the kingdom and was a King. His words and works were even verified by John the Baptist, the wise men, and fulfilled prophecies relating to the kingdom (riding the colt into Jerusalem for instance - Matt. 21:2-5). Who would have guessed any different? Larkin explains:

> From the Prophets "viewpoint" they saw the Birth of Jesus, the Crucifixion, the Outpouring of the Holy Spirit, the Antichrist, Christ coming as the "Sun of Righteousness," the Kingdom, as peaks of one great mountain, they did not see what we standing off to the side now see, that those peaks belonged to two different mountains separated by the "Valley of the Church."[14]

CONTRASTS BETWEEN THE TWO

The contrasts of the first and second advents are abundant:

FIRST ADVENT	SECOND ADVENT
BORN AS A BABY	RETURNS AS A KING
WOUNDED BEAT AND KILLED	WOUNDS, BEATS AND KILLS
MAN OF SORROWS	MAN OF VICTORY
SENT TO SAVE	RETURNS TO JUDGE
FIRST ADVENT WAS SECRETLY	SECOND ADVENT IS PUBLIC
BORN TO DIE	RETURNS TO LIVE AND REIGN

As an evangelist sang: "When He first came as a baby, His mama laid Him in a manger. But what a sight, on horses white, He will return as the Lone Ranger."

---

[14] Larkin, *Rightly Dividing the Word of Truth*, 69.

The principles of right division are so critical with regard to these Old Testament prophecies of Christ. In fact, the validity of Jesus' own claims are at stake. Was He to fulfill BOTH the suffering prophecies, as well as the "glory" prophecies? He was tempted by Satan to get ahead of the program of God by manifesting His "glory," and even the Pharisees and rulers of the Jews were looking for the "**Lord of glory**" (1 Cor. 2:8). [Note: all three temptations of Christ are directly related to the second advent.]

JESUS TAUGHT IT!

The division, or gap between the two advents (separated by a mere comma is some Old Testament passages), was intentionally taught by the Lord Jesus Christ. In Luke 4:18,19, Jesus quotes Isaiah 61:1,2, a segment where both advents of the Messiah are depicted. Instead of reading the entire passage, He stops after the prophecies of the earthly ministry of the Messiah (or the first advent) are given, and closes the book of scripture. He never reads the part about the second advent: "**and the day of vengeance of our God**." Note Scofield's comment:

> A comparison with the passage quoted, Isa. 61:1,2, affords an instance of the exquisite accuracy of Scripture. Jesus stopped at, "the acceptable year of the Lord," which is connected with the first advent of and the dispensation of grace ... "the day of vengeance of our God" belongs to the second advent (Deut. 30:3; Acts 1:11, note) and judgment.[15]

---

[15] *Scofield Reference Bible*, 1077.

BOTH ADVENTS IN ONE VIEW

In the Old Testament many times both the first and second advents were mentioned together. This is why the disciples were looking for the visible Davidic kingdom during the earthly ministry of Christ. And since the Church Age was a "parenthetical age" between the 69th and 70th week of Daniel, they also thought Jesus would restore the kingdom after He arose (see Acts 1:6).

Below are the verses that give both advents in one view:

I. Genesis 3:15

Gen 3:15 **And I will put enmity between thee and the woman, and between thy seed and her seed; it shall bruise thy head, and thou shalt bruise his heel.**

The first coming is mentioned by the fact that a woman will have a "**seed.**" And the bruising of the head of the serpent is definitely a future fulfillment of the second coming. See: Rom. 16:20; Ps. 68:21; 110:6; Hab. 3:13.

II. Genesis 49:11

Gen 49:11 **Binding his foal unto the vine, and his ass's colt unto the choice vine; he washed his garments in wine, and his clothes in the blood of grapes:**

Jesus rode the ass's colt during the latter part of His ministry in the first advent, but will wash "**his clothes in the blood of the grapes**" at Armageddon. See: Isa. 63:1-6; Rev. 14:20.

III. <u>Isaiah 40:1-5</u>

Isa 40:1-5
**1 Comfort ye, comfort ye my people, saith your God.
2 Speak ye comfortably to Jerusalem, and cry unto her, that her warfare is accomplished, that her iniquity is pardoned: for she hath received of the LORD's hand double for all her sins.
3 The voice of him that crieth in the wilderness, Prepare ye the way of the LORD, make straight in the desert a highway for our God.
4 Every valley shall be exalted, and every mountain and hill shall be made low: and the crooked shall be made straight, and the rough places plain:
5 And the glory of the LORD shall be revealed, and all flesh shall see it together: for the mouth of the LORD hath spoken it.**

Notice in the passage that the iniquity of Israel is "**pardoned**" at the first advent of Christ. This is proven by the baptism of John to the nation of Israel "**for the remission of sins,**" a phrase utilized FIVE times in scripture to show that someone's sins HAD BEEN forgiven. [Note the following: Matt. 26:28; Mark 1:4; Luke 3:3; Acts 2:38; Rom. 3:25.]

Observe also the commission of John the Baptist, as quoted in Matt. 3:1-3, that took place during the first advent of Christ. If you will recall, John had a problem with seeing only the "**glory that should follow,**" and questioned the Lord as to why the kingdom was not manifested:

Matt 11:3 **And said unto him, Art thou he that should come, or do we look for another?**

John could not distinguish between the "iniquity being pardoned," and the "**glory of the LORD shall be revealed**," which is clearly a second advent reference (Rev. 1:7 - "**every eye shall see him**").

IV <u>Genesis 49:24</u>

Gen 49:24 **But his bow abode in strength, and the arms of his hands were made strong by the hands of the mighty God of Jacob; (from thence is the shepherd, the stone of Israel:)**

Here we see "**the shepherd**" (first advent - John 10); and the smiting "**stone of Israel**" (second advent).

V. <u>Matthew 21:44</u>

Matt 21:44 **And whosoever shall fall on this stone shall be broken: but on whomsoever it shall fall, it will grind him to powder.**

The two advents in this verse (a time gap of AT LEAST 2,000 years) are separated by only a comma!

It is apparent that the command to "rightly divide the word of truth" is not just a "King James Only" reading and preference in translating. It was practiced by the Lord Jesus Christ Himself, and has been demonstrated to be the proper *key* to unlocking Old Testament prophecies concerning the first and second advents of the Messiah.

The importance and significance of the two advents will be expounded upon later. But suffice it to say that they are equally important (and equally LITERAL). You cannot have one without the other. As the greatest day for any sinner, was the day that Jesus said "**It is finished**," so the greatest day for the Saviour will be when the Father says, "you're enemies ARE you're footstool," (Ps. 110:1; Matt. 22:44) and He receives the GLORY that is due Him.

> *Rev 5:12* **Saying with a loud voice, Worthy is the Lamb that was slain to receive power, and riches, and wisdom, and strength, and honour, and glory, and blessing.**

[I believe George Frederick Handel (1685-1759) will lead the chorus!]

RAPTURE AND REVELATION

A clear distinction between the revelation of Jesus Christ (the literal return of Christ to the earth bodily), and the rapture of the body of Christ is indispensable to accurate Bible interpretation. Too many times we hear of prophecy preachers abstracting verses concerning the revelation and applying them to the rapture. They will say that the rapture is close because we are seeing the "signs" such as earthquakes, wars, and other *Tribulation* signs! If you read Matthew 24 you will find out that those "signs" are addressed to those IN the first half of the Tribulation and are called "**the beginning of sorrows**." They cannot be addressed to the church because the narrative is a continuous dialogue! Those in the "**beginning of sorrows**" are the ones that, having seen the wars and famines are to buckle down and get ready "**to endure unto the end**" (Matt. 24:13).

While it is true that 1 Tim. 4 and 2 Tim. 3 indicate certain features of the "**last days**," there is a danger in observing "signs" as prefatory to the rapture. I am sure the Dark Ages seemed like the "**last days**" to the martyrs.

It is important to note that the revelation can be considered in TWO stages, with the first part being the rapture, and the latter the literal bodily return of Christ. Paul *does* refer to the rapture as **"the coming of our Lord Jesus Christ"** (1 Cor. 1:7). This is easily proven as a valid Bible interpretation when one considers that the first coming of Christ was spoken of in *TWO phases*. The first being His birth (Micah 5:2), and the second stage, His death (Psalm 22). Since both stages are spoken of as His first coming, and they are separated by an interval of thirty-three years; why would it be strange for His *second* coming to be separated by at least seven years?[16]

MISAPPLICATION

Overlooking the differences between the rapture and the revelation, many often exploit verses aimed at the second advent and apply them to the rapture. There are a few verses dealing with the second advent that are so often taken out of context, that without fail somebody will quote them to you during a conversation about the "last days," or the return of the Lord (i.e. rapture). Even the master **"workman"** Clarence Larkin uses these verses to prove that "the rapture will be a surprise."[17] They are:

> *Matt 24:36* **But of that day and hour knoweth no man, no, not the angels of heaven, but my Father only.**
>
> *Matt 24:42* **Watch therefore: for ye know not what hour your Lord doth come.**
>
> *Matt 24:44* **Therefore be ye also ready: for in such an hour as ye think not the Son of man cometh.**

---

[16] McGee, J. Vernon, *He is Coming Again* (Pasadena: Thru the Bible Books, 1980) 18.
[17] Larkin, Clarence, *The Second Coming of Christ* (Glenside: Rev. Clarence Larkin Est., 1918) 13.

Mark 13:32-33
**32 But of that day and that hour knoweth no man, no, not the angels which are in heaven, neither the Son, but the Father.
33 Take ye heed, watch and pray: for ye know not when the time is.**

The context of Matthew 24:36 cannot point to the passing away of the heaven and earth (vs. 35), but to the "**coming of the Son of man**" (vs. 27): the second advent (the revelation). If you make it the passing away of the heavens and the earth, you are jumping from the second advent clear over the millennial reign to what the Bible calls, "**the day of God**" (2 Pet. 3:12) when the heavens and earth are destroyed by FIRE (Rev. 20:15). This takes place 1,000 years later, *after* the kingdom age.

KNOWING THE DAY AND HOUR

It is the principle of *wrong division*, or *no division* that manufactures this "you cannot know the day or hour of the rapture," when the verse is talking about the revelation. The Bible teaches that you can *know* the "**times and seasons**" (1 Thess. 5:1) of the "**day of the Lord**," even though you might not be able to pinpoint the hour, week or day. To use the previous verses to teach the "imminent" return of Christ, in the rapture is akin to using "**whether there be tongues, they shall cease**," (1 Cor. 13:8) to disprove the tongues movement. Simply because Paul the apostle was watching and waiting for the rapture does not mean that those living during the last "**watch of the night**" will not *know* they are about to be translated. Bible scholars soon forget that it is at "**the last trump**" out of a *series* of trumpet calls (Num. 10:4; Josh. 6:5), when the dead are raised and the saints go up. Furthermore, "**the day of Christ**" (which we will get into later) is marked by TWO noticeable, identifiable events: "**a falling away**," and the appearance of "**the man of sin.**"

> *2 Thess 2:2-3*
> **2 That ye be not soon shaken in mind, or be troubled, neither by spirit, nor by word, nor by letter as from us, as that the day of Christ is at hand.**
> **3 Let no man deceive you by any means: for that day shall not come, except there come a falling away first, and that man of sin be revealed, the son of perdition;**

This *view* is taking for granted that the phrase, "**day of Christ**" means the rapture. It is worthy of notice that Elijah AND Elisha AND the "**sons of the prophets**" *knew* when Elijah would be translated (raptured). Also it is intriguing that Joshua and his armies *knew* the exact DAY when they would "**ascend up.**" It was after the "**long blast with the ram's horn**" and after the "**shout with a great shout.**" This took place in the SIXTH book of the Bible (Joshua) in the SIXTH chapter of the book, in the FIFTH verse, just *prior* to 666!

Not Simultaneously

The rapture and the revelation are undeniably two separate events, with two separate purposes, and two entirely different outcomes. The rapture produces joy and comfort among God's people (1 Thess. 4:18), while the second advent brings "**wrath against the day of wrath and revelation of the righteous judgment of God**" (Rom. 2:5). Lindsey lists several reasons why that "the Bible distinguishes between the Rapture and the second coming of Christ, and why they do not occur simultaneously:"[18]

1. "A great distinction between God's purpose for the nation of Israel and his purpose for the church."[19] The Tribulation period is called "**the time of Jacob's trouble**" (Jer. 30:7) not the "churches trouble." When Jesus returns at the second advent He will return as "**the son of Man**" (Matt. 24 - His Jewish designation) to save Israel, NOT the church!

   Rom 11:26 **And so all Israel shall be saved . . .**

2. "The second coming is said to be visible to the whole earth. . . in the rapture, only the Christians see Him - it's a mystery, a secret."[20]

3. "When Christ comes at the second coming it is at the height of a global war . . . .when Christ comes for the believers, it will not necessarily be at the time of a war."[21]

4. "If the rapture took place at the same time as the second coming, there would be no mortals left who would be believers; therefore, there would be no one to go into the Kingdom and repopulate the earth."[22] This point is taking for granted that all unbelievers are killed at the second advent. Not only do you have mortals in the Millennium, you have them in *eternity* with the new heavens and the new earth; for, lo and behold, the tree of life pops up *again* in Rev. 22, in order to give eternal life to mortals, who do

---

[18] Lindsey, Hal, *The Late Great Planet Earth* (Grand Rapids: Zondervan, 1970) 142.
[19] *Ibid.*, 142.
[20] *Ibid.*, 143.
[21] *Ibid.*
[22] *Ibid.*

not have a glorified body like Christ. Instead, they have one like Adam had in the garden of Eden!

SUMMARY

The revelation and rapture are two, distinctly different events. Dr. Ruckman summarizes:

> The Rapture is a secret event (1 Thess. 4:15-17) when the Lord comes for His saints and they meet Him in the air. The Revelation, to the contrary, is a public view (Rev. 1:7) when the Lord comes with His saints to set up the millennial reign (1 Thess. 3:13) . . . the first time the Lord Jesus Christ came, he appeared first in secret, to His own disciples, and only saved people saw His birth in the manger. Then thirty years later, He appeared publicly to His enemies, at the ministry of John the Baptist. In like manner, the Second Coming of Christ will be in private to those who know Him, His saints; then seven years later, at the end of Daniel's Seventieth Week, He will appear in wrath before His enemies.[23]

Keep in mind also, that the rapture of the church is just *that:* the rapture of THE CHURCH. It does *not* include the resurrection of Old Testament saints! Dave Hunt thinks Abraham and John "die[d] with faith in Christ, looking forward to redemption through Him,"[24] and therefore will be included in the rapture:

> Thus they must be among "them which sleep in Jesus," whose bodies Christ will resurrect at the Rapture. If not, they would never be resurrected, because the only other

---

[23] Ruckman, Peter S., *Theological Studies Vol. I* (Pensacola: Bible Baptist Bookstore, 1995) 417,418.
[24] Hunt, Dave, "Q&A," *TheBerean Call* 02/2005: 5.

persons who are resurrected are those who died as martyrs at the hands of the Antichrist (Rev. 20:5,6).[25]

Mr. Hunt forgot that the first resurrection is divided into three parts (firstfruits, harvest, and gleanings – see 1 Cor. 15:22-25; Deut. 16:16). These correspond with a resurrection in Matt. 27:53, 1 Thess. 4:13-18, and John 5:24 (referring to a resurrection *just prior* to the Millennium). He also failed to understand that along with a *rapture* of Jewish Tribulation saints (*prior* to the Millennium), there is a *resurrection* of Old Testament saints (see Ezek. 37,38). Finally, he places Abraham and John in Christ's body, *before* Christ had a body!

Ps 2:7 I will declare the decree: the LORD hath said unto me, Thou art my Son; <u>this day</u> have I begotten thee.

No one in the Old Testament was "**in Jesus**" (1 Thess. 4), and no one in the Old Testament was "**born again!**" The Holy Spirit could leave a person in the Old Testament (Ps. 51:11; 1 Sam. 16:14), and there is no promise that Old Testament saints will have a body "**conformed to the image of his son**" (Rom. 8:29).

The misinformation given by Keith Mathison that "the doctrine [of the pretribulation rapture] was never taught before 1830"[26] has already been shot down (Part One: *Pre-trib Rapture in 3rd Century* page 60) where I quoted source material substantiating the opposite. Paul the apostle taught about the pretribulation rapture (1 Thess. 1:10; 5:9), and recorded the doctrine as early as 50 A.D.

---

[25] *Ibid.*
[26] Mathison, Keith A., *Dispensationalism* (New Jersey: P&R Publishing, 1995) 115.

CHAPTER 5

Dispensational Salvation

OLD TESTAMENT VS. THE NEW

> The basis of salvation in every age is the death of Christ; the requirement for salvation in every age is faith; the object of faith in every age is God; the content of faith changes in the various dispensations.[1]

Is the above statement true or false? Ryrie insists that it explains the "dispensationalists position" on salvation. While the above explanation may be the accepted viewpoint, it is nonetheless *unbiblical.* Although the Bible concedes the fact that it is the *blood of Christ,* that *clears* the sins of every saint from every age (**it is not possible that the blood of bulls and of goats should take away sins** - Heb 10:4), it still does not reverse the fact that some saints (*excepting* those in the Church

---

[1] Ryrie, Charles C., *Dispensationalism* (Chicago: Moody Press, 1995) 115.

Dispensational Salvation

Age) were placed in a position of having their sins cleared by the blood based on their WORKS.

Furthermore, no saint in the Millennial age will be saved by faith in Christ, because **"faith is ... the evidence of things NOT seen"** (Heb. 11:1). Every "believer" will literally SEE the Lord Jesus Christ during the Millennial age because they will be required to assemble at Jerusalem, (Zech. 14:16) **"the city of the great King"** (Ps. 48:2).

[By the way, "scholars" refuse to discuss the person in eternity who gets his eternal life from the **"tree of life,"** and gets to partake of it because of **"do[ing] his commandments"** (Rev. 22:14). That verse bothers them so much they *change* it. More discussion under *Salvation in the Tribulation*, page 147.]

UNSCRIPTURAL CLICHÉS

The adage, "people in the Old Testament were saved by looking forward to the cross, while people in the New Testament are saved by looking back to the cross," is akin to crafty statements such as: "God loves the sinner but hates the sin," and "If He is not Lord of all, He is not Lord at all." These insidious, and devious illusions form such a blockade against *solid Bible doctrine*, that once a person adheres to these clichés, the truth *appears* grossly immoral and heretical. Modern entertained Christians who believe "God loves the sinner but hates the sin," would require mental medication if they ever heard a sermon from Ps. 5:5; Deut. 7:10; Ps. 11:5; 139:21; and James 4:4. Those verses ACCLAIM that God hates sinners, *NOT sins!*

So, even though the concurring "dispensational position" (see Ryrie) is based on a faulty cliché, it does not cancel out the truth, or the facts regarding dispensational salvation.

Some people under different dispensations *have been* "saved," and *will be* "saved" not as we are today **"by grace**

through faith" (Eph. 2:8) in the sacrifice of Christ, but by their works plus their faith! This will be proven and validated with scripture:

> *1 Sam 3:9* . . . **Speak, LORD; for thy servant heareth.**

"SAVED," "SAVE"

As a preliminary background to "soteriology" (the study of salvation), the Bible believer should understand that the words "save," and "saved," are not always used in the spiritual "soul saving" sense that Christians are accustomed to. In fact, in the Old Testament those words are NEVER used with the spiritual soul saving intention in mind. [For the sake of space, I leave it up to you to check the references in a concordance.] Even in the New Testament they are used many times in a broader sense than we find in Romans 10:

1. Matt. 10:22; 24:13 - relating to the preservation of life (Mark 13:20 - "**no flesh should be saved**") AND eternal salvation by endurance and refusal of the mark of the beast. [See: Rev. 22:14; 12:17; 14:12]

2. Matt. 27:42 - relating to physical salvation and deliverance from death.

3. Luke 1:71 - relating to deliverance from enemies.

4. Luke 18:42 - relating to physical healing.

5. 1 Peter 3:20; 2 Peter 2:5; Acts 27:20,31 - relating to deliverance from natural disasters.

6. Rom. 11:26 - relating to the national salvation (or "deliverance") of Israel from the Antichrist.

7. 1 Tim. 2:15 - relating to being saved from deception.

8. Jude 5 - relating to the deliverance of Israel from Egypt.

9. Rev. 21:24 - relating to the corporate nations that followed Christ during the Millennial age.

With those Bible facts in mind let us chronicle the *opinions* of the leading dispensationalists regarding Old and New Testament salvation.

NSRB "CORRECTING" SCOFIELD

Scofield's note under John 1:17 was a death blow for passive dispensationalists, because it stated that, "the point of testing is no longer legal obedience as the condition of salvation, but acceptance or rejection of Christ . . ."[2] Knowing that the note blatantly hinted at two different "conditions" of salvation, the *New Scofield Reference Bible* board decided to doctor up the *dead editors* note, to clarify what he would say if he were alive today. Ryrie comments:

> Undoubtedly the charge persists because dispensationalists have made unguarded statements that would have been more carefully worded if they were being made in the light of today's debate. . . . Scofield did write, "The point of testing is no longer legal obedience as the condition of salvation, but acceptance or rejection of Christ." But Scofield also wrote some other things, and what would he write today if he were alive and answering

---

[2] *Scofield Reference Bible* (New York: Oxford, 1909) 1115.

present-day critics of dispensationalism? The New Scofield Bible clarified the note:[3]

The *New Scofield Reference Bible* did not "clarify the note," it CHANGED IT. Observe:

> Prior to the cross man's salvation was through faith (Gen. 15:6; Rom. 4:3), being grounded on Christ's atoning sacrifice, viewed anticipatively by God . . .' now it is clearly revealed that salvation and righteousness are received by faith in the crucified and resurrected Savior.[4]

The NSRB does a great deal more "clarifying" than just the note in John 1:17. In the first note on dispensations (Gen. 1:28 - heading) they "elaborate" (to quote Ryrie) on Scofield's original definition of a dispensation:

> These different dispensations are not separate ways of salvation. During each of them man is reconciled to God in only one way, i.e. by God's grace through the work of Christ that was accomplished on the cross and vindicated in His resurrection. Before the cross *man was saved in prospect of Christ's atoning sacrifice, through believing* the revelation thus far given him. Since the cross man has been saved by believing on the Lord Jesus Christ in whom revelation and redemption are consummated.[5] *[emphasis added]*

How could a man be reconciled to God through Christ's work on the cross in the Old Testament when Christ was not even born yet? Answer: He could not.

The NSRB (1967) also adds to C.I. Scofield's original note on the four gospels (Rev. 14:6) stating that, "Grace is the basis for salvation in all dispensations, and is under all circumstances

---

[3] Ryrie, *Dispensationalism*, 107.
[4] *New Scofield Reference Bible* (New York: Oxford, 1967) 1124.
[5] *Ibid.*, 3.

the only way of salvation from sin."[6] The notes in the NSRB complement the beliefs of covenantal amillennialists. Covenant Theology "maintains that Old Testament believers did exercise faith in Christ . . ."[7] The scholars only see things from God's prospective ("in prospect of Christ's atoning sacrifice) *after* redemption is accomplished. They think that way because most of them are Calvinists. If Old Testament saints were saved "in prospect" why didn't God allow them to go to heaven when they died? The "lamb was already slain" was He not? The Old Testament saint was NOT allowed into heaven until the death of Christ. The atoning sacrifice of Christ took place in TIME, not eternity! This explanation (along with others) attempts to be scriptural by inserting "believing the revelation thus far given," and implies what Ryrie said, "the content of faith changes in the various dispensations."[8] If the "content of faith changes," how can it be the same?

Ryrie quotes Chafer defending the "saved the same way scenario:"

> This is to assert that God never saved any one person or group of persons on any other ground than that righteous freedom to do so which the Cross of Christ secured. There is, therefore, but one way to be saved and that is by the power of God made possible through the sacrifice of Christ.[9]

Gerstner, the anti-dispensationalist Reformed Calvinist, points out contradictory statements between Pentecost, Chafer and Walvoord regarding Old Testament saints being regenerated. He quotes Pentecost as saying, "the fact of new

---

[6] *Ibid.*, 1366.
[7] Gerstner, John H., *Wrongly Dividing the Word of Truth*, (Morgan: Soli Deo Gloria Publications, 2000) 186.
[8] Ryrie, *Dispensationalism*, 115.
[9] *Ibid.*, 108.

birth had not been revealed in the Old Testament,"[10] then quotes Chafer and Walvoord saying, "an Old Testament saint who was truly born again was just as saved as a believer in the present age."[11] He later goes on to correctly ask, "If these (Israel and the church) are two different people, how can they have the same salvation?"[12] The answer to which is: they do not! The Old Testament Jew was not "converted" nor "saved" nor "born again" (see John 7:38,39) in the New Testament sense. They were taught the law, not the gospel of the grace of God (see: Neh. 8:9; 2 Chron. 17:9).

Pentecost, although right about the absence of a new birth in the Old Testament, is off the mark in relation to Noah's preaching:

> During that extended interval Noah was a preacher of righteousness, who evidently proclaimed a coming judgment and exhorted people to escape by offering them salvation through faith.[13]

How could Noah offer "salvation through faith," when Noah himself was said to be **"saved by water"** (1 Pet. 3:20)? We understand that the "salvation" of Noah was not primarily *spiritual*, but physical. Many times in the Old Testament (the books, not the covenant), physical salvation is indicated (see Ps. 3:7,8; 31:16, et. al). As a result of their faith (Noah believed God), plus their works (Noah built the ark), their spiritual soul was saved at death *from* hell. They went to paradise to await the redemption on Calvary, which they would not have to wait for if the dispensational Calvinists were right. They did not get to paradise by faith *alone*. It IS true, that ultimately their sins are *cleared* by the blood of Christ, but they

---

[10] Gerstner, *Wrongly Dividing the Word of Truth*, 152.
[11] *Ibid.*, 153.
[12] *Ibid.*, 235.
[13] Pentecost, J. Dwight, *Thy Kingdom Come* (Grand Rapids: Kregel, 1995) 43, 44.

put themselves into that category by their obedience to the truth dispensed to them, and their obedience of it – works. While the obedience of Noah, Moses and Abraham (Gen. 22 – concerning his *justification* – James 2) entailed *works*, ours is "**obedience of faith**" (see Rom. 16:26 with Rom. 10:16,17; Rom. 1:5).

NOAH'S PREACHING

Noah was not preaching a soul condemning judgment of life after death, Hebrews 9:27, sermon! He was preaching an impending physical judgment of physical life! If the people refused the message of the "**preacher of righteousness**" (2 Pet. 2:5), they died physically *and* they went to hell. The message was not the same in Adam's, Noah's, Abraham's, or Moses' day, as it is now! The Old Testament placed the emphasis *first* on the visible, physical, outward "salvation," whereas, the New Testament starts at the heart (Rom. 10) dealing with a spiritual "salvation."

SCARED OF THE TRUTH

Most dispensationalists go out of their way (even though they are denying the word of God) in order to escape the allegation, that true dispensationalism supports more than one plan of salvation. Evidently they would agree with Covenant theologians that, "if Dispensationalism does this [teaches different plans of salvation in different dispensations], then Dispensationalism is a cult and not a branch of the Christian church."[14]

Charles Ryrie approaches the topic by attempting to defend dispensationalists themselves (like Scofield and Chaffer)

---

[14] Gerstner, *Wrongly Dividing the Word of Truth*, 169.

instead of the "dispensational system." He does this because, logically, he knows the dispensational system, in fact, leads to multiple ways of salvation as the Reformed anti-dispensationalists allege. Note Gerstner:

> Nevertheless, the presupposition of the difference between law and grace, between Israel and the church, between the different relations of God to men in the different dispensations, <u>when carried to its logical conclusion will inevitably result in multiple forms of salvation - that men are not saved the same way in all ages.</u>[15] *[emphasis added]*

> Dispensationalists, whatever they may say about 'dispensations,' are also insistent in their claims that they entertain no other method of salvation in any dispensation than by grace . . . However frequently they affirm their loyalty to the indispensable way of salvation in the blood of Jesus Christ, their system of doctrine relentlessly militates against this.[16]

Gerstner and other Reformed anti-dispensationalists, often cite Scofield's note in John 1:17 where he comes almost as close as Bullinger did (Deut. 6:25 note) in admitting at least TWO plans of salvation. We have already commented on how Ryrie and the NSRB tried to cover up the "advanced revelation," sweeping the "logical conclusions" under the rug. Ryrie even admits that, "all [dispensationalists of his camp] desire to maintain the doctrine of salvation by grace at all times."[17] Should the "desires" of dispensational theologians and recognized scholars be "maintained," at the expense of making a liar out of God? That is exactly what is done when a format of "saved the same" is coerced into "Bible teaching."

---

[15] Bass, Clarence B. *Backgrounds to Dispensationalism* (Grand Rapids: Baker Book House, 1960) 34.
[16] Gerstner, *Wrongly Dividing the Word of Truth*, 170,171.
[17] Ryrie, *Dispensationalism*, 111.

To further register the foreboding panic of dispensational scholars, note the foreword to the *Dictionary of Pre-millennial Theology:*

> This dictionary has been compiled in order to explain the major tenets of dispensationalism as it has been taught historically and to show that certain false accusations against the system are nothing more than straw men. In some cases, such accusations against dispensationalism have been based upon awkward sentences **[referring to Scofield in John. 1:17]** pulled from their context. For instance, some claim dispensationalists believe in various ways of salvation . . . [18] **[words in bracket added]**

It is unmistakable that what matters to these dispensational authors, are the historical opinions and systems of men, instead of the written words of God. The *Dictionary* goes on to fight an invisible man on the subject of salvation:

> A dispensational view of salvation has been misunderstood when it was inferred that the administrations (dispensations) of law and of grace involved two ways of salvation.[19]

Following Ryrie's breakdown of dispensational salvation (basis, requirement, object, content), leads the naive into thinking salvation is the same because only the *content* of the faith changes. M.H. Tabb concurs with Ryrie saying, "the difference has been in the object of faith - what the faith is placed in."[20] As Gerstner points out, this simply does not "fly," because, if the "content of faith changes," then "one

---

[18] FOREWORD, *Dictionary of Premillennial Theology:* 10.
[19] "Salvation, Dispensational View Of," *Dictionary of Premillennial Theology:* 388.
[20] Tabb, M.H. *Dispensational Salvation* (Ft. Walton Beach, Fl: Foundation Ministries, 1991) 1.

would not be talking about the same thing - about the same requirement."[21]

Some faith in the Old Testament had to be accompanied by works, or it was no good (James 2; 2 Sam. 22:21; Ps. 7:8). Ryrie and Tabb fail to mention that the word "faith" only appears *twice* in the whole Old Testament canon. Neither did they point out the difference in *personal* faith (Hab. 2:4 - "**his faith**") in the Old Testament and the "**faith of the Son of God**" (Gal. 2:20), which is simply called "**faith**" (Rom. 1:17). [The quotation of Hab. 2:4 in Rom. 1:17 and Gal. 3:11 omit the word "**his**."]

Furthermore, no one in the future Millennial Age will be saved by faith, since "**faith is . . . not seen**" (Heb. 11:1). Everyone in the Kingdom Age will literally, physically SEE Jesus Christ - the "object," or "content" of faith:

> *Zech. 12:10* **. . . they shall look upon me whom they have pierced...**

The *Tim LaHaye Prophecy Study Bible* (with an article written by Robert Dean) likewise misrepresents Old and New Testament salvation:

> Though each dispensation has distinct and identifiable characteristics, the truths and principles of God's revelation and plan for redemption are constant. Salvation is by grace through faith in Christ alone. Prior to the cross, faith anticipated fulfillment of the divine promise of salvation through the work of Messiah. Since the crucifixion of Jesus Christ, faith looks back to His finished, substitutionary atonement on the cross.[22]

---

[21] Gerstner, *Wrongly Dividing the Word of Truth*, 185.
[22] "Dispensations," *Tim LaHaye Prophecy Study Bible:* AMG, 2000, 10.

Dean's explanation differs some from Ryrie and Pentecost. At least Ryrie admitted that:

> Jesus Christ was not the conscious object of their faith, though they were saved by faith in God as he had revealed Himself principally through the sacrifices that he instituted as part of the Mosaic Law.[23]

The student of dispensationalism should notice the progression of error. They began by admitting that Old Testament believers were saved by "obedience" (Scofield's note in John 1:17). They also admitted that no Old Testament believer was ever born again (Pentecost). Then, they said they were saved by faith in Christ, although they were not conscious of it (Ryrie). Now, they say Old Testament believers were anticipating the cross, understanding it, and looking forward to it for their salvation. The modern overall dispensational summation is:

> *People in the Old Testament were saved*
> *by looking forward to the cross,*
> *while we are saved by looking back at the cross.*

"Not according to the Bible!"

In order for someone to fully adhere to that conjecture, Calvinism must be embraced, and plain passages of scripture rejected. Notice the Calvinism "flavor" in Tabb's comment:

> We have proven conclusively that a person is saved by faith alone in any dispensation. There has only ever been one plan of salvation, and it was worked out and settled before the foundation of the world . . .[24]

---

[23] Ryrie, *Dispensationalism*, 119, 120.
[24] Tabb, *Dispensational Salvation*, 90.

For, if the fact of Jesus being "**slain from the foundation of the world**" (Rev. 13:8), makes Old Testament salvation the same, why were the believers still in the holding tank (paradise, Abraham's bosom - Luke 16; Eph. 4) until the TIME of the actual crucifixion? The fact of the matter remains, that although no person will ever be "saved" apart from the blood of Christ; Old Testament saints had to *exercise* their own *personal* faith (Hab. 2:4) which was *works* in order to eventually have their sins *cleared*!

OLD TESTAMENT FAITH

With all of the colloquy about faith in the Old Testament, "Bible scholars" disregard the lack of references to "faith" in the Old Testament canon. As we have said, it only occurs *twice*. The first reference (Deut. 32:20) is negative, and the other one (Hab. 2:4) is not the "**faith of the Son of God**" (Gal. 2:20). This is evident because Paul, writing under the inspiration of the Holy Ghost, *removes* the pronoun "his" from the quotation of Hab. 2:4 in Rom. 1:17. The obvious *change* illustrates the *change* in Old and New Testament salvation. [Notice that the *translation* in the New Testament does not match the *original* Old Testament quote yet it is inspired as well.] There is a "**righteousness of the law**" (see Rom. 2:26; 8:4) and there is a "**righteousness of God**" (Rom. 1:17; 3:5; 3:21; 3:22; 10:3; 2 Cor. 5:21). This personal righteousness (Deut. 6:25 - "**our righteousness**") was the basis for the believer's eternal destiny, and if he was "**righteous**" (Ezek. 18:20) he would "make it," and if he was "**wicked**" (Ezek. 18:20) he would be "**turned into hell**" (Ps. 9:17).

The *Tim LaHaye Prophecy Study Bible* tangles up the truth in the *Glossary* section as well:

Dispensationalism - A system of theology that interprets Scripture literally and from the perspective of God's interaction with humanity through successive ages. This view of biblical history, maintains one plan of salvation in which God reveals Himself to man and deals with humanity in different ways in each successive period of their relationship or economy (dispensation) of time.[25]

"One plan of salvation?" Do they not see a difference in the "plan" for the young rich ruler (Matt. 19) and Nicodemus (John 3)? Two different ways for a person to get "eternal life." The only explicable reason is that the times of application are DIVIDED! If 2 Tim. 2:15 is NOT employed the integrity of scripture is nullified. There are *four* "plans of salvation" in the book of Acts alone! Or, I should say, four different ways people get the Holy Ghost. Let it be surveyed, however, that the above definition in the *Tim Lahaye Prophecy Bible* leaves room for the breeding of unorthodoxy and perplexity!

ISRAEL AND THE OLD TESTAMENT LAW

Many dispensationalists, like J. Dwight Pentecost, appeal to a false sense of understanding of the Old Testament Law in order to shoot down salvation by faith and works under it. The whole crux of the matter is what we mentioned at the onset of our discussion. In the Old Testament, the prophets were not preaching a judgment after death; at least not *primarily*. They were not focusing on the eternal life after death future, but rather, the future of the nation (corporately) on a physical piece of literal ground. Pentecost demonstrates his own confusion when he says, "the Law of Moses was given to a redeemed people, not to redeem a people."[26] A "redeemed people?" Redeemed in what way? They were redeemed, but that was in

---

[25] "Glossary of Prophetic Terms," *Tim LaHaye Prophecy Study Bible:* AMG, 2000, 1407.
[26] Pentecost, *Thy Kingdom Come*, 87.

the PHYSICAL sense, not spiritual. This "typology teaching" (though it makes good preaching) overlooks the primary reason for scripture – doctrine.

Pentecost goes on to say that the law "was not to save souls,"[27] but fails to give ONE verse reference in the entire thirty-nine books of the Old Testament on how a soul was saved! Like others, he goes to Hebrews 11 (the faith chapter) in an attempt to prove they had faith for salvation, even though that faith was for PHYSICAL things (i.e. crossing the Red Sea).

GALATIANS "CATCH ALL"

The book of Galatians is the constant drum beat of every normative dispensationalists, because in it Paul tells us that the Law does NOT save. Note that Paul did not say that the Law *never* (in previous dispensations) had a part in anyone's salvation. In fact, the "**righteousness of the Law**" was required for a person to be declared "**righteous**" in the Old Testament. Even unsaved Gentiles that did not have the "**oracles of God**" were declared righteous by their keeping (works) of the law:

> *Rom 2:12-15*
> **12 For as many as have sinned without law shall also perish without law: and as many as have sinned in the law shall be judged by the law;**
> **13 (For not the hearers of the law are just before God, but the doers of the law shall be justified.**
> **14 For when the Gentiles, which have not the law, do by nature the things contained in the law, these, having not the law, are a law unto themselves:**

---

[27] *Ibid.*, 87.

15 Which shew the work of the law written in their hearts, their conscience also bearing witness, and their thoughts the mean while accusing or else excusing one another;)

Still there are those who say that the law played no part in the "salvation" of Old Testament believers. Note Charles Ryrie again: "People were saved under the Law economy but not by the law . . . the law contained the revelation that brought people to a realization that their faith must be placed in God the Savior."[28]

ROMANS TWO

Paul said, in Romans 2, that people in the Old Testament economy were justified by being a "doer of the law." The commentator will immediately cry out, "That portion is relating to the heathen, not the Jew." That does not change the fact that **"the doers of the law shall be justified."** The Jew is even said to be **"judged by the law"** in verse twelve, not by his "faith . . . in God the Savior." Commentators fail to understand that Romans and Galatians are transitioning the Jews from the works of the law, and the Gentiles from following their conscience, to faith alone in Jesus Christ. If you couple Paul's statements in Romans 2 with those of Christ during His earthly ministry, it all makes perfect sense. Christ told people to keep the law and they would have eternal life (Matt. 19:17), and that works were necessary in order to avoid hell fire (Matt. 18:9).

Luke 10:28 **And he said unto him, Thou hast answered right: <u>this do</u>, and thou shalt live.**

---

[28] Ryrie, *Dispensationalism*, 117.

THE DEFINITIVE "WORKS" CHAPTER: EZEKIEL 18

This takes us to one of the greatest passages on *works* under the Old Testament dispensation: Ezekiel 18. In this section of scripture, God clearly lays down the law and gives "life" to those who "keep" his laws, and "death" to those who refuse to *work*. Dr. Ruckman comments on Ezek. 3:20 and 18:24:

> Under the Law, a saint not only is not "cleared" (Exod. 34:7), but his sins are not "taken away" (Heb. 10:4). And if that were not enough, he dies "in his sins" if he does not live right. . . . A sinner who dies "in his sins" (John 8:24) cannot go where Jesus Christ went (John 8:21). . . . Under the Law, the righteous saint (see text) dies in his sins with his iniquities on him. They are NOT imputed to Christ.[29]

When faced with the obvious, the classic answer is: "He is talking about this life, not eternal life."[30] Question: Did the righteous man in the passage go to hell? Of course not! How was he "righteous?" By faith in the substitutionary blood atonement of Christ? No, he was righteous by his OWN GOOD DEEDS! Commentators are so obsessive trying to prove salvation by faith alone *in this age*, that they reject what the Bible says about Old Testament salvation. Jamieson, Fausset and Brown do not understand the difference between Old Testament righteousness of the law, and the "**righteousness which is of faith.**" Notice:

> in his righteousness . . .he shall live - in it, not for it, as if that atoned for his former sins; but "in his righteousness" he shall live, as the evidence of his being already in favor

---

[29] Ruckman, Peter S., *Ruckman's Bible References* (Pensacola: Bible Baptist Bookstore, 1997) 127, 129.
[30] McGee, J. Vernon, *Thru the Bible with J. Vernon McGee Vol. 3* (Pasadena: thru the Bible Radio, 1983) 474.

with God through the merit of Messiah, who was to come.[31]

LUKE 16 WITH EZEKIEL 18

We understand that their motive was to "help God out" with regards to salvation is *this age* (compare John R. Rice's comment on Rev. 22:14); but enough is enough. The fact of the matter is, that God gave physical rules for physical life, and they DID play a part in a person's SPIRITUAL salvation *after* death! Even in Luke 16 the basis for the rich man going to hell was his BAD WORKS! Read the story! Even though some preachers think Lazarus prayed *the sinner's prayer* after hearing Moses and the prophets preach a message on "justification by faith" that is simply not the case. The rich man went to hell because he "**oppressed the poor and needy**" (Ezek. 18:12).

How come most "recognized scholars" missed the cross-reference in Luke 16 to Ezekiel 18:12? They missed it because they are not concerned with "**what saith the scripture**" (Rom. 4:3)! They could care less what the Book is really saying. Instead they develop their personal scholarly opinions and theological suppositions, and extract verses to secure and guard their points.

MORE EVIDENCE

When faced with the evidence from scripture that teaches *works and faith* in the Old Testament, dispensational scholars refuse comment. This is readily seen with the following verses:

---

[31] Jamieson, Fausset, Brown, *Commentary on the Whole Bible* (Grand Rapids: Zondervan, 1961) 695.

I. <u>Deuteronomy 6:25</u>

Deut 6:25 **And it shall be our righteousness, if we observe to do all these commandments before the LORD our God, as he hath commanded us.**

As we have said before, E.W. Bullinger (along with Scofield's note in John 1) hinted at a plain obvious difference in Old and New Testament salvation. Others may have recognized it, but they did not have the courage to teach "**all the counsel of God**" (Acts 20:27). Notice Bullinger's accurate observation:

> **our righteousness.** This is superseded by Rom. 10:4,5; Gal. 3:12. That true then: this true now. No discrepancy if the Dispensations are rightly divided according to 2 Tim. 2:15.[32]

The *Ryrie Study Bible* transfers the "**righteousness**" in the passage from a personal righteousness to a covenant right of the nation of Israel for a physical land inheritance:

> *it shall be our righteousness.* i.e., obedience to the law could not guarantee eternal life, but such obedience constituted the right to the blessings of the covenant, particularly title to the land.[33]

Although the point is well taken that the obedience to the law granted the conditional blessings of possessing the land under the Palestinian Covenant, it also determined whether or not a person was considered a "righteous man," or a "wicked man." No one was ever promised eternal life in the Old Testament (apart from the Messianic promise to Jesus Christ in

---

[32] *Companion Bible* (Grand Rapids: Kregel, 1990) 248.
[33] *Ryrie Study Bible* (Chicago: Moody Press, 1976) 285.

Ps. 21:4 with Titus 1:2), and if they were, they were not "guaranteed eternal life." There was no *eternal security* before Jesus rose from the dead (John 7:38,39)!

The Old Testament makes a distinction between the "righteous" and the "wicked:"

Deut. 25:1 **. . . then they shall justify the righteous, and condemn the wicked.**

Gen 18:23 **And Abraham drew near, and said, Wilt thou also destroy the righteous with the wicked?**

2 Sam 4:11 **How much more, when wicked men have slain a righteous person . . .**

1 Kings 8:32 **Then hear thou in heaven, and do, and judge thy servants, <u>condemning the wicked</u>, to bring his way upon his head; and <u>justifying the righteous</u>, to give him according to his righteousness.**

Ps 1:6 **For the LORD knoweth the way of the righteous: but the way of the ungodly shall perish.**

Prov 10:11 **The mouth of a righteous man is a well of life: but violence covereth the mouth of the wicked.**

Eccl 3:17 **I said in mine heart, God shall judge the righteous and the wicked: for there is a time there for every purpose and for every work.**

The appeal made in Isaiah 64:6, to prove a person in the Old Testament did not have righteousness by works, is despicable Bible exegesis. The previous verse (Isa. 64:5) mentions a man that "**worketh righteousness**" and "righteous" individuals are discussed about ten times in Isaiah alone! Isa. 64:6 is a great soul-winning verse to prove the New Testament truths of Romans 3:10,23, but in context refers to the nation of Israel (note: "we" of verse six; "us" of verse 7; "our father" of verse 8; "Zion," and "Jerusalem" of verse 10").

II. Psalm 7:8; 18:20; 35:24; 86:2

Ps 7:8 **The LORD shall judge the people: judge me, O LORD, according to my righteousness, and according to mine integrity that is in me.**

Ps 18:20 **The LORD rewarded me according to my righteousness; according to the cleanness of my hands hath he recompensed me.**

Ps 35:24 **Judge me, O LORD my God, according to thy righteousness; and let them not rejoice over me.**

Ps 86:2 **Preserve my soul; for I am holy: O thou my God, save thy servant that trusteth in thee.**

The preceding verses, in an unambiguous fashion teach *works* under the Old Testament economy. While we understand their sins were not cleared until Calvary, the Old Testament saint still had to maintain personal righteousness *for* justification. To get around these clear verses inconsistent dispensationalists forfeit the saint's righteousness as having any part in their future eternal home. This is done by stating, as Ryrie does, that "eternal salvation was by grace and that the means of temporal life was by law."[34] The personal righteousness is then only good for earthly life and rewards. Note M.H. Tabb in *Dispensational Salvation* where he uses Isa. 64:6 to prove David was not justified by his own righteousness.[35] To reach a conclusion that Old Testament righteousness was simply for earthly life and had no bearing on eternity, one must overlook the following Bible facts:

1. The phrase "everlasting life" is only cited ONE time in the thirty-nine books of the Old Testament canon, and that being Dan. 12:3 - a reference to the resurrection, NOT a personal present possession upon belief as in John 3:16; 3:36; 5:24.

2. The word "eternal" is only listed twice, and neither time does it refer to the life of an Old Testament saint (Deut. 33:27; Isa. 60:15).

3. Dispensationalists who teach people were "saved the same" confound Old Testament righteousness with *sinlessness.* An Old Testament saint could be "righteous," but he was certainly NOT *sinless.* Solomon, after writing that **"there is not a just man upon earth, that doeth good, and sinneth not"** (Eccl. 7:20), still insisted that there were "righteous" men (see: Eccl. 8:14; 9:1,2). The Old Testament Jew made sure his standing was that of "forgiven" by being "righteous" and "obedient" to the Law by doing the things prescribed in the law when he sinned.

---

[34] Ryrie, *Dispensationalism*, 117.
[35] Tabb, *Dispensational Salvation*, 48.

4. Many dispensationalists also overlook the fact that David's preservation was based on his *personal holiness*, and not the holiness of God. It is hard to say that David was referring to physical life when he used the word "soul." Tabb attempts to nullify the importance of the Old Testament saint's righteousness in Ezekiel 14:14,20 by stating that "soul is used many times in the Old Testament with reference to the physical life."[36] So what if it means "physical life." What would happen to a "wicked" man who died *physically*? Would he go to paradise (Abraham's bosom) or hell? If a man was not considered "holy" under the Old Testament economy his soul was not "preserved," and he had no guarantee of eternal security.

III. Ezekiel chapters 3 and 18

Ezek 3:20 **Again, When a righteous man doth turn from his righteousness, and <u>commit iniquity</u>, and I lay a stumblingblock before him, he shall die: because thou hast not given him warning, he shall die in his sin, and his righteousness which he <u>hath done</u> shall not be remembered; but his blood will I require at thine hand.**

Ezek 18:5, 9 **But if a man be just, and <u>do that</u> which is lawful and right . . . . Hath walked in my statutes, and <u>hath kept</u> my judgments, to deal truly; he is just, he shall surely live, saith the Lord GOD.**

Ezek 18:19 **Yet say ye, Why? doth not the son bear the iniquity of the father? When the son hath <u>done</u>**

---

[36] *Ibid.*, 58.

that which is lawful and right, and hath <u>kept</u> all my statutes, and hath done them, he shall surely live.

Ezek 18:20-28
20 The soul that sinneth, it shall die. The son shall not bear the iniquity of the father, neither shall the father bear the iniquity of the son: the <u>righteousness</u> of the righteous shall be upon him, and the <u>wickedness</u> of the wicked shall be upon him.
21 But if the wicked will turn from all his sins that he hath committed, <u>and keep</u> all my statutes, <u>and do</u> that which is lawful and right, he shall surely live, he shall not die.
22 All his transgressions that he hath committed, they shall not be mentioned unto him: <u>in his righteousness</u> that he hath done he shall live.
23 Have I any pleasure at all that the wicked should die? saith the Lord GOD: and not that he should return from his ways, and live?
24 But when the righteous turneth away from his righteousness, and committeth iniquity, and <u>doeth according</u> to all the abominations that the wicked man doeth, shall he live? All his righteousness that he hath done shall not be mentioned: in his trespass that he hath trespassed, and <u>in his sin</u> that he hath sinned, in them shall he die.
25 Yet ye say, The way of the Lord is not equal. Hear now, O house of Israel; Is not my way equal? are not your ways unequal?
26 When a righteous man turneth away from his righteousness, and <u>committeth iniquity</u>, and dieth

in them; for his iniquity that he hath done shall he die.

27 Again, when the wicked man turneth away from his wickedness that he hath committed, and <u>doeth that</u> which is lawful and right, he shall save his soul alive.

28 Because he considereth, and turneth away from all his transgressions that he hath committed, he shall surely live, he shall not die.

The above passages are by far the most informative verses on the topic of Old Testament salvation. We have briefly commented on them earlier, but are driven back to them since they reinforce true salvation under the Law. They also reprimand dispensationalists who snub their nose at a *works plus faith* salvation in the Old Testament, with multiple *gridlocks*. The toughest one being the fact that a righteous man could *lose his salvation* and go to hell.

The arguments against the truths in the passages are typical for those who try to cover up the truth with circular reasoning. As Dr. Stauffer correctly avows, "The passage deals with the soul dying or living, not simply the physical life of an individual."[37] Nevertheless, notice how Barnes *changes* the meaning of the verses to fit his *private interpretation*. He contends that the words "soul" and "live" relate only to the physical temporal realm:

> [Live ... die] In the writings of Ezekiel there is a development of the meaning of "life" and "death." In the holy land the sanctions of divine government were in great degree <u>temporal</u>; so that the promise of "life" for "obedience," the threatening of "death" for "disobedience," in the Books of Moses, were regarded

---

[37] Stauffer, *One Book Rightly Divided*, 224.

simply as **temporal and national** . . . . The word "soul" denotes a "person" viewed as an "individual," possessing the "life" which God breathed into man when he became a "living soul" (Gen. 2:7); i.e., it distinguishes "personality" from "nationality," and this introduces that fresh and higher idea of "life" and "death," **which is not so much "life" and "death" in a future state**, as "life" and "death" as equivalent to communion with or separation from God - that idea of life and death which was explained by our Lord in the Gospel of John (John 8), and by Paul in Rom 8.[38] **[emphasis added]**

Tabb abuses Ezekiel 3 and 18 by saying that the wicked man not only dies physically, but goes to hell; while the righteous man who becomes a wicked man only dies physically:

> The wicked in verses 18 and 19 is the lost man. If he will not repent . . . He will die (physically) in his iniquity, and go to hell . . . The righteous man in verse 20 is saved. When the saved man turns from his good works (his righteousness), and goes into sin (commit iniquity), he shall die (physically) in his sin. But if he refrains from sin in his life, he shall surely live (physically).[39]

Tabb is teaching exactly *opposite* to what the passage is stating. "**When the righteous turneth away from his righteousness, and committeth iniquity,**" he dies "**in his sin**" (18:24)! No one can escape hell who dies "**in his sin!**" To say someone has died "**in his sin**" is equivalent to saying he was UNSAVED:

> *John 8:24* **I said therefore unto you, that ye shall die in your sins: for if ye believe not that I am he, ye shall die in your sins.**

---

[38] (from Barnes' Notes, Electronic Database. Copyright (c) 1997 by Biblesoft)
[39] Tabb, *Dispensational Salvation*, 59.

The **"righteous"** in the passage who **"turn[s] from his righteousness"** *becomes* **"wicked."** Where do the **"wicked"** go at death? You have one guess: Ps. 9:17; Isa. 5:11-14; Ps. 55:15; Prov. 9:18; 15:11; 15:24.

Dispensationalists like McGee, will affirm that the "life" in Ezekiel is only physical life, yet they will insist (and rightly so) that life in John 1:4; 5:26; 5:29; 5:40; 6:33; 6:35; 6:51; 6:53; 6:63; and 8:12 is eternal life even though the words "eternal," or "everlasting" are NOT in the verses. Could this be a double standard? Bullinger (commenting on **Lev 18:5** *Ye shall therefore keep my statutes, and my judgments: which if a man do, he shall live in them: I am the LORD.*) notes that the phrase,

> 'he shall live in them' (Lev. 18:5) is "resurrection life . . . The Chaldaen paraphrase = shall live by them to life eternal . . . Cp. The other passages where 'live' is used in this sense: Ezek. 13:21; 20:11; Luke 10:28; Rom. 10:5; Gal. 3:12; Neh. 9:29; Hab. 2:4; Rom. 1:17; Heb. 10:38 . . . . . .Thus 'eternal life,' by faith, is set in contrast with eternal life by works.[40]

Another approach toward private interpretation is to apply the "never was" technique. Baptists are awfully familiar with this. If a person got saved, and did not "pan out" (or do the things a believer *"should"* - Rom. 6:4), then the assumption is forced that they never were saved to begin with. You must understand that this technique is essential if you refuse to "rightly divide the word of truth." For, if every one is saved the same way, then the application of Ezekiel 18 would still apply for New Testament saints today. And, lo and behold, those "righteous" men in the passage could become "wicked,"

---

[40] *Companion Bible*, 158.

and be **"turned into hell."** The "never was" tactic is then adopted to resolve the sticky situation.

Matthew Henry employs this in Ezek. 18:21-29 by stating that the righteous man who became wicked, "never was in sincerity a righteous man."[41] We will find the "never was" policy executed in scores of passages where the indolent Bible student declines God's method of proper division (i.e. Tribulation salvation, and the transition periods).

IV. Galatians 3:12; Romans 9:32; 10:5; 11:6

Gal 3:12 **And the law is not of faith: but, The man that doeth them shall live in them.**

The very idea of saying Old Testament saints under the Law were saved exclusively by "faith" (see any major treatise on the subject) is contrary to Romans AND Galatians. Since when did "doeth" become "faith?" Dr. Ruckman summarizes:

> The Old Testament saint under the law must perform the works (Deut. 28:14) as an evidence of his faith (James 2:21). These works do not justify him (Gal. 3:11) unless faith accompanies them (Heb. 11:39,40). He lives by doing (Ezek 18), and when he quits "doing" (Ps. 51:11), he has "had it" (Jud 16:20). God can take the spirit from him permanently (Saul) or temporarily (Samson) or not at all (David), but even under the law exceptions are made (2 Sam. 12:13). Grace is everywhere manifest in the life of Samson who never repents, confesses, or restores anything one time in a lifetime of continued transgression. But "Eternal Security" is unknown in the Old Testament apart from the Psalms of David (Ps 91:14-16), who was given "sure mercies" (Acts 13:34) that other men were

---

[41] (from Matthew Henry's Commentary on the Whole Bible: New Modern Edition, Electronic Database. Copyright (c) 1991 by Hendrickson Publishers, Inc.)

not given (2 Sam. 7;14). Even in the Old Testament the Just lives by faith, but it is "his faith" (Hab. 2:4); whereas the New Testament believer is living by "the faith OF THE SON OF GOD who loved . . ." (Gal. 2:20).[42]

Rom 9:32 **Wherefore? Because they sought it not by faith, but as it were by the works of the law. For they stumbled at that stumblingstone;**

Rom 10:5 **For Moses describeth the righteousness which is of the law, That the man which doeth those things shall live by them.**

Rom 11:6 **And if by grace, then is it no more of works: otherwise grace is no more grace. But if it be of works, then is it no more grace: otherwise work is no more work.**

Grace, even though demonstrated all throughout scripture, is not expressly applied in the fullest sense where works is involved. As we have already seen (Ps. 86:2), the Old Testament saint was not protected by grace, but preserved by his own holiness. Romans 11:6 explains the fact that grace and works cannot appropriately fit together. Maybe stretching things, Stauffer comments:

> The first half of Romans 11:6 refers to the transition from the law to the current Church Age. During the Church Age, salvation is no more of works. Salvation once included works (under the law), but is no more of works (during the Church Age). The second half of the verse will pertain to the Tribulation period still yet to come. During this time it will be "no more of grace." In other

---

[42] Ruckman, Peter S., *Galatians, Ephesians, Philippians, Colossians* (Pensacola: Bible Believers Press, 1973) 91,92.

words, it was once of absolute grace (during the Church Age), but will be no more of grace (in the Tribulation).[43]

Note: This chart reflects the two dispensations termed "the Law," and "the Church Age" and are represented by "Old Testament" and "New Testament." They do not cover the period of about 2500 years *before* the giving of the Law, nor do they include the *transitional periods*, the Tribulation period or the Kingdom Age.

OLD AND NEW TESTAMENT COMPARED

OLD TESTAMENT	*NEW TESTAMENT*
Holy Spirit could leave, and did not perform his sealing work: 1 Samuel 10:5,6; 16:14; 18:10; 19:9; Ps. 51:11	**Holy Spirit abides** with the believer for ever and seals the believer until the "day of redemption." Eph. 1:13; 4:30; John 14:16,26 15:26; 16:7.
Content of message: Adam (don't eat); Noah (build an ark); Abraham (believe and offer your son); Moses (keep the law) Works are an integral part of the Old Testament sacrificial system. Deut. 6:25; Ex. 19:8; Ezek. 3:20; 18; Num. 5:3.	**Content of message:** Believe on the sacrificial atoning death of Jesus Christ, and His resurrection for complete redemption. Justified by faith. The works of the law cannot justify in this age. Rom.3:21,22; Gal. 3:12,13 Eph. 2:8,9; 1 Cor. 15:1-4.

---

[43] Stauffer, *One Book Rightly Divided*, 154.

Day, Place and Manner of Worship: Sabbath a sign for the Jewish nation (Ex.31). Jerusalem chosen for the place of worship, and the temple is the habitation of God. 1 Kings 8:12,18,29; Deut 15:20; 2 Chron. 7:12.	**Day, Place and Manner of Worship:** The first day of the week for believers. The temple of the Christian is the body. John 20:1,19; Acts 20:7; 20:18; 1 Cor. 16:2; 1 Cor. 3:16; 6:19.
Literal FEAST observed in the Old Testament Deut. 16	**Christ our FEAST.** 1 Cor. 15.
The Levites handled scriptures. Neh. 8:8; 2 Chron. 17:7; 2 Chron. 30:22; 35:3; Ezra 7:25.	**Priesthood of believers** determine what books belong in the canon of the New Testament: 1 Peter 2
Many sacrifices that cannot "take away sin."	**One sacrifice.** Heb. 10:10-12
Many ordinances. Ezek. 43:18	**Freedom** in Christ. Col. 2:10-23
A system of **Law** with works. Ps. 18:20,24; 2 Sam. 22:21,22; Prov. 28:18.	Salvation by **grace** through faith alone. Eph. 2:8,9; Acts 13:38,39; Gal. 3:23-25.
Old Testament saints went to **paradise** (Abraham's bosom) after death. Luke 16; Eph. 4; Job 3:17,18; Ezek. 31:15; Isa. 14:11; Gen. 44:31; Job 17:13; Isa. 38:10	New Testament saints go directly into the **presence of Jesus Christ.** 2 Cor. 5:1-8; Phil. 1:23.

SALVATION IN THE TRIBULATION

Despite the fact that most dispensational authors (Ryrie, Pentecost, Ironside, LaHaye, Lindsey, Walvoord, Ice, Hitchcock, Dave Hunt et. al.) cannot expound with any detail how a person is saved during the Tribulation is no surprise. Most prominent dispensational authors have long ago rejected the God blessed English text of the Authorized Version. Once THE Book was abandoned for scholarship, so was advanced light and revelation about the future. The so-called prophecy experts like LaHaye, Van Impe, Hitchcock, Walvoord, and Lindsey combined, could not produce ONE prophecy truth that Larkin did not published before they were born. Furthermore, there is not *one* dispensational truth taught by the well-known authors listed above, that cannot be proven from the King James text without the assistance of *any* Hebrew or Greek.

Tribulation salvation, as found in the Bible, is a faith and works plan. And to teach this *Biblical truth* incites cries of "heresy," and "heretic" from nearly all sides. According to Dr. Ruckman, "[n]o biblical doctrine was ever labeled 'heresy' as much as this one, especially by Baptists and Charismatics."[44]

WHAT'S THE BIG DEAL?

Tribulation salvation is a paramount doctrine because it is a key that unlocks many difficult passages and adds momentum to the Church Age doctrine of eternal security. Most verses used to teach that a person can lose his salvation are actually Tribulation passages, not related to the Church Age at all. While believing in salvation by grace through faith, Baptists and other "evangelicals" often impose verses out of Matthew, Hebrews, James and Revelation that perceptibly teach faith

---

[44] Ruckman, Peter S., *22 years of the Bible Believer's Bulletin Vol. 3*(Pensacola: Bible Baptist Bookstore, 2000) 79.

plus works, on the Church Age. Then they either avoid them, by refusing to comment, or *change them* (like Rice in Rev. 22:14) to match their ideas. Baptists also get in a jam with Tribulation references that teach a man can lose his salvation. When they come to these passages, instead of "determining the correct doctrinal application,"[45] they spiritualize them, or use the "never was" scheme.

As we examine what some of the leading dispensationalists have said about Tribulation salvation, let us "**search the scriptures**" (John 5:39), and "**let God be true, but every man a liar**" (Rom. 3:4).

TRIBULATION SALVATION IN REVELATION

I. Revelation 1:3

Rev 1:3 **Blessed is he that readeth, and they that hear the words of this prophecy, and keep those things which are written therein: for the time is at hand.**

The first three chapters of the book of Revelation are generally taught (because of 1:19) as Church Age doctrine, although they are plainly for someone who is living at "**the time**" that is "**at hand.**" Understanding that all verses of scripture have *three* applications (doctrinal, historical, and devotional) compels the Bible believer to ask: "What kind of doctrine is taught in the first three chapters of Revelation?" If it is Church Age doctrine then it should match the Church Age epistles teaching salvation by grace *without* works. That is simply NOT the case.

---

[45] Stauffer, *One Book Rightly Divided*, xiii.

Now, we understand that the first three chapters are addressed to "churches." But the word "church" does not demand the body of Christ, unless you are a Baptist brider. There was a "church" before Jesus was born, called "Israel" (Acts 7:38), and it was no more in Christ's body than Methuselah, Lamech, and Noah. There are TWO designations for the word "church" in the New Testament. One being the local called out assembly, and the other the spiritual body of Jesus Christ. After the rapture of the church (not local churches) there will still exist "churches" who will need a message from the Spirit (i.e. Rev. 2:7,11,17,29; 3:6,13,22) that includes instructions on how to "**endure unto the end**" (Matt. 24:13).

Revelation 1:3 promises a blessing to those who "keep" something. Notice the personal WORK on behalf of the person. The "blessing" in the passage deals with more than "spiritual blessings" (Eph. 1:3) found in the Church Age. You know this by running the references in the book of Revelation on the word "blessed" (see: Rev. 14:13; 16:15; 19:9; 20:6; 22:7; 22:14). The blessed person keeps the commandments of God *plus* the faith of Christ, sings the song of Moses, and gains access to the tree of life *for* his eternal life by WORKS!

I am afraid we have gotten too loose with the typology of John being caught up in Revelation chapter four *after* the messages to the "churches." This devotional application places all material in chapters 1-3 as Church Age doctrine. All premillennial, pretribulational dispensationalists use the fact that the word "church" does not appear *after* chapter four as a catapult for the pretribulation rapture. Larkin as well as Scofield, Ironside and other pretribulational dispensationalists follow this reasoning. LaHaye explicates:

> The church is mentioned 17 times in the first three chapters of Revelation, but after John (a member of the

church) is called up to heaven at the beginning of chapter 4, he looks down on the events of the Tribulation, and the church is not mentioned or seen again until chapter 19, when she returns to the earth with her Bridegroom at His glorious appearing.[46]

While it is true that the word church does not appear in chapters 4-21, Rev. 22:16 states that the entire message of the book of Revelation was for the seven churches:

> *Rev 22:16* **I Jesus have sent mine angel to testify unto you <u>these things in the churches</u>. I am the root and the offspring of David, and the bright and morning star.**

Either you have Church Age doctrine in chapters 4-21 with the church (body of Christ) going through the Tribulation, or the churches of Rev. 1-3 *doctrinally* are NOT "Church Age churches," saved by grace through faith alone.

The best way to handle Rev. 1-3 is to break it down three ways: historically, devotionally, and doctrinally. John obviously wrote in history to seven literal churches of his day. That is the historical division. The devotional division would fall in line with what most are familiar with as *periods of church history:*

> The first of these [periods] (Ephesus, Rev. 2:1) can be denominated the Apostolic Period, beginning with the first local new Testament church called out in Matthew 10 and ending somewhere around 90 A.D . . . .The second period of time (Smyrna, Rev. 2:8) corresponds generally to the time between 90 A.D. and 325 A.D. . . . and the third period (Pergamos, Rev. 2:12) from 325 A.D. to 500 A.D. . . The fourth period of church history (Thyatira,

---

[46] LaHaye, Tim, Ice, Thomas, *Charting the End Times* (Eugene, Oregon: Harvest House Publishers, 2001) 108.

Rev. 2:18) runs roughly from Leo "the Great" to the times of the Crusades (approximately 500-1000 A.D.) . . . The fifth period (Sardis, Rev. 3:1) goes from 1000-1500 A.D. . . . .And the sixth period (Philadelphia, Rev. 3:7) will take history into the Reformation (1500-1900 A.D.). . . . At around 1900 A.D. (1884 and 1901 will bracket the date) the seventh and final period (Laodicea, Rev. 3:14) begins.[47]

The doctrinal portion would apply to literal churches in the Tribulation period. This is no problem, for there was at least one literal church during Christ day before the forming of the spiritual body of Christ (see Matt. 18:17). If this approach is NOT taken you must either *pretend* the verses that teach *works plus faith* are NOT THERE, or *change them*. Tabb eliminates their meaning by saying they are talking about rewards instead of salvation.

Pentecost has an interesting twist on things. He says the Philadelphia church is the "true church" that is raptured, and the Laodicean church is the false "professing church" which is left behind. Now, he does this in order to dodge around the passages that teach some of these "churches" could go into the Tribulation. Notice he says that,

> the true church terminates with the Philadelphia church, which is removed from the earth according to the promise of Revelation 3:10 before the tribulation begins, and the false professing church, from which the true has been separated by rapture, is left behind, rejected by the Lord, and vomited out into the seventieth week to reveal the true nature of her profession so that such may be rejected justly by the Lord.[48]

---

[47] Ruckman, Peter S. *The History of the New Testament Church, Vol. 1*, (Pensacola: Bible Believers Press, 1984) ii.
[48] Pentecost, J. Dwight, *Things to Come* (Grand Rapids: Zondervan, 1958) 213.

So, instead of the Laodicean church being in type and devotion, the age prior to the rapture of the church, it becomes a false church of professors, not possessors. This is the "never was" syndrome.

Pentecost invents this idea because he cannot see the fact that some people in literal churches during the Tribulation could be spewed out of God's mouth, lose their salvation and go to hell. Doctrinally, his scheme does not work because there are churches other than Laodicea that are in danger of going into the Tribulation, or losing their salvation. Notice:

1. Rev. 2:5 - Ephesus could lose their candlestick.

2. Rev. 2:10 - Smyrna is said that they will "**have tribulation ten days,**" and the only way to survive is to DIE.

3. Rev. 2:16 - Pergamos is on the boarder of an outright "**fight**" with Jesus Christ himself.

4. Rev. 3:22 - members ("servants" of verse 20) of the church of Thyatira are warned that they will be "**cast . . . into great tribulation, except they repent of their deeds.**"

5. Rev. 3:5 - members of the church of Sardis can possibly have their names blotted out of the book of life if they do not "overcome." The implications are there.

Pentecost also failed to mention that the church of Philadelphia was granted the promise of deliverance because of their *works*, not their faith: "**Because thou hast kept the word of my patience...**" (Rev. 3:10)

At this juncture, we see that "**dividing the word of truth**" (2 Tim. 2:15) goes deeper than simply placing Rev. 1-3 as the Church Age. Conversely, to "rightly divide" the scriptures also goes beyond eliminating Rev. 1-3 from ANY Church Age doctrine, which hyper-dispensationalists will do:

> . . . when these passages are compared with Paul's epistles, Ephesians in particular, one sees a completely different tone . . . .For the above reasons, some dispensationalists believe these seven epistles are addressed to seven churches which will be established during the future period of the Tribulation. . . ."[49]

So, at least hyper-dispensationalism has something right! But what about Revelation 1:5? Can hypers honestly say that Rev. 1:5 is NOT "body of Christ" material? To formulate a chart grouping the books of Hebrews through Revelation as "Tribulation, Second Coming, Millennium, Eternity,"[50] is equally as wrong as stating that Hebrews through Revelation chapter 3 *is* Church Age doctrine. For example, if you say the book of Hebrews is completely for the Tribulation (as hypers do), then you have just dumped all of the passages on the eternal sacrifice of Christ for the believer *now*. Hebrews 10:14-17 is the New Covenant for New Testament Christians in the body of Christ, not *Tribulation saints!* Hebrews 8:10-12 is the New Covenant for Hebrew Tribulation saints, and it is the same quotation (aside from the phrase, "**house of Israel**") from Jeremiah 31. If you learn this "book grouping" format, you will place John 3:16 under the kingdom message, and also forbid Christians to confess their sins (1 John 1:7-9).

---

[49] Baker, Charles F. *A Dispensational Synopsis of the New Testament* (Grand Rapids: Grace Publications, 1989) 189.
[50] Stauffer, *One Book Rightly Divided*, 12.

The first three chapters of Revelation certainly relate a faith and works salvation program for the seven churches that will embark into the Tribulation Period:

II. Revelation 2:7

Rev 2:7 **He that hath an ear, let him hear what the Spirit saith unto the churches; To him that overcometh will I give to eat of the tree of life, which is in the midst of the paradise of God.**

Here, Revelation 2:7 gives numerous inconsistencies with *our* salvation. First of all, our "overcoming" is not futuristic. We have already overcome (John 16:33; 1 John 2:13,14; 4:4; 5:4) through the merits of Jesus Christ. Those in the Tribulation will only overcome if they **"hold fast"** (Heb. 3:6). Also, notice that the Tribulation saint receives "eternal life" orally. He must **"eat of the tree of life"** in order to **"inherit everlasting life"** (Matt. 19:29). A person in the Church Age gets eternal life by BELIEF (Rom. 10:10-13). Moreover, the New Testament Christian has eternal life as a present possession (John 5:24; 3:36; Rom. 6:23), instead of waiting for it to be granted **"in the world to come"** (Matt. 10:30).

The New Scofield Reference Bible (1967) tries to make the tree of life the cross! Note:

> In the New Testament the word translated 'tree' (Gk. xulon) is used of the cross (Acts 5:30; 10:39; Gal. 3:13; 1 Pet. 2:24). It is through Christ death on the tree that mankind may have eternal life.[51]

Van Impe handles the verse like you would on the street dealing with a Charismatic who was trying to convince you

---

[51] *New Scofield Reference Bible* (New York: Oxford, 1967) 1353.

that you could lose your salvation. He says, "How can one be an over-comer? By trusting in the merits of the shed blood of Jesus Christ."[52] While there is some truth in his statement (all Tribulation saints must have *faith* in Christ as well as works), he is basically attempting to shove the passage back into the Church Age.

M.H. Tabb claims that Rev. 2:7 along with 2:11,17, and 26 has "to do with rewards,"[53] and thinks that just because the historical church of Ephesus is mentioned, "verse 7 is aimed at the Ephesian period of church history, which is the period of the apostles [who were] under grace, just as we are today."[54] He then goes on to say that we are overcomers (from 1 John) but fails to mention the glaring fact that the "eternal life" in the passage comes off of *a tree*.

The most popular prophecy *"expert,"* Tim LaHaye, attempts to make the verse apply to a Christian, saying, "Believers in heaven will have access to that tree forever."[55] The "tree of life" is NOT located in "heaven" at all. Read the references and their contexts: Rev. 2:7, 22:2; 22:14.

Oliver Greene ties **"the paradise of God"** to the third heaven where Paul was caught up. He does this, like all others, to eliminate the Tribulation reference and force it to teach "rewards."[56]

III. Revelation 2:11

Rev 2:11 **He that hath an ear, let him hear what the Spirit saith unto the churches; He that overcometh shall not be hurt of the second death.**

---

[52] Van Impe, Jack, *Revelation Revealed* (Royal Oak: Jack Van Impe Ministries, 1982) 31.
[53] Tabb, *Dispensational Salvation*, 81.
[54] *Ibid*.
[55] *Tim LaHaye Prophecy Study Bible*, AMG: 2000, 1366.
[56] Greene, Oliver B., *Revelation* (Greenville: The Gospel Hour, 1963) 70.

Our second example of Tribulation salvation in the book of Revelation lists a prerequisite for escaping the lake of fire (Rev. 20:15) and it is NOT belief. It is "overcoming." The obvious implication is, that the person who does not "overcome" will go to hell. Charismatics have used this verse with Rev. 3:5 time and time again (*out of context*) to prove a person can lose their salvation. The problem is not the fact that some Bible verses teach *someone* can lose their salvation (over "90 percent of professing Christians"[57] admit that); but WHO are those verses aimed at, and what dispensational AGE is under discussion? If it is the Church Age, then you have a disarray of bewilderment, with a Bible full of contradictions and mistakes. On the other hand, if the scriptures are "**rightly divid[ed]**" the honor and dignity of the word of God is retained.

Once any Baptist Bible teacher or commentator allows Rev. 1-3 for the Church Age, he is then forced to maneuver his way around the obvious implications in order to teach eternal security. The same is done in Matthew, James and Hebrews. Instead of utilizing God's tool of proper division, they create confusion and contradictions.

IV. Revelation 2:17

> *Rev 2:17* **He that hath an ear, let him hear what the Spirit saith unto the churches; To him that overcometh will I give to eat of the hidden manna, and will give him a white stone, and in the stone a new name written, which no man knoweth saving he that receiveth it.**

---

[57] Ruckman, *22 years of the Bible Believer's Bulletin Vol. 3*, 80.

To place this verse *doctrinally* in the Church Age, for the body of Christ, denies the very foundation of the futurists principles. Oliver Greene, for instance, does what every "saved the same" preacher does; he devotionalizes the "manna," and the "white stone," so he can find application for us:

> We then have a promise to the overcomer, concerning special and personal rewards of hidden manna, and a white stone . . . Overcoming the world, the flesh, and the devil is an individual matter. WE must be overcomers. Overcoming refers to individuals, not to a group.[58]

The above exposition overlooked the cross-referencess to manna being given to the "overcomers" *literally* during the Tribulation: Job 38:22,23; Micah 7:14; Ps. 74:14; Rev. 12:6; Matt. 14:15-21. This tribulation event is typified by Jesus feeding the five thousand (which is recorded in *all four* of the gospels). Satan even tempts Jesus to turn a STONE into this bread, *in the wilderness* (see Matt. 4:1-11).

V. Revelation 2:26

Rev 2:26 **And he that overcometh, and keepeth my works unto the end, to him will I give power over the nations:**

How much plainer can the Bible be concerning Tribulation salvation. The deepest dispensationalists out there (excluding hypers), still insist that the context is the rapture of the Church (not "churches"). They do this by making the phrase "till I come" refer to the rapture instead of the revelation. Once the application is understood to be the revelation, and the phrase

---

[58] Greene, *Revelation*, 89.

"**the time is at hand**" (Rev. 1:3) is taken literal, there is no "problem" with the verse.

When the Baptist sees "works" he immediately cries out - "rewards not works" (see Tabb's reasoning). The argument is, that the result of keeping the works is "**power over the nations**" NOT eternal life. It seems that could be an easy application for the Church Age saint (taking into account Rom. 8:17 and 2 Tim. 2:12). The "elders" of Rev. 5:10-24 *may* represent Church Age saints, but it must remembered that Tribulation saints ALSO reign during the Kingdom Age: Rev. 20:6; Rev. 20:4 with Rev. 6:9.

The honest Bible student, cannot help but notice that the phrase "**unto the end**" matches: Matt. 10:22; 13:39,40,49; 24:3,6,13,14. This "end" is not the end of somebody's life, but the end of a period of time (Dan. 7:26; 8:17 - "**time of the end:**" 8:19; 9:26; 11:27; 11:35; 11:40; 12:4, 6, 8, 9, 13).

VI. Revelation 3:3

Rev 3:3 **Remember therefore how thou hast received and heard, and hold fast, and repent. If therefore thou shalt not watch, I will come on thee as a thief, and thou shalt not know what hour I will come upon thee.**

Here, Bullinger hit the nail on the head, stating, "These words are not addressed to the members of the 'church which is His body' (Eph 1:22,23), . . . We do not 'watch' for the 'thief', but 'wait' for the Lord."[59] The second advent is what is in view, *not* the rapture of the Church! "Not knowing the day or hour" refers to the revelation, not the *rapture*.

---

[59] *Companion Bible*, 1888.

Note that the references of "hold fast" in Heb. 3:6; 3:14; 4:14; 6:18; and 10:23 are connected with Tribulation salvation, enduring to the end, and NOT taking the mark of the beast.

VII. <u>Revelation 3:5</u>

Rev 3:5 **He that overcometh, the same shall be clothed in white raiment; and I will not blot out his name out of the book of life, but I will confess his name before my Father, and before his angels.**

How does the preacher who believes in eternal security in every dispensation, handle the *implication* in the verse above? He refuses to. If a Holiness, or Church of God member attempted to use this verse against most Baptist preachers, they would respond by saying, "The verse does not say God will blot out anyone's name." Then, he might use the 1 John 4:4; 5:4 maneuver. [To be honest, 1John 4:4; 5:4 *is* the best way to handle someone who thinks you can lose it - because they will not understand the basics of dispensationalism. They probably do not know the difference between a "dispensation" and a "deportation."]

The cold hard facts of the verse are:

1. This "white raiment" is given based on works. Notice the corollary passage where a guest at the wedding does not have this "wedding garment" - Matt. 22:11,12. Also note Rev. 3:4 where these garments can be stained by bad works.

2. Overcoming is related (except in 1 John - the only other mention of the word) to dying a martyr's death: Rev. 3:21; Rev. 12:11.

3. The promise to "not" blot the name out entails the risk of one's name *being blotted out.* You would have to wear blinders to miss that. In the Old Testament God could "blot out" names - Ex. 32:32-33; Deut. 9:14; Ps. 69:28; Ps. 109:13.

4. The confession is alluded to in Matt. 10:32,33, and there the reverse is also true, demonstrating that a person can lose their salvation in the Tribulation, if they deny Christ:

Matt 10:33 **But whosoever shall deny me before men, him will I also deny before my Father which is in heaven.**

Rev 3:8 **I know thy works: behold, I have set before thee an open door, and no man shut it: for thou hast a little strength, and hast kept my word, and hast not denied my name.**

VIII. Revelation 3:11-12

Rev 3:11-12
11 Behold, I come quickly: hold that fast which thou hast, that no man take thy crown.
12 Him that overcometh will I make a pillar in the temple of my God, and he shall go no more out: and I will write upon him the name of my God, and the name of the city of my God, which is new Jerusalem, which cometh down out of heaven from my God: and I will write upon him my new name.

Notice in our eighth example, that the promise of preservation *from* the impending Tribulation Period (vs. 10), is granted by *works.* Various authors freely "correct" the

Authorized Text in these verses stating that the Greek word εκ should be "out of." Even though they do this with a motive of defense for the pretribulation position (c.f. the change in 2 Thess. 2:7), they *completely change* the passage.[60] As the text stands, the church of Philadelphia "overcomes" in order to be kept from **"the hour of temptation."** Furthermore, there is no definite proof that the phrase **"hour of temptation"** can be defined as the Great Tribulation Period. The church is still commanded to **"hold fast"** (vs. 11).

IX. <u>Revelation 3:21</u>

> *Rev 3:21* **To him that overcometh will I grant to sit with me in my throne, even as I also overcame, and am set down with my Father in his throne.**

Tabb asserts that these passages refer to rewards, and NOT Tribulation salvation. He says, "no one inherits salvation"[61] even though the Bible says:

> *Matt 19:29* **And every one that hath forsaken houses, or brethren, or sisters, or father, or mother, or wife, or children, or lands, for my name's sake, shall receive an hundredfold, and shall <u>inherit everlasting life</u>.**

In the passage *someone* has to FORSAKE every physical thing in order to GET eternal life. This inheritance of salvation is opposed to the idea of someone possessing it presently. Notice the *future tense*, in Hebrews 1:14.

---

[60] Pentecost, *Things to Come*, 216.
[61] Tabb, *Dispensational Salvation*, 82.

Heb 1:14 **Are they not all ministering spirits, sent forth to minister for them who shall be <u>heirs of salvation</u>?**

Mark 10:17 **And when he was gone forth into the way, there came one running, and kneeled to him, and asked him, Good Master, what shall I do that I may <u>inherit eternal life</u>?**

The Lord Jesus Christ did NOT correct the man by telling him, "No, you must repent of your sins and believe that I have atoned for your sins by my future death on the cross." This man was looking for an inheritance of everlasting life, as was a lawyer in Christ's day:

Luke 10:25 **And, behold, a certain lawyer stood up, and tempted him, saying, Master, what shall I do to <u>inherit eternal life</u>?**

"No one inherits salvation?" Tabb neglected to locate simple cross-references that related to his comments! He failed to provide any information on "overcoming" and "inheriting eternal life."

THE "BIG THREE"

The three most obvious and clear verses that teach faith plus works in the Tribulation, found in the book of Revelation are: 12:17; 14:12; and 22:14. They undoubtedly affirm a different *plan* of salvation than the one found in Paul's epistles (like in Romans 10 and Galatians 3).

X. Revelation 12:17

Rev 12:17 **And the dragon was wroth with the woman, and went to make war with the remnant of her seed, which keep the commandments of God, and have the testimony of Jesus Christ.**

Tabb (whom equates Tribulation saints with "Old Testament saints"[62]) employs the "never was" alibi, maintaining that Tribulation saints

> are simply saved, obedient, saints. Is not that our case today? Are we who are saved not also obedient to the Lord? [We certainly should be, if we are not!] Do we not have the testimony of Jesus Christ <u>and</u> keep the commandments of God?! We do if we are faithful to our Lord.[63]

Tabb's comment presents the "Lordship salvation" error, and sidesteps what the verse *says!* He thinks they "keep the commandments" *because* they are saved. That is NOT what the verse said at all. And, if you read Rev. 12:17 with 22:14 all qualms are dispelled; for, in 22:14 keeping the commandments (people kept them under the Old Testament) is a requirement for eating the "tree of life," and entering New Jerusalem.

XI. Revelation 14:12

Rev 14:12 **Here is the patience of the saints: here are they that keep the commandments of God, and the faith of Jesus.**

---

[62] *Ibid.*, 83.
[63] *Ibid.*

Here, the "faith and works" *layout* is awfully plain. The only truth most commentators (like Ironside) get out of it, is that these are Jewish believers:

> . . . these converts will be Jewish believers. They keep the commandments of God, as made known in the Old Testament, and yet the faith of Jesus as declared in the New. Their part is not in the body of Christ: that glorious truth of the present dispensation is not for them . . .[64]

Tabb compares these Tribulation saints with martyrs during the Spanish Inquisition, attempting to prove that "patience" and "keeping" is the same as "endur[ing] during trial."[65] He forgets that those who do NOT **endure unto the end** (Matt. 24:13) go to hell. He never hints around, or poses the question: What happens to the saints who do NOT "keep the commandments?" He would merely say, like most Baptist today: "they were never saved to begin with."

XII. Revelation 22:14

Rev 22:14 **Blessed are they that do his commandments, that they may have right to the tree of life, and may enter in through the gates into the city.**

The last passage we will site in the book of Revelation is by far the most stupendous. This passage, as it stands in the KJV, unmistakably teaches faith *plus* works. In fact, most scholars and dispensational theologians *know* this and admit it. But, instead of accepting this biblical doctrine of eschatology, they

---

[64] Ironside, H.A., *Revelation* (New Jersey: Loizeaux Brothers, 1920) 263.
[65] Tabb, *Dispensational Salvation*, 84.

change the Authorized Version and accuse it of errors. Note the "walking Bible" Van Impe:

> According to Dr. C.I. Scofield, <u>a better rendering is</u>: "Blessed are they that wash their robes that they may have right to the tree of life." If one is seeking rights to the tree of life by commandment-keeping, he is planning to arrive in the eternal state by his works. This, of course, is impossible as we have learned through Titus 3:5, Romans 4:5 and numerous other texts. . . . Dr. A.C. Gaebelein, Dr. H.A. Ironside, Dr. J.A. Seiss and practically all noted Bible scholars also translate the verse: "Blessed are they that wash their robes [in the blood of the Lamb] that they may have right to the tree of life . . ."[66] *[emphasis added]*

Jack Van Impe took the opinions of leading dispensationalists over the ONE book that was responsible for his salvation. He followed the system he was taught more than the words of God.

Observe Oliver Greene's remark:

> Greek authorities tell us that in the original language this <u>should read</u>, "Blessed are they who have washed their robes," not "blessed are they that do His commandments," because certainly we know that eternal life does not depend upon keeping the commandments.[67]

So, everyone *knows exactly* what the King James reading is teaching. *That* is not the problem. The problem is that no one wants to accept it, because they do not understand it *dispensationally.* Note how Ironside "sidestepped" the truth with the corrupt Revised Version:

> The 14th verse, it is well to notice, is differently rendered in the Revised Version, and that in accordance with the

---

[66] Van Impe, *Revelation Revealed*, 252.
[67] Greene, *Revelation*, 535.

best manuscripts. It is thus: "Blessed are they that wash their robes, that they may have right to the tree of life, and may enter in through the gates into the city." The promise rests on no legal grounds. It is not doing that gives one title to that home of the saints.[68]

"The best manuscripts?" According to whom? Ironside? He did not mention the fact that these "best manuscripts" (Siniaticus: 330 A.D., and Alexandreanus: 400-450 A.D.) both contain part of the Apocrypha as inspired *within the text*. Are we to trust those corrupted texts?

[Note: the King James translators understood that the Apocrypha was not inspired, so they placed it *between* scripture.]

Furthermore, the King James reading is defended by "𝔐" (classifying the "majority of manuscripts), the Harclean Syriac, the Bohairic (a Coptic version) and the church father Tertullian, who quoted it in 220 A.D. (*prior* to the inception of ℵ and A). [See Nestle's critical apparatus for documentation.]

Notice John R. Rice's confession as to what the English KJV teaches. Also note his contemptuous criticism:

> One mistranslation of the King James Version in Revelation 22:14 would make salvation by works and it is obviously wrong. It says . . . But the Bible certainly does not teach that anybody earns a right to heaven by keeping the commandments. And that mistranslation is corrected in the American Standard Version . . . The Episcopalian translators there, who did not fully understand the doctrine of salvation by grace, evidently did not check the manuscripts carefully enough to get the translation right in the King James Version.[69] *[emphasis added]*

---

[68] Ironside, *Revelation*, 364.
[69] Evans, Herbert F., *Dear Dr. John: Where is my Bible?* (Harlingen, TX: Wonderful Word Publishers, 1976) 3, 4.

Rice failed to understand that the passage (along with Rev. 12:17 and 14:12) concerns Tribulation saints, *not Church age saints!* Ruckman clarifies:

> **1.** No Christian has any "robes" washed.
> **2.** No Christian has to partake of a "tree of life."
> **3.** No Christian has to do anything to "enter" into any city.
> **4.** No Christian has to "do his commandments" to get eternal life.
> **5.** The admonition was not aimed at one human being on the face of this earth between A.D. 33 and A.D. 1997.
> **6.** The people whose "ROBES ARE WASHED" are in Daniel's Seventieth Week (Rev. 7:13).
> **7.** Every sinner saved from A.D. 33 to A.D. 1997 got eternal life from a Saviour who DIED ON A TREE: NOT FROM ANY TREE.
> **8.** Every Christian is already IN "the city," for it is the dwelling place of "the Lamb's wife" (Rev. 21:9-10).
> **9.** The commandments to be "kept" by someone are in Revelation 14:12 and have nothing to do with any Christian, living or dead, who breathed air between A.D. 33 and A.D. 1997.[70] **[Note: 1997 was the year of the publication of the book from which the quotation is derived.]**

The believer in the Church Age does NOT fall under the category of Rev. 22:14 because (in addition) WE have been washed (Rev. 1:5; 1 Cor. 6:11; 1 Pet. 1:18,19; 1 John 1:7) "**not by works of righteousness which we have done**" (Titus 3:5). And if our "robes" were washed, we did not wash them, they were washed by HIM. Even if we accepted the corrupted verse ("they that wash their robes"), works are evident. The "washing of the robes" was a WORK (Rev. 7:14) done by the saints, not the Saviour!

---

[70] Ruckman, *Ruckman's Bible References*, 384, 385.

It is interesting that M.H. Tabb's book, *Dispensational Salvation* supposedly covers "the passages from the book of Revelation used to teach a works salvation in the Tribulation period and the coming kingdom age"[71] but neglects to discuss Rev. 22:14.

Henry Morris, attempts to get around the passage, although he favors the KJV reading. He states that " . . .it is surely true that any person who is genuinely saved will love His commandments and seek to keep them."[72] The verse did NOT say that! The qualification of "DOING his commandments" grants two things: partaking of the tree of life (which gives eternal life - Gen. 3:22) and entering into New Jerusalem. The believer in the Church Age is granted eternal life by FAITH, through the ear canal, not orally through the digestive system! Furthermore, we are not waiting to go through the gate, we ARE the gate.

> *Rev 21:9-10* **. . . Come hither, I will shew thee the bride, the Lamb's wife . . . shewed me that great city, the holy Jerusalem, descending out of heaven from God,**

TRIBULATION SALVATION IN HEBREWS

Without covering all the material relating to the nature and dispensational theme of Hebrews, suffice it to say that the book of Hebrews is one of the most arduous books of the New Testament. Along with Matthew, Acts and James, Hebrews supplies heretics with plenty of proof texts. Hyper-dispensationalists simply compartmentalize Hebrews as *all* Tribulation material; while the nominal dispensationalists classifies it as Church Age doctrine. As we have said before,

---

[71] Tabb, *Dispensational Salvation*, 3.
[72] *The Defenders Study Bible* (Grand Rapids: Word, 1995) 1468.

"**rightly dividing the word of truth**" reaches farther than simple groupings and classifications of books. Hebrews ten, for instance, teaches *both* Church Age truths *and* Tribulation doctrine!

I. <u>Hebrews 2:1 and 2:3</u>

Heb 2:1 **Therefore we ought to give the more earnest heed to the things which we have heard, lest at any time we should let them slip.**

Heb 2:3 **How shall we escape, if we neglect so great salvation; which at the first began to be spoken by the Lord, and was confirmed unto us by them that heard him;**

In our first example of Tribulation salvation in Hebrews, notice the key word: "lest." Many times "lest" in Hebrews has a "Tribulation flavor." Take note of the following references: Hebrews 2:1; 3:12; 3:13; 4:1; 4:11; 11:28; 12:3; 12:13; 12:15; 12:16.

Notice also in Hebrews 2:3 that Paul is using the plural pronoun "we." He is *not* referring to Gentiles in the body of Christ, but rather to Hebrews that are "in danger of letting something slip away from them and it will cause them to 'neglect salvation' (v.3)."[73] Dr. Ruckman precisely comments:

> No reader of the Bible would mistake such a discourse **[Hebrews 2:1-4]** for Pauline salvation for half of a second. This is not Paul's doctrinal revelation to the Gentiles (Rom. 1-10) or to the church (Eph. 1-5). Paul was no more worried about "neglecting salvation" by

---

[73] Ruckman, Peter S., *Hebrews* (Pensacola: Bible Baptist Bookstore, 1986) 36.

letting it "slip" than by neglecting Santa Claus through "flipping" (see Rom. 8, for example).[74]

II. Hebrews 3:6 and 3:14

Heb 3:6 **But Christ as a son over his own house; whose house are we, if we hold fast the confidence and the rejoicing of the hope firm unto the end.**

Heb 3:14 **For we are made partakers of Christ, if we hold the beginning of our confidence stedfast unto the end;**

In our second example, the demands given are marked by "**if.**" The phrase "**the end**" is also used extensively in Hebrews (3:6; 3:14; 6:8; 6:11; 9:26; 13:7) in the same context it is used in Matt. 10:22; 24:3; and 24:13. And, as we have previously averted, this "time of the end," is a definite period of time (see: Dan. 7:26; 8:17 - "**time of the end**"; 8:19; 9:26; 11:27; 11:35; 11:40; 12:4,6,8,9,13).

The book of Hebrews was addressed to *Hebrews* "**in these last days**" (Heb. 1:2), and has *primary* application to Hebrew believers in the Tribulation Period.

The "ifs" in Hebrews can easily be dismissed as no problem when the profanation of Calvinism is adopted. [Calvinism is directly or indirectly responsible for at least 90% of all theological errors and perversions.] The Calvinist simply believes the elect will persevere unto the end anyway, so what Paul is saying could be summarized as:

> if we are sons of God and if we are partakers of the heavenly calling, we will be faithful and we will hold fast. This is the proof that we are of God's house.[75]

---

[74] *Ibid.*, 36.

It may sound good, and many non-Calvinists are duped into this line of reasoning. But it makes the verse read differently! The verse does not say that a partaker of Christ will hold fast, it says a person who holds fast will be made (future) a partaker. In other words, the man is not 100% "saved" until he endures! The only dispensation this will fit is the Great Tribulation.

Before we move to the third example, the Bible believer should take note of the following contrast:

1. The "**house**" in Hebrews 3:6 is NOT a present possession. In 2 Cor. 5:1 Christians are said to "**have**" this "**house**." The "**house**" in Hebrews is something hoped for, while the house of the Christian is stedfast and "**eternal**."

2 Cor 5:1 **For we know that if our earthly <u>house</u> of this tabernacle were dissolved, <u>we have</u> a building of God, an house not made with hands, <u>eternal</u> in the heavens.**

2. In Colossians 1:12 Paul confirms that we have already been made "**partakers**," instead of hoping to make it "**unto the end**."

Col 1:12 **Giving thanks unto the Father, which <u>hath made us meet to be partakers</u> of the inheritance of the saints in light:**

III. <u>Hebrews 4:1</u>

Heb 4:1 **Let us therefore fear, lest, a promise being left us of entering into his rest, any of you should seem to come short of it.**

---

[75] McGee, J. Vernon, *Thru the Bible with J. Vernon McGee Vol. 5* (Pasadena: thru the Bible Radio, 1983) 524.

Here in Hebrews 4:1 the command is to FEAR. This is *contrary* to every command for the New Testament Christian in the body of Christ! Why, in Paul's other epistles believers are told to NOT fear:

> *Rom 8:15* **For ye have not received the spirit of bondage again to fear; but ye have received the Spirit of adoption, whereby we cry, Abba, Father.**
>
> *2 Tim 1:7* **For God hath not given us the spirit of fear; but of power, and of love, and of a sound mind.**

Those who teach the "saved the same" doctrine will emphasize and stress the references to fearing God in Paul's epistles (Rom. 3:18; Rom. 11:20; 2 Cor. 7:1; Eph. 5:21). They does this to harmonize Hebrews 4:1 with Romans - Ephesians. The only problem is that the "fear" in Hebrews 4:1 relates to the promises of God, NOT the "fear of God" in the father - son relationship. These promises are only given "**after ye have done the will of God**," (Heb. 10:36). "Devotionalizers" and "emotionalizers" twist the verse by connecting the "fear" of Hebrews 4:1 with "**godly fear**" (Heb. 12:28) and the "**entering into his rest**" with, "going to heaven." The "rest" concerns a physical piece of land for a literal race of people - Hebrews (see: 3:11,18; 4:1,3,4,5,8, 9,10,11).

IV. <u>Hebrews 4:9-11</u>

Heb 4:9-11
**9 There remaineth therefore a rest to the people of God.
10 For he that is entered into his rest, he also hath ceased from his own works, as God did from his.**

Dispensational Salvation

11 Let us labour therefore to enter into that rest, lest any man fall after the same example of unbelief.

In this example "labour" is necessary "to enter into that rest." To make this "rest" "a heavenly rest" (see most commentaries) is to "devotionalize" the verse. This is a millennial rest. It is a rest that is JEWISH and is obtained by works (labour). The cross-referencess are found in the context:

1. The sabbath is mentioned in verse four. The sabbath was a sign to the *Jewish nation*: Ezek. 20:20.

2. The "people of God" during the time of Moses and Joshua (see the context) would be *Jews*. See Hebrews 11:25 where this is used exclusively for Israelites.

3. Joshua is mentioned (verse 8) with his Greek name "Jesus." This shows that the second time (see Acts 7:13) Israel goes into the land it will be under their new "captain" (Heb. 2:10) – Jesus.

4. Those in the passage who "fall" (verse 11) do not make it into the land. Their carcasses stay in the wilderness!

Commentators will convert "the people of God" from Jews (Heb. 11:25) to the "body of Christ" (like in Titus 2:14 and 1 Peter 2:10); and "that rest" into a heavenly rest. Then they just pretend the "labour" in the passage is Christian service. Notice McGee:

> Here the writer is projecting into the future when all the people of God are going to find a heavenly rest. Heaven will be a place of deep satisfaction, of real joy, and real blessing. . . . I think the supreme satisfaction that can

come to a child of God is that he is in the will of God, doing the work of God, and trusting and just resting in Him . . . Someone will say, "Do I have to labor to enter into rest?" Yes, my friend . . . To lay hold of God in prayer, and in faith, and to be used of Him. Oh, my Christian friend, let us labor toward that end.[76]

The above example is the procedure of nearly every Bible teacher and commentator, and proves that their systems are contrary to the scripture.

V. Hebrews 5:9

Heb 5:9 **And being made perfect, he became the author of eternal salvation unto all them that obey him;**

Our fifth example of Tribulation salvation in Hebrews concerns obedience. Although the scriptures manifestly teach that the Lord is **"the Saviour of all men"** (1 Tim. 4:10), Hebrews 5:9 intimates that *this* "eternal salvation," will be given only to obedient men. Compare Hebrews 12:14 where a person's clean living determines his "seeing God."

VI. Hebrews 6:4-12

Heb 6:4-12
**4 For it is impossible for those who were once enlightened, and have tasted of the heavenly gift, and were made partakers of the Holy Ghost,
5 And have tasted the good word of God, and the powers of the world to come,**

---

[76] *Ibid.*, 532, 533.

6 If they shall fall away, to renew them again unto repentance; seeing they crucify to themselves the Son of God afresh, and put him to an open shame.
7 For the earth which drinketh in the rain that cometh oft upon it, and bringeth forth herbs meet for them by whom it is dressed, receiveth blessing from God:
8 But that which beareth thorns and briers is rejected, and is nigh unto cursing; whose end is to be burned.
9 But, beloved, we are persuaded better things of you, and things that accompany salvation, though we thus speak.
10 For God is not unrighteous to forget your work and labour of love, which ye have shewed toward his name, in that ye have ministered to the saints, and do minister.
11 And we desire that every one of you do shew the same diligence to the full assurance of hope unto the end:
12 That ye be not slothful, but followers of them who through faith and patience inherit the promises.

Despite the statement by Paul that "**the inward man is renewed day by day**" (2 Cor. 4:16), implying Hebrews 6:4 *cannot* apply to a Christian, this portion of scripture has been used to teach a person can lose his salvation. The fact that at least 90 percent of all professing Christians believe you can lose your salvation, should not go unnoticed. Every major denomination outside of Baptists and Presbyterians (except for a few non-denominational "evangelicals") reject eternal security. Dr. Ruckman puts it well:

> Are we to assume that 90 percent of professing Christians, including John Wesley, Francis Asbury, Henry C. Morrison, Peter Cartwright, Bob Schuler, Sam Jones, and their converts, had no Scriptural BASIS or Scriptural GROUNDS for their belief?[77]

These groups DO have scriptural authentication to verify that *someone* can lose their salvation. The only dilemma they have, is that the *someone* is not THEM. Verses that teach a person can lose their salvation are *never* AIMED at a saved person in the body of Jesus Christ. So is the case with Hebrews chapter six.

"Inconsistent dispensationalists" (correctly labeled so by Reformed Calvinists) close their eyes to the obvious verses, like Hebrews six, that unmistakably teach *someone* can lose their salvation. The *New Scofield Reference Bible* (1967) presents nearly all views and attitudes about the passage except the correct one:

> The major interpretations are: (1) The warning is directed to some of the Jewish people who professed to be believers in Christ but stopped short of true faith in Him after advancing to the threshold of salvation. (2) The admonition presents a hypo-thetical case: if one could "fall away" (v. 6), it would be impossible to renew him again to repentance; for, in such an instance, it would be necessary for Christ to be crucified a second time. Obviously this will not occur (Heb. 10:12-14); thus to fall away is impossible. (3) The warning is directed toward believers who have fallen into sin to such an extent that they have crucified to themselves the Son of God afresh (v. 6) and are therefore disapproved and will lose their reward (see 1 Cor. 9:27, note). And (4) the warning is to those who are believers in the Lord Jesus Christ and are in danger of falling away, through unbelief or sin, and losing their salvation. . . . . Scripture abundantly affirms

---

[77] Ruckman, *22 years of the Bible Believer's Bulletin Vol. 3*, 80.

Dispensational Salvation **177**

the Christian's eternal security; therefore this passage must not be interpreted as teaching that believers in Christ can lose their salvation."[78]

The first interpretation the NSRB lists was that of C.I. Scofield and the *Old Scofield Reference Bible* (see page 1295). It was also embraced by Larkin who says "these words do not apply to Christians. They were spoken to apostate Jewish professors of Christianity who had never been born again . . ."[79]

Scofield compared the "professors" (modern cliché: "professor not possessor") with the spies at Kadesh-barnea. But, as Ruckman points out,

> no spy at Kadesh-barnea had been made a "**PARTAKER OF THE HOLY GHOST**" . . . they tasted of no "**heavenly gift**" whatsoever; if they had eaten the grapes (Num. 13) they would have "tasted" an earthly gift.[80]

Scofield says that the "professed believers . . .halt short of faith in Christ."[81] How can a person be a "**partaker of the Holy Ghost**" and not have "faith in Christ?" No *recognized* scholar will answer. Neither will they address the fact that to "taste" something is more than a "profession." If "taste" means a shallow profession, then are we to assume that the Lord Jesus did not really die? Hebrews 2:9 says he "**taste[d] death for every man.**"

The person in Hebrews six is said to have been "enlightened," which matches a conversion. Note the following verse:

---

[78] *New Scofield Reference Bible*, 1315.
[79] Larkin, Clarence, *Rightly Dividing the Word of Truth*, (Glenside: Rev. Clarence Larkin Est., 1920) 7.
[80] Ruckman, *Hebrews*, 117.
[81] *Scofield Reference Bible*, 1295.

Eph 1:18 **The eyes of your understanding being enlightened; that ye may know what is the hope of his calling, and what the riches of the glory of his inheritance in the saints,**

The person in Hebrews six is a "**partaker of the Holy Ghost,**" which definitely means he is saved (although not in the body of Christ). The student of the word of God should not forget how the words "save," and "saved" are used in the gospels of Matthew through Luke. See: Matt 10:22; 19:25; 24:13; 24:22; 27:42; Mark 10:26; 13:13; 13:20; 15:31; 16:16; Luke 1:71; 7:50; 8:12; 13:23; 18:26; 18:42; 23:35.

The person in Hebrews six has repented before ("**again unto repentance**") thus proving he is a convert, not merely a professor.

Titus 1:15-16
**15 Unto the pure all things are pure: but unto them that are defiled and unbelieving is nothing pure; but even their mind and conscience is defiled.
16 They profess that they know God; but in works they deny him, being abominable, and disobedient, and unto every good work reprobate.**

The text (Heb. 6), is not relating to a "professed believer," but rather to someone in the Tribulation that has to worry about *keeping* his "profession," in order to have a "possession."

Heb 4:14 **Seeing then that we have a great high priest, that is passed into the heavens, Jesus the Son of God, let us hold fast our profession.**

Heb 10:23 **Let us hold fast the profession of our faith without wavering; (for he is faithful that promised;)**

The second interpretation given by the NSRB, was the one adopted by Oliver B. Greene.[82]

> (2) The admonition presents a hypothetical case: if one could "fall away" (v. 6), it would be impossible to renew him again to repentance; for, in such an instance, it would be necessary for Christ to be crucified a second time. Obviously this will not occur (Heb. 10:12-14); thus to fall away is impossible.[83]

What kind of jibber jabber is this? If this is even a feasible option, where else in scripture are we presented with a hypothetical doctrinal dissertation similar to this one? It does not exist. We would be better off to imagine that *this interpretation* is hypothetical.

The third analysis of Hebrews six, listed by the NSRB, complements the view of Dr. M.R. DeHaan,[84] and confuses rewards with salvation:

> (3) The warning is directed toward believers who have fallen into sin to such an extent that they have crucified to themselves the Son of God afresh (v. 6) and are therefore disapproved and will lose their reward (see 1 Cor. 9:27, note).[85]

This departure from "**sound doctrine**" (2 Tim. 4:3) demonstrates the lack of real, serious Bible study by the board members of the NSRB. They neglected the cross-references

---

[82] Ruckman, *Hebrews*, 118.
[83] *New Scofield Reference Bible*, 1315.
[84] Ruckman, *Hebrews*, 118.
[85] *New Scofield Reference Bible*, 1315.

confirming that the works and rewards were not the "**thorns and briers,**" but rather the people: "**those who were ONCE enlightened.**" Notice:

> *Mal 4:1* **For, behold, the day cometh, that shall burn as an oven; and all the proud, yea, and all that do wickedly, shall be stubble: and the day that cometh shall burn them up, saith the LORD of hosts, that it shall leave them neither root nor branch.**

> *2 Sam 23:6-7*
> **6 But the sons of Belial shall be all of them as thorns thrust away, because they cannot be taken with hands:**
> **7 But the man that shall touch them must be fenced with iron and the staff of a spear; and they shall be utterly burned with fire in the same place**

> *Ps 118:12* **They compassed me about like bees; they are quenched as the fire of thorns: for in the name of the LORD I will destroy them.**

> *Isa 9:18-19*
> **18 For wickedness burneth as the fire: it shall devour the briers and thorns, and shall kindle in the thickets of the forest, and they shall mount up like the lifting up of smoke.**
> **19 Through the wrath of the LORD of hosts is the land darkened, and the people shall be as the fuel of the fire: no man shall spare his brother.**

> *Matt 3:10* **And now also the axe is laid unto the root of the trees: therefore every tree which bringeth**

not forth good fruit is hewn down, and cast into the fire.

Matt 3:12 **Whose fan is in his hand, and he will throughly purge his floor, and gather his wheat into the garner; but he will burn up the chaff with unquenchable fire.**

These standardized interpretations are fostered to preserve the teaching that people are saved the same in all ages as they are in the Church Age. Once the "saved the same" *lie* is accepted, then the principles and doctrines of the Church Age (namely *eternal security*) must apply to *all* ages. When this is done uniformly, you become a non-dispensationalist in reality. For, if someone in the Old Testament was "saved the same" as someone in the Church Age, and had eternal security, then why were they not in the body of Christ? Why any distinction between Israel and the Church? All classic dispensationalists (Darby, Scofield, Gaebelein, Pember, Larkin, Chaffer, Walvoord, Pentecost, Ryrie) make a clear concise division between Israel and the Church. This division is even said to be one of the demarcations of dispensationalism. Well, if a Jew is not in the body of Christ, how can he have eternal life (eternal security) since *that* doctrine is only promised to Church Age saints?

Without any answers to the above questions from the renowned Bible teachers of today, we move on to the fourth explanation of Hebrews six as given by the *New Scofield Reference Bible:*

> And (4) the warning is to those who are believers in the Lord Jesus Christ and are in danger of falling away, through unbelief or sin, and losing their salvation. . . . . Scripture abundantly affirms the Christian's eternal

security; therefore this passage must not be interpreted as teaching that believers in Christ can lose their salvation.[86]

This rationalization of Hebrews six contains some truth, except for the fact that the groups who propose this interpretation, believe you can get it back after you lose it (Methodists, Assemblies of God, Churches of Christ, and Catholics). The text plainly states that if a person "**falls away**" he has had it: "**it is impossible**." The quandary then, of those who hold this conjecture, is the definition of "fall away." Is it adultery, fornication and murder? Or gossip, envy and pride? Whatever it is, once you have "fallen away" you cannot be restored! We agree that "believer's in Christ" cannot lose their salvation, but those in the tribulation certainly can!

Now, we must address the problematic interpretation of M.H. Tabb.

Tabb claims that "no one loses salvation in Hebrews six, but neither do they earn rewards."[87] He makes a big deal out of the "it" in verse four, saying, "the it of verse four refers to God's permission in verse three."[88] If what he says is true, the verse would read, "For God's permission is impossible for those who were once enlightened." Tabb then goes on to say that Hebrews six

> refers rather to a saved person to whom God will not grant permission to go on to perfection. It will not be granted because he has already refused to go on beyond the basic principles of Christianity.[89]

In order to make this *fit* the context, he ignores the cross-references to verse 8 (which we have listed) and concurs with

---
[86] *Ibid.*, 1315.
[87] Tabb, *Dispensational Salvation*, 78.
[88] *Ibid.*, 78.
[89] *Ibid.*, 79.

DeHaan, that the "works go up in smoke."[90]

To put the icing on the cake, Tabb makes an appeal to the Greek (even though he is supposedly a KJV Bible believer) to prove that "fall away . . . implies simply not making the grade."[91]

The basic grammatical structure of Hebrews six forbids the surreptitious analysis of Tabb. The pronoun "it" cannot refer to God's permission in verse three, or it would be ambiguous. The personal pronoun "it," must point clearly to the correct antecedent. Tabb's manipulation produces this:

For, God's permission is impossible . . . . to renew them again unto repentance (those who have fallen away).

When you test the pronoun (by substituting the antecedent for the pronoun), Tabb's grammar gets an "F." The pronoun "it" can only correctly be interchanged with "to renew them again unto repentance," not "God's permission." This accurate structure could be reworded as follows, and still make perfect sense:

For, to renew them again unto repentance is impossible . . . . If they shall fall away.

Tabb alters and misrepresents basic English grammar in order to insert his private interpretations. Tabb believes anything *but* the text of Hebrews six, and is inane with his allegations.

---

[90] *Ibid.*, 79.
[91] *Ibid.*, 80.

BIBLE INTERPRETATION OF HEBREWS SIX

The only way to "handle" the passage is to follow the orders in 2 Tim. 2:15, and divide Hebrews, as a "Tribulation epistle aimed primarily at Tribulation Hebrews."[92] This portion of scripture must relate to a Tribulation saint, rather than a Church Age believer in the body of Christ. Note:

1. The **"powers of the world to come"** have absolutely NO application for *any* Church Age saint. If it does, then *who* has these "powers," and *where* are these "powers" seen today?

    A. These powers are related to the "**kingdom**" and the "prayer for the kingdom."

Matt 6:13 . . . **For thine is the kingdom, and the power, and the glory, for ever. Amen.**

   B. These powers are related to "healing."

Matt 9:6-8 . . . . **then saith he to the sick of the palsy,) Arise, take up thy bed, and go unto thine house.**
7 And he arose, and departed to his house.
8 But when the multitudes saw it, they marvelled, and glorified God, which had given such power unto men.

Luke 5:17 **And it came to pass on a certain day, as he was teaching, that there were Pharisees and doctors of the law sitting by, which were come out**

---
[92] Ruckman, *Hebrews*, 126.

of every town of Galilee, and Judaea, and Jerusalem: and the <u>power of the Lord</u> was present to heal them.

Acts 10:38 **How God anointed Jesus of Nazareth with the Holy Ghost and with power: who went about doing good, and healing all that were oppressed of the devil; for God was with him.**

Acts 6:8 **And Stephen, full of faith and <u>power</u>, did great <u>wonders and miracles</u> among the people.**

    C. These powers were given to the twelve apostles, as they preached the "**gospel of the kingdom.**"

Matt 10:1 **And when he had called unto him his twelve disciples, he gave them <u>power</u> against unclean spirits, to cast them out, and to heal all manner of sickness and all manner of disease.**

    D. This "power of God" is connected with the literal, bodily resurrection that will take place in "**the world to come.**"

Matt 22:29-30
**29 Jesus answered and said unto them, Ye do err, not knowing the scriptures, nor the power of God.
30 For in the resurrection they neither marry, nor are given in marriage, but are as the angels of God in heaven.**

    E. These "**powers of the world to come**" were given in Acts 2, as promised by the Lord. It is significant that the book of Hebrews was almost certainly written during this early Acts period. Peter and Paul identify the apostolic signs as "**power**."

Luke 24:49 **And, behold, I send the promise of my Father upon you: but tarry ye in the city of Jerusalem, until ye be endued with <u>power from on high.</u>**

Acts 3:12 **And when Peter saw it, he answered unto the people, Ye men of Israel, why marvel ye at this? or why look ye so earnestly on us, as though by our own <u>power</u> or holiness we had made this man to walk?**

Rom 15:19 **Through mighty <u>signs and wonders</u>, by the<u> power</u> of the Spirit of God; so that from Jerusalem, and round about unto Illyricum, I have fully preached the gospel of Christ.**

2. The "**world to come**" is a reference to the Millennial Age, *not* the Church Age. See: Matt. 12:32; Mark 10:30; Luke 18:30; Heb. 2:5.

3. The "**falling away**" of the passage could only refer to taking the "mark of the beast." There is no other "**sin unto death**" that cannot be repented of in scripture. If a Tribulation saint takes the mark, he has lost his salvation and goes to hell.

Rev 14:11 **And the smoke of their torment ascendeth up for ever and ever: and they have no rest day nor night, who worship the beast and his** image, and whosoever receiveth the mark of his name.

4. This is the only explanation that maintains the integrity of scripture. The other clues that identify this as a Tribulation reference are:

> **A.** Verse seven: "the rain." The "RAIN at the end of the Tribulation which precedes the Advent."[93] See: 2 Sam. 23:4; Ps. 68:9; Joel 2:23; James 5:7,8; 1 Ki. 18:45 with Rev. 11:6.
>
> **B.** Verse eight: "rejected," "cursing," "burned." The rejection of the "tares," or "thorns" in the passage is taken care of by burning, *not* "separation of God" (see any modern preacher).

Matt 13:40 **As therefore the tares are gathered and burned in the fire; so shall it be in the end of this world.**

Mal 4:1 **For, behold, the day cometh, that shall burn as an oven; and all the proud, yea, and all that do wickedly, shall be stubble: and the day that cometh shall burn them up, saith the LORD of hosts, that it shall leave them neither root nor branch.**

---

[93] *Ibid.*, 127.

VII. Hebrews 10:23-27

Heb 10:23-27
**23 Let us hold fast the profession of our faith without wavering; (for he is faithful that promised;)
24 And let us consider one another to provoke unto love and to good works:
25 Not forsaking the assembling of ourselves together, as the manner of some is; but exhorting one another: and so much the more, as ye see the day approaching.
26 For if we sin wilfully after that we have received the knowledge of the truth, there remaineth no more sacrifice for sins,
27 But a certain fearful looking for of judgment and fiery indignation, which shall devour the adversaries.**

Here is a passage which most Baptist preachers take out of context. They will use verse 25 to bolster church attendance, and verse 26 to "retread" some of their members that are already saved. This substandard treatment of Hebrews 10:23-27 is akin to the common interpretation of 1 John 3:9. [They say "Whosoever is born of God doth not habitually practice sin." See Scofield's note.] Dispensational authors insist on these changes and bogus explanations because the verses simply do NOT match *their* soteriology! Rather than admitting the validity of certain verses, which teach a man can LOSE his salvation (in other ages), they tip toe around them, change them, and privately interpret them.

Verse 26 is a problem for those who refuse the doctrinal Tribulation application in Hebrews, because inherently *everyone who sins* does it willingly. To escape this logic, some of the brethren advocate "sinless perfection." They profess to be sinless after salvation. They do not "sin wilfully," because *they do not sin.* [If you could hear them as they work on their used car, I guarantee you would think otherwise!]

The doctrinal, Tribulation truths found in the passage are as follows:

1. The "we" are Hebrews (see 2:3; 3:14; 4:11; 6:3). The two applications would be the early Acts period when the book was written (to Hebrews), and Jewish Tribulation saints. If you run the references on "we" in Hebrews you will see that they are not addressed to saved, born again members of the body of Christ.

2. There are "sacrifices" being offered in the Tribulation on a literal altar in Jerusalem (Rev. 6:9; 2 Thess. 2:3-8; Matt. 24:15). The New Testament believer's redemption is complete in the ONE SACRIFICE of Jesus Christ. The two are NOT the same.

3. The proof positive way that a Jewish Tribulation saint could "sin willfully" where there was "no more sacrifice," would be to take the mark of the beast. Ruckman again:

> Hebrews 10:26-31 is aimed at a tribulation Jew who gets saved and takes the mark of the beast (or turns back to sin-Luke 21:34) and LOSES HIS SALVATION. This interpretation meets all of the demands of every word in every verse in the passage.[94]

4. The references to verse 27, will more than prove that the context is the second advent: Isa. 5:24; 26:11; 30:27;

---

[94] *Ibid.*, 227.

33:12; Jer. 50:32; 51:58; Ezek. 38:22; Hos. 8:14; Matt. 3:10-12; 13:30; Zeph. 1:18; 3:8; Mal. 4:4; 2 Thess. 2:8,9.

5. Moses is mentioned in verse 28, which demonstrates the connection between "keeping the commandments and the faith of Jesus." The "song of Moses" (Deut. 32) is sung by Jewish Tribulation saints (Rev. 15:3) *not* Church Age saints.

6. **"His people"** (verse 30) always refers to the Jewish nation, even in Paul's epistles: Rom. 11:1,2; 15:10.

7. How could it be **"fearful"** for us **"to fall into the hands of the living God,"** when Paul said:

2 Tim 1:7 **For God hath not given us the spirit of fear; but of power, and of love, and of a sound mind.**

We understand that Paul preached **"the terror of the Lord"** (2 Cor. 5:11) relating to the Judgment Seat of Christ (for Christians), but never did he preach the **"fiery indignation"** that **"devour[s]"** the people (**"adversaries . . . he"** - 27,28)! Paul taught that the fire devoured the works (wood, hay, stubble - 1 Cor. 3).

VIII. Hebrews 12:14-15

Heb 12:14-15
14 Follow peace with all men, and holiness, without which no man shall see the Lord:

15 Looking diligently lest any man fail of the grace of God; lest any root of bitterness springing up trouble you, and thereby many be defiled;

In our last example (Hebrews 12:14-15), it stipulates "holiness" as a requirement for "seeing God" (although collectively the entire race will "see God" - Rev. 1:14; Rev. 20:11-15). Attempting to force the passage into the Church Age perverts the idea of the "grace of God" as a "free gift" (Rom. 6:23; Eph. 2:8,9). It is apparent that those in the verse can "**fail of the grace of God**;" something a Christian cannot. Verse seventeen confirms what Hebrews chapter six taught about the impossibility of repentance.

TRIBULATION SALVATION IN MATTHEW

There are several other bold portions of scripture that teach Tribulation salvation as a faith *plus* works set-up. Some of them include:

1. James 1:12; 1:27; 2:24; 4:4; 4:11; 5:7-9; 5:12; 5:19,20.

2. 1 Peter 1:5; 1:7; 1:9; 1:13; 1:20: 2:3 (with Heb. 6:4); 2:8 (with Matthew); 2:12; 4:5; 4:7; 4:13; 4:17; 4:19; 5:1; 5:4; 5:10 (with 4:12,16; 1:7).

3. 2 Peter 2:20.

4. 1 John (*Possible Tribulation References*) 2:3-9; 2:8; 2:13-14; 2:17; 2:18; 2:24; 2:28.

The other outstanding references are found in the book of Matthew.

I. Matthew 5:8

Matt 5:8 **Blessed are the pure in heart: for they shall see God.**

Our first case in Matthew can be crossed with Hebrews 12:14. It displays a prerequisite of *good works* in order to "**see God.**" No New Testament child of God will see the Lord based on the purity of his heart. He sees the Lord based on the righteousness of Jesus Christ.

II. Matthew 10:22

Matt 10:22 **And ye shall be hated of all men for my name's sake: but he that endureth to the end shall be saved.**

Here, you must place this in the Tribulation, or you will have works as part of a Christian's salvation!

This is *not* "the fact that the Lord will be able to keep His own for the three-year period of His ministry."[95] Neither does it refer to the Lord being able "to keep His own during the Great Tribulation period."[96] The Lord is not keeping anybody! The verse did not say, "the Lord endureth!"

III. Matthew 10:32-33

Matt 10:32-33
32 Whosoever therefore shall confess me before men, him will I confess also before my Father which is in heaven.

---

[95] McGee, J. Vernon, *Thru the Bible with J. Vernon McGee Vol. 4* (Pasadena: thru the Bible Radio, 1983) 59.
[96] *Ibid.*

33 But whosoever shall deny me before men, him will I also deny before my Father which is in heaven.

Our third case in Matthew teaches a man can lose his salvation by denying Christ. You would have to be a tulip picking Calvinist to think that no Christian has ever denied Christ. For, every saved person would have to persevere to prove they were one of the elect. If a man in the Tribulation denies the Lord, and takes the mark; he will be denied, *no matter how many times he prays the "sinners prayer."*

[Could it be that today, Satan is deceiving the world by telling them works are a part of salvation, and in the Tribulation he will deceive them by telling them it is "**by grace through faith**?" The *Left Behind* series propagates that LIE, and nearly all professing Christians think a person can simply pray to be saved in the Tribulation Period!]

IV. Matthew 19:29

Matt 19:29 **And every one that hath forsaken houses, or brethren, or sisters, or father, or mother, or wife, or children, or lands, for my name's sake, shall receive an hundredfold, and shall inherit everlasting life.**

This is an obvious Tribulation reference showing "**everlasting life**" as an INHERITANCE, instead of a *present possession* (John 5:24; 3:36 ect.). The Tribulation saint must forsake everything (including food - Rev. 13) in order to make it.

V. Matthew 24:13-14

Matt 24:13-14
13 But he that shall endure unto the end, the same shall be saved.

14 And this gospel of the kingdom shall be preached in all the world for a witness unto all nations; and then shall the end come.

The context of Matthew 24 is clearly *not* the Church Age, but the Tribulation. Note:

1. Verse 3 - "**end of the world.**" Notice this is prior to "**the world to come**" of Hebrews 2 and 6.

2. "**The end**" (verses 3,6,13,14) is the perspective of the narrative.

3. The "**gospel of the kingdom**" is being preached, NOT the gospel of 1 Cor. 15:1-4, called the "**gospel of the grace of God**" (Acts 20:24).

4. There is a temple in Jerusalem, and the Antichrist is PRESENT ON THE EARTH (verse 15).

The Jewish Tribulation saint must "flee" (verse 16) from the persecution of the Antichrist, believe on the Lord Jesus and refuse to take the mark of the beast. The Jewish Tribulation saint must "**keep the commandments of God**" (Rev. 12:17; 14:12; 22:14) AND believe in Christ as the Saviour and Messiah. They are typified as the servants of Matthew 24 and 25, who have to BUY their oil (a Christian cannot buy the Holy Spirit - Acts 8:20), live holy (Heb. 12:14), "watch" (Matt. 24:42), and "**endure unto the end**" in order to be saved. They will be judged "**according to [their] works**" (Rev. 20:11-15) to determine if they "held fast" (Heb. 3:6; 4:14; 10:23; Rev. 2:13; 2:25; 3:3; 3:11) TO "THE END" (Heb. 3:6). You would have to read the Bible with your eyes closed to think *that* matches the plan of salvation for a sinner in *this Age!*

SALVATION IN THE MILLENNIAL KINGDOM

Those who think "everyone is saved by faith in every age,"[97] overlook the obvious fact that people in the Millennial Age will "walk by sight," instead of faith. This is apparent since the Lord Himself is literally, physically, visibly, present on the earth. The vast host of dispensational scholars (Couch, Gromacki, Hindson, Ice, LaHaye, Ryrie, Towns, McGee, Ankerberg, Breese, Dave Hunt, David Jeremiah, Lutzer, Pentecost, Adrian Rogers, Van Impe, Zane Hodges, and John Walvoord) forgot the key element of faith, and its definition:

Heb 11:1 **Now faith is the substance of things hoped for, the evidence of things <u>not seen.</u>**

Note the "distinguished Professor Emeritus of Bible exposition at Dallas Theological Seminary, J. Dwight Pentecost:"[98] " . . .salvation in the millennium will be based on the value of the death of Christ and will be appropriated by faith . . ."[99]

According to WHAT and WHOM? According to the Bible? Of course not. That statement is according to an ideology of *anti-biblical* sentiments, and an unknown bias *against* the integrity of scripture. No one is saved by FAITH in the Millennium! People will not be "living by faith," but by

---

[97] Stauffer, *One Book Rightly Divided*, 225.
[98] "Pentecost, J. Dwight," *Dictionary of Premillennial Theology:* 293.
[99] Pentecost, *Things to Come*, 530.

SIGHT, since Jesus Christ Himself will be present. Read John 1:51; Zech. 14:16; 12:10; Isa. 11:1-9; Matt. 25:31; and Isa. 2:3.

Without covering all the material, notice some of the characteristics of the Millennial Age, that have absolutely *nothing* to do with the Church Age:

1. Israel has been "saved" (delivered physically and spiritually) and gathered back into their land: Rom. 11:27-31.

2. The sins of Israel, *nationally and corporately* have been "blotted out" and "forgiven:" Acts 3:19; Isa. 44:22; Jer. 50:20.

3. Temple worship, along with *bloody sacrifices* are restored: Col. 2:17; Ezek. 40-48.

4. Jesus Christ is literally sitting upon **"the throne of David"** ruling as King of the universe: Matt. 25; Luke 1.

5. All unclean spirits are departed: Zech. 13:2.

6. Satan is bound for the period of the Kingdom Age (1000 years): Rev. 20:1-6.

7. A literal lake of fire is located on the earth in Edom, south of the Dead Sea: Matt. 5:30; Isa. 34:5-10.

Why would you even remotely consider the likelihood that salvation in the Millennium would be similar to that of the Church Age? Nothing else is similar. There is no *spiritual* "body of Christ" in the Millennium, for the body of Christ is seated on the throne, and those who were members of His body during the Church Age are reigning with Him! The gospel message is not 1 Cor. 15:1-4, it is Matthew 5-7 (the constitution of the kingdom).

Salvation in the Millennial Age is 100% works, as found in the *Sermon on the Mount* and scores of places in Psalms (like Ps. 24:1-7). If a person fails to do good works, then he is liable for "hell fire." Undoubtedly the judgment for millennial saints is the white throne judgment (Rev. 20:11-15) where they are **"judged every man according to their works."**

The fact that all major dispensational premillennial scholars teach otherwise is a sad commentary. Instead of simply *believing* the Bible they exalt their preconceived systems of study. When scholars and professors disagree with the Bible, students should take them as serious as a panda bear does the scouting reports for major league baseball.

TRANSITIONAL PERIODS

The word "transition" is defined as:

> a movement, passage, or change from one position, state, stage, subject, concept to another; a change... a passing from one key to another; modulation.[100]

There are distinct, divisible, transitions in the Bible that move the doctrinal content from one dispensation to the next. Failure to recognize these transitions engender primarily the *two* following ideologies:

1. Since there are no transitions, everyone in the Bible is "saved the same" way. The unheard of implications are that all people throughout the scripture attended "worship services," heard the gospel message, responded at the "invitation" (even

---

[100] "Transition," *The Random House College Dictionary:* 1396.

though they were not made popular until around Moody's time), prayed the "sinners prayer," and were "born again."

2. Since there are no transitions (chiefly in the book of Acts), the workings of the Holy Spirit in the book of Acts (along with tongues and healing) are still pertinent for today. No Assembly of God preacher believes in any transition in the book of Acts. If he did, it would hurt his doctrine and income.

THREE MAJOR TRANSITIONS

The three major transitions in scripture are listed below:

1. A transition from the Old Testament to the New Testament. It includes the ministry of Jesus Christ, and relates extensively to the Kingdom. Stauffer terms this the "Age of Readiness."[101]

2. A transition from Israel to the Church Age. This is found throughout the book of Acts.

3. A transition from the Church Age to the Tribulation. This is found chiefly in Hebrews.

FROM OLD TO NEW TESTAMENTS

The breakdown of the various dispensations, are not so clearly marked as many dispensationalists would have you believe. Many times, dispensationalists (mostly hypers) will divide whole books of the Bible into various dispensations (see

---

[101] Stauffer, *One Book Rightly Divided*, 240.

One Book Rightly Divided by Stauffer[102]). The following chart reflects this ideology:

Old Testament	Church Age	"Age of Readiness"	Age of Kingdom	Eternity future
Matt. - John	Rom. - Philemon	Heb. - Rev. 19	Rev. 20	Rev. 21-22

Unfortunately, the Bible does not conform to little "package deals" like some want. For instance, if you include all of the gospels as "Old Testament," the problems are abundant:

1. Jesus never participated in the animal sacrifices, nor commanded His disciples to.

2. The New Testament is instituted at the Last Supper, and is "**of force**" (Heb. 9:17) at the end of each gospel, not in Acts 2!

3. The words of Jesus in John 3 cannot apply to the Old Testament legal obedience to the law. It is a clear message of salvation by grace through faith! [John had all of Paul's epistles when he wrote the gospel of John. To say that he did not know "the mystery" (as hypers do) is unwarranted and ignorant. John 14:17,20; 15:4,7 all attest to the contrary.]

This type of division leaves no room for *transition*. Since dispensations are NOT periods of time (although they operate *during* specific time brackets), they are not so certainly distinguished as the above chart indicates. If you only followed Stauffer's charts, you would think the doctrinal material in Hebrews matches with that of Matthew through

---

[102] *Ibid.*, 181.

John, since it is classified as the same "age" ("the age of Readiness"). As previously noted, Hebrews contains Church Age material even though some of it is doctrinally for the Tribulation.

Correspondingly, Matthew contains Old Testament material, but also transitions to the *New Testament Kingdom Age*. Here, we leap from first base to third. Dispensationalists forget, that the Kingdom is *part of* the New Testament. Israel, in the Kingdom, will have their sins forgiven by the blood of Christ (Acts 3:19), and have a resurrected King (Ezek. 34:23) reigning over them (Acts 2:36). *All* of John certainly does not apply to the "Age of Readiness," nor does all of 1 John - Jude.

The books of Matthew, Mark and Luke specifically record this transition from the "old bottles" to the "new bottles" (Matt. 9:17). And because John was written *after* Paul's revelation, it contains mostly Church Age material. Notice the comparison:

Matt - Luke	John
Matt 19:17 . . . *if thou wilt enter into life, keep the commandments.* **Mark 10:21** . . . *go thy way, sell whatsoever thou hast,* **Luke 18:18,20** . . . *what shall I do to inherit eternal life? . . . Thou knowest the commandments,* "Believe" occurs 23 times in Matthew - Luke combined.	**John 3:36** *He that believeth on the Son hath everlasting life: and he that believeth not the Son shall not see life; but the wrath of God abideth on him.* **John 20:31** *But these are written, that ye might believe that Jesus is the Christ, the Son of God; and that believing ye might have life through his name.* "Believe" occurs 52 times in John.

Matthew through Luke are transition books that deal with the impending Kingdom Age and consequently give

Tribulation material. The Tribulation comes *prior* to the Kingdom. Salvation is NOT presented as a spiritual transaction "**by grace through faith**" in the blood atonement of Christ in the books of Matthew - Luke. [A "monkey wrench" is given in Luke 7:48-50 where a woman has her sins forgiven, and Christ says, "**Thy faith hath saved thee.**" This is an example of "Church Age salvation" occurring directly in the middle of the "gospel of the kingdom." The woman perceptibly did not understand the blood atonement of Christ, only that He could forgive her sins. This, along with Matthew 15 (where Jesus steps out of His dispensational program and ministers to a Gentile) disengages the "book bracketing" of the "dry-cleaners" (hyper-dispensationalists).]

SALVATION IN THE TRANSITIONS (MATT-LUKE)

1. In Matthew 19, the disciples understand salvation being applicable to those whom God had blessed physically through prosperity.

Matt 19:24-25
24 And again I say unto you, It is easier for a camel to go through the eye of a needle, than for a rich man to enter into the kingdom of God.
25 When his disciples heard it, they were exceedingly amazed, saying, Who then can be saved?

This was the Old Testament arrangement, not the set-up under Pauline revelation. In the Old Testament a man's relationship to God was seen by his physical prosperity and riches. See: Gen. 21:22; 2 Chron. 9:4; 32:27; Job 4:7; 8:6; 9:4; Job 11:14-20; 36:11; Ps. 37:3; Ps. 112:1-3; 128:1-6; Prov. 3:9,10; 10:3.

2. In Luke 1, salvation was physical deliverance from the enemies of Israel.

Luke 1:71 **That we should be saved from our enemies, and from the hand of all that hate us;**

Paul and Silas were not preaching physical deliverance when they said "**Believe on the Lord Jesus Christ, and thou shalt be saved, and thy house**" (Acts 16:31).

3. In Luke 18:42 Jesus mentions salvation by faith, but it refers to physical deliverance from darkness.

Luke 18:42 **And Jesus said unto him, Receive thy sight: thy faith hath saved thee.**

4. Tribulation salvation is explained in Matthew - Luke as "enduring to the end."

Mark 13:13 **And ye shall be hated of all men for my name's sake: but he that shall endure unto the end, the same shall be saved.**

5. The chief priests and scribes understood that Jesus "**saved others;**" but they understood it in the physical sense, not the spiritual, soul-saving idea of Rom. 10:9-13.

Mark 15:31 **Likewise also the chief priests mocking said among themselves with the scribes, He saved others; himself he cannot save.**

6. The element of the New Testament that concerns the forgiveness of the sins of Israel, through Christ is explained, but has no reference to the individual atonement through belief (as in John). For, Israel will be forgiven at the second advent, and her sins "**blotted out**" corporately, as a nation: "**all Israel shall be saved**" (Rom. 11:26).

Matt 1:21 **And she shall bring forth a son, and thou shalt call his name JESUS: for he shall save his people from their sins.**

PROGRESSION OF REVELATION IN MATT-LUKE

In summary, the four gospels present a transition from the Old to the New Testament, and consequently they progress in revelation, as follows:

1. Matthew closes with the resurrection - relating to the nation of Israel - the Hebrews. [See Acts 26:7-8 for the Jewish connection to the resurrection.]

2. Mark closes with the ascension of Christ.

3. Luke closes with the ascension and a mention of Pentecost, which begins the missionary movement (Acts 1:8).

4. John closes with a reference to John being caught up (in type - the rapture of the Church).

TRANSITIONS IN THE BOOK OF ACTS

The fact that the book of Acts presents truth in a transitory manner is evident. The book moves from a church that is *entirely Jewish*, to the Jews rejecting the gospel message (Acts 28). The setting aside of Israel, and the transition of the gospel to the Gentiles is the key to the book. Peter is the apostle to the Jews, while Paul **"turns to the Gentiles"** (Acts 13:46). It must be remembered that Paul also had a burden for the Jews, and constantly preached to them, even rebelling against the Holy Ghost to do so. He obeyed Romans 1:16 and went to the Jews first, but after the four official rejections by the nation (Acts 7,13,18,28) Paul focused primarily on Gentile believers.

The "hyper hang up" that Peter and Paul preached two different gospels *at the same time* is pure nonsense. The Bullingerites, and Stamites have Peter preaching Acts 2:38 *while* Paul is preaching the **"gospel of the grace of God"** (Acts 20). The dry-cleaners forget that when Paul referred to "**the gospel of the uncircumcision**," and "**the gospel of the circumcision**" (Gal. 2:7), the meeting in Acts 15 had already taken place. Peter declared in Acts 15 that salvation was by grace alone *without* baptism! You will not find the message of Acts 2 (a messianic message) preached by Peter any more after Acts 8!

> *Acts 15:11* **But we believe that through the grace of the Lord Jesus Christ we shall be saved, even as they.**

After the matter of salvation by grace through faith was settled in Acts 15, Peter went to the Jews and Paul to the Gentiles (see Gal. 2:7). They did not go with different gospels. They just went to different groups. This is clear in Galatians:

> *Gal 2:9* **. . . that we should go unto the heathen, and they unto the circumcision.**

Acts, then, presents the transition of the recipients of the gospel from Israel over to the Church. This is observed by the transitions of ordinances (Acts 10,11), sabbath observance

(Acts 20:7), the priesthood (Acts 6:7), animal sacrifices (Col. 2:15), and affiliation between Jews and Gentiles (Acts 10; Gal. 2:14,15).

The most evident proof that this transition existed, regards pneumatology (the study of the Holy Spirit). Below are the scriptural facts teaching indeed a shift (relating to salvation) in how the Holy Spirit was "given" to people in the book of Acts. These facts dispel any myth that "salvation was always the same."

1. The Holy Spirit was given by water baptism in Acts chapter two.

> *Acts 2:38* **Then Peter said unto them, Repent, and be baptized every one of you in the name of Jesus Christ for the remission of sins, and ye shall receive the gift of the Holy Ghost.**

Most scholars, theologians and Baptist preachers will insist that the whole salvation process is summarized in "repent." To say, "such repentance brings salvation"[103] relieves the importance of the baptism. The same procedure is done (not respecting the word of God) in Mark 16 where Jesus insisted on water baptism as a condition for salvation:

> *Mark 16:16* **He that believeth and is baptized shall be saved; but he that believeth not shall be damned.**

The response given by most Baptist preachers (within a 100 mile radius) is, "If a person is saved they will want to be baptized," or "the verse does not say if a person is not baptized

---

[103] *Ryrie Study Bible*, 1542.

he is damned, only if he does not believe." While the purpose of such statements is to shield the doctrine of salvation by faith, they actually malign the dignity and verity of the scriptures. If they would "rightly divide the word of truth," instead of twisting it to suit what they *know* to be true, the confusion would disappear.

The verse teaches *someone* gets the Holy Ghost by repentance PLUS baptism. If the man repented and was not *physically* water baptized he would not get the "gift." That is what the verse SAYS! Although this does not match *your* conversion, and how *you* got the "gift," it does not abolish its truthfulness. The book of Acts is a transitional book, and "this was a temporary setup in accordance with the truth revealed up to that time."[104]

Not only is salvation different between the Old Testament and the New Testament, it is not even identical in ONE BOOK. Here, in Acts 2, no one speaks in tongues when they receive the gift, and they got it by repentance and water baptism (a continuation of John's baptism to Israel). In other instances, tongues are required as evidence that the Holy Spirit was given (Acts 19:1-9).

[Without covering the doctrinal material and dispensational nature of Acts 2, suffice it to say that Peter's message to Israel includes the death, burial and resurrection of Christ as Messiah and King, but excludes the substitutionary atonement for sin. Peter does not preach Eph. 2:8,9. In fact, the blood atonement for individual sins is not proclaimed until Acts 8!]

   2. Laying on of hands was necessary in order to receive the Holy Ghost. Notice, there are no tongues as "evidence."

---

[104] Ruckman, Peter S., *Acts* (Pensacola: Bible Believers Press, 1974) 118.

Acts 8:17-18
**7 Then laid they their hands on them, and they received the Holy Ghost.
18 And when Simon saw that through laying on of the apostles' hands the Holy Ghost was given, he offered them money,**

Here the "gift of the Holy Ghost" is given by *physical contact* with an apostle. Is that how *you* were saved? Some may argue that the verse did not say they were saved, only that they got the Holy Ghost. Can a person be saved and NOT have the Holy Ghost? There is an obvious difference in the administration of the Holy Ghost in the book of Acts, and consequently a difference in how people were saved throughout the book of Acts. It is a progressive revelation of truth beginning with the Jews and going to the Gentiles.

Rom 1:16 **For I am not ashamed of the gospel of Christ: for it is the power of God unto salvation to every one that believeth; to the Jew first, and also to the Greek.**

Acts 28:28 **Be it known therefore unto you, that the salvation of God is sent unto the Gentiles, and that they will hear it.**

3. Baptism, laying on of hands, *then* speaking in tongues was a sign to the Jews.

Acts 19:2 **He said unto them, Have ye received the Holy Ghost since ye believed? And they said unto him, We have not so much as heard whether there be any Holy Ghost.**

Acts 19:6 **And when Paul had laid his hands upon them, the Holy Ghost came on them; and they spake with tongues, and prophesied.**

Notice that they were baptized in the name of Jesus, as in Acts 2, instead of the name of the Father, Son, and Holy Ghost (Matt. 28). Apollos was a Jew, and his disciples were Jews, or they would not have been baptized by John.

4. The last "plan of salvation" in the book of Acts concerns a man who is saved by believing in the blood atonement. He is baptized only *after* he is converted. This man does NOT speak in tongues, and is converted *before* the apostle Paul.

Acts 8:35-37
**35 Then Philip opened his mouth, and began at the same scripture, and preached unto him Jesus.
36 And as they went on their way, they came unto a certain water: and the eunuch said, See, here is water; what doth hinder me to be baptized?
37 And Philip said, If thou believest with all thine heart, thou mayest. And he answered and said, I believe that Jesus Christ is the Son of God.**

Why the Differences?

In summary, the transitional nature of Acts can be explained with one word: Jew. There are absolutely NO Gentiles being preached to in Acts 2:38, and certainly no "gospel of the grace of God." Acts 2 is a message addressed to the Jews who crucified *their* Messiah. Since their sins were forgiven as a nation ("**for the remission**" always means "because of") they were to be baptized by Peter and follow Christ through the ministry of the apostles. This "forgiveness" was granted after Christ's prayer on the cross (Luke 23:34), making Peter's baptism an "extension" of John's.

[Note the prophesy of forgiveness along with John's commission in Isaiah 40:9.]

Acts 8:17-18 presents a case where the converts "believed," were "baptized," and still did not have the Holy Ghost until the apostles laid hands on them. The answer to this marked peculiarity borders on what the God-denying world lables: hate, racism, prejudice, and discrimination. Ruckman aptly comments:

> The Samaritans believed and were baptized (vs. 12) according to Mark 16:16. Simon is included in this group of converts (vs. 13). However! The "gift of the Holy Ghost" does not show up here (vss 15,16). There has been a transitional shift between Acts 2 and Acts 8 . . . The Samaritans are half-breeds who rebelled against the authority of Jerusalem by building a rival temple on Mt. Gerizim (John 4:20). To reinforce the ancient authority of Jerusalem as the capitol of Palestine . . . the Lord withholds the holy Spirit from the Samaritans until His Coming is connected with the apostolic authority from Jerusalem.[105]

People are "saved the same" all throughout the scriptures? They do not even get the Holy Ghost the same in the book of Acts!

The next example (Acts 19:1-6) lays emphasis again on the laying on of hands. These Jewish disciples (from Apollos - Acts 18:25; 19:1,7,8) have been baptized by John, but do not have the Holy Ghost. [The "Baptist Briders" think John was a Christian preacher, even though people who were baptized by him did not have the Holy Spirit. I guess to them John was

---

[105] *Ibid.*, 276-277.

baptizing lost people.] The disciples in Acts 19 get re-baptized, this time according to Acts 2:38 (in the "name of Jesus") but still do not get the Holy Ghost until the Paul lays his hands on them. These Jews are different than the ones in Acts 2:38. They never rejected their Messiah, and they were not responsible for His crucifixion. They speak in tongues (similarly in all cases) as a "sign" to the Jews (vss. 8,9) in the area.

The last "plan of salvation" in the book of Acts deals with an Ethiopian Gentile (Acts 8:37,38). This man believes the substitutionary death of Christ "**according to the scriptures.**" Philip does not preach a national "blotting out" of sins (Acts 3:19); but rather, the individual blood atonement for sinners. This Gentile believes, and his baptism follows his conversion. Since there are no Jews present (except for Philip) the "sign gift" of tongues is not manifested, as in Acts 10:44-46 with Cornelius.

THE TRANSITION BOOKS

It is safe to say that Matthew, Acts, and Hebrews are the core transitional books in the New Testament. As stated earlier, Matthew records the transition from the Old Testament to the New Testament, Acts details the setting aside of Israel for the Church, and Hebrews shifts from the Church Age to the Tribulation.

The most hazardous book for a new Christian is by far the book of Acts. It furnishes the "proof texts" for hyper-dispensationalists, Campbellites, Charismatics, and Calvinists. Or, a *softer* way to express it:

> The Acts of the Apostles! The great stumbling block for water dogs, blabber mouths, religious quacks, self

righteous humanitarians, dead-orthodox dispensationalists, and theological librarians![106]

Acts is so treacherous because the *doctrinal content* differs WITHIN one dispensation. This occurs minutely in Matthew, but not to the same extent.

---

[106] *Ibid.*, xiv.

DISPENSATIONALISM

Part Three:
EXPOSITORY

COVENANTS AND DISPENSATIONS

CHAPTER 6

A Beginning Summary

COVENANT EXAMINATION

In this section we will examine the various covenants and dispensations. Since no one could ever improve upon Larkin's classic work, *Dispensational Truth*, or Ruckman's "kingdom theme" in *The Sure Word of Prophecy*, we will not even attempt it. Neither will we give an exhaustive analysis of each dispensation. Much of the foundational material was covered either in chapter one: *Definition, Description and Distinction* (page 2), chapter four: *Some Basic Divisions* (page 78), or chapter five: *Dispensational Salvation* (page 116). Although this portion will skip some of the established material, it will probe into the "meat" (Heb. 5:12,14) of each covenant, by laying out a concise analytical breakdown of the vital events and foundational teachings.

How Many Dispensations

The breakdown and classification of the assorted dispensations vary from author to author. Ryrie comments:

> Most dispensationalists see seven dispensations in God's plan (though throughout the history of dispensationalism they have not always been the same seven). Occasionally a dispensationalists may hold as few as four, and some hold as many as eight.[1]

The common *seven* dispensations (made popular by Scofield) are:

1. Innocence
2. Conscience
3. Human Government
4. Promise
5. Law
6. Grace (or Church Age)
7. Kingdom

Larkin adds the eighth as the "Perfect Age," and identifies it as the "dispensation of the fullness of times."[2]

Nine Dispensations

It is interesting to note that the Tribulation "Age" is completely overlooked by the classic authors of dispensationalism (like Scofield, Larkin, Chaffer, and Ironside) as a separate dispensation. Dr. Ruckman explains why:

---

[1] Ryrie, Charles C., *Dispensationalism* (Chicago: Moody Press, 1995) 46.
[2] Larkin, Clarence, *Dispensational Truth* (Glenside: Rev. Clarence Larkin Est., 1920) 43.

> ... they fail to go into the details of salvation in the 'end time,' which would include The Great Tribulation and the Millennium.... When any of these Bible scholars hit Hebrews 3, 6 and 10; Matthew 24 and 25; Revelation 12, 14, and 22, they tend to 'fizzle out.'[3]

Most dispensationalists (not including hypers) simply mention the Great Tribulation as occurring *after* the rapture of the Church (since most are pretribulational); but they neglect to position it as an independent dispensation. Ryrie admits that the Tribulation cannot be placed in the Church Age dispensation or the Kingdom (or Millennial) dispensation. He even proposes the idea, though he does not accept it, that the Tribulation "is itself a distinguishable economy in the outworking of God's purpose."[4]

Stauffer (with his system of *nine* dispensations) names the Tribulation dispensation, the "Age of Readiness" differentiating it as an isolated dispensation.[5] Stauffer creates confusion however; when he claims the Church Age "splits" this "Age of Readiness" which began in the book of Matthew. If these two transition periods (after Malachi before the cross, and after the rapture of the Church) coincide, the plans of salvation would be similar. They are NOT. As we have proven, during the Tribulation a man is saved by faith in the blood of Christ *plus* his works (keeping the commandments). During Christ's earthly ministry, NO ONE was saved by faith in the blood of Christ. The blood had not been shed. Furthermore, there was no "mark of the beast" to avoid during Christ's earthly ministry.

While there *are* some similarities between the time of Christ's earthly ministry (3 ½ years), and that of the Great

---

[3] Ruckman, Peter S., *How to teach Dispensational Truth* (Pensacola: Bible Believers Press, 1992) 7.
[4] Ryrie, *Dispensationalism*, 50.
[5] Stauffer, Douglas D., *One Book Rightly Divided* (Millbrok: McCowen Mills Publishers, 1999) 181.

Tribulation (3 ½ years); there is not enough to bond them together as the same dispensation, or age. If someone has a different "plan or arrangement," they are in a different dispensation! [We must be careful here, because *transitions* are not considered dispensations. For instance, in Acts (a transitional book) the dispensation is the same, but the *revelation* of truth is progressive. Hypers confuse the two.]

Because of the *disorder* in the neat packaged dispensational schemes (whether you have seven, eight, or nine), the best way to study dispensations is by the *covenants*. Note, Dr. Ruckman:

> Since the Bible is, basically, a history book that deals with God's dealing with mankind in regards to a Kingdom . . . the covenants are the best ways to mark off the "dispensations." [6]

Covenants relate to *history* and more clearly section the Bible off far better than dispensations do, and provide a more systematic methodology.

A Brief Overview

Any good dispensational study by a King James Bible believer will suffice for a brief overview. The only problem with small summaries, are the impressions they leave that each dispensation abruptly ends where the next one picks up. As we shall see, many truths from past dispensations are still relevant today, and "in force" today for New Testament believers.

On the following pages is a summary of the covenants along with their corresponding dispensations, similar to what you will find in many works:

---

[6] Ruckman, *How to teach Dispensational Truth*, 19.

I. The Edenic Covenant (*Innocence*)

    A. Purpose: to fix the problem of rebellion of Satan and the sons of God (Gen. 1:2).

    B. Test: abstain from the "tree of knowledge of good and evil."

    C. Result: Failure.

II. The Adamic Covenant (*Conscience*)

    A. Purpose: to deal with the results of fallen man.

    B. Test: do good and sacrifice animals for sin.

    C. Result: "every imagination only evil continually" – Failure: The Flood.

III. The Noahic Covenant (*Human Government*)

    A. Purpose: to replenish the earth, and maintain order.

    B. Test: multiply and scatter.

    C. Result: they did not scatter, so the Lord scattered them: The tower of Babel.

IV. The Abrahamic Covenant (*Promise*)

    A. Purpose: to bless the world through one man, one seed, and one race.

    B. Test: dwell in the promised land.

    C. Result: went down into Egypt and became slaves.

V. The Mosaic Covenant (*Law*)

    A. Purpose: to follow God as a nation under statues and commandments.

    B. Test: keep the law as a personal righteousness.

    C. Result: broke the law, and dispersed worldwide.

VI. The Davidic Covenant (*Kingdom*)
   A. Purpose: to establish the kingdom of heaven under kings of Judah, until the KING OF KINGS takes over the throne.
   B. Test: to keep the law and "do right in the sight of the Lord."
   C. Result: kings failed and fall under a curse (Jer. 22:29,30).

VII. The New Covenant
FIRST DIVISION (*Church*)
   A. Purpose: a new order of salvation by faith Jesus Christ.
   B. Test: keep the faith, be witnesses everywhere.
   C. Result: apostasy, and a lost world.
SECOND DIVISION (*Jew and Gentile*)
   A. Purpose: to return the kingdoms of this world to their rightful owner
   B. Test: to serve and worship the Lord Jesus Christ as King.
   C. Result: rebellion and worldwide revolt; ends with a destruction by fire.

VIII. The Eternal Covenant (*fullness of times*)
Purpose: to re-establish the original plan and purpose of God with a redeemed creation and NO SIN, DEATH, or DEVIL.

   Right away, the flaws of such a concise explanation (if you can call it that) are evident. The dispensational content of the New Covenant gets especially "hairy" because there is a Jewish and an Ecclesiastical application that *must* be divided. Notice also, that normally, the transition periods (i.e. Malachi through the crucifixion; and the Tribulation Age) are left out as identifiable dispensations.

Chapter 7

Before Eden

TOO MUCH!

The considerations, and, many times senseless reflections, regarding history prior to the creation of man, is enough for a "knock out." As William Grady states: "The ability to rightly divide scripture is a humbling experience, as it fosters an ever-increasing awareness of just how little we really do know."[1] The more a Bible believing dispensationalist learns, the more he cannot grasp. Answered questions generate more questions. The over-whelming consensus after a *believing* evaluation of the Bible, is summed up by Job and David:

> *Job 42:3* **Who is he that hideth counsel without knowledge? therefore have I uttered that I**

---

[1] Stauffer, Douglas D., *One Book Rightly Divided* (Millbrok: McCowen Mills Publishers, 1999) xii.

understood not; things too wonderful for me, which I knew not.

Ps 139:6 **Such knowledge is too wonderful for me; it is high, I cannot attain unto it.**

Paul said it this way:

Rom 11:33 **O the depth of the riches both of the wisdom and knowledge of God! how unsearchable are his judgments, and his ways past finding out!**

When we begin to delve into the time *prior* to the Edenic Covenant, we pioneer on ground with little scriptural support. This is dangerous. Many times, speculation, assumption, opinion, and emotion take precedence over scripture (or the lack thereof). Frequently, interpretations are embraced merely because they were made popular by past dispensational authors, or because the arguments are presented in a convincing manner. While some are resolved to the NON-study of such topics, the Bible student knows it is necessary if he is to "**live by . . . every word of God**" (Luke 4:4).

GAP THEORY, OR FACT?

The importance and significance of whether or not there was a "gap" between Gen. 1:1,2 cannot be overvalued. In fact, Biblical veracity reconciled to true *geological science* pivots heavily upon the validity or error of such a "gap."

With the "gap," the historical objectives and goals of Satan and God are clearly played in accordance with the book of Revelation. And the scientific integrity of scripture is retained. Without the gap "creation evangelists" turn Noah's flood into the answer for any "old earth" scientific evidence. To the "anti-gapers" *all* geologists, physicists, and other scientists (evolutionists or not) are wrong if they espouse the view of an old earth.

Anti-gap arguments are not hard to find. Materials from *ICR* (*Institute for Creation Research*), *Creation Science Evangelism* (Kent Hovind), or *Answers in Genesis* (Ken Ham) are defiantly against the gap. Hovind goes as far to call the gap "godless"[2] indicting it for the furtherance of "communism, humanism, and Nazism."[3] He says:

> The acceptance of the gap theory opened the floodgates for these ideologies, which have caused untold suffering as well as hundreds of millions of deaths in the last two centuries.[4]

Does not the above assertion boarder on extremism? Hovind should *document* and verify his outlandish accusations.

Some advocates of a 6,000 year old earth indict the gap theory as being a innovation of the early nineteenth century. Notice the misleading quote from Hovind:

> Thomas Chalmers (1780-1847), a notable Scottish theologian and first moderator of the Free Church of Scotland, is credited with being the first proponent of the gap theory. His proposal of the theory was first recorded in 1814 in one of his lectures at Edinburgh University. Until 1814, no theologian had put forth the idea of a gap between Genesis 1:1 and 1:2.[5]

Have we not heard this familiar tune before? "Fact deniers" like to pinpoint a doctrine or teaching to a specific man at a precise date. In doing so, they think they have repudiated the

---

[2] Hovind, Kent; Lawwell, Stephen, *Are there billions of years between Genesis1:1 & 1:2?* (www.dr.dino.com)
[3] *Ibid.*
[4] *Ibid.*
[5] *Ibid.*

credibility of the teaching. Even though other "young earth" supporters like John Whitcomb admit that "the Gap Theory had been advocated in one form or another spasmodically for centuries,"[6] Hovind still claims "Chalmers . . . created the gap theory."[7]

The Bible verifies a "gap" between Gen. 1:1,2 even if modern dispensationalists, or "creation evangelists" disown it. The Bible (AV 1611) will always be the most unusual book on the planet, and will never curve or bend to flatter and soothe *professional* scholars.

GAP PROOFS

The following Bible facts demonstrate the legitimacy of a definite "gap" in Gen. 1:1,2:

GAP PROOF 1
God would not create the earth in a state of chaos.

> *Isa 45:18* **For thus saith the LORD that created the heavens; God himself that formed the earth and made it; he hath established it, he created it not in vain, he formed it to be inhabited: I am the LORD; and there is none else.**

To those who think Gen. 1:2 does not imply or suggest chaos, the cross-references for **"without form and void"** should be studied. We list them below with comment:

---

[6] Whitcomb, John C., *The Early Earth* (Grand Rapids: Baker, 1972) 115.
[7] Hovind; Lawwell, *Are there billions of years between Genesis1:1 & 1:2?* (www.dr.dino.com)

Jer 4:23 **I beheld the earth, and, lo, it was without form, and void; and the heavens, and they had no light.**

Jer. 4:23 is obviously a Tribulation reference using the phrase "**without form**" to describe chaos and destruction.

Although Jeremiah chapter four is a great proof text for the undertone of "**without form and void**," it has been misapplied far too often. Ruckman on Jeremiah 4:23:

> Often wrongly applied, doctrinally, to Genesis 1:2. If it is a reference to Jeremiah observing what happened at that time, his vision changes immediately in the context of two verses, for "**the birds of the heavens**" (vs. 25) were not there in Genesis 1:2. Nor were there any "**cities**." There are no cities till Genesis chapter 4. The doctrinal reference is prophetic. It is aimed at the condition of this earth in the tribulation (note vss. 26-30 and especially vs. 31).[8]

Notice Scofield's affirmation of "the gap" with his comment on Jer. 4, where he unites it with Gen. 1:2:

> Jer. 4:23-26; Isa. 24:1; and 45:18, clearly indicate that the earth had undergone a cataclysmic change as the result of a divine judgment. The face of the earth bears everywhere the marks of such a catastrophe. There are not wanting intimations which connect it with a previous testing and fall of angels.[9]

Ps 89:39 **Thou hast made void the covenant of thy servant: thou hast profaned his crown by casting it to the ground.**

---

[8] Ruckman, Peter S., *Ruckman's Bible References* (Pensacola: Bible Baptist Bookstore, 1997) 115.
[9] *Scofield Reference Bible* (New York: Oxford, 1909) 3.

> *Nah 2:10* **She is empty, and void, and waste: and the heart melteth, and the knees smite together, and much pain is in all loins, and the faces of them all gather blackness.**

To "**make void the covenant**" (according the cross-references) does *not* mean "unformed, and unexercised, not yet ready for habitation."[10] And to be "**empty, and void, and waste**," does not carry a *positive insinuation!*

Would God create the earth in such a state as "**without form and void?**" That is the question, and the crux of the matter. A lengthy disputation regarding the Hebrew word for "was" is non-essential. Bullinger claims that "was" means "became" and is so used in scripture[11] (i.e. Gen. 2:7; 4:3; 9:15; 19:26; Ex. 32:1; Deut. 27:2; 2 Sam. 7:24). Conversely, Whitcomb lists verses where this logic would not make sense[12] (i.e. Gen. 2:25; Zech. 3:1-3). And, any tabulation or twisting of the *sense* of Gen. 1:1-3 is "private interpretation."

Whitcomb reduces the significance of Gen. 1:2, by tying it to the creative week:

> He did not allow it to remain in the empty and formless condition in which He first created it, but in six creative days filled it with living things and fashioned it to be a beautiful home for man.[13]

According to Whitcomb, and other creation scientists (who *all* change the King James text) the verse should easily read: *When God began creating the heaven and the earth, it was without form and void with darkness all over the waters.*

Notice the vast difference from the actual text:

---

[10] *The Defenders Study Bible* (Grand Rapids: Word, 1995) 4.
[11] *Companion Bible* (Grand Rapids: Kregel, 1990) 3.
[12] Whitcomb, *The Early Earth*, 121,122.
[13] *Ibid.*, 123.

Gen 1:1-2

1 In the beginning God created the Heaven and the earth.

2 And the earth was without form, and void; and darkness was upon the face of the deep. And the Spirit of God moved upon the face of the waters.

GAP PROOF 2
The word "create" can refer back to Gen. 1:1 <u>or the re-creation</u>

Pember, as well as Scofield, noted the difference between "create" and "made." Pember assumed that the "morning stars" of Job 38 were the same "stars" that show up on the Fourth Day; thus they would have been created when the foundation of the earth (Gen. 1:1) was laid:

> We are next told that God prepared - not created - the stars also . . . perhaps by the concentration of light into the sun, that the stars then first appeared, or re-appeared, in it. . . . At the close of the Third Day earth was finished and ready for the reception of life, while the stars are not mentioned till the Fourth Day. But in a passage of Job we are told that the morning stars were admiring witnesses when God laid the foundation stone of the earth, and sang together for joy at its completion . . . They must, therefore, have been pre-existent.[14]

This variation confuses the "light" of Genesis 1:3 with the sun of Genesis 1:16. While it is possible that our "sun" is included in the "heaven" of Gen. 1:1, it is obviously re-created in 1:16. Notice how "made" is used interchangeably with "created." See: Gen. 1:7; 1:16; 1:25; 1:31; 2:2; 2:4; 2:22; 3:1 *with* Gen. 1:21; 1:27; 2:3; 5:1.

---

[14] Pember, G.H., *Earth's Earliest Ages* (Grand Rapids: Kregel, 1975) 68.

Gen 2:3-4
**3 And God blessed the seventh day, and sanctified it: because that in it he had rested from all his work which God <u>created and made</u>.
4 These are the generations of the heavens and of the earth when they <u>were created</u>, in the day that the LORD God <u>made the earth and the heavens</u>,**

Gen 1:27 **So God <u>created</u> man in his own image, in the image of God created he him; male and female created he them.**

Gen 9:6 **Whoso sheddeth man's blood, by man shall his blood be shed: for in the image of God <u>made he</u> man.**

Isa 45:12 **I have <u>made</u> the earth, and <u>created man</u> upon it: I, even my hands, have stretched out the heavens, and all their host have I commanded.**

Morris and other young earth promoters claim Exodus 20:11 must revert back to Genesis 1:1, therefore canceling out a gap. What they fail to understand is that the word "created" can be used when something (or someone) is created out of matter already available! Without wasting time with the Hebrew, note that Adam is said to be "**created**" (Gen. 1:27); and "**made**" (Gen. 5:1). Our "young earth" friends forget that Adam was formed out "**of the dust of the ground**" that was *already in existence!*

While it is emphatically declared that Adam is the first man (1 Cor. 15:45), what about plant and animal life? Some (like Pember) attribute elements of the fossil record to beasts before Adam:

Not merely had its fruitful place become a wilderness, and all its cities broken down; but the very light of its sun had been withdrawn . . . the beasts of the earth were not always as they now are . . . Since, then, the fossil remains are those of creatures anterior to Adam, and yet show evident tokens of disease, death, and mutual destruction, they must have belonged to another world, and have a sin-stained history of their own, a history which ended in the ruin of themselves and their habitation.[15]

Henry Morris, Kent Hovind, and other creation scientists disclaim the gap, insisting that it was invented in hopes that "these ages could be pigeon-holed and forgotten as far as biblical exegesis was concerned."[16] They also consider the teaching of the gap as an

attempt to ignore or explain away the supposed great age of the earth [and] makes an unnecessary and abortive compromise with evolutionism.[17]

Young earth enthusiasts must shift all geological evidence of a catastrophe to Noah's flood, and reject plain references to an inhabited earth *prior* to Adam (such as Gen. 1:28).

GAP PROOF 3
Darkness is not GOOD

Anti-gap proponents use Genesis 1:31 (**and God saw every thing that he had made, and, behold, it was very good**) as an attempt to impede a gap. They claim that at the end of the six days, there was no sin, Satan had not fallen, and the earth had not been "**overflowed with water**" (2 Peter 3:6). But the problem remains with them and their "model." *What about the*

---

[15] *Ibid.*, 34,35.
[16] *The Defenders Study Bible*, 3.
[17] *Ibid.*

darkness? Willing ignorant, they claim the darkness is good, even though the Bible says *nothing* of the kind (see Gen. 1:4). If it was "good," why did God "**divide**" it from the light? The idea that "**darkness**" in the verse could have a good connotation is illogical and unfeasible. Whitcomb refers to Ps. 104:19-24, to prove his point.[18]

Ps 104:20 **Thou makest darkness, and it is night: wherein all the beasts of the forest do creep forth.**

The fact that God made the darkness does not mean that it is good! *He made everything!* Is *hell* therefore "good" because God made it? The logic of Morris, Whitcomb, and Hovind is unreasonable. They are not "*thimking.*" The "**darkness**" in the passage is located in the firmament ("outer space") which was created on the second day. Further, the phrase, "**God saw that it was good**" is NOT GIVEN for day two. You have one guess as to *why*. Check out the following scriptures and note the correlation between darkness, the firmament and *Leviathan*: Ephesians 6:12; Job 41; Isa. 24:21; Psalm 74:13,14.

The "**thick darkness**" that is associated with God (Ex. 20:21; Deut. 4:11; 1Ki. 8:12; 2 Chron. 6:1; Ps. 18:8-11 and Ps. 97:2) is not there because it is "good," but rather to *divide* between Himself and His sinful creation. To claim that the darkness is good because God created it ignores the purpose and intent behind its inception.

The subsequent chart catalogs references to "darkness" in scripture, showing their obvious *negative* association:

---

[18] Whitcomb, *The Early Earth*, 126.

REFERENCES TO THE "DARKNESS"

Genesis: 1:2; 1:4; 1:5; 1:18; 15:12;	**Exodus**: 10:21,22; 14:20; 20:21
Deuteronomy 4:11; 5:22; 5:23; 28:29	**Joshua** 24:7
1 Samuel 2:9	**2 Samuel** 22:12; 22:29
2 Chronicles 6:1 **Psalm** 18:9; 18:11; 18:28; 82:5; 88:6; 88:18; 91:6; 97:2; 104:20; 105:28; 107:10; 107:14; 112:4; 139:11; 139:12; 143:3	**Job** 3:4; 3:5; 3:6; 5:14; 10:21; 10:22; 12:22; 15:22; 15:23; 15:30; 17:12; 18:18; 19:8; 20:26; 22:11; 23:17; 28:3; 29:3; 30:26; 34:22; 37:19; 38:9; 38:19
Prov. 2:13; 4:19; 20:20	**Eccl.** 2:13; 2:14; 5:17; 6:4; 11:8
Isaiah 5:20; 5:30; 8:22; 9:2; 29:18; 42:7; 42:16; 45:3; 45:7; 47:5; 49:9; 50:10; 58:10; 59:9; 60:2	**Jeremiah** 2:31; 13:16
Lamentations 3:2	**Ezekiel** 32:8
Daniel 2:22	**Joel** 2:2; 2:31
Amos 4:13	**Micah** 7:8
Nahum 1:8	**Zephaniah** 1:15
Matthew 4:16; 6:23; 8:12; 10:27; 25:30; 27:45	**Mark** 15:33
Luke 1:79; 11:34; 11:35; 12:3; 22:53; 23:44	**John** 1:5; 3:19; 8:12; 12:35; 12:46
Acts 2:20; 13:11; 26:18	**Romans** 2:19; 13:12
1 Corinthians 4:5	**2 Corinthians** 4:6; 6:4
Ephesians 5:8; 5:11; 6:12	**Colossians** 1:13
1 Thessalonians 5:4; 5:5	**1 Peter** 2:9
2 Peter 2:4; 2:17	**I John** 1:5; 1:6; 2:8; 2:9; 2:11
Jude 6, 13	**Rev.** 16:10.

GAP PROOF 4
There was an inhabited earth prior to Adam.

Even though Adam was the first man (1 Cor. 15:45 - there is no pre-Adamite race of *men*), there was someone here before Adam was created. [Larkin was wrong to assume that the original earth was "inhabited . . . with human life."[19] He also insinuates that they were destroyed by fire and "their escaping spirits became the demons."[20]] Adam was told to "**replenish**" the earth that this "someone" had once filled.

> *Gen 1:28* . . . **Be fruitful, and multiply, and <u>replenish the earth</u>, and subdue it** . . .

If one is so foolish to doubt the unadorned meaning of "replenish," the commission to Noah (after the flood) clarifies it precisely:

> *Gen 9:1* **And God blessed Noah and his sons, and said unto them, Be fruitful, and multiply, and <u>replenish the earth</u>.**

You can go to the Hebrew, and maintain that "the verb in the Hebrew text (maleh) simply means 'to fill,' with no suggestion of a repetition."[21] You could even call the KJV a "misleading translation"[22] like Morris does. Or, you could do as Hovind and claim that:

> In 1611, the time of the King James translation, English dictionaries defined the word *replenish* as "to supply

---

[19] Larkin, Clarence, *Dispensational Truth* (Glenside: Rev. Clarence Larkin Est., 1920) 22.
[20] *Ibid.*, 24.
[21] Whitcomb, *The Early Earth*, 130.
[22] *The Defenders Study Bible*, 7.

fully, to fill." Nearly a century later, a second definition arose, "to fill or build up again."[23]

Hovind lacks basic comparative skills. He should have noticed the fact that the AV translators used the definition **"fill"** for the Hebrew word מלא (male′) in Genesis 1:22; just six verses prior to where they used "**replenish**." They knew the differences between the two words, and were well aware of the implications and assertions of "**replenish**." Their translation was correct then, as well as now. In fact, the ASV of 1901 retains "**replenish**" in Gen. 1:28; 9:1; Ezek 26:2 and Ezek 27:25. The NKJV uses "**replenish**" in Jer. 31:25; and the RSV translates "male′" as "replenish" in Ezek 26:2. Out of 16 occurrences of the Hebrew word in Genesis the translators pick "replenish" when the context regarded human procreation. They knew precisely what they were doing.

Why "Replenish"

A. The English word "replenish," or "replenished" *never* means "to fill something that was not filled before" in the KJV: Gen. 1:28; 9:1; Isa. 2:6; Isa. 23:2; Jer. 31:25; Ezek. 26:2; Ezek. 27:25.

B. The new "bibles" (except the ASV) change the King James reading in Gen. 1:28, removing the cross-reference to Gen. 9:1.

C. Noah and Adam receive similar commissions (Gen. 1 and Gen. 9) in that they both have to refill the earth, and both follow a flood.

---

[23] Hovind; Lawwell, *Are there billions of years between Genesis1:1 & 1:2?*)

D. The parallels between Noah and Adam are too numerous and noteworthy to discount. They substantiate the worth of the word "replenish" in both commissions. Dr. Ruckman comments:

> --- They both were sole possessors of the earth.
> --- They both had a direct commission from God.
> --- They both replaced races which God did not want controlling the earth.
> --- They both had three sons by name.
> --- One of their sons was a type of Christ.
> --- One was a type of Antichrist.
> --- Shem and Abel are connected with Christ.
> --- Cain and Canaan are both cursed.
> --- Adam is naked when he sins, exactly as Noah.
> --- Adam and Noah partake of "forbidden fruit."
> --- Adam's prohibition is a vine, and Noah's prohibition is blood.[24]

E. Adam and Eve were not shocked at the mention of other beings on the earth called "gods" (Gen. 3) that could *not* populate on their own (Gen. 6:1-4). [The "King James user" may cry, "Oh, but does not the Hebrew word translated 'gods' in the AV really mean 'God?'" What is the *final authority?* Is it the AV English text (as it stands) or possible definitions of Hebrew words? Examples like this separate Bible believers from "Bible users."]

F. The "sons of God" are said to be present and alive on the creation morning (Job 38:7) *before* Adam is made.

GAP PROOF 5
2 Peter 3:1-7 corroborates with Gen. 1:2 teaching an obvious "gap."

---

[24] Ruckman, Peter S., *Genesis* (Pensacola: Bible Believers Press, 1969) 234.

2 Peter 3 is NOT a reference to Noah's flood (see Morris). There are too many incongruities between the flood of 2 Peter 3 and that of Noah's day.

A. The reference in 2 Peter 3 is to "**the beginning of the creation**" and Noah's flood took place 1700 years after the "beginning."

B. The "**earth standing out of the water and in the water**" could not refer to the "earth" of Noah's day because the "earth" of Noah's day, and of today, is suspended in outer space in a solar system:

Job 26:7 **He stretcheth out the north over the empty place, and hangeth the earth upon nothing.**

C. The "heavens" were not destroyed during the flood of Noah, but are said to have been affected and changed *after* this catastrophe of 2 Peter 3: "**heavens of old . . . heavens . . . which are now.**"

D. The importance of the difference in the singular "heaven" of Gen. 1:1 and "heavens" of 2 Peter 3 cannot be emphasized enough. 2 Peter 3 chronicles three distinct "heavens and earth." The first is identified in Gen. 1:1; the second is from Gen. 1:2 to the present ("**the heavens and earth which are now**"); and the "**new heavens and a new earth**" is yet future. The "heaven" of Gen. 1:1 is to be distinguished from the "heaven" of Gen. 1:8. The heaven of Gen. 1:8 is not said to be "good" (as the other creative days) because Satanic powers inhabit it (see Ephesians 6)!

It is also worthy to note that the creation of Gen. 1:1 is not spoken into existence as the rest of the "re-creation" is. The "creation" in the six days comes from things already there (see

Gen. 1:11,12 – Adam came from the ground, and Eve came out of Adam).

AN ARGUMENT

Some try to link the words "destroy," and "perish" as found in Gen. 6:7,13,17; 7:4; 9:11,15 with 2 Peter 3:6. Larkin said "the world of Noah's day did not perish,"[25] but the "earth" of Noah's day is said to be destroyed in Genesis. How much closer can you get to "perish," than the word "destroy?" 2 Peter 2 says that God "**spared not the old world, but saved Noah**" indicating a "perishing" of the "world" of Noah. Therefore, it seems plausible that the "world" that *perished* (mentioned in 2 Peter 3:6) was the old world prior to Noah's flood.

Several items are overlooked in that contention. First of all, the "old heavens" in 2 Peter 3 are said to be affected as well as the earth. The "heavens" were completely different in Gen. 1:1. They are said to be singular in number, and the earth was co-existing with the literal presence of God; instead of separated by the darkness (c.f. Matt. 27:45).

The context is the "beginning," and as pointed out previously, the flood of Noah was over 1700 years *after* "the beginning."

It is certainly acceptable to say that the world of Noah "perished." But it does not oblige 2 Peter 3 into the same flood. In the first flood of Gen. 1:2, the world "perished" along with the "heavens" (compare the future -Rev. 20:11). Only the physical globe was "destroyed" in Noah's day. The destruction of Gen. 1:2 was to such a magnitude that God had to re-create and restore the earth and the heavens to make it suitable for life. When the flood of Noah was finished, man's longevity of

---

[25] Larkin, *Dispensational Truth*, 24.

life was stunted (due to the atmospheric pressure change), but it did not require a re-making.

GAP PROOF 6:
If there is no gap, when did the devil fall, and sin enter the universe?

We concur with Hovind that "the timing of Satan's fall is extremely important to the integrity of the gap theory."[26] The question of the source of sin, and its entrance into the universe is most crucial to the gap, dispensationalism, and eschatology (the study of last-things). For, if you want to learn *why* things are happening *now*, and *what* is going to happen in the *future*, you must study the past.

When we look for answers from the so-called "prophecy experts" (like LaHaye and Pentecost) or the young earth creationists (like Morris, Whitcomb and Hovind) we come up empty. Although everyone forfeits the fact that Satan sinned and fell, *most* modern dispensationalists and *all* creation science evangelists, do NOT place his fall between Gen. 1:1 and 1:2.

Morris says that Satan was still sinless when Adam and Eve were created, that "he had been created to serve"[27] them. Hovind includes Satan and the angels in the phrase "**and all that in them is**" - Ex. 20:11) maintaining, "since everything was made in the six days, then obviously Satan was also made then."[28] Tim LaHaye and Thomas Ice (though they practically copied Larkin on most everything) reject the gap stating:

---

[26] Hovind; Lawwell, *Are there billions of years between Genesis1:1 & 1:2?*)
[27] *The Defenders Study Bible*, 11.
[28] Hovind; Lawwell, *Are there billions of years between Genesis1:1 & 1:2?*) (www.dr.dino.com)

> Satan and the angels were likely created during the six days of creation. . . . Satan fell somewhere between Genesis chapters 2 and 3.[29]

Disregarding the fact that Satan and the sons of God were said to be present *prior* to the "**foundations**" of the earth being laid (Job 38:6,7), Hovind asserts that Isaiah 14 disproves a Genesis 1:2 fall:

> Isaiah 14:14, records the words of Satan at the time of his fall - *"I will ascend above the heights of the clouds; I will be like the most High."* Since the clouds could not have formed prior to God's creation of water on day one, Satan fell after day one. Referring back to Job 38:4-7 that Satan was "shouting for joy" as the foundations were being laid, his fall must have occurred after day two or day three. Isaiah 14:13 also reveals to us that Satan's fall must have occurred after the creation of the "stars," which occurred on day four.[30] *[emphasis added]*

First of all, Hovind assumes Isaiah 14 refers to the past "casting out" of Satan, when it most likely refers to the *future*. Notice verse 16, where Lucifer is manifested in the flesh as a MAN: "**Is this the man.**" We are familiar with him in scripture as the "son of perdition," or the "seed" of the serpent (Gen. 3).

Second, notice that Hovind's logic assumes Satan could not fall until *after* the formation of "clouds." According to his own creation model, he has inadvertently placed the fall of Satan *after* Noah's flood! There were NO CLOUDS *during* the antedeluvian age!

---

[29] LaHaye, Tim, Ice, Thomas, *Charting the End Times* (Eugene, Oregon: Harvest House Publishers, 2001) 31.
[30] Hovind; Lawwell, *Are there billions of years between Genesis1:1 & 1:2?*) (www.dr.dino.com)

Gen 2:6 **But there went up a mist from the earth, and watered the whole face of the ground.**

Finally observe that the "stars" being present when Satan falls is no problem to the Bible believer. Stars were created in Genesis 1:1 ("heaven") *prior* to Satan falling.

If you follow this paradoxical analysis you wind up with a *sinless* Satan in the garden of Eden with Adam and Eve. Note Hovind: "The clues of Scripture confirm that Satan could not have possibly fallen until after day six."[31]

Since modern "creation scholarship" goes amiss from "the beginning" we must go to the scriptures:

A. Satan was created as **"the anointed cherub that covereth"** (Ezek. 28:14).

The word "anointed" is the same Hebrew word as "messiah." [This is why the Mormons claim that Jesus and Lucifer are brothers.] The fact of the matter is, Lucifer will manifest himself in the person of his "seed" (Gen. 3:15; 2 Thess. 2) as his "son," and is indeed another Christ (not equal though - Luke 2:26 - **"the Lord's Christ"**).

B. Satan was **"perfect"** (Ezek. 28) when he was created, and was the most powerful being in the universe outside of God Himself.

[Henry Morris failed to list the cross-references to "**holy mountain of God**" (Ex. 3:1; 1 Kings 19:8-11; Isa. 27:13; 2 Peter 1:18; Matthew 17:1). The "mountain" is "holy" (Ex. 3:5) long before Moses, Joshua, or even Christ touches it!] Satan was in charge of this world *prior* to the creation of man, and

---

[31] *Ibid.*

remains the "**god of this world**" (2 Cor. 4:4) possessing the power and control of "**the kingdoms of the world**" (Luke 4:5), until Jesus returns to take them back (Rev. 11:15). Notice the connection of Satan's musical instruments *in his body* (Ezek. 28). As the choir leader and full orchestra, Lucifer led the first congregational song on creation morning:

Job 38:7 **When the morning stars sang together, and all the sons of God shouted for joy?**

C. Satan indeed rebelled against God, and "**iniquity was found**" (Ezek. 28) in him.

Whether or not Isaiah 14, refers to this event is doubtful and debatable. Ezekiel 28 certainly does. Isaiah 14 more than likely refers to the future kingdom of Satan under the dominance of his seed, through the son of perdition (note "**man**" -Isa. 14:16). If Isaiah 14 does speak of time past, then it is correct to presuppose there were literal "**kingdoms**" (Isa. 14:16) and "**nations**" (Isa. 14:12) composed of (not humans) "sons of God." [Note the connection of "**son of the morning**" with "**morning stars,**" and "**sons of God.**"] It is favorable that the remains of such kingdoms are left behind in the structures of the pyramids (a phenomena of unexplainable proportions). The change in 2 Peter 3 from "earth" to "world" also indicates that there was a "system" in operation before Adam.

Revelation 12 is definitely a future reference, and has no bearing on our study of Satan's fall. The fact that most Bible teachers refer to Rev. 12 when teaching on Satan's fall demonstrates how influenced Christian scholarship is by the opinions of un-regenerated minds. No doubt Milton's *Paradise Lost* is responsible for much faulty Bible exposition.

D. This "**iniquity**" of Satan took place *before* Adam was created, and of necessity took place *prior* to the re-creation after Gen. 1:2.

The question as to why God made the Devil was answered by Larkin who said, "He did not make him, he made himself."[32] God is NOT a Calvinist. He might have *known* that Satan would fall, but He did not *cause* his fall.

It is also irrational to suppose Satan (along with the "sons of God" - Job 1,2; Gen. 6) sinned and the earth was not affected. Remember, there is "evil" in the *tree,* which grew "**out of the ground**" Gen. 1:9).

The fall of Satan must take place in Gen. 1:2. There is no other "time bracket" to place it in. If we are to be "workmen" of scripture, then we cannot force something that does not "work!" If you have Satan falling in the garden of Eden, there would be "evil" in the "tree of knowledge of good and **evil**" *before* Satan sinned!

The magnitude of Satan's fall calls for a Gen. 1:2 time placement. Satan was so powerful, that he caused the entrance of sin into the universe. This explains the division between the light and the darkness, and the glaring separation of God from His creation. If there was no gap, *why* did God separate the earth, and the "heavens" from Himself? Why did He plunge a perfect and sinless earth and universe into utter darkness when He created it? Answer: He did not. Even though the separation between God and man occurred in the garden of Eden, the separation of God, His earth, and the physical universe occurred in Gen. 1:2.

E. Sin, then, enters the universe through the fall of Satan, and effects the physical creation of Gen. 1:1.

---

[32] Larkin, Clarence, *Spirit World* (Glenside: Rev. Clarence Larkin Est., 1921) 12.

The fall of man, even though it influenced the earth's reproductive system of crops, and added thorns, weeds and thistles, did not affect the "**heavens and the earth**" (2 Peter 3) as the fall of Satan did. Are we to assume (like Whitcomb and Morris do) that the destructive evidence on the Moon, Mars, and other planets demonstrates a creative act? No, rather, it spells out destruction and disaster.

F. The earth was also impinged on by the fall of Satan.

The fact that "evil" existed in a tree, on the "perfect earth" should send up red flags. As pointed out earlier, it grew "**out of the ground**" (Gen. 2:9). Another glaring fact that refuses to go away is the timing of the creation of hell. If Gen. 1:2 is not connected with Satan's rebellion and fall, "pray tell me," *why* and *when* did God put hell in its core? [Hell *is* in the center of the earth: Job 28:5; Ps. 63:9; Isa. 14:9; Ezek. 31:14; Num. 16:33; Matt. 12:40 with Acts 2:27-31.]

Do the pieces of the puzzle fit together good enough to say that "hell" (that is inside the earth) was "**prepared for the devil and his angels?**" Although Matthew 25:41 points to "**everlasting fire,**" (c.f. "**the lake of fire**" – Rev. 20:10-15), do not forget that the "fire" *in* the lake of fire is said to be "**hell fire:**"

Mark 9:47-48
47 And if thine eye offend thee, pluck it out: it is better for thee to enter into the kingdom of God with one eye, than having two eyes to be cast into <u>hell fire</u>:
48 Where their worm dieth not, and the fire is not quenched.

[The student of scripture must be aware also, that there is "a" lake of fire on the earth during the Millennial Age. This "**burning pitch**" (Isa. 34:9) will be located south of the Dead Sea area. Jesus referred to this in Mark 9:47-48; Matt. 5:22 (where it is called "**hell fire**"); Matt. 5:30 and 10:28 (where a "body" can be put in there); Matt. 13:50; and Matt. 18:8. The detailed passages regarding the forming of this "lake of fire," and its timing are found in Isa. 30:30-33; 66:23-24; Rev. 19:19-20; 20:10. Notice that hell (in the center of the earth) *plus* "a lake of fire" *on the earth* (Rev. 19:19-20) are both cast into "**the lake of fire**" (Rev. 20:11-15.]

With regard to the study of geology, Genesis 1:2, is obviously the best "time frame" of the creation of hell *and* "hell fire." If there is "no gap," there is "no sense."

G. Another conspicuous truth involves the "**tree of life**."

Why would Adam and Eve need to partake of the tree of life, if they had not sinned, and there was no sin or *death* in the universe? There is no indication, however, that Adam and Eve ever ate of the tree of life. In fact, the contrary is noted: "**lest he put for his hand, and take also of the tree of life, and eat, and live for ever.**" (Gen. 3:22).

Was there physical death already in the universe, just not yet applicable to man? While Romans 5:12 tells us that "**death passed upon all men**" because of Adam, it does not tell us that death passed upon the living organisms such as trees, vegetation and animals. If the living trees, plants and "garden amenities" *were* subject to death, that would explain why Adam would have to "keep" the garden. Was there already a curse of some kind (not related to "thorns and thistles") on the earth *before* Adam? Whereas, the scriptures attribute sin *in the world* to Adam (Rom. 5:12), they say nothing about sin *in the earth*.

Do not forget that the tree of life shows up again in the Eternal Age (Rev. 22:2,14) *after* "death and hell" (and sin presumably) are in the lake of fire! There is more to Genesis 1:2 than meets the eye, or the comprehension.

THE ORIGINAL PLAN AND PURPOSE

Taking all the relevant Bible verses (registered above) in summary, this is the conclusion:

1. God created the heaven and the earth closely connected to His throne or abode (note the division and separation of the "light" from the "darkness" in Gen. 1). This **"beginning"** is different from **"the beginning of the creation"** (Mark 10:6). We have seen how the word "creation" many times refers to the "making" found in the six days, and not the "creation" of Genesis 1:1. There is a certain amount of "looseness" here. For, Adam and Eve were said to be made at the **"beginning of the creation"** (Mark 10:6), when in fact they were made on the sixth day – the end, or last day! So, there is a conspicuous distinction between **"the beginning"** in Genesis 1:1, and **"the beginning of the creation"** found in Genesis 1:3-31. Notice the reference to **"the beginning"** (Gen. 1:1) in Proverbs, that entails time *prior* to **"the beginning of the creation"** of the earth:

   Prov 8:23 **I was set up from everlasting, from the beginning, or ever the earth was.**

2. This creation included "morning stars," and "sons of God." These "sons of God" *could* be different than angels. Since they were a "male only species" they could not reproduce. They are mentioned in a good positive way

on the creation morning, but in a negative way *after* Gen. 1:2 (see Gen. 6 and Job 1,2 - they are with Satan).

3. Lucifer ("light bearer") was the "anointed one" that "covered," and had rule over this creation. The "kingdoms" of this pre-Adamite civilization were delivered to Satan, and he was the "king." He also once had the current job of every Christian alive today: *reflecting the light of the glory of God.* Read Ezek. 28!

4. Satan sinned, and was not merely "kicked out of heaven" (modern cliché), but his habitation itself was "destroyed." The expulsion of Satan and the sons of God (whether they first sinned with Satan, or only later in Gen. 6 is not clear) included a "drowning of the earth" in the great deeps (note: "the waters" of Gen. 1:3 are separate from the earth!).

5. After the fall of Satan and the FAILURE of this dispensation, God began anew with a "re-creation" of "**the heavens and the earth, which are now**" (2 Peter 3:7) and a new order: man.

6. This new "son of God" (Luke 3:38) was different than the previous "sons of God," in that he was made in God's image (Gen. 1:26).

7. This new "son of God" takes the "kingship" away from Satan, and was given "dominion" over the earth that Satan once ruled (Gen. 1:26).

8. He is different than the "sons of God" in the respect that he has a "better half" - Eve. He can reproduce "after his kind." The sons of God could not, prior to Gen. 6. When Eve is made from Adam she is named "Adam."

Gen 5:2 **Male and female created he them; and blessed them, and <u>called their name Adam,</u> in the day when they were created.**

9. Adam is given a commission to "**replenish**" what God had destroyed (implying most of the sons of God died, or were made incapable of reproducing), and given a tree of life to sustain this new population.

   a. BUT, when everything is going according as planned, Satan steps into the scene and deceives the woman ruining the possibility of a pure seed and through her, gets to Adam. Adam had a choice: Eve or God. He chose Eve, and the rest is history. The countless speculations are useless and vain. One thing is for certain. Satan wanted to corrupt the SEED, (seeds are in fruit too) and he did! Somehow, *now* he would have the capability of reproduction, through a "seed." Undoubtedly 1 John 3:12; 2 Cor. 11:3; and Ps. 109:14 are linked to this.

   b. Adam loses his shirt, (actually, he has to put one on) and the kingship (of the kingdom of heaven) returns to Satan who is called "the god of this world."

The Lord God Almighty will not be defeated though:

Acts 15:18 **Known unto God are all his works from the beginning of the world.**

The Lord promises to defeat the serpent and his seed with His *own* seed (Gen. 3:15). The "**only begotten**" Son of God comes into the world as THE "**image of God**" (2 Cor. 4:4; Heb. 1:3; Phil. 2:6; Col. 1:15) to restore the "image" that Adam lost. [Remember, Seth was in the image of Adam - Gen. 5:3.] He does this through reproduction of the spiritual seed (1 Pet. 1:23) with a spiritual bride (Rom. 7:4). These "sons of God" (John 1:11,12) will eventually be "manifested" (Rom. 8:19; 1 John 3:1-3) and return with their "elder brother" (Heb. 2); the "**first begotten of the dead**" (Rev. 1:5) to reclaim the kingdoms of this world (Rev. 11:15) and "**destroy the works of the devil**" (1 John 3:8).

Chapter 8

Edenic
&
Adamic

WHY EDEN?

The Edenic Covenant (dispensation of Innocence) was established in order to fix the problem of Gen. 1:2. God created "a new order - man," and decided to "replenish" the earth with a holy race of men rather than the "sons of God."

The teaching that Satan fell *after* the creation of man is inaccurate. Morris says, "His fall from heaven to the earth could only have been after God's universal 'very good' proclamation."[1] While Gen. 1:31 proclaims the "goodness" of the re-creation, it does not reverse the omission of "good" for day two. The negative connotation for the second day is implied because the "firmament" made on the second day is

---

[1] *The Defenders Study Bible* (Grand Rapids: Word, 1995) 8.

home to Satanic powers! For reference see: Job 41; Eph. 6; Col. 2; Ps. 74:13; and Isa. 24:21.

THE NATURE OF THE COVENANT

There is not much disagreement among dispensational authors as to the nature and content of the Edenic Covenant. Most understand that Adam was responsible for the following:

> (1) To replenish the earth with a new order - man; (2) to subdue the earth to human uses; (3) to have dominion over the animal creation; (4) to eat herbs and fruits; (5) to till and keep the garden; (6) to abstain from eating of the tree of knowledge of good and evil; (7) the penalty - death.[2]

Since the NSRB (1967ed.) changes "replenish" to "fill" in Gen. 1:28, and they remove Scofield's original note regarding Gen. 1:2 (in favor of the gap); they are forced to change his note under the Edenic Covenant. They alter "replenish the earth with a new order - man" to read: "to propagate the race."[3] Nothing could be further from the truth. So, changes in the new bibles *are* significant! In fact, modern versions read 100% opposite than the AV in Gen. 1:28. Consequently, they BEGIN the storyline *off track*. The devil wants to cover up something about the "seed" (see Gen. 6).

THE GOSPEL OF EDEN

Dispensationalists neglect to see that the "plan of salvation" in the Edenic Covenant was *pure* WORKS! Adam was NOT "**saved by grace through faith**" (Eph. 2)! His possessing eternal life was dependent upon his NOT EATING one tree,

---

[2] *Scofield Reference Bible* (New York: Oxford, 1909) 6.
[3] *New Scofield Reference Bible* (New York: Oxford, 1967) 5.

and EATING (works) another one. He did not even have an animal to sacrifice in order "to look forward to the cross."

What is the result of the first covenant? *"It was broke."* God commands Adam NOT to eat of the tree, he does, and he dies.

It is important to note that the edict pronouncing *physical* death was given *after* the fall of man:

> *Gen 3:19* **In the sweat of thy face shalt thou eat bread, till thou return unto the ground; for out of it wast thou taken: for dust thou art, and unto dust shalt thou return.**

The declaration of *death* specified prior to the fall (Gen. 2:17) was *spiritual*. This is confirmed because God told Adam that he would die on the very DAY that he ate of the forbidden fruit. We all know that he lived to be 930 years old (Gen. 5:5)! Since Adam died *spiritually,* all those **"in Adam"** (1 Cor. 15:22) have dead spirits, and **"must be born again"** (John 3:3) *spiritually* (John 3:6).

Overlapping the dispensation of Innocence (so named because Adam was created "innocent") is the commission to replenish. This is evident by the fact that marriage is a viable institution still established and verified for New Testament believers (see 1 Cor. 7; Heb. 13:4; Eph. 5). This commission is eventually carried out (after Rev. 21) with sinless bodies (unlike those of today) that must eat of the tree of life in eternity:

> *Rev 22:14* **Blessed are they that do his commandments, that they may have right to the tree of life, and may enter in through the gates into the city.**

Luke 1:33 **And he shall reign over the house of Jacob for ever; and of his kingdom there shall be no end.**

Isa 9:7 **Of the <u>increase</u> of his government and peace there shall be no end, upon the throne of David, and upon his kingdom, to order it, and to establish it with judgment and with justice from henceforth even for ever. The zeal of the LORD of hosts will perform this.**

THE ADAMIC COVENANT

While some dispensational teachers refuse to acknowledge the existence of the Adamic Covenant, since the word "covenant" is not used; *their definition* allows for an Adamic covenant to be identified: "A covenant is an agreement between two parties and represents relationships formed between God and man, man and man, or nation and nation."[4]

The Adamic Covenant relates to the result of the fall of man, and how specifically God deals with a sinful race of people. It is interesting, that while they *die*, they are not extinguished because God Himself purposed to be born through this "new order - man."

The dispensation of Conscience is so named because there was no written law to go by, and man had come "to a personal and experimental knowledge of good and evil."[5] If there is any doubt that conscience had entered, a close comparison of Gen. 2:25 with 3:10 will dispel these reservations. The word "conscience" means "with knowledge." There is an indication that God required a blood sacrifice during this "age." He *did* shed blood to clothe Adam and Eve, and evidently (see Gen. 4)

---

[4] "Covenants, The" *Dictionary of Premillennial Theology:* 72.
[5] *Scofield Reference Bible,* 10.

Cain and Able were aware of this concept. In this respect, salvation during this age, was by faith in the bloody animal sacrifice, and not of works. Cain's fruits (works) were not accepted.

According to Romans 2, this idea of conscience (with no law) has application to Gentiles during the time of the Age of the Law as well. Could it be that TWO separate dispensations can operate during the same *time period*? Well, in the Tribulation, there are TWO gospels preached. A "**gospel of the kingdom**" to the Jews, and "**the everlasting gospel**" to the Gentiles (Rev. 14). Also, during Christ's earthly ministry to the Jews, there were times when He moved out of his "dispensational bracket" toward the Gentiles (see Matt. 15:22-28; 12:18; John 12:20-22).

[Hypers stretch this line of reasoning in order to prove Peter and Paul preach two separate gospels at the same time. They differentiate between the "**gospel of the circumcision**," and the "**gospel of the uncircumcision**." We know that they are the SAME gospel, just preached to different groups because of the agreement at the council in Jerusalem. There, Peter himself granted that salvation was "**by grace through faith**," as Paul had been preaching (see Acts 15:11).]

We do know, according to Romans 2, the Gentiles during the Age of the Law were judged by their conscience. This was done, because they only had the "law written in their hearts":

> *Rom 2:14-15*
> **14 For when the Gentiles, which have not the law, do by nature the things contained in the law, these, having not the law, are a law unto themselves:**
> **15 Which shew the work of the law written in their hearts, their conscience also bearing witness, and their thoughts the mean while accusing or else excusing one another;)**

Notice that by the "works of the law" written in their hearts, they were justified:

> *Rom 2:13* **For not the hearers of the law are just before God, but the <u>doers of the law</u> shall be justified.**

COVENANT OVERLAPS

All covenants and dispensations have overlaps. [Like the overlaps of the Church Age (i.e. "churches" in the Great Tribulation).] The Adamic covenant contains much material that is still binding today:

1. The ground is still cursed.

2. Woman still labor in pain during childbirth.

3. The man is to be the head of the wife, even during the Church Age.

4. Men still die and return to the ground.

CORRUPTED SEED

This covenant lasted nearly 1700 years and climaxed with Satan and the sons of God attempting to "**mingle themselves with the seed of men**" (Dan. 2:43). This crazed obsession of Satan to corrupt the seed of man runs clear throughout scripture. Notice the tracing of this endeavor:

1. There *may* (notice "may") be an attempt to corrupt Adam's seed through Cain.

1 John 3:12 **Not as Cain, who was of that wicked one, and slew his brother. And wherefore slew he him? Because his own works were evil, and his brother's righteous.**

2 Cor 11:3 **But I fear, lest by any means, as the serpent beguiled Eve through his subtilty, so your minds should be corrupted from the simplicity that is in Christ.**

2. There is an obvious attempt to kill the seed of the woman in the murder of Abel, but God gives Seth.

3. The intermarriage of the sons of God with the daughters of men, would result in an offspring. The offspring would become a great army to go against the seed of the woman.

4. When Satan knew that the seed of the woman would come through Abraham, he supplanted the Canaanites in the promised land (Gen. 12:6).

5. He then went after Abraham through Hagar thwarting the assurance of a promised seed (Gen. 16:1-3).

Bullinger chronicles this "attempt of corruption" further:

- The destruction of the chosen family [was] by famine, (Gen. 50:20)
- The destruction of the male line in Israel [was another attempt], Ex. 1:10; 15. Cp. Ex. 2:5; Heb. 11:2.
- [Next was] [t]he destruction of the whole nation in Pharaoh's pursuit, Ex. 14.
- [Then] ... David's line was singled out (2 Sam. 7) . . . Satan's first assault was in the union of

Edenic and Adamic

Jehoram and Athaliah by Jehoshaphat, notwithstanding [2 Chron. 17:1] Jehoram killed off all his brothers (2 Chron. 21:4).

- ❖ The Arabians slew all his children, except Ahaziah (2 Chron. 21:17; 22:1).
- ❖ When Ahaziah died, Athaliah killed 'all the seed royal' (2 Chron. 22:10).
- ❖ Hezekiah was childless, when a double assault was made by the King of Assyria and the King of Terrors (Isa. 36:1; 38:1).
- ❖ In captivity Haman was used to attempt the destruction of the whole nation (Est. 3:6,12,13).
- ❖ Joseph's fear was worked on (Matt. 1:18-20). Notwithstanding the fact that he was 'a just man', and kept the Law, he did not wish to have Mary stoned to death (Deut. 24:1); hence Joseph determined to divorce her. But God intervened: 'Fear not.'
- ❖ Herod sought the young Child's life (Matt. 2).
- ❖ At the Temptation, 'Cast thyself down' was Satan's temptation [to destroy God's seed –Jesus Christ].
- ❖ At Nazareth, again (Lk 4), there was another attempt to cast Him down and destroy Him.
- ❖ The two storms on the Lake were other attempts [to annihilate the seed].
- ❖ At length the cross was reached, and the sepulcher closed; the watch set; and the stone sealed. But 'God raised him from the dead.'

The irruption of the 'fallen angels' .... was directed against the whole human race. When Abraham was called, then he and his seed were attacked. When David was enthroned, then the royal line was assailed. And when 'the Seed of the woman' Himself came, then the storm burst upon Him.[6] **[words in brackets added]**

---

[6] "Appendix 23," *Companion Bible*: Grand Rapids: Kregel, 1990

THE SONS OF GOD

During the Adamic Covenant, one of the causes of the judgment of Noah's flood, was the intermarrying of the "sons of God" and the "daughters of men." To assume as Scofield, that the "sons of God" were "the godly line of Seth" hides the purpose of God (Eph. 2) and veils eschatological information related to the Antichrist, the ten kings, and the current interest in cloning and genetics. Scofield states:

> Some hold that these "sons of God" were the "angels which kept not their first estate" (Jude 6). It is asserted that the title is in the Old Testament exclusively used of angels. But this is an error (Isa. 43:6). Angels are spoken of in a sexless way. No female angels are mentioned in Scripture, and we are expressly told that marriage is unknown among angels (Matt. 22:30). The uniform Hebrew and Christian interpretation has been that verse 2 marks the breaking down of the separation between the godly line of Seth and the godless line of Cain, and so the failure of the testimony to Jehovah committed to the line of Seth (Gen. 4:26).[7]

In answer to Scofield's popular note:

1. The verse that Scofield used (Isa. 43:6) is not relevant to the topic at all. For, as Ruckman points out:

> The "sons and daughters" of Isa. 43 are all Israelites, not Pre-Deluge sons of Seth! Seth had plenty of descendants who were not Israelites.[8]

The phrase in Isa. 43:6 is not even the same as Gen. 6. "Sons and daughters" are hardly "sons of God." Gen. 6

---

[7] *Scofield Reference Bible*, 13.
[8] Ruckman, Peter S., *Genesis* (Pensacola: Bible Believers Press, 1969) 175.

Edenic and Adamic **255**

makes the clear distinction by using the expression "daughters of men."

2. The verses that mention the "sons of God" identify them as NOT the sons of Seth! See: Gen. 6:2; Gen. 6:4; Job 1:6; Job 2:1; Job 38:7. Were Seth's sons (or *any* "godly line") present with the Devil *in heaven* arguing about Job?

3. Angels are NOT "spoken of in a sexless way." They are always identified as MALE: Gen. 18:1,2; 19:1,5,8,10,15; Gal. 4:14; Acts 27:23; Rev. 21:17; Judg. 13; Acts 1:10; Luke 24:4,23.

4. Angels do not marry, not because they are "sexless," but because marriage is impossible between the members of the same sex (unless you live in America). Larkin affirms:

> Angels as far as we know were created "en masse," and as they are immortal, and never die, there is no necessity for marriage among them. Marriage is a human institution to prevent the extinction of the race by death."[9]

It is also worthy of notice, that "the teaching that angels 'cannot reproduce' is arrived at by changing the reading in Matthew 22:30 to omit the words 'in heaven.'"[10] Angels *have* reproduced ON EARTH, and will in the future (Dan. 2). Why do you think the Antichrist is called, " the **son of** perdition." He will be "born" by a reproductive act of Satan!

5. Scofield claimed his interpretation was "uniform," even though there were many well-known writers before him

---

[9] Larkin, Clarence, *Spirit World* (Glenside: Rev. Clarence Larkin Est., 1921) 27.
[10] Ruckman, *Genesis*, 176.

who held the "Angelic Interpretation." Larkin (1850-1924), Bullinger (1837-1913), and Pember (1876) did not *invent* this teaching. Furthermore, there is no "godly line" mentioned *anywhere* in scripture.

6. How can Seth be a "godly line" when he bears the image of Adam, and not God. For, no one was "born again" in the Old Testament. Every unsaved man is in the image of Adam (Rom. 5:12). When a person is born again (male or female) they have the image of God restored to them. The image of God is Jesus Christ Himself: Heb. 1:3; 2 Cor. 4:4. Man was created in the "**image of God**" but lost this image. Hence Seth retains "Adam's image." Note:

> *Gen 5:3* **And Adam lived an hundred and thirty years, and begat a son in his own likeness, after his image; and called his name Seth:**

Scampering to Gen. 9:6 ("**image of God**") to prove that mankind is still in the image of God is erroneous. Gen. 9:6 refers back to the original creation of man, and is not a doctrinal record of *current* men. Otherwise the tense of the verb would be in the present instead of *past!*

7. If the "sons of God" were the "godly line of Seth" how could their intermarriage with women produce GIANTS? Some, like McGee, deliberately teach contrary:

> I do not know why it is assumed by so many that the offspring were giants . . . It says, "There were giants in the earth in those days," but it does not say they are the offspring of the sons of God and the daughters of men. . . The record makes it clear that the giants were in the earth

before this took place, and it simply means that these offspring were outstanding individuals.[11]

Even the NSRB board understood that the intermarriage produced giants as offspring! The verse plainly states *how* the giants were produced: **"when the sons of God came into the daughters of men."** McGee does not even see the magnitude of them being called "sons of God." He assumes "evil angels could never be designated as 'sons of God.'"[12] They are called "sons of God" so you would *know* that they are not HUMAN. In fact, the term "son of God" is not used in relation to a *man* anywhere in the Old Testament! He could have said "evil angels" (if they indeed are the "angels" of Jude and 2 Peter); but He identified them as God's children (evil or not):

Ps 82:6-7
6 I have said, Ye are gods; and all of you are children of the most High.
7 But ye shall die like men, and fall like one of the princes.

The overall *purpose* of God has been distorted by those who proliferate Scofield's faulty view. Ruckman fittingly expounds:

> God's original purpose was to populate an infinite universe with a people "made in his image," subject to Him as Almighty Sovereign. This first trial ends in Gen. 1:2 with a rebellion of these spiritual beings and a recreation and re-commission for man ["made lower than the angels"] to begin the work anew. This trial ends in Genesis 3:1-13.[13]

---

[11] McGee, J. Vernon, *Thru the Bible with J. Vernon McGee Vol. 1* (Pasadena: Thru the Bible Radio, 1983) 36, 37.
[12] *Ibid.*, 36.
[13] Ruckman, Peter S., *Charts and Outlines* (Pensacola: Bible Believers Press, 1997) 3.

OTHER NOTES OF INTEREST

Other study material of import (skipping over the "norm") relating to the Adamic Covenant would include:

1. Other representatives from Satan's original class (called cherubim) were on the earth, along with the sons of God. They remained on the earth guarding the tree of life up to the time of the flood.

   Gen 3:24 **So he drove out the man; and he placed at the east of the garden of Eden Cherubims, and a flaming sword which turned every way, to keep the way of the tree of life.**

   The Bible often delves deep into the realm of "other life forms." The books of Daniel and Revelation contribute much to this multifaceted subject.

2. This "paradise" (the garden of Eden) may have been relocated to the center of the earth (Abraham's bosom) until *after* the resurrection of Christ.

   Luke 23:43 **And Jesus said unto him, Verily I say unto thee, To day shalt thou be with me in paradise.**

   2 Cor 12:4 **How that he was caught up into paradise, and heard unspeakable words, which it is not lawful for a man to utter.**

   2 Cor 12:2 **I knew a man in Christ above fourteen years ago, (whether in the body, I cannot tell; or whether out of the body, I cannot tell: God** knoweth;) such an one caught up to the third heaven.

Ezek 31:18 **To whom art thou thus like in glory and in greatness among the trees of Eden? yet shalt thou be brought down with the trees of Eden unto the nether parts of the earth: thou shalt lie in the midst of the uncircumcised with them that be slain by the sword. This is Pharaoh and all his multitude, saith the Lord GOD.**

3. Capitol punishment for death is NOT instituted during this covenant. In Gen. 4:11,12 Cain is merely penalized from farming, and becomes a vagabond (although he builds a city - Gen. 4:16,17). [The assumption that Cain and Abel were twins is not necessarily biblical. See Gen. 38:3-5 where duplicate phrases are used and one son (Shelah - Gen.38:12) is considerably younger than the others.]

4. During this Adamic Covenant the "**presence of the Lord**" (Gen. 4:16) is still abiding on the earth (possibly close to the cherubim). See: Gen. 3:8, 24; 4:16, 26.

5. During the Adamic Covenant men lived noticeably *longer* than in any other covenant. This may be a result of the atmospheric conditions (no rain, just a "mist" - Gen. 2:6). Their diet (men were to only eat fruits and vegetables) obviously did not require the minerals that animal flesh now provides after the flood. It is also highly possible that the longevity of life also applied to animals. If certain lizards and other reptilian creatures lived to be over two and three hundred years old, would they be as large as dinosaurs? Obviously Noah would only take the small ones on the Ark.

THE FLOOD

The "set-up" during the Adamic Covenant ends with the destruction of the earth (Gen. 6:13) by water *the second time.* This time, all flesh (except Noah and his family) that breathed died, along with the "sons of God."

[The suggestion that Gen. 9:11 "mentions two previous floods; one of which cut off 'all flesh,' the other of which destroyed the earth itself"[14] is incorrect. Gen. 6:13 states that one of the purposes of Noah's flood *was* to destroy the earth.]

Voluminous information can be obtained regarding Noah's flood, legitimizing the biblical record, and defending the historical and scientific accuracy of the account. It is incompetent for anyone to claim that the biblical explanation is not scientific. Suffice it to say that the flood dramatically changed civilization, and left its marks all over the globe.

---

[14] Tibbetts, Jeffrey A., *Genesis 1:1-3* (Pensacola: Tibbetts Publications, 1997) 59.

CHAPTER 9

Noahic & Abrahamic

STARTING OVER AGAIN

God's second plan to "repeople" the earth through one man, begins after the flood, with Noah. As pointed out earlier, Noah and Adam parallel each other in that (among several) they both follow a flood, have three named sons, and both get in trouble *naked* in a garden with *forbidden fruit*.

Noah nonetheless is called a **"preacher of righteousness,"** and is chosen because he is **"righteous"** before God (Gen. 7:1). Noah is a righteous man, not purely because he sacrificed animals (Gen. 4, 8) but because he OBEYED God (works) by doing what *He said.*

Compare to the Mosaic Covenant, where God's mercy is NOT by faith, but by works:

Ps 103:17-18 **But the mercy of the LORD is from everlasting to everlasting upon them that fear him . . . To such as <u>keep his covenant</u>, and to those that remember his commandments <u>to do</u> them.**

NOAH'S SALVATION

Some assume Noah's obedience only led to his physical salvation. This is an error. God said that Noah was "righteous," while those who perished were "ungodly" (2 Peter 2:5). Noah's righteousness is even attributed to HIM (Ezek. 14:14), not to God, or Christ (as in Rom. 10). This connection between the physical *and* spiritual salvation of Old Testament saints, "confounds the wise" (1 Cor. 1:27). If you disconnect the two, then you could say that some of the "ungodly" who drowned *physically*, may have been *spiritually* saved. [See notes and comments under Ezekiel 18.] Pentecost boldly alleges this dogma:

> Noah was a preacher of righteousness (2 Peter 2:5) who evidently proclaimed a coming judgment and exhorted people to escape by offering them salvation through faith.[1]

Noah did not preach "salvation through faith." He preached salvation through a BOAT! Granted, Noah had to have faith in what God said (Heb. 11:7) but the *visible* ark was their way of "salvation." Noah did not have his faith in the finished work of Jesus Christ, nor did he preach it. His faith was in God's warning (the words "dispensed" to him) of a FLOOD! That is NOT the same "gospel" we preach today!

---

[1] Pentecost, J. Dwight, *Thy Kingdom Come* (Grand Rapids: Kregel, 1995) 43-44.

The Noahic Covenant gets underway with a visible SIGN, in the form of a rainbow, and sets up the dispensation of Human Government. A few changes that are noticeable are:

1. Man's relationship to the animals is definitely different. Now, men can EAT animals (Gen. 9:3). This continues up to, but not during the Millennial Age.

2. Capitol punishment is instituted (Gen. 9:5). This carries on through the rest of the "ages," until death and sin are eliminated. [For a Jehovah's Witness, or a Mennonite to assert that warfare is identical to "murder" exhibits their inability to compare scripture with scripture. Jesus defines **"Thou shalt not kill"** as **"murder"** and NOT warfare in Matt. 19:18. God Himself commanded the "killing" of thousands of "innocents" in the Old Testament. That was warfare, *not* murder.]

3. The grouping of *three* distinct "races" of people is outlined with Noah, and the dispensation of Human Government. Under this covenant the prophecy of Noah regarding slavery was honored and blessed by God. This arrangement was considered viable and "fair" under both Testaments. See: Lev. 27, and 1 Tim. 6.

THE LEGS OF "PELEG" & TOWER OF BABEL

Between the calling of Noah and the calling out of Abraham, the Bible (as it often does - see Gen. 1:16) seems to "underestimate" a dramatic event; an event proportionate to that of the flood.

Gen 10:25 **And unto Eber were born two sons: the name of one was Peleg; for in his days <u>was the earth divided</u>; and his brother's name was Joktan.**

Here are the cross-references:

1 Chron 1:19 **And unto Eber were born two sons: the name of the one was Peleg; because in his days the earth was divided: and his brother's name was Joktan.**

Deut 32:7-8
**7 Remember the days of old, consider the years of many generations: ask thy father, and he will shew thee; thy elders, and they will tell thee.
8 When the most High divided to the nations their inheritance, when he separated the sons of Adam, he set the bounds of the people according to the number of the children of Israel.**

Acts 17:26 **And hath made of one blood all nations of men for to dwell on all the face of the earth, and hath determined the times before appointed, and the bounds of their habitation;**

In view of the fact that Gen. 1:9 only recognizes ONE land mass, and the people in Babel could not be "scattered" across the oceans, there must have been a time (or "days") when the continents were separated. If you look at a map you can easily notice how neatly the continents would fit together like a puzzle.

Whether or not this division in Gen. 10 refers to that *is* questionable. If this is indeed the supposed "continental drift theory" promoted by Alfred Wagner, does it make sense that three chapters (Gen. 6-9) would have been given to the flood, while only a few verses to this event (which is as great, or of *greater* magnitude)? Ruckman:

> Two verses to describe the shift of four continents, plus islands, does not seem to be the tenor of Genesis 6-9, which has just taken three chapters to describe a flood.[2]

We are reminded, though, how the Bible nonchalantly cites extraordinary events and outstanding occasions (i.e. the miracles of Jesus).

Morris supposes that this "dividing of the earth" refers to Babel, and not the "drift theory:"

> It should be remembered, however, that the continental drift hypotheses has by no means been proved, and the verse seems to refer more directly to the division into families countries and languages. Furthermore, even if the continents have separated from a single primeval continent, such a split more likely would have occurred in connection with the continental uplifts terminating the global deluge (Psalm 104:6-9).[3]

Since there is an allowance for the chronology of Gen. 10 to follow the events of chapter eleven (given that chapter ten is registering genealogies); the above argument is credible. Especially since sometimes the word "earth" *is* used to signify the population, and not simply the land mass:

Gen 11:1 **And the whole earth was of one language, and of one speech.**

It is strange, however, that the division at Babel would be

---

[2] Ruckman, Peter S., *Genesis* (Pensacola: Bible Believers Press, 1969) 286.
[3] *The Defenders Study Bible* (Grand Rapids: Word, 1995) 31.

identified with one man - Peleg. For that matter, it seems bizarre that the busting up of the land mass would be connected to one man. What is momentous about "his days?" [If you run to Gen. 6:3 for "his days" it will not yield much insight.]

So, whether or not the division took place at Babel, or the flood, it took place as a result of God's judgment. God, is a God of *division, separation, and segregation.* See: Deut. 32:7, 8; Isa. 5:8; Luke 12:51; 2 Cor. 5:14-17. Until **"God may be all in all"** (1 Cor. 15:28) He will continue to bust up, separate, and divide:

> *Gen 1:4* **And God saw the light, that it was good: and God divided the light from the darkness.**

The "one world" movement of the tower of Babel illustrates perfectly the Laodicean Age in which we live. We have come from the "evil imagination" (Gen. 6) to "no restraint" in "imagination:"

> *Gen 11:6* **And the LORD said, Behold, the people is one, and they have all one language; and this they begin to do: and now nothing will be restrained from them, which they have imagined to do.**

The connection between Nimrod (Gen. 10:9,10), Babel, and the future Antichrist at "mystery Babylon" should not be ignored. The word "Babel" first rears its ugly head in Gen. 10:10. Ten is the number of the Gentiles. The last Gentile world power will consists of 10 kings, represented by the 10 toes of Daniel chapter two.

THE ABRAHAMIC COVENANT

When you arrive at Genesis twelve, there is a distinct change of events. God selectively calls out *one man* (Abram) and promises to bless or curse the world through him, and his descendents. Ryrie points out that "the title Promise comes from Heb. 6:15 and 11:9, where it is said that Abraham obtained the promise and sojourned in the land of promise."[4]

The promises are *unconditional and everlasting:*

> *Judg 2:1* **And an angel of the LORD came up from Gilgal to Bochim, and said, I made you to go up out of Egypt, and have brought you unto the land which I sware unto your fathers; and I said, <u>I will never break my covenant with you</u>.**

> *Gen 17:7-8*
> **7 And I will establish my covenant between me and thee and thy seed after thee in their generations <u>for an everlasting covenant</u>, to be a God unto thee, and to thy seed after thee.**
>
> **8 And I will give unto thee, and to thy seed after thee, the land wherein thou art a stranger, all the land of Canaan, <u>for an everlasting possession</u>; and I will be their God.**

The unconditional nature of this covenant is evident by the blood covenant where only God "passes through the pieces" (Gen. 15:17) instead of both parties (see Gen. 31 - Jacob and Laban). The covenant relates to a physical piece of land. See:

---

[4] Ryrie, Charles C., *Dispensationalism* (Chicago: Moody Press, 1995) 53.

Gen. 13:16,17; 15:7,8; 22:17. This land grant was given to Abraham, Isaac, and Jacob (Israel), no matter what the U.N. or the Muslim world thinks of it. The land promised to Abraham and his "seed" (Gen. 12:7; 13:15,16; 15:5) stretches from Kadesh (below Tamar) over to the Mediterranean, up to Hamath, over to the Euphrates and all the way down to Ur (see Ezek. 46-48). The current return of the Jews to *part* of their land, falls under the restoration in *unbelief* (Ezek. 20:33-38; 22:17-22; 36:22-24; Isa. 11-12; Zeph. 2:1-2; Ezek. 38-39); while the Millennial Age will satisfy God's promise in full to Abraham and his seed. For a restoration *before* the Millennium see: Deut. 4:29-31; 30:1-10; Isa. 27:12-13; 43:5-7; Jer. 16:14-15; 31:7-10; Ezek. 11:14-18; Amos 9:14-15; Zech. 10:8-12; Matt. 24:31.

CIRCUMCISION – THE SIGN

Abraham is given the sign of "circumcision," as an outward, visible sign of the covenant. This "sign" relates to the "seed," because it is a cutting away of the *reproductive* organ. [The problem with Adam was *his* seed; hence "**her seed**."] A new "race" is born, and *typifies* a new race of "sons of God" by the new birth. The New Testament epitomizes this by an *operation* called "**the circumcision of Christ**," where the old man is "cut off." [The idea that water baptism replaces this Jewish rite is ludicrous. If that were the case, only *males* could be baptized!] To clarify that the "land of promise" (Heb. 11:9) is not ascribed to everyone who is circumcised (Ishmael for example), God names Isaac, Jacob and their seed exclusively:

> *Gen 50:24* **And Joseph said unto his brethren, I die: and God will surely visit you, and bring you out of this land unto the land which he <u>sware to Abraham, to Isaac, and to Jacob.</u>**

Satan, *knowing* God's plan, endeavors to corrupt this seed again (with a Hamite - Hagar) and doubtless had a role in the attempt of Isaac's life by Abraham (c.f. the book of Job, where God "tries" Job because of Satan's accusations). Isaac lives and the seed continues to Jacob and his twelve sons, where famine tries its hand at destroying the pure seed. The dispensation of Promise (or the dispensation of the Patriarchs) ends with Egyptian bondage.

ABRAHAM'S SALVATION

The *excepting* examples of God's grace on Abraham and David have instigated more "saved the same" rhetoric, than any other examples in the Old Testament. Observe Tabb's remarks:

> Some argue that because Abraham was before law he was under grace. That is true: he was before law. But the law is right in this same passage of Romans chapter four, and David under law is shown to have been saved exactly the same way in which Abraham was.[5]

Tabb does not understand that the imputed righteousness given to Abraham was based on his "belief," while his justification came later when he offered his son (James 2). Romans 4 and James 2 are talking about *two* separate events. "Paul draws his illustration from Gen. 15:6; James from Gen. 22:1-19."[6] The "justification" in Rom. 4 relates to his "belief" (Gen. 14); while James 2 assures us his *works* "justified" him.

Any effort to force Abraham's salvation experience to match yours is a misrepresentation of scripture. When you were saved, you were justified *and* given imputed

---

[5] Tabb, M.H. *Dispensational Salvation* (Ft. Walton Beach, Fl: Foundation Ministries, 1991) 6.
[6] *Scofield Reference Bible* (New York: Oxford, 1909) 1196.

righteousness (Rom. 4) AT THE SAME TIME. Abraham was not!

Sure, Abraham was given righteousness by belief. But *what* did he believe? Did he believe that "Christ died for our sins" (1 Cor. 15:1-4)? Of course not! He believed what God told him (that He would multiply his seed) so God imputed righteousness to him. Just because an Old Testament saint is given righteousness does not mean his salvation matches ours! Phinehas had righteousness counted ("imputed") to him because he stabbed and killed two fornicators (Ps. 106:30,31; Num. 25:7)!

There are admonitions in the Old Testament that typify our salvation, but Paul only uses these to develop New Testament doctrine as different from Old Testament doctrine. The very fact that Paul had to clarify the difference in works and faith demonstrated the *understood* change in God's arrangement (dispensation). The entire book of Galatians expresses this.

CHAPTER 10

Mosaic & Davidic

A NATION WITH LAWS

The next great division in scripture surfaces with the emergence of Israel as a nation. Even though God's "commandments," "statutes," and "laws" were said to be kept by Abraham (Gen. 26:5); the Mosaic Law was formulated because of the disobedience of Israel as a corporate nation (Ezek. 20:8-11). **"It was added because of transgressions"** (Gal. 3:19).

WHAT IS "THE LAW?"

What we call the Mosaic Law entails not only social laws (how to treat your neighbor), but religious laws (how to approach unto God). The idea that the dietary, ceremonial, and moral laws should be distinct and separated, leads to error and possible heresy. The ill-advised Seventh-Day Adventists are guilty of this.[1] Notice, that *all of it* is called "the law:"

1. The ceremonial ordinances of Leviticus 1 are called "the law" in Hebrews 9:19.

2. The Old Covenant, called "**the first covenant**" is said to include, not only sacrifices but dietary laws:

   Heb 9:1 **Then verily the first covenant had also ordinances of divine service, and a worldly sanctuary.**

   Heb 9:9-10
   **9 Which was a figure for the time then present, in which were offered both gifts and sacrifices, that could not make him that did the service perfect, as pertaining to the conscience;
   10 Which stood only in <u>meats and drinks</u>, and divers washings, and carnal ordinances, imposed on them until the time of reformation.**

3. Breaking the sabbath day, is considered breaking "the law."

   Matt 12:5 **Or have ye not read in the law, how that on the sabbath days the priests in the temple profane the sabbath, and are blameless?**

   If one broke this "moral law," they were to be put to death (Num. 15:33-35)!

---

[1] Marcussen Jan A., *National Sunday Law* (Thompsonville, Il: Amazing Truth Publications, 1996) 89.

4. The social aspect of "the law," loving God and neighbor is considered "the law:"

Matt 22:36-40
36 Master, which is the great commandment in <u>the law</u>?
37 Jesus said unto him, Thou shalt love the Lord thy God with all thy heart, and with all thy soul, and with all thy mind.
38 This is the first and great commandment.
39 And the second is like unto it, Thou shalt love thy neighbour as thyself.
40 On these <u>two commandments hang all the law</u> and the prophets.

5. The sabbath day is considered a "moral," and a "ceremonial" law. Notice in Leviticus 19 (the "ceremonial law") that the law written in STONE (the "moral law") is included:

Lev 19:3 **Ye shall fear every man his mother, and his father, and <u>keep my sabbaths</u>: I am the LORD your God.**

So, whether you have a "ceremonial law," "moral law," or "dietary law," they are all included as "the law!" This "law of Moses" covers massive territory, and is *totally* done away with (regarding salvation) under the Church Age:

Eph 2:15 **Having abolished in his flesh the enmity, even the law of commandments contained in ordinances; for to make in himself of twain one new man, so making peace;**

Col 2:14 **Blotting out the handwriting of ordinances that was against us, which was contrary to us, and took it out of the way, nailing it to his cross;**

Col 2:20-22
**20 Wherefore if ye be dead with Christ from the rudiments of the world, why, as though living in the world, are ye subject to ordinances,
21(Touch not; taste not; handle not;
22 Which all are to perish with the using;) after the commandments and doctrines of men?**

Heb 8:13 **In that he saith, A new covenant, he hath made the first old. Now that which decayeth and waxeth old is ready to vanish away.**

The law then, was Jewish in nature, and the Gentile was to follow his conscience during this "period of time" (see Romans 2:12-15). While Paul rightly states "**no man is justified by the law in the sight of God,**" (Gal. 3:11) he also states that, "**the doers of the law shall be justified**" (Rom. 2:13). The explanation for this supposed contradiction is simple. Romans chapter two is dealing with the Old Testament "period of time" when men were declared outwardly "righteous" (see Zacharias - Luke 1:5,6) and consequently were "justified" by being a "**doer of the law.**" Galatians chapter three concerns *this age*. If a man *today* attempts to be "**justified by the law,**" he will "fall from grace," and go to hell. The entire book of Galatians illuminates this.

The Mosaic Law also built upon the foundation of the Abrahamic Covenant regarding the promises to enter the land. The difference is that the promises in Deuteronomy were conditional upon obedience, whereas the promises to Abraham,

Isaac, and Jacob were not. These "conditional promises" have been termed by some as the "Palestinian Covenant." See: Deut. 28-30 and Lev. 26:14-39.

THE CAPTIVITIES AND DISPERSION

Concerning the disobedience of the Mosiac Law, captivity was impending. The northern tribes (10 in number) were carried away captive to Assyria in the eighth century B.C. and the southern tribes were taken to Babylon in the sixth century B.C. This captivity, though foretold countless times (through the prophets Isaiah and Jeremiah especially) is not to be confused with the dispersion of the Jews as a result of their rejection of the Messiah (A.D. 70 - Luke 21:20-24). The Jews did return (partly) under Ezra and Nehemiah, but the re-gathering in unbelief began *after* 1918 with the signing of the *Balfour Declaration*.

The Mosaic Law dispensation runs approximately 1500 years and becomes corrupted (by religious groups such as the Pharisees, Saducees, Herodians, and Essenes) prior to the time of Christ' earthly ministry. As elaborated on earlier, the Law was still in effect during Christ days (Matt. 5:17), but was in a "transitory form," preparing the way for the "new wine" (Matt. 9:17).

THE DAVIDIC COVENANT

Under the Davidic Covenant the dispensation of the Law was still under operation. There were, nonetheless, certain "enhancements" the Davidic Covenant made in relation to the kingdom of heaven.

1. David's seed was to build a temple and "establish the kingdom" (2 Sam. 7:12).

2. Eternal security was a guarantee given in this covenant, not given anywhere else in the Mosaic Law (2 Sam. 7:14,15). This "eternal life" applied directly to David's "seed" (possibly Solomon), and found fulfillment in Jesus Christ (who was promised eternal life - Titus 1:2 with Ps. 21:4).

3. The "**throne of David**" would continue forever. "Progressive dispensationalists" have David's throne in heaven with no literal one in Jerusalem. They think just because Jesus is sat down in heaven, that He sat on a throne. The scriptures teach that Jesus is "**set on the right hand of the throne**" (Heb. 8:1), not on the throne itself! See: Rom. 8:34; Eph. 1:20; Col. 3:1; Heb. 4:14; 10:12; 12:2; and 1 Peter 3:22.

CORRUPTION

The crisis of the apostasy in the southern kingdom, culminated with a wicked king named Jehoiakim. He was so wicked that he destroyed the inspired word of God (Jer. 36:23), so God gave him a "**burial of an ass**" (Jer. 22:19), and cursed his seed (Coniah, also called Jehoiachin):

Jer 22:29-30
29 O earth, earth, earth, hear the word of the LORD.
30 Thus saith the LORD, Write ye this man childless, a man that shall not prosper in his days: for no man of his seed shall prosper, sitting upon the throne of David, and ruling any more in Judah.

INCENTIVE FOR VIRGIN BIRTH

The previous passage shows the importance of the virgin birth of Jesus Christ. For, if Christ had been born of the "seed" of Joseph (which traced back to David through Conaih), He would have been disqualified. Jesus Christ "**was made of the seed of David according to the flesh**" (Rom. 1:3), but it was through Mary's *fleshly* lineage, and God's *spiritual* lineage that made the kingship of Christ possible.

The promise of the Davidic Covenant will be fulfilled literally as outlined by Gabriel to Mary:

> *Luke 1:32-33*
> **32 He shall be great, and shall be called the Son of the Highest: and the Lord God shall give unto him the throne of his father David:**
> **33 And he shall reign over the house of Jacob for ever; and of his kingdom there shall be no end.**

This literal, physical, visible, throne will be in Jerusalem, and is also called the "**throne of his glory**" (Matt. 19:28; 25:21), and "**David's throne**" (Acts 2:29,30). It is imperative that the reference to Christ sitting on a throne in Rev. 3:21 is either future, or a reference to the close of the Church Age, when He finishes the intercessory work (Heb. 7:25). This "throne" in Rev. 3:21 cannot be David's throne because it is in heaven and is said to be God's!

Because Jesus wore the "**crown of thorns**" (from dead wood – corruptible) instead of the kingly crown (from gold – representing deity – incorruptible); the Davidic Covenant awaits fulfillment in the Millennial Kingdom Age. Notice "**now**" in John 18:36:

John 18:36 **Jesus answered, My kingdom is not of this world: if my kingdom were of this world, then would my servants fight, that I should not be delivered to the Jews: but <u>now</u> is my kingdom not from hence.**

DAVID'S SALVATION

David is the second outstanding exception of Old Testament salvation because he deserved to DIE according to the Law. Grace was shown to David, not because he was "**saved by grace through faith**" in the finished work of Christ, but because God had given him "**sure mercies.**"

Isa 55:3 **Incline your ear, and come unto me: hear, and your soul shall live; and I will make an everlasting covenant with you, even the <u>sure mercies of David.</u>**

Ps 89:20, 24 **. . . I have found David my servant; with my holy oil have I anointed him . . . . But my faithfulness and <u>my mercy shall be with him</u>: and in my name shall his horn be exalted.**

2 Sam 12:13 **And David said unto Nathan, I have sinned against the LORD. And Nathan said unto David, <u>The LORD also hath put away thy sin</u>; thou shalt not die.**

Moreover, David understood that he could have LOST his salvation: "**take not thy holy spirit from me**" (Ps. 51:11). That does NOT match Church Age salvation at all.

Chapter 11

New Covenant & Beyond

"Line Upon Line"

With the study of the New Covenant, the "workman" of scripture learns what Solomon meant when he said: "**much study is a weariness of the flesh**" (Eccl. 12:12). The student also discovers that the Bible is not a systematic book, like many dispensational charts and outlines *seem* to indicate. It certainly does not "divide" up as easily as the hypers would have you to believe. One good example is found in Isa. 65:17-20, where the "sinless" new heavens and earth are mentioned, alongside of earthly Jerusalem (said to have been "created") that contains "accursed sinners." If you fail to "rightly divide" the Millennial Jerusalem from the New Jerusalem, you wind up with sin in eternity. I have heard *that* taught.

TWO APPLICATIONS

While some dispensationalists contend that there are "two new covenants"[1] (Lewis Sperry Chafer); and some, insist that "the church has no relationship to the new covenant"[2] (Darby); the fact remains that the New Covenant has a "dual nature"[3] valid for Israel *and* the Church.

The Dictionary of Premillennial Theology defines the New Covenant as:

> an administrative covenant promised to Israel by God, during the late precipice and exilic periods, as the instrument that would govern the nation's spiritual and political life during the future messianic kingdom.[4]

It also points out that "the full realization of the covenant remains future."[5]

"TO THE JEW FIRST"

The fact that the New Covenant relates *primarily* to Israel is unmistakable. Ryrie documents, the following promises, of the New Covenant (first announced in Jer. 31), pointing out the Jewish distinctive:

> (1) putting God's law into Israelites' hearts; (2) no necessity to teach His people; (3) forgiveness of Israel; (4) Israel restored to favor and guaranteed everlasting existence; (5) God's Spirit upon the people; (6) material

---

[1] "New Covenant, Dispensational Views of the" *Dictionary of Premillennial Theology:* 281.
[2] *Ibid.*, 281.
[3] Ruckman, Peter S., *How to teach Dispensational Truth* (Pensacola: Bible Believers Press, 1992) 57.
[4] "New Covenant, Theology of the" *Dictionary of Premillennial Theology:* 278.
[5] *Ibid.*

blessing in the land of Israel; (7) peace; (8) God's sanctuary rebuilt.[6]

FOR THE CHURCH ALSO

The New Covenant "is applied to the church (Matthew 6:27-28; Luke 22:20; 2 Cor. 3:6) because it provides the forgiveness of sins and a spiritual dynamic that is not reserved solely for the nation of Israel."[7] This impairs the Reformed Calvinistic view (Israel = Church); and those dispensationalists who avow that "the New Covenant only applies doctrinally to '**the house of Israel**' and '**the house of Judah**' (Jer. 31:31; Heb. 8:8)."[8]

To the dispensationalist who insist that New Covenant "has nothing to do with the born again believer or the present Dispensation of Grace,"[9] a careful comparison of Hebrews 10:14-17 and Hebrews 8:10-12 is in order. The "covenant" in Hebrews 10 (quoting Jeremiah) "appl[ies] to anyone who has put their trust and faith in the once-and-for-all (v. 10) offering of the ONE (v. 12) true sacrifice which the Lord Jesus made."[10] You know this because the phrase, "**house of Israel, and with the house of Judah**" (from Heb. 8) is OMITTED. To those who say, "them" refers to Israel, we point out the Jewish background of "whosoever" in Rom. 10:13 (which is a quote from Joel 2:32)! Paul (under the inspiration of the Holy Ghost) gave an *alternate doctrinal meaning* applicable to the Church Age in the body of Christ. He not only did this with Jer. 31, but in the following verses:

1. Hab. 2:4 (where he omitted "his" in Rom. 1:17 and Gal. 3:11).

---

[6] Ryrie, Charles C., *Dispensationalism* (Chicago: Moody Press, 1995) 171.
[7] LaHaye, Tim, Thomas Ice, *Charting the End Times* (Eugene, Oregon: Harvest House Publishers, 2001) 81.
[8] Morton, Timothy S. *The Difference is in the Dispensations* (http://members.citynet/moton/)
[9] *Ibid.*
[10] Ruckman, Peter S., *Hebrews* (Pensacola: Bible Baptist Bookstore, 1986) 211.

2. Hab. 1:5 (where he applies a prophesy of the Babylonian captivity to unbelieving Jews in the Church Age - Acts 13:40,41).

3. Hos. 1:10, 11 (where the regathering of "**the children of Judah and the children of Israel**" is applied to Gentiles - Rom. 9:24,25).

Even the Lord Jesus Christ suggested that Gentiles would have a part in the New Covenant (see Matt. 8:11; 12:10; 12:18-21; 12:40-42; Luke 4:23-27; John 10:16-18).

The fact that the New Covenant has application to the nation of Israel, *and* the body of Christ is true, but confusing. One of the reasons for the confusion is that the blood of Jesus Christ sanctions and seals *both* groups. Peter applies the blood of Jesus Christ to the national atonement of Israel (which is yet future) in the early part of Acts:

> *Acts 3:19* **Repent ye therefore, and be converted, that your sins may be blotted out, when the times of refreshing shall come from the presence of the Lord;**

This "conversion" matches the "promise" (Acts 2:39) of the national restoration of Israel and the atonement of their sins as a corporate entity. It is then ("**after those days**" - Tribulation) that "**all Israel shall be saved**" (Rom. 11), and the national atonement realized (see Isa. 43:23-28; 44:22; Isa. 33:24; Isa. 4:4; Ps. 130; Micah 7:18; Zech. 3:9).

Later, in the book of Acts the blood atonement is employed in a message to a Gentile for *individual salvation*:

> *Acts 8:32* **The place of the scripture which he read was this, He was led as a sheep to the slaughter;**

and like a lamb dumb before his shearer, so opened he not his mouth:

Acts 8:35 **Then Philip opened his mouth, and began at the same scripture, and preached unto him Jesus.**

Here, in Acts 8, is the first "linking" of Isaiah 53 and individual salvation (apart from John's statement in John 1:29). This "Old Testament" passage (Isa. 53:3-5) *does indeed* apply to Israel (see the "our" - John 1 - "**his own**"); but in Acts 8 the Holy Spirit shows (before Paul's revelation) that there is an application of the blood atonement for the individual sinner whether "**Jew or Greek**" (Rom. 10:12).

This application of the New Covenant (partly because of Israel's rejection in Acts) moves from the historic, visible, nationalistic promises to the non-visible (John 3:8), spiritual promise of eternal life as a free gift, based on the blood of the covenant - Col. 1:14. [Some say that the "kingdom" goes into "mystery form" (see Matt. 13 in a Scofield Bible), thus having application to the Church.]

Paul, in 2 Corinthians 3 claims to be living under the "**new testament**" even professing to be a "minister" in this "**new testament**" (vs. 6). So, to claim that the New Testament is strictly Jewish (remember Paul was the apostle to the Gentiles) boarders on heresy, and only tells a part of the truth.

THE CHURCH IS NOT ISRAEL

It is agreed, that one of the main tenets of dispensationalism is that "the church is distinct from Israel."[11] "The doctrine of

---

[11] "Dispensationalism" *Dictionary of Premillennial Theology:* 94.

the church is the touchstone of dispensationalism."[12] This is obvious for a number of reasons:

1. "The term Israel is not used in the Scriptures to describe anyone but the physical descendants of Abraham."[13] They (as Gentiles) are spoken of as a *different class* than the "church." "Israel is addressed as a nation in contrast to Gentiles *after* the church was established at Pentecost (Acts 3:12; 4:8,10; 5:21, 31,35; 21:28)."[14]

   1 Cor 10:32 **Give none offence, neither to the Jews, nor to the Gentiles, nor to the church of God:**

2. The Church is a living "organism" that has absolutely NO physical ethnicity.

   Gal 3:28 **There is neither Jew nor Greek, there is neither bond nor free, there is neither <u>male nor female</u>: for ye are all one in Christ Jesus.**

$\epsilon\kappa\lambda\eta\sigma\iota\alpha$

Local Church	Universal Church
Contains unsaved	Only saved members
Local Churches—plural	One body– singular
Ends in Apostasy	Ends in Glory
No Baptist Bride	No Baptist Bride
Unassembled Believers are called a "church" (Acts 8:3; 12:5)	Paul includes himself with the same body he wrote to (Rom. 12:5; 1 Cor. 12:13; Eph. 5:30)

---

[12] Ryrie, *Dispensationalism*, 123.
[13] Pentecost, J. Dwight, *Thy Kingdom Come* (Grand Rapids: Kregel, 1995) 173.
[14] Ryrie, *Dispensationalism*, 127.

3. The Church is different from Israel in that it is not "**under the law**" as Israel was, and shall be (Col. 2:16,17).

Rom 6:14 **For sin shall not have dominion over you: for ye are not under the law, but under grace.**

If Calvinism and the "saved the same" scenario is true, why was the law ever imposed to start with? If people were saved by faith in the blood of Christ (*anticipatory faith*), why not skip the Law, and enact the ordinances of the Church? The very fact of *alteration,* from the Old to the New controverts that deviation.

4. The work of the Holy Spirit is different with regards to the church. No Jew in Israel was "sealed" and guaranteed the Holy Spirit in the Old Testament (Ps. 51:11).

Eph 1:13 **In whom ye also trusted, after that ye heard the word of truth, the gospel of your salvation: in whom also after that ye believed, ye were sealed with that holy Spirit of promise,**

5. The content of the message is drastically different in the Church Age, than in any other age. The Church Age is *the only age* whereby a man is saved (presently) by faith in the death, burial and resurrection of Christ as an atonement for his sins. In the future Tribulation Age, men are saved by faith and works, and in the Millennium, NO MAN will be saved by faith: Jesus Christ will be present visibly!

Eph 2:8-9
**8 For by grace are ye saved through faith; and that not of yourselves: it is the gift of God:
9 Not of works, lest any man should boast.**

Note that, the Church Age is incorrectly called "the dispensation of Grace" (Scofield). Grace is disseminated in every dispensation (to some degree).

6. In the Church Age, there is no literal temple for worship (as in the Old Testament) but the body of the believer is the **"temple of the Holy Ghost"** (1 Cor. 6:19).

There are dozens of other dissimilarities between Israel and the church that identify it as a "new program." Examples would include Sunday assembly instead of "sabbath" worship (Matt. 28; 1Cor. 16) and direct entrance into the "third heaven" instead of the "holding tank" called "Abraham's bosom" (1 Cor. 12; Phil. 1; Luke 16).

The Church (*not* the idea of local assembly - Matt. 16:18; 18:17; Acts 7:38; and 19:37- which is an unsaved assembly) is a "mystery" (Rom. 16:25; Eph. 3:3) and is NOT Israel, nor the "kingdom." Larkin suitably stated:

> The church is never confounded with the Kingdom in the Scriptures. The Church is compared to a "House" (1 Tim. 3:15), to a "Temple" (1 Cor. 3:16,17), to a "Body" (1 Cor. 12:27-31), but never to a kingdom. Christ is the "HEAD" of His Church (Eph. 1:22; 4:15; Col. 1:18), but He is never spoken of as its King. The Church's relation to Christ is to be that of a "Bride," Eph. 5:23-31; Rev. 21:2, 9, 10.[15]

This "parenthetical age" (called so because it divides the 69th and 70th week of Daniel's prophecy[16]) will end with the rapture of the saints. The rapture will *precede* the Tribulation Period.

---

[15] Larkin, Clarence, *Dispensational Truth* (Glenside: Rev. Clarence Larkin Est., 1920) 74.
[16] Larkin, Clarence, *Daniel* (Glenside: Rev. Clarence Larkin Est., 1929) 194.

THE PRETRIBULATION RAPTURE

Any serious dispensationalist who is premillennial, believes in the pretribulation rapture of the Church. The major "premise" upon which the pretribulation rapture view rests is "the literal method of interpretation of the Scriptures."[17] This literal method forces and distinguishes Israel from the Church and views the book of Revelation in an unembroidered way. Below are some of the "essential arguments" by Pentecost favoring the pretribulation rapture:

1. The literal method of interpretation: This is true biblical interpretation, and includes "**rightly dividing**."

2. The nature of the seventieth week: This nature includes wrath, judgment; punishment; hour of trial; hour of trouble; destruction and darkness.

3. The scope of the seventieth week: This is the "time of Jacob's trouble."

4. The purpose of the seventieth week: This is to try, or test the earth and the preparation of Israel for their King.

5. The unity of the seventieth week: It is impossible to permit the existence of the church in the week as a unit.

6. The nature of the church: There is a distinction between the church and Israel:

> The church is manifestly an interruption of God's program for Israel, which was not brought into being until

---

[17] Pentecost, J. Dwight, *Things to Come* (Grand Rapids: Zondervan, 1958) 193.

Israel's rejection of the offer of the Kingdom.[18]

7. The doctrine of imminence: Many signs were given to the nation Israel . . . To the church no such signs were ever given.[19]

Other evidence for a pretribulation rapture are:

A. There are no "Jews" in the Church. If a person has been born again, they are **"neither Jew nor Greek"** (Gal. 3:28).

B. There is no "gospel of the kingdom" during the Church Age. A different gospel is preached during the Tribulation Period. If the Church goes through the Tribulation, there is a "cursed angel" in Rev. 14 (see Gal. 1:8).

C. It is called the **"time of Jacob's trouble**," not the "Churches trouble."

D. The rapture cannot occur at the same time as the resurrection in Rev. 20, because the "resurrection" is not called "a mystery" (1 Cor. 15).

E. There is no "song of Moses" in the Church Age.

2 THESS. 2 AND THE IMMINENT RETURN

The doctrine of the imminent return of Christ (that He could come at *any* time) remains under attack:

> David Webber proclaimed on his *Southwest Radio Church of the Air* broadcast that the Antichrist will be

---

[18] *Ibid.*, 201.
[19] *Ibid.*, 193-203.

revealed to believers before they go up in the rapture.[20]

Those who hold to this view assert that 2 Thessalonians 2 teaches this "revelation" of the Antichrist prior to the rapture. Here is the passage:

2 Thess 2:1-12
**1 Now we beseech you, brethren, by the <u>coming</u> of our Lord Jesus Christ, and by our <u>gathering together</u> unto him,
2 That ye be not soon shaken in mind, or be troubled, neither by spirit, nor by word, nor by letter as from us, as that the <u>day of Christ</u> is at hand.
3 Let no man deceive you by any means: for <u>that day</u> shall not come, except there come a falling away first, and that man of sin be revealed, the son of perdition;
4 Who opposeth and exalteth himself above all that is called God, or that is worshipped; so that he as God sitteth in the temple of God, shewing himself that he is God.
5 Remember ye not, that, when I was yet with you, I told you these things?
6 And now ye know what withholdeth that he might be revealed in his time.
7 For the mystery of iniquity doth already work: only he who now letteth will let, until he be taken out of the way.
8 And then shall that Wicked be revealed, whom the Lord shall consume with the spirit of his**

---

[20] MacPherson, Dave., *The Incredible Cover-Up* (Medford: Omega Publications, 1975) 143.

mouth, and shall destroy with the brightness of his coming:

9 Even him, whose coming is after the working of Satan with all power and signs and lying wonders,

10 And with all deceivableness of unrighteousness in them that perish; because they received not the love of the truth, that they might be saved.

11 And for this cause God shall send them strong delusion, that they should believe a lie:

12 That they all might be damned who believed not the truth, but had pleasure in unrighteousness.

The argument is based upon the phrase "**day of Christ**," and insists that it refers to the rapture of the Church. Once the "**day of Christ**" is defined as the rapture, then the passage demands a "sign" (more than an interpretive "**falling away**," but the revealing of the Antichrist) *before* the rapture.

What is even worse, is that apostate bibles (and corrupt Greek texts) change the phrase to read "day of the Lord," thus dispelling any thought of the Bible believer that the "**day of Christ**" could refer to the "day of the Lord." [See Scofield's dishonest note - it is not a "mistranslation" but a different choice of Greek readings: the "Textus Receptus" has "Christ."]

The argument continues that everywhere in the New Testament the "**day of Christ**" refers to the rapture, or the judgment seat of Christ, so here it must also. See the references: 1 Cor. 1:7,8; 1 Cor. 3:11-15 (the day); 1 Cor. 5:4,5; 2 Cor. 1:14; 1 Thess. 2:19; Phil. 1:6,10; 2:16; 2 Tim. 1:12,18 (that day). The claim that John the apostle (being a type of the church) had the "son of perdition" revealed to him *before* his rapture, and that Elijah *knew* when he was to be raptured also supports this view.

To soften this risky interpretation, some have implied that the church will not be around "too long" after this "revelation." [How long is too long?] Others have shifted the "revelation" from the person of the Antichrist to the church *receiving a revelation*. Both are bad errors.

Below are the following biblical reasons this view must be rejected:

1. The passage is speaking, not only of the "**gathering together**" (like 1 Thess 4:17 - "meet the Lord in the air"), but about "**the coming of our Lord**" (second advent). You know that this "coming" *is* the second advent because of verse eight:

   2 Thess 2:8 **And then shall that Wicked be revealed, whom the Lord shall consume with the spirit of his mouth, and shall destroy with the brightness of <u>his coming</u>:**

2. Paul was in effect telling them, that if they would have missed the "**gathering together**" then the events in verses 3,4, and 5 would have been unfolding.

3. The object of the "revelation" (verses 3,6, and 8) is the Antichrist, *not* the church. It is the Antichrist who is "revealed," not the church *receiving revelation!* This is understood by the way "revealed" is used in 2 Thessalonians 1:7 about the "**revelation of Jesus Christ**" (Rev. 1:1).

   2 Thess 1:7 **And to you who are troubled rest with us, when the <u>Lord Jesus shall be revealed</u> from heaven with his mighty angels,**

The revealing of the Antichrist takes place at one specific time and locality. This is outlined in the passage. If a prerequisite for the rapture is the "revealing" of the Antichrist, then the church will be on earth during that **"time"** (vs 6 – **"his time**," not "Christ's time," or the "church's time"). Further, the church would be in danger of taking the mark of the beast, given out during this "time" (see Rev. 1:3; 12:12; 12:14).

This inconsistent interpretation would then force you to say that the church would be raptured *just prior* to the institution of the mark. Remember, a person in the Tribulation can lose their salvation if they take the mark of the beast (Matt. 24:13; Rev. 14:11).

4. The phrase **"day of Christ"** (a correct translation from the right line of manuscripts) refers to the rapture, or the judgment seat of Christ, in every case BUT THIS ONE.

The context (plus other scripture) demands a different meaning. Some may think it is stretching things a bit to make this claim. But this is not an isolated case, where a phrase can mean one thing 99% of the time, and something else 1% of the time.

Eph. 2:13 uses the phrase **"far off"** to refer to Gentiles, while that quotation (from Dan. 9:7) is referring to the Jews of the dispersion. If you apply **"far off"** to Gentiles in Acts 2 (where Peter quotes Dan. 9), then you have Gentiles speaking in tongues, and Acts 2:38 applicable for Gentiles! Eph. 2 is the ONE EXCEPTION, and the context demands it. So it is here in 2 Thessalonians 2.

5. The historical *timeframe* of the writing of 2 Thessalonians must be considered with regard to this phrase. If 1 and 2 Thessalonians were indeed written earlier than any of the

other epistles (notwithstanding Galatians), then the law of first mention would apply *here*, not in Corinthians.

6. Moreover, if you allow "**day of Christ**" to by synonymous with the rapture, then you nullify the verses aimed at New Testament believers, commanding them to LOOK FOR JESUS CHRIST (not "signs"):

John 14:3 **And if I go and prepare a place for you, I will come again, and receive you unto myself; that where I am, there ye may be also.**

Acts 1:11 **Which also said, Ye men of Galilee, why stand ye gazing up into heaven? this same Jesus, which is taken up from you into heaven, shall so come in like manner as ye have seen him go into heaven.**

1 Cor 15:51-52
**51 Behold, I shew you a mystery; We shall not all sleep, but we shall all be changed,
52 In a moment, in the twinkling of an eye, at the last trump: for the trumpet shall sound, and the dead shall be raised incorruptible, and we shall be changed.**

He did not say "in a moment directly after the revealing of the Antichrist," or "in a moment just before the mark is given!"

Phil 3:20 **For our conversation is in heaven; from whence also we look for the Saviour, the Lord Jesus Christ:**

We are to LOOK for the Saviour, not the son of Satan!

Col 3:4 **When Christ, who is our life, shall appear, then shall ye also appear with him in glory.**

The imminent appearing is what we are looking for.

1 Thess 1:10 **And to <u>wait for his Son</u> from heaven, whom he raised from the dead, even Jesus, which delivered us from the wrath to come.**

1 Tim 6:14 **That thou keep this commandment without spot, unrebukeable, until the appearing of our Lord Jesus Christ:**

Titus 2:13 **<u>Looking for that blessed hope</u>, and the glorious appearing of the great God and our Saviour Jesus Christ;**

1 Thess 5:6 **Therefore let us not sleep, as do others; but let us <u>watch</u> and be sober.**

Phil 4:5 **Let your moderation be known unto all men. The Lord is at hand.**

Notice how the "day of Christ" could NOT be at hand in 2 Thess 2, but "the Lord is at hand" in Phil. 4. This proves beyond any shadow of a doubt that **"the day of Christ"** in 2 Thess. 2 is the same as the "day of the Lord."

2 Thess 3:5 **And the Lord direct your hearts into the love of God, and into the <u>patient waiting for Christ</u>.**

Rom 13:11 **And that, knowing the time, that now it is high time to awake out of sleep: for now is <u>our salvation nearer</u> than when we believed.**

1 Cor 1:7 **So that ye come behind in no gift; <u>waiting for the coming of our Lord Jesus Christ</u>:**

1 John 3:2-3
2 Beloved, now are we the sons of God, and it doth not yet appear what we shall be: but we know that, when he shall appear, we shall be like him; for we shall <u>see him</u> as he is.
3 And every man that hath <u>this hope</u> in him purifieth himself, even as he is pure.

Ruckman lists seven things some Christians are looking for instead of Jesus Christ:

> 1. America to be 're-Christianized' by 'Reconstructionists' (i.e., The Chalcedon Ministry).
> 2. A great revival to come by political activity of the 'Christian Right' ('right wing' of Christianity).
> 3. Daniel's Seventieth Week to show up.
> 4. The temple to be rebuilt.
> 5. The Son of Perdition to show up.
> 6. Russia to invade Palestine.
> 7. And now (with Rosenthal's muddled nonsense), waiting to enter the last half of Daniel's Seventieth Week after going through Revelation chapters 6-15, without getting into Revelation chapter 16-19 . . . . That is, in the twentieth century, the Lord's 'flock' has been led astray and deceived into looking for ANYTHING except the One they were told to look for . . . It is not the work of the Holy Spirit.[21]

---

[21] Ruckman, Peter S., *The Two Raptures* (Pensacola: Bible Baptist Bookstore, 1996) 20, 21.

WHY "DAY OF CHRIST?"

Why did the Holy Spirit use "**the day of Christ**" instead of "**the day of the Lord**?" The answer is found in the book of Acts where the Old Testament phrase, "**thus saith the LORD**" is substituted with "**thus saith the Holy Ghost**" (Acts 21:11). In Acts 21 the deity of the Holy Ghost is verified with the replacement. In 2 Thessalonians 2 the deity of Jesus Christ is confirmed. The substitution is "Christ" for "LORD" (Jehovah of the O.T). That explains the real intent by Satan to attack this verse in the corrupt manuscripts (and new versions). The AV reading is a revelation that Jesus Christ is the LORD JEHOVAH, and will be the LORD of the "day" discussed in the Old Testament [Dispensational authors who accepted the change did so because they *knew* the passage had to be the "day of the Lord" doctrinally. They rejected the AV on insufficient grounds, and in the process missed a revelation on the deity of the Lord Jesus Christ.]

WHO IS "HE?"

Most dispensational authors insist that "**he who now letteth will let**" is the Holy Spirit. Regardless of whether or not they call Him "the sealing Holy Spirit," or "the only One who could do such a restraining ministry,"[22] they still say the "he" is the Holy Spirit. Larkin said, "the holy Spirit will have gone back with the 'Raptured Ones'[23]), and Scofield boldly proclaimed, "this Person can be no other than the Holy Spirit."[24] Lahaye, Pentecost, and even Stauffer maintain that "the indwelling and sealing Holy Spirit will leave this world with the Christians."[25]

---

[22] Pentecost, *Things to Come*, 205.
[23] Larkin, *Dispensational Truth*, 80.
[24] *Scofield Reference Bible* (New York: Oxford, 1909) 1272.
[25] Stauffer, Douglas D., *One Book Rightly Divided* (Millbrok: McCowen Mills Publishers, 1999) 188.

This interpretation made its way in the NKJV which capitalizes the "h" to make him deity. And if this "he" is really the "man of sin" as the context proves, then someone is guilty of substituting the spirit of the Antichrist for the Spirit of Jesus Christ!

How could the Holy Spirit be gone from the earth, when He is said to be speaking to "post Church Age churches" (see comments under *Rev. 1:3*) during and just *prior* to the Tribulation? See: Rev. 2:7,11,17,29; 3:6,13,22 – "**He that hath an ear, let him hear what the Spirit saith unto the churches.**"

That is not all. Elijah and Moses (the two witnesses) are raised from the dead by the "**Spirit of life from God**" (Rev. 11:11).

To say that it is "the Holy Spirit in the Church, who will 'be taken out of the way' in the Rapture,"[26] is peculiar to say the least! You cannot just remove the third person of the Godhead. David said:

Ps 139:7 **Whither shall I go from thy spirit? or whither shall I flee from thy presence?**

Knowing this, some claim that the Holy Spirit does not "cease to be omnipresent . . .but the restraining ministry does cease."[27] Pentecost (at all cost) has transformed "he" from a person to a "ministry." The text says *NOTHING* of the kind! You cannot have Him leaving, yet "him" NOT leaving!

The only real "answer" to the problem of the "he" is found in the context, where "he" is used. Verses four and six use the "he" as the antecedent to "the man of sin" of verse three. The insertion of the Holy Spirit in verse seven, (even if it was to propagate a truth – the pretribulation rapture) has no

---

[26] *Tim LaHaye Prophecy Study Bible*, AMG: 2000; 1292.
[27] Pentecost, *Things to Come*, 205.

corroboration or authentication at all! The best *interpretation* links verse seven to verse three. The one that is to "**be taken out of the way**" is "**the man of sin**" so the "**son of perdition**" can be revealed. This supports the idea (found in Daniel) that during the first 3½ years of the Tribulation the "man of sin" (called "**a vile person**") will *bring* peace to the earth, while during the next 3½ years the "**son of perdition**" ("perdition" means destruction) will "*take* **peace from the earth**" (Rev. 6:4). Many refer to the complete era as the Tribulation period, and the last 3½ years as "the Great Tribulation."

> *Dan 11:21* **And in his estate shall stand up a vile person, to whom they shall not give the honour of the kingdom: but he shall come in peaceably, and obtain the kingdom by flatteries.**

THE TRIBULATION PERIOD

Without giving an exhaustive dissertation on eschatology (passing over some of the established teachings); we move into some of the highlights of the Tribulation Period.

CHRONOLOGY OF THE TRIBULATION

This period (called "**the time of Jacob's trouble**" - Jer. 30:7) is divided and sectioned off into two 3½ periods of time, equaling seven years (see any standard work). The teaching, however, that the Tribulation Period begins *directly* after the Rapture is not biblically founded. In fact, scripture seems to indicate just the opposite: that there will be a period of time (how long????) prior to the seventieth week of Daniel. Notice the future tense in the following verses:

Rev 2:22 **Behold, <u>I will</u> cast her into a bed, and them that commit adultery with her into great tribulation, except they repent of their deeds.**

Rev 3:10 **Because thou hast kept the word of my patience, I also <u>will keep thee</u> from the hour of temptation, which shall come upon all the world, to try them that dwell upon the earth.**

This "silent time" accounts for the transitional material found in the book of Hebrews, and logically follows other "gaps" in the prophetic calendar (such as "a 50 year gap in the 70 weeks <u>before</u> the '62' begin - Ezra 6:15; Ezra 7:17"[28]).

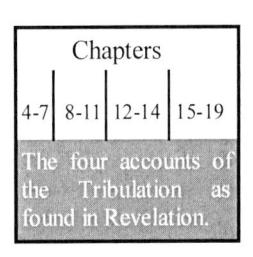

Chapters			
4-7	8-11	12-14	15-19
The four accounts of the Tribulation as found in Revelation.			

Most dispensational authors and teachers (including all the prophecy "experts" - LaHaye, Van Impe, Walvoord ect.) maintain a continuous chronology for the book of Revelation. Larkin says that "the Book of Revelation is written in chronological order."[29] That is simply NOT the case. Even Pentecost, who says chapter twelve through nineteen "surveys the period a second time"[30] falls short.

Dr. Ruckman suitably outlines the book of Revelation as *four separate accounts* of the Tribulation Period: first account (4-7); second account (8-11); third account (12-14); fourth account (15-19).[31] This is the safest chronological system for the Book of Revelation.

When you impose a linear chronological system to the book of Revelation, the following *problems* rear their ugly head:

---

[28] Ruckman, Peter S., *Charts and Outlines* (Pensacola: Bible Believers Press, 1997) 67.
[29] Larkin, *Dispensational Truth*, 14.
[30] Pentecost, *Things to Come*, 188.
[31] Ruckman, *Charts and Outlines*, 78.

1. *Three* separate earthquakes (Rev. 6:12; 11:13; 16:18) of great magnitude. We know that Jesus mentioned "earthquakes" (plural in Matthew 24:7); but THREE "***great* earthquakes**???"

2. Reconciling Revelation 6:12-14 with the first part of the Tribulation. Matthew 24:29 indicates that the celestial bodies are distressed at the *end* not the beginning:

    Matt 24:29 **Immediately <u>after</u> the tribulation of those days shall the sun be darkened, and the moon shall not give her light, and the stars shall fall from heaven, and the powers of the heavens shall be shaken:**

3. An actual appearance of Jesus Christ to His enemies (Rev. 6:16) matching the second advent (at the end of the Tribulation).

4. Rev. 7:14 where people are already "**come out of great tribulation.**"

5. Rev. 8:12 where a "third part" of the stars are "smitten" matching Rev. 12:4.

6. The obvious Armageddon reference in Rev. 9 (200 million man army). Notice the citing of "Euphrates" - Rev. 9:14 and 16:12. If Rev. 9 is chronologically *in tune* with the remaining storyline, then when does Armageddon take place: chapter nine, sixteen or nineteen???

7. When the seventh angel sounds, *that is* "**the end**" according to Rev. 10:6,7. The second advent of Jesus Christ is found in Rev. 11:15-19, where the great white

throne judgment is expounded upon as well. There are not TWO white throne judgments: one in Rev. 11 and one in Rev. 20!

8. There is an evident reference to Armageddon *again* in Rev. 14:20, along with another reference on the appearing of Jesus Christ (14:14).

9. Reference to the sea becoming "blood" *twice:* Rev. 8:8 and Rev. 16:3.

10. Babylon "falling" *three times:* Rev. 14:8 demonstrates that the events of Revelation cannot be chronological. For, Babylon is said to have fallen in 14:8, how can it fall again in 17 and 18?

OTHER CONSIDERATIONS

The only other chronological considerations relate to the dividing of this period into two sections (i.e The "Tribulation" – the first 3½ years, and the "Great Tribulation" – the second 3½ years).

That the entire Tribulation is not just 3½ years is evident. In Revelation 11:3 and 12:6, the Tribulation is well underway, when 1260 days are mentioned as in the future. [Note: The placement of which 3½ years the two witnesses fall under determines either a "mid" or "post" Tribulation rapture of Tribulation saints.]

REVELATION 12 – THE MAN CHILD

Why most authors revert back over 1900 years (vowing that the "**man child**" is Christ) is puzzling. Although there are similarities between the "man child" and Christ; the fact that

John was to "**write . . . the things which shall be hereafter**" (Rev. 1:19 - all pretribulationalists categorize chapters 4-22 as "hereafter") *must cancel out* Christ as the "man child." Also, if the man child is Christ, the Catholic interpretation of "the woman" (as Mary) could be endorsed.

The man child is possibly one of the following:

1. A literal "man child" sent during the Tribulation to deliver Israel (like Moses and Elijah) on the political scale: Gen. 17:9-14; 1 Sam. 1:11; Job 3:3; Isa. 66:7; Jer. 1:6; Matt. 16:14; Lam. 4:20. Possibly David: Ezek. 34:23,24; 37:24,25.

2. A representation of the 144,000 Jewish male virgins that are raptured up preceding the second advent: Rev. 14:1-5.

3. A personification of the nation of Israel giving birth as a nation: Hos. 13:13; Isa. 54.

He is definitely NOT Jesus Christ. If you make him Christ, then the subsequent material in chapter twelve had to take place in the early part of Acts. It just will not *work*.

Rapture of Tribulation Saints

Outside of material from Dr. Peter S. Ruckman, the teaching of a rapture of Tribulation saints is completely missing from any *major* books on prophecy, the rapture, or commentaries on the book of Revelation.

Below are the facts relating to this post-tribulation rapture of Tribulation saints:

1. Throughout the book of Revelation there is a "pre-advent" appearance of Jesus Christ. It is also referred to in Hebrews:

Rev 6:16 **And said to the mountains and rocks, Fall on us, and hide us from the <u>face of him</u> that sitteth on the throne, and from the wrath of the Lamb:**

Rev 14:14 **And I looked, and behold a white cloud, and upon the cloud one sat like unto the Son of man, having on his head a golden crown, and in his hand a sharp sickle.**

Heb 1:2 **Hath in these <u>last days spoken unto us by his Son</u>, whom he hath appointed heir of all things, by whom also he made the worlds;**

Remember that the "us" are Hebrews, not New Testament Christians in the body of Christ. Ruckman draws on a type:

> Paul's conversion is a type of that appearance of Christ (Acts 9:1-5), which explains his **'born out of due time'** statement in 1 Corinthians 15:8. This appearance is foreshadowed in places like Isaiah 60:1-3; Joel 3:16; and Psa. 50:2. It is God 'shining forth, brighter than the sun' (Psa. 67:1; Matt. 17:2; Acts 22:6).[32]

Heb 12:25-26
25 See that ye refuse not him that speaketh. For if they escaped not who refused him that spake on earth, much more shall not we escape, if we turn away from him that speaketh from heaven:

---

[32] Ruckman, *The Two Raptures*, 16.

26 Whose voice then shook the earth: but now he hath promised, saying, Yet once more I shake not the earth only, but also heaven.

2. The requirements one must meet, in order to be raptured in the Tribulation are:

   a. Holiness:

   Heb 12:14 **Follow peace with all men, and holiness, without which no man shall see the Lord:**

   b. Watchful waiting:

   Heb 9:28 **So Christ was once offered to bear the sins of many; and <u>unto them that look for him</u> shall he appear the second time without sin unto salvation.**

   c. A pure heart:

   Matt 5:8 **Blessed are the pure in heart: for they shall see God.**

3. These requirements are linked to keeping "**the commandments of God**" (Rev. 12:17; 14:12; 22:14) and refusing to take the mark of the beast (Rev. 14:11; Hebrews 6).

4. The post-tribulation rapture verses in the gospels (Matt.-Luke) are often misapplied to the Church Age rapture:

   Matt 24:31 **And he shall send his angels with a great sound of a trumpet, and they shall gather** together his elect from the four winds, from one end of heaven to the other.

These are not just "advent references" (like most prophetic, dispensational scholars claim) they DO refer to a "rapture."

Matt 24:40-42
40 Then shall two be in the field; the one shall be taken, and the other left.
41 Two women shall be grinding at the mill; the one shall be taken, and the other left.
42 Watch therefore: for ye know not what hour your Lord doth come.

Matt 24:44 **Therefore be ye also ready: for in such an hour as ye think not the Son of man cometh.**

5. The "translation" (Heb. 11:5) of Tribulation saints is crystal clear in Rev. 7 and 14. In chapter seven, they are on the earth, in chapter fourteen they have been raptured, and are standing on "**mount Sion.**"

6. The post-tribulation rapture is identified with the resurrections of Moses and Elijah (Rev. 11) *after* the second 3½ years.

7. This rapture is called a "harvest" in Rev. 14:14,15 and is different than the "reaping" of 14:18-20.

Rev 14:14-15
14 And I looked, and behold a white cloud, and upon the cloud one sat like unto the Son of man, having on his head a golden crown, and in his hand a sharp sickle.

15 And another angel came out of the temple, crying with a loud voice to him that sat on the cloud, Thrust in thy sickle, and reap: for the time is come for thee to reap; for the harvest of the earth is ripe.

Jesus referred to this very event in Matthew 13:

Matt 13:39 **The enemy that sowed them is the devil; the <u>harvest is the end of the world</u>; and the reapers are the angels.**

Some may argue that the Tribulation is not the "end of the world." But the scriptures teach that it is. The Millennium is said to be the "world to come," and the Tribulation Period is referred to as "the end" in Matthew 24:13. In fact the "end of time," is said to be at the end of the Tribulation. Read Rev. 10:6! The harvest takes place precisely prior to the second advent, and matches the **"gleanings of thy harvest"** (Lev. 19:9). The Tribulation saints are raptured and resurrected in the first resurrection (Rev. 20:6) before the Millennial kingdom begins.

> **Post-tribulation rapture of Tribulation Saints:**
> Rev. 6:16; 14:14; Heb. 1:2; 12:14; 9:28; Matt. 5:8; 24:31; Rev. 7 with Rev. 14.

DIFFERENCES BETWEEN THE TWO RAPTURES

This "second" rapture, relates to the **"virgins"** (Matt. 25) who are waiting to **"meet the bridegroom."** It does not involve a "**chaste virgin**" (2 Cor. 11:2); that is going to "MARRY HIM" (Rev. 19)!

The post-tribulation rapture is a calling with the "**great sound of a trumpet**" (Matt. 24:31) which is the seventh trumpet (Rev. 11:15) and the body of Christ (the bride) is called with the "**trump of God**" (1 Thess 4:16), matching the voice of God. See: Rev. 4:1; John 12:29; and Job 37:4.

Misapplying the rapture of the Church for the post-tribulation rapture is what formulated the "post-tribulation rapture of the Church." It has also brewed the anti-eternal security sentiments in most Protestant denominations (outside of Baptist and Presbyterian). The verses used to teach a person can lose his salvation are mostly doctrinal verses aimed at someone in the Tribulation Period. Wrongly dividing, or NOT dividing, produces 90% of all heresies.

THE MILLENNIAL AGE

The Kingdom Age (or Millennial Age) finds fulfillment for the Davidic, Mosaic, Abrahamic, and New covenants. The constitution of this kingdom era is found in the Sermon on the Mount (Matt. 5-7) where orders and regulations under the monarchy are instituted. Several outstanding features of this epoch are as follows:

1. A judgment of the nations commencing this kingdom age:

> *Matt 25:32* **And before him shall be gathered all nations: and he shall separate them one from another, as a shepherd divideth his sheep from the goats:**

2. The restoration of Israel to their land, and the "realization" of the unconditional promises to Abraham Isaac and Jacob:

Ezek 37:25 **And they shall dwell in the land that I have given unto Jacob my servant, wherein your fathers have dwelt; and they shall dwell therein, even they, and their children, and their children's children for ever: and my servant David shall be their prince for ever.**

3. The establishment of the Davidic throne in Jerusalem with the son of David (Jesus Christ) ruling with a rod of iron.

Matt 5:35 **Nor by the earth; for it is his footstool: neither by Jerusalem; for it is the city of the great King.**

Ezek 48:35 **It was round about eighteen thousand measures: and the name of the city from that day shall be, The LORD is there.**

4. The lifting of the "ground curse" (Gen. 3:17), and the releasing of the animals from their "bondage" (Rom. 8:15):

Isa 11:7 **And the cow and the bear shall feed; their young ones shall lie down together: and the lion shall eat straw like the ox.**

Amos 9:13 **Behold, the days come, saith the LORD, that the plowman shall overtake the reaper, and the treader of grapes him that soweth seed; and the** mountains shall drop sweet wine, and all the hills shall melt.

5. The "blotting out" of the sins of Israel (Acts 3:19) and the national forgiveness granted under the New Covenant. The animal sacrifices in the temple at Jerusalem will be part of national atonement for the sins of the nation:

Ezek 43:18 **And he said unto me, Son of man, thus saith the Lord GOD; These are the ordinances of the altar in the day when they shall make it, to offer burnt offerings thereon, and to sprinkle blood thereon.**

Ezek 45:15 **And one lamb out of the flock, out of two hundred, out of the fat pastures of Israel; for a meat offering, and for a burnt offering, and for peace offerings, to make <u>reconciliation for them</u>, saith the Lord GOD.**

6. The placement of a literal lake of fire on the earth, to deter rebellion:

Mark 9:43 **And if thy hand offend thee, cut it off: it is better for thee to enter into life maimed, than having two hands to go into hell, into the fire that never shall be quenched:**

Isa 66:23-24
23 And it shall come to pass, that from one new moon to another, and from one sabbath to another, shall all flesh come to worship before me, saith the LORD.

24 And they shall go forth, and look upon the carcases of the men that have transgressed against me: for their worm shall not die, neither shall their fire be quenched; and they shall be an abhorring unto all flesh.

7. The reinstatement of the longevity of life. There will be literal flesh and blood bodies on the earth during the Millennial Age. Since longevity of life will be restored (as the pre-flood era) the commission of "replenishing the earth" will be well underway when "the thousand years are expired."

PEOPLE IN THE MILLENNNIUM

Since the Lord destroys the wicked at His second coming (Matthew 25:41-46; 2 Thess. 2:8-12), the question arises: "Where do these fleshly bodies come from?" This question has been used as a noteworthy argument against the faulty post-tribulation rapture of the *church*:

> It is impossible for the Rapture to occur at the end of the Tribulation, for if it did, there would be no one left on earth in a natural body who can populate the Millennial kingdom. [33]

When we "rightly divide" the two raptures we come up with a couple of biblical explanations:

1. They are the bodies of the raptured and resurrected Tribulation saints (Rev. 6:9).

It is a misnomer (from Luke 20:35,36) that a resurrected body cannot reproduce. Those who teach this forget that

---

[33] LaHaye, Tim, *The Rapture* (Eugene, Oregon: Harvest House Publishers, 2002) 130.

Lazarus, Jarius's daughter, and the woman of Nain's son, were all resurrected and later reproduced (assumingly) and then died. Their resurrection was different because they were NOT in the body of Christ. Tribulation saints will not be in the body of Christ either. This explains the appearance of "the tree of life" in eternity. While we get our eternal life by faith, others will obtain it physically by eating fruit off a tree (Rev. 2:7; 22:2; 22:14; Gen. 2:9; 3:22,24).

[The only problem with *the above* theory is that "the resurrection" of Luke 20 *could* refer to these very saints!]

2. The bodies that inhabit the Millennial kingdom will consist of a literal resurrection of the nation of Israel as found in Ezekiel 37, and 38.

This would clear up the "problem" of the resurrected bodies of Tribulation saints reproducing. The wording of Ezekiel 37 and 38 is persuasive:

> *Ezek 37:12* **Therefore prophesy and say unto them, Thus saith the Lord GOD; Behold, O my people, I will open your graves, and cause you to come up out of your graves, and bring you into the land of Israel.**

3. They may be the offspring of the "sheep" found in Matthew 25. Those who treated the Jews right will go into the Kingdom and reproduce in fleshly bodies.

THE ETERNAL COVENANT

> *1 Cor 15:28* **And when all things shall be subdued unto him, then shall the Son also himself be subject**

unto him that put all things under him, that God may be all in all.

Eph 1:10 **That in the dispensation of the fulness of times he might gather together in one all things in Christ, both which are in heaven, and which are on earth; even in him:**

The complications of the fleshly bodies in the Millennial Age remain with the establishment of the "Eternal Covenant." The very fact of the necessity of the "tree of life" (Rev. 22:2) proves the possibility of DEATH in eternity (or does it? - it was here before Adam sinned!). But, since "death" is cast into the lake of fire (Rev. 20:11-15) it is assumed that all sin is gone as well.

The dilemma (as we have seen throughout) is connected to a "seed." Somehow the seed of man (carried over from Adam via. the Millennial saints) must be restored to purity and eradicated from the tainting of sin passed down from Adam (Rom. 5:12). Ruckman speculates:

> You see a New Planet. It has been renovated by fire, exactly as an old car is mashed, molten, and poured anew. This new earth is populated by 12 nations of men who are segregated and bounded, as God originally intended (Deut 32:7,8). Over them stands Israel, reigning supreme in the pyramid tract of land stretching from Babylon to Cairo, and from Mt. Ararat to the base line. These all live in natural human bodies. They are born and they grow and then at the point of 33 ½ years of age - oh, brother! - they enter the new Jerusalem on the appointed month, and are healed of the old sin-cursed Adamic nature. Where any refuse to go, or rebel, they die off. Where they obey they live forever; in a few thousand years (probably 33,000), all are living forever. They reproduce, they are fruitful, they multiply, they replenish the earth. In 5000 years they

over-run the earth . . . Out go the earthlings, carried two at a time, each to be placed on a new home - a new 'garden of Eden.' Eden, restored a million times! Ten million times! Ten billion times! One hundred trillion times! Oh, Lord my God, how great Thou art![34]

There are a few problems with the above synopsis:

1. How can anyone die, when death is in the lake of fire? See: Rev. 20:11-15.

2. There is no proof that the "tree of life" can heal the "sin curse." The "**leaves**" of the tree of life are for the "**healing of the nations**" and may be a reference to the Gentile nations. How could there be any nations after Rev. 20:11-15 unless it simply refers to non-Jewish descendents? Genesis 3:22 indicates that the purpose of the tree of life is to give PHYSICAL eternal life.

As the postulation of history *before* Eden is often baffling and futile, so is a view into the Eternal Covenant, when you go beyond the bounds of scripture. Suffice the following verses to speak for themselves:

> *Dan 2:44* **And in the days of these kings shall the God of heaven set up a kingdom, which shall never be destroyed: and the kingdom shall not be left to other people, but it shall break in pieces and consume all these kingdoms, and <u>it shall stand for ever</u>.**

---

[34] Ruckman, Peter S., *The Sure Word of Prophecy* (Pensacola: Bible Believers Press, 1969) 232.

Matt 13:43 **Then shall the righteous shine forth as the sun in the kingdom of their Father. Who hath ears to hear, let him hear.**

Rev 22:3-5
**3 And there shall be no more curse: but the throne of God and of the Lamb shall be in it; and his servants shall serve him:
4 And they shall see his face; and his name shall be in their foreheads.
5 And there shall be no night there; and they need no candle, neither light of the sun; for the Lord God giveth them light: <u>and they shall reign for ever and ever</u>.**

Isa 65:17 **For, behold, I create new heavens and a new earth: and the former shall not be remembered, nor come into mind.**

Ps 93:1-2
**1 <u>The LORD reigneth</u>, he is clothed with majesty; the LORD is clothed with strength, wherewith he hath girded himself: the world also is stablished, that it cannot be moved.
2 Thy throne is established of old: thou art from everlasting.**

Rev 19:6 **And I heard as it were the voice of a great multitude, and as the voice of many waters, and as the voice of mighty thunderings, saying, Alleluia: for <u>the Lord God omnipotent reigneth</u>.**

Dispensationalism

Part Four:
Apologetic

Answering Errors

CHAPTER 12

Hyper-dispensationalism

THEIR FOUNDING FATHERS

As detailed previously, hyper-dispensationalism (or ultra-dispensationalism) arose primarily from the teachings of E.W. Bullinger (1837-1913), and was later Americanized by J.C. O'Hair, Charles F. Baker, and Cornelius R. Stam (1908-2003). Modern day "Bereans" believe those men "recover[ed] the truth of Pauline revelation."[1] The Berean Bible Society publishes the hyper's periodical: *The Berean Searchlight*.

"ULTRA," OR "HYPER"

Whether you use the Greek prefix (hyper) or the Latin (ultra), makes no difference. Shelton Smith (editor of *The*

---
[1] Sadler, Paul M. "From the Editor," *The Berean Searchlight* 05/03: 4.

Sword of the Lord) creates his own definition by differentiating between an "ultra," and a "hyper" dispensationalist: "By my definition, an ultra dispensationalist is somewhere between a dispensationalist and a hyper dispensationalist."[2] Smith's label is aimed at Bible believing soul-winning Baptists, who reject the "saved the same" scenario. Smith knows they are not "hypers," but he disagrees with them; hence, the label "ultra."

Classic hyper-dispensationalism is a *dead end* divergence that *kills* any real "Bible Study." Articles in *The Berean Searchlight* include such titles as: "Are the Twelve Apostles in the Body of Christ," "No Other Doctrine But Right Division," "Why Paul," "The Confession of Sins," "Paul, The Apostle of Grace," "At What Age was Jesus Baptized," and "The Devil and the Mystery."

WHAT IS "PAUL'S GOSPEL?"

Instead of "Paul's gospel" *including* the message of salvation by "**grace through faith**," (with an *emphasis* on the mystery of the body of Christ and the rapture) hypers attribute the doctrine of substitutionary atonement to Paul alone. Ricky Kurth of the *Berean Bible Society* answers the question: "Did Philip preach 'Christ died for our sins' to the Ethiopian eunuch?"

> It is tempting to think that Philip preached this to the eunuch when we read that he "*preached unto him Jesus*" from Isaiah 53 (Acts 8:26-35). However, this message that was later given to the Apostle Paul (1 Cor. 15:3,4) had not yet been revealed. Thus we know that Philip rather preached Christ according to the kingdom program.[3]

---

[2] Smith, Shelton., "*One Book Rightly Divided* Reflects Ultra-dispensationalism," *The Sword of the Lord* 07/05/02: 8B
[3] Kurth, Ricky. "Question Box," *The Berean Searchlight* 03/05: 21.

THE "ISSUE"

A person can easily be identified as a hyper by their unorthodox view of *when* the body of Christ began. In fact, this is "the issue."[4]

Stam states their position:

> We believe, and are sure, however, that the present dispensation began, not with Peter and the eleven at Pentecost, but with Paul, to whom the risen, glorified Lord later reveled His will and program for our day.[5]

Ryrie correctly notes that most "Dispensationalists say that the church began at Pentecost, while ultra dispensationalists believe that it began with Paul sometime later."[6] Whether or not they hold to the "Acts 28" view (Bullinger), or the Acts 18 view (O'Hair) or the so-named "mid Acts" view (Acts 9 - Stam and Sadler) makes no difference. They all add an extra dispensation between Acts 2 and Paul. This is done to eliminate w*ater baptism.* [Bullinger, and his followers also did away with communion since they only held Paul's prison epistles (of which 1 Cor. 11 is not included) as doctrine for the Church Age.]

Ironside, in his classic pamphlet *Wrongly Dividing the Word of Truth,* categorizes the errors of hypers who took Bullinger's position:

1. The "four gospels are entirely Jewish."[7]

2. The church in the book of Acts "is simply an aspect of the

---

[4] Ruckman, Peter S., *Hyper-Dispensationalism* (Pensacola: Bible Baptist Bookstore, 1985) 6.
[5] Cornelius R. Stam "True Spirituality," *The Berean Searchlight* 02/05: 11.
[6] Ryrie, Charles C., *Dispensationalism* (Chicago: Moody Press, 1995) 197.
[7] Ironside, H.A., *Wrongly Dividing the Word of Truth* (New York: Loizeaux Brothers, 1938) 9.

kingdom and is not the same as the Body of Christ."[8]

3. Only Paul's prison epistles are Church Age material. "Paul did not receive his special revelation of the mystery of the body until his imprisonment in Rome."[9]

4. "The entire book of Revelation has to do with the coming age and has no reference to the Church today."[10]

[Note: The fact that some of the doctrinal verses in Rev. 1-3 teach a person can lose his salvation imposes at least a primary application to the Tribulation, with a historical and devotional relevance to the Church Age. See: Rev. 4:1- "**things which must be hereafter**."]

5. The bride of Jesus Christ is NOT the body of Christ, but "Jewish."[11]

6. "The Christian ordinances . . . Have no real connection with the present economy."[12]

Ruckman outlines the teachings of hyper-dispensationalism as follows:

> **1.** There is a period of time called "THE GRACE OF GOD" which began in Acts 9 (Stam, Baker, Moore, Watkins) or in Acts 18 (O'Hare and others) or in Acts 28 (Bullinger . . .
> **2.** Water baptism is not for "THIS AGE" since "THIS AGE" began in Acts 9 or Acts 13 or Acts 18 or Acts 28.

---

[8] *Ibid.*
[9] *Ibid.*
[10] *Ibid.*
[11] *Ibid.*
[12] *Ibid.*

3. Bible-believing Baptists are heretics who do not follow PAULINE teaching (1 Ti. 1:16).
4. Since Paul did not COMMAND anyone to be baptized, it is UNSCRIPTURAL.
5. Since Paul was not "SENT TO BAPTIZE," water baptism is PRE-PAULINE (1 Cor. 1).
6. The "ONE BAPTISM" of Ephesians 4 automatically cancels water baptism.[13]

"IN THE BODY OR OUT OF THE BODY?"

As we have demonstrated before (see *The Transition Periods*) the Bible does not "chop up" as neatly as the hypers would have you to believe. They want the so-called "Dispensation of the Grace of God" to begin with Paul so they can seemingly get away from the different plan of salvation found in Acts 2:38. Note Sadler's flawed comment:

> The early chapters of Acts are merely a continuation of the earthly ministry of Christ to Israel... We must ask, who of the Acts 2 persuasion, preaches Acts 2:38 as the terms of salvation today?[14]

Well, who of the "mid Acts" position (following Paul) preaches Acts 19:6 as the terms of receiving the Holy Ghost? Biblical facts show *four* different "plans of salvation" (or "ways to get the Holy Ghost") in the book of Acts before and *after* Paul's conversion (see: Acts 2,8,16,19). All four "plans of salvation" fall under ONE dispensation. Hypers confuse the *dispensing* of truth with the *revelation* of truth during the transition from Jew to Gentile (see Romans 11) in Acts!

The beginning of the body of Christ is easy to determine when the Bible is taken at face value, instead of the *understanding* of men (i.e. Paul being "revealed" the mystery).

---
[13] Ruckman, *Hyper-Dispensationalism*, 20.
[14] Sadler, *The Berean Searchlight* 03/03: 3.

The way for the spiritual body of Christ was made at Calvary (Eph. 2:14-16), even though it "hinged" upon the glorification and ascension of His physical body. While it found full manifestation on the day of Pentecost, it did not necessarily begin there, and certainly did not begin *after* Pentecost. Ruckman:

> The "**ONE BODY**" did not begin with Paul at all. The verse (vs. 16) says that the reconciliation of Jew and Gentile (see "**the mystery**" given in 3:4-6) began at CALVARY: "**in the one body by the cross.**"[15]

Observe the following verses:

Eph 2:14-16
14 For he is our peace, who hath made both one, and hath broken down the middle wall of partition between us;
15 Having abolished in his flesh the enmity, even the law of commandments contained in ordinances; for to make in himself of twain one new man, so making peace;
16 And that he might reconcile both unto God in one body by the cross, having slain the enmity thereby:

John 16:7 **Nevertheless I tell you the truth; It is expedient for you that I go away: for if I go not away, the Comforter will not come unto you; but if I depart, I will send him unto you.**

---

[15] Ruckman, Peter S., *Ruckman's Bible References* (Pensacola: Bible Baptist Bookstore, 1997) 297.

John 7:39 **(But this spake he of the Spirit, which they that believe on him should receive: for the Holy Ghost was not yet given; because that Jesus was not yet glorified.)**

John 17:21 **That they all may be one; as thou, Father, art in me, and I in thee, that they also may be one in us: that the world may believe that thou hast sent me.**

Luke 24:49 **And, behold, I send the promise of my Father upon you: but tarry ye in the city of Jerusalem, until ye be endued with power from on high.**

Acts 1:4-5
**4 And, being assembled together with them, commanded them that they should not depart from Jerusalem, but wait for the promise of the Father, which, saith he, ye have heard of me.
5 For John truly baptized with water; but ye shall be baptized with the Holy Ghost ...**

1 Cor 12:13 **For by one Spirit are we all baptized into one body, whether we be Jews or Gentiles, whether we be bond or free; and have been all made to drink into one Spirit.**

The facts that believers were **"added to the church"** (Acts 2:47), and also **"added to the Lord"** (Acts 5:14) before Paul's conversion, indicate that the body existed *prior* to Paul. [Stam does NOT comment on Acts 5:14 in his commentary,[16] nor

---

[16] Stam, C.R. *Acts Dispensationally Considered Vol. I, II* (Germantown Wisconsin: Berean Bible Society, 1954) 184-189.

does Sadler in his booklet *The Historical Beginning of the Church!*] Additionally, 1 Cor. 12:13 proves that Paul was preaching the mystery of the body *before* Acts 18! Other verses that prove conclusively that the body of Christ was present *before* Paul are listed below:

> *Rom 16:7* **Salute Andronicus and Junia, my kinsmen, and my fellowprisoners, who are of note among the apostles, who also <u>were in Christ before me</u>.**

> *Gal 1:13* **For ye have heard of my conversation in time past in the Jews' religion, how that beyond measure I persecuted the <u>church of God</u>, and wasted it:**

> *Acts 9:5* **And he said, Who art thou, Lord? And the Lord said, <u>I am Jesus whom thou persecutest:</u> . . .**

Romans 16:7 is so clear that hyper-dispensationalists must make a difference between being "in Christ," and "in the body of Christ." Joel Finck writes in *The Berean Searchlight:* "Being 'in Christ' is not necessarily the same as being 'in the body of Christ.'"[17] This is a grave inaccuracy. Paul said that the Corinthians were "**in Christ**" (1 Cor. 1:30) and also that they *were* "**the body of Christ**."

> *1 Cor 12:27* **Now ye are the body of Christ, and members in particular.**

Galatians 1:13 and Acts 9:5 confirm that the body of Christ was on the earth as "the church." Otherwise, how could Paul

---
[17] Finck, Joel W. "Are the Twelve Apostles in the Body of Christ," *The Berean Searchlight* 08/03: 19.

(as an unsaved man) persecute Jesus when He was at the right hand of God? Hypers assume that the body of Christ could not exist until it was revealed to Paul. What they do not understand, is that revelation of a truth has nothing to do with the reality of the particular truth. For instance, the death of Jesus was an atonement for individual sinners, even though it was not revealed as such until Acts 8. Paul never said the body of Christ began with him, he only said that the "mystery" of it was "revealed" to him (Eph. 3:3,4).

What hypers eventually do is invent another other "body" (one before Acts 9) called the "Kingdom Church."[18] Those in the "Kingdom Church" would include Peter, James and John. Since Peter, James and John were baptized by the Spirit in Acts 2 (which would place them *in the body*), hypers are forced to "teach two or three baptisms of the Spirit."[19]

Hypers fail to associate John 17:21 (**"that they also may be one IN US"**) with the promise of Luke 24:49 and Acts 1:4,5 (which see). While Baker admits the apostles were baptized with the Holy Spirit, he denies that it placed them in the "body of believers, as described in 1 Corinthians 12:13."[20]

Furthermore, hypers must get around the fact that Peter was writing to those **"in Christ"** (1 Pet. 3:16; 5:14), thus proving he was in the body. Finck alleges that Peter uses the phrase "in a redemptive sense rather than the dispensational sense of being in the body of Christ."[21] He does this to discount Peter's epistles for Church Age doctrine.

Hypers must also ignore plain references to other Jews (remember Paul was a Jew) living during Paul's time that were said to be a part of the **"one body."**

---

[18] Sadler, Paul M., *The Historical Beginning of the Church* (Germantown, WI: Berean Bible Society, 1996) 15.
[19] Ruckman, *Hyper-Dispensationalism*, 21.
[20] Baker, Charles F. *A Dispensational Synopsis of the New Testament* (Grand Rapids: Grace Publications, 1989) 33.
[21] Finck, *The Berean Searchlight* 08/03: 19.

Rom 12:5 **So we, being many, are one body in Christ, and every one members one of another.**

Finck" comments: "Paul is not saying in Rom. 12:5 that every believer living at that time was a member of the body of Christ."[22] Hypers invent a special class of "body mystery believers" converted under Paul. According to their system Romans 12:5 might read this way: "So, those Gentiles who were converted after *my* conversion and revelation of the mystery, are one body, which is different than the kingdom body of Jewish believers who received a different gospel by Peter to the circumcision." They fail to remember that Peter's GENTILE converts, were saved just like Paul's converts (see Acts 10)!

"ONE BAPTISM"

Their attempt to prove the body of Christ is not in Acts 2 is not their only impairment. They insist: "water baptism ends"[23] in Acts 28 with the rejection of the gospel from Israel. They assert: "Paul, the apostle of the Gentiles, the teacher of the Church, never once commands us to be baptized with water?"[24] They answer the question, "Should I be baptized" with:

> While many pastors would say "yes," the Apostle Paul says "no." Water baptism was once a part of God's program for His people Israel, but it is not a part of God's program for His people today, the Body of Christ.[25]

---

[22] *Ibid.*
[23] Stam, C.R. *Water Baptism* (Germantown Wisconsin: Berean Bible Society, 1998) 10.
[24] *Ibid.*, 12.
[25] Kurth, Ricky *Now That I Believe (Part 2)* (Germantown Wisconsin: Berean Bible Society, 2004) 17.

Although Paul never answered that question in his writings, hypers emphatically answer "in his name." Paul answered with his works (he was baptized, and he baptized others)!

They lump baptism in with circumcision (Jewish), miracles (sign to the Jews), healing, and tongues. They think the reason Paul was "thankful" that he did not baptize any more converts (other than Crispus and Gaius) was because he was NOT to do any more baptisms.[26] They believe Eph. 4:4,5 cancels out any water baptism for this age.

HUNG UP TO DRY

Below are the Bible answers to this anti-baptism (dry-cleaning) fixation:

ANSWER ONE

The commission in Matthew 28 is NOT distinctly Jewish, or the word "nations" would not have been used. [All the confusion over the different "commissions" overlooks the fact that Paul is the only apostle that fulfilled the "Tribulation commission" of Mark 16:16-18 (all except drinking the poison).]

ANSWER TWO

The mode of baptism in Matt. 28 is NOT the same as Acts 2:38. All three names of the Godhead are used in Matt. 28 while only the name of "Jesus Christ" is used in Acts 2.

ANSWER THREE

All three names (plural) are said to be a "name" (singular). This is interesting, because in Acts 10:48 Gentiles are baptized

---

[26] Stam, *Water Baptism*, 14.

by Peter, not in the name of Jesus Christ, but in the "name (singular) of the Lord" - "Father, Son, and Holy Ghost."

ANSWER FOUR

Church history testifies to the fact of believers baptism (immersion) *after* conversion. Hypers believe that the truth was missing all these years, and was finally revealed and "recovered."[27]

ANSWER FIVE

Paul was baptized, and we are to follow Paul. To this contention, hypers may respond, "Paul was circumcised too, but we should not get circumcised." This comparison is not justifiable. For, Paul was circumcised as a Jew, but baptized as a believer in Jesus Christ. Baptism was something NEW CONVERTS did! Paul was a new convert, placed into the "one body," and was baptized as a "new creature," not a Jew or Gentile! As Ruckman states, "Paul COMMANDED NO ONE to attend church, pass out tracts, proselyte Baptists who are already saved, or argue about water baptism."[28]

ANSWER SIX

Furthermore, Peter, James, and John were all baptized, and so was Jesus Christ. Hypers claim that Christ's baptism was his priestly "anointing."[29] They go to the Greek and are thereby confused with "washing" and "baptism." Jesus was not anointed as a priest on earth! His earthly ministry was that of a prophet (John 1:25; 4:19; 6:14; 7:40; Deut. 18:18). The priestly role of Jesus Christ took place *after* He died and rose again! See: Heb. 2:17; 3:1; 4:14.

---

[27] Sadler, Paul M. "From the Editor," *The Berean Searchlight* 05/03: 4.
[28] Ruckman, *Hyper-Dispensationalism*, 20.
[29] *Companion Bible* (Grand Rapids: Kregel, 1990) 1313.

Answer Seven

Paul baptized his own converts, AFTER Acts 9! The meaning of 1 Cor. 1:17 is *clear* if one adheres to the context. A verse without a context is useless. Christ did not send ANYONE *just* to baptize, but to preach!

Answer Eight

Just because the phrase "one baptism" is used, does not annul water baptism. If it did, Paul would not have baptized anyone, and would have COMMANDED believers NOT to be baptized in water.

The context again clears up any misunderstanding. Notice the framework is *unity:* "one another," (vs. 2); "unity of the Spirit" (vs. 3); and seven "ones" in the passage (verses 5,6). Paul is saying that there is only one "saving baptism." This would match Rom. 6:3; Gal. 3:27; Col. 2:12; 1 Cor. 12:13 and Matt. 3:11. That must be the correct "interpretation," since we know there are MANY "lords," MANY "faiths" and MANY "spirits:"

> *1 Cor 8:5-6*
> **5 For though there be that are called gods, whether in heaven or in earth, (as there be gods many, and lords many,)**
> **6 But to us there is but one God, the Father, of whom are all things, and we in him; and one Lord Jesus Christ, by whom are all things, and we by him.**

> *Mark 3:11* **And unclean spirits, when they saw him, fell down before him, and cried, saying, Thou art the Son of God.**

CONFESSION OF SIN

As alluded to earlier, hypers sever the word of God up into such thin slices, that ONLY Paul's epistles (and maybe only his *prison* epistles) are allowed for Church Age doctrine. Once that presupposition is taken, Peter, James and John are not allowed in the body of Christ, although they are "in Christ" (1 Peter 3:16; 5:14). To them, Peter's epistles cannot contain ANY Church Age doctrine, nor can 1 John through Jude.

This brings us to an important question: Should a Christian confess his sins to God for forgiveness according to 1 John 1:9? While the hypers do not believe in sinless perfection (like some Holiness groups), they do, however, preclude a Christian confessing his sins, distort the Grace of God, and fail to understand the "standing and state" of the believer.

Hyper Ken Lawson, says that 1 John. 1:9 "has caused untold harm and detriment to the people of God."[30] He thinks a Christian should not feel guilty about his sins (after salvation) since "God wishes for us to enjoy the gift of salvation."[31] He claims that God will not "continue to show him [the believer] the cold shoulder"[32] if he "fails to confess wrongdoing."

So, hypers do not believe a Christian's fellowship with Jesus Christ is based on *their* personal, holy walk. Lawson's arguments against the "Father, son, relationship" understanding of 1 John 1 are as follows:

> It is based on a performance system of conditional blessing, and shifted my gaze away from Christ and His grace to my own faithfulness (or usually failure) to confess.[33]

---

[30] Lawson, Ken, "The Confession of Sin," *The Berean Searchlight* 01/03: 14.
[31] *Ibid.*, 16.
[32] *Ibid.*, 17.
[33] *Ibid.*

Repentance, and confession of sin (both of which hypers snub) are CLEARLY a part of the believer's fellowship with God the Father, *in every dispensation!* Peter had to confess his love to Jesus Christ, before he could be restored (John 21), and we are not any better than him! Who (but hypers) would think that sin was not acknowledged (Ps. 51:13) with Peter's *three confessions* in John 21?

Over and over again, fellowship (not salvation) is predicated upon repentance - the stem of confession. Hypers do NOT believe in REPENTANCE. Note the following verses:

> *Lev 5:5* **And it shall be, when he shall be guilty in one of these things, that he shall confess that he hath sinned in that thing:**

> *Isa 64:6-7*
> **6 But we are all as an unclean thing, and all our righteousnesses are as filthy rags; and we all do fade as a leaf; and our iniquities, like the wind, have taken us away.**
> **7 And there is none that calleth upon thy name, that stirreth up himself to take hold of thee: for thou hast hid thy face from us, and hast consumed us, because of our iniquities.**

> *Prov 28:13* **He that covereth his sins shall not prosper: but whoso confesseth and forsaketh them shall have mercy.**

> *Num 5:7* **Then they shall confess their sin which they have done: and he shall recompense his trespass with the principal thereof, and add unto it the fifth part thereof, and give it unto him against whom he hath trespassed.**

Lev 26:40 **If they shall confess their iniquity, and the iniquity of their fathers, with their trespass which they trespassed against me, and that also they have walked contrary unto me;**

Neh 1:6 **Let thine ear now be attentive, and thine eyes open, that thou mayest hear the prayer of thy servant, which I pray before thee now, day and night, for the children of Israel thy servants, and confess the sins of the children of Israel, which we have sinned against thee: both I and my father's house have sinned.**

Ps 32:5 **I acknowledged my sin unto thee, and mine iniquity have I not hid. I said, I will confess my transgressions unto the LORD; and thou forgavest the iniquity of my sin. Selah.**

Ps 38:18 **For I will declare mine iniquity; I will be sorry for my sin.**

Josh 7:19 **And Joshua said unto Achan, My son, give, I pray thee, glory to the LORD God of Israel, and make confession unto him; and tell me now what thou hast done; hide it not from me.**

Dan 9:4 **And I prayed unto the LORD my God, and made my confession, and said, O Lord, the great and dreadful God, keeping the covenant and mercy to them that love him, and to them that keep his commandments;**

Hos 5:15 **I will go and return to my place, till they acknowledge their offence, and seek my face: in their affliction they will seek me early.**

2 Sam 12:13 **And David said unto Nathan, I have sinned against the LORD. And Nathan said unto David, The LORD also hath put away thy sin; thou shalt not die.**

Isa 6:5 **Then said I, Woe is me! for I am undone; because I am a man of unclean lips, and I dwell in the midst of a people of unclean lips: for mine eyes have seen the King, the LORD of hosts.**

Matt 3:6 **And were baptized of him in Jordan, confessing their sins.**

1 Cor 11:31 **For if we would judge ourselves, we should not be judged.**

Acts 19:18 **And many that believed came, and confessed, and shewed their deeds.**

The last two references are during the "dispensation of the mystery." How do you "judge" yourself without confessing and repenting of your sins? Answer: you cannot, and some do not, therefore, they fall under the chastening hand of Almighty God according to Hebrews 12 (which hypers disregard for the Church Age).

The real Berean who "**rightly**" divides, (instead of "wrongly shredding the word") will notice that the people who confess in Acts 19 do so under Paul's preaching. If they confessed publicly to men, you KNOW they had to confess to God! In

Hyper-dispensationalism 333

fact Paul attributed God's presence to himself while he was preaching and teaching the word.

> *2 Cor 2:17* **For we are not as many, which corrupt the word of God: but as of sincerity, but as of God, in the sight of God speak we in Christ.**

> *1 Thess 2:13* **For this cause also thank we God without ceasing, because, when ye received the word of God which ye heard of us, ye received it not as the word of men, but as it is in truth, the word of God, which effectually worketh also in you that believe.**

The next problem that Lawson has with the word of God, concerns prayer and *honesty*.

> If what I believed concerning confession was true, I was probably 'out of fellowship' much of the time, and so were most believers.[34]

Yes, "most believers" are "out of fellowship" with the Lord, for only through a constant "cleansing of ourselves" (2 Cor. 7:1) through PRAYER (1 Thess. 5:17) can we be "in fellowship." Notice Lawson's excuse: "I had to honestly admit to myself that I found it extremely difficult to confess all my daily sins on a consistent basis." So, since prayer and confession is "difficult," hypers find scriptural alibis to disobey 1 John 1:7-9, as well as *Paul's command* to "**pray without ceasing.**"

Note also, that the verse does not stipulate confession of **every** sin. It simply states a fact: When you mess up, you can

---

[34] *Ibid.*

go to the Lord, confess, and the blood of Jesus (the basis for forgiveness) will clean you.

> *Heb 9:14* **How much more shall the blood of Christ, who through the eternal Spirit offered himself without spot to God, purge your conscience from dead works to serve the living God?**

Lawson (as all hypers do) reverts to Paul for a defense:

> Paul, the apostle of the Gentiles, is silent in all his writings on confession of sins for forgiveness, parental or otherwise.[35]

Paul never forbad the practice either. Should we not observe the omissions as well as the commands? As pointed out earlier, Paul did NOT rebuke the Ephesians from "confessing" (Acts 19) when he preached. In fact, Paul's preaching pivoted upon the message of REPENTANCE (which is the heart of confession):

> *Acts 20:21* **Testifying both to the Jews, and also to the Greeks, repentance toward God, and faith toward our Lord Jesus Christ.**

> *Acts 26:20* **But shewed first unto them of Damascus, and at Jerusalem, and throughout all the coasts of Judaea, and then to the Gentiles, that they should repent and turn to God, and do works meet for repentance.**

Going further from the truth, Lawson tries to prove 1 John 1 is not relevant to a Church Age saint, because "A believer

---

[35] *Ibid.*, 18.

cannot walk in darkness any more than an unbeliever can walk in the light."[36] Has he failed to read the favorite book of hyper-dispensationalists - Ephesians?

> *Eph 5:8* **For ye were sometimes darkness, but now are ye light in the Lord: walk as children of light:**
>
> *Eph 5:11-14*
> **11 And have no fellowship with the unfruitful works of darkness, but rather reprove them.**
> **12 For it is a shame even to speak of those things which are done of them in secret.**
> **13 But all things that are reproved are made manifest by the light: for whatsoever doth make manifest is light.**
> **14 Wherefore he saith, Awake thou that sleepest, and arise from the dead, and Christ shall give thee light.**

If the Lord commands us to "**walk as children of light**" (Eph. 5:8), then obviously there are believers who are NOT "walking in the light." The "sleeper" in Eph. 5:14, is NOT an unbeliever, he is a Christian. Paul often edified the believer to "walk in the light" *instead* of darkness:

> *Rom 13:11-13*
> **11 And that, knowing the time, that now it is high time to awake out of sleep: for now is our salvation nearer than when we believed.**
> **12 The night is far spent, the day is at hand: let us therefore cast off the works of darkness, and let us put on the armour of light.**

---

[36] *Ibid.*, 19.

13 Let us walk honestly, as in the day; not in rioting and drunkenness, not in chambering and wantonness, not in strife and envying.

1 Thess 5:4-8
4 But ye, brethren, are not in darkness, that that day should overtake you as a thief.
5 Ye are all the children of light, and the children of the day: we are not of the night, nor of darkness.
6 Therefore let us not sleep, as do others; but let us watch and be sober.
7 For they that sleep sleep in the night; and they that be drunken are drunken in the night.
8 But let us, who are of the day, be sober, putting on the breastplate of faith and love; and for an helmet, the hope of salvation.

While it is true that *positionally*, every child of God is "in the light" (in Christ, in heavenly places), practically 1 John 1 applies *along with* Paul's epistles (Ephesians, Romans, and 1 Thessalonians) in a doctrinal manner to the New Testament saint. [Hypers forget that good "sound doctrine" (1 Tim. 1:10) refers not only to the revelation of the "Pauline mystery," but to BEHAVIOR! Read 1 Tim. 1:9]

Some hypers may not believe in "sinless perfection" (like some Holiness groups) but they do believe in "constant fellowship." Notice Lawson again:

> If any believers were living in a state of broken fellowship, it was the Corinthians.
> A. There were carnal divisions and contentions among them (1 Cor. 1:10-13; 3:1-3).
> B. They were infatuated with worldly wisdom (1 Cor. 1:28-2:5; 3:18-23).

C. They were judging things which they should not and failing to judge things which they should (1 Cor. 4:1-5; 5:6).

D. They were allowing sexual immorality in the local church and were proud of it (1 Cor. 5:1,2).

E. They were taking each other to court before the unbelievers (1 Cor. 6:1-12).

F. They were visiting harlots (1 Cor. 6:13-20).

G. They were proud of their knowledge and causing weaker brethren to stumble (1 Cor. 8).

H. They were questioning Paul's authority and apostleship (1 Cor. 9:1-6)

I. They were prone to idolatry by lusting after evil things (1 Cor. 10).

J. They had disorders at church, including making a mockery of the Lord's Supper (1 Cor. 11).

K. They were enamored with the spiritual gifts but were failing to exercise them in love (1 Cor. 12-14).

L. They were doubting the resurrection (1 Cor. 15:12-19).

M. If all this was not enough, they were stingy in their contribution to the poor saints (2 Cor. 8:9).

. . . . Moreover, there is no command to confess their sins in order to receive forgiveness and restoration to fellowship. On the contrary, Paul assures them that 'God is faithful, by whom ye were called unto the fellowship of His son Jesus Christ our Lord' (1 Cor. 1:9). It is a fellowship based upon God's faithfulness.[37]

So, basically, Lawson is teaching that the immoral living Corinthians were in sweet fellowship with a holy God. Anyone who can read the letter to the Corinthians from Paul, and get *that* summation, would probably think the Koran contains good marital advice! Read the following verses and note how they *drive at* confession and repentance: 1 Cor 3:1-4; 1 Cor 3:17; 1 Cor 4:2; 1 Cor 4:6; 1 Cor 4:14; 1 Cor 4:18-20; 1

---

[37] Lawson, Ken, "The Confession of Sin Cont'd," *The Berean Searchlight* 02/03: 15, 16.

Cor 5:1-2; 1 Cor 5:6-7; 1 Cor 5:13; 1 Cor 6:5; 1 Cor 6:18; and on and on.

The very fact of their repentance (given in 2 Corinthians) stipulates confession:

> *2 Cor 7:9* **Now I rejoice, not that ye were made sorry, but that ye sorrowed to repentance: for ye were made sorry after a godly manner, that ye might receive damage by us in nothing.**
>
> *2 Cor 7:11* **For behold this selfsame thing, that ye sorrowed after a godly sort, what carefulness it wrought in you, yea, what clearing of yourselves, yea, what indignation, yea, what fear, yea, what vehement desire, yea, what zeal, yea, what revenge! In all things ye have approved yourselves to be clear in this matter.**
>
> *2 Cor 12:21* **And lest, when I come again, my God will humble me among you, and that I shall bewail many which have sinned already, and have not repented of the uncleanness and fornication and lasciviousness which they have committed.**

Hypers teach Satan (not the Lord) burdens the believer with conviction of sin and guilt:

> Guilt is a killer, a killer of our joy, our peace, and our enjoyment of intimacy with God. If Satan can use guilt (which our Lord has already taken away) to use as a wedge to separate us from God, his strategy to take us as a captive in the battle is secure. . . . Our fellowship with Jesus Christ our Lord can never be broken.[38]

---

[38] *Ibid.*, 18, 20.

They disregarded Paul's comment: **"ye sorrowed after a godly** [not devily] **sort"** (2 Cor. 7:1), and the repercussion of broken fellowship in the life of the believer - the Judgment Seat of Christ. *Why* the Judgment Seat of Christ, if a believer is never out of fellowship? Adam was saved by "grace" and "the blood of a lamb" (Gen. 3:21) and he was OUT OF FELLOWSHIP with God! Hypers abandon the distinction ("rightly dividing" right?) between the Christian's *standing* and *state*. Scofield appositely comments: "Positionally he [the believer] is 'perfected forever' (Heb. 10:14), but looking within, at his state, he must say, ' Not as though I had already attained, either were already perfect' (Phil. 3:12)."[39]

This "unfatherly grace" of hypers culminates with a hollow answer to the problem of sin in the life of a believer:

> . . . .even the most mature Christians do sin. When this happens, the first thing to remember is our complete forgiveness in Christ Jesus. This will prevent us from going on another guilt trip. . ."[40]

Was the "godly sorrow" (2 Cor.) just a "low self esteem" guilt trip? Or, was it true repentance and confession of sin? Lawson continues:

> When a Christian sins, we should agree with God's Word that it is wrong (confess) and forsake the behavior or attitude . . . So we confess our sins, not in order to receive forgiveness, but because we wish to be properly attuned to grace and to thus glorify Him who has forgiven us all trespasses.[41]

---

[39] Scofield, C.I., *Rightly Dividing the Word of Truth* (New Jersey: Loizeaux Brothers, 1896) 53.
[40] Lawson, Ken, "The Confession of Sin Cont'd," *The Berean Searchlight* 02/03: 21.
[41] *Ibid.*, 22.

What is all this "behavior," and "attitude" garbage? Is it Bible? "We wish to be properly *attuned*?" After writing two articles with the intent of impeding the confession of sin to God, Lawson says that we should confess our sins (but not for forgiveness)! Do you think the Corinthians just "properly attuned" themselves, or did they actually CONFESS THEIR SINS because they wanted restored fellowship? How could they "repent" without confession? A hyper no more believes in repentance for today (Church Age) than he does sabbath worship.

Lawson's conclusion about the doctrinal meaning of 1 John 1:9 is as shallow as a teardrop:

> Our key verse in 1 John 1:9 is found to be a salvation verse for Israel looking for the return of Christ to establish His earthly, Davidic, Millennial Kingdom . . . In conclusion, 1 John 1:9 is a salvation verse which fits 'hand in glove' with the Prophecy program of the Gospel of the kingdom.[42]

If it is a salvation verse for Israel in the Tribulation, why is the word "all" used in 1 John 1 "all sin" (vs. 7); "all unrighteousness" (vs. 9). Rev. 14:11 explains that there is NO REMEDY (confession or otherwise) for taking the mark of the beast. A person will no more be washed from "all sin" in the Tribulation by the confession of it, than a person NOW can be saved by the golden rule!

If 1 John 1:9 is a salvation verse for Israel in the Tribulation, why are the believers in 1 John said to be **"sons of God"** awaiting the "appearing" (not advent) of the Lord. No Tribulation saint will **"be like he is"** (1 John 3) because no Tribulation saint will be a member of the body of Christ.

---

[42] *Ibid.*, 17,22.

"The blood of Jesus Christ" did NOT cleanse anyone during the gospel of the kingdom message in Matthew, Mark or Luke. 1 John cannot be applied to Israel. [This brings up a difference between the "gospel of the kingdom" *prior* to the cross, and "the gospel of the kingdom" *after* the cross, preached during the Tribulation. In the Tribulation, the "gospel of the kingdom" will include the **"faith of Jesus Christ"** (Rev. 13:10; 14:12). That is, a person must believe that Jesus Christ is not only Messiah, but the Saviour. Belief in the substitutionary atonement of Christ is crucial to a person's salvation in the Tribulation period.]

FRUITS OF HYPER-DISPENSATIONALISM

The heresies of hyper-dispensationalists produce such "deep Bible study," that its adherents drown under its influences. Their teachings are inconsistent with the scriptures, and manufacture Christians *inactive*. Wining lost souls to Jesus Christ is not the "drive" of hypers, even though it *was* for the apostle Paul. They are obsessed with *stopping* water baptism, and "following Paul" *nowhere*. As Dr. Ruckman suitably summarizes: "The only theme song they have is "How dry I am, how dry I am," and their teaching and preaching is as dry as their baptism"[43]

---

[43] Ruckman, *Hyper-Dispensationalism*, 20.

CHAPTER 13

Answers for the Critics

1 Peter 3:15 **But sanctify the Lord God in your hearts: <u>and be ready always to give an answer</u> to every man that asketh you a reason of the hope that is in you with meekness and fear:**

In this chapter of our apologetic section, we are going to examine a few books that are decidedly anti-dispensational and against the pre-trib rapture. We have chosen a few of the more "popular" works, ones you might find in circulation at a local Christian bookstore.

BOOK ONE: *THE INCREDIBLE COVER-UP*
(Exposing the Origins of Rapture Theories)
BY: DAVE MACPHERSON

MELODRAMATIC NONSENSE!

Our first book under examination is *The Incredible Cover-Up* by Dave MacPherson. First published back in 1975, this book remains influential in the dispensational/covenantal debate. The premise behind this volume hinges upon rejection of *biblical final authority* and acceptance of *available church history*.

Dave MacPherson claims that the pretrib rapture originated by a vision from a demon possessed Scottish teen-aged girl in 1830:

> We have seen that a young Scottish lassie named Margaret Macdonald had a private revelation in Port Glasgow, Scotland, in the early part of 1830 that a select group of Christians would be caught up to meet Christ in the air *before* the days of Antichrist.[1]

He then claims that Darby learned this doctrine from her, and began teaching it as his own system:

> Darby borrowed from her, modified her views, and then popularized them under his own name without giving her credit . . . . Darby, then, did his part to draw attention away from the real origin of his special teaching.[2]

There are several glitches in MacPherson's deceptive sentiments, but the most obtrusive regards what this Scottish girl actually taught in her "vision."

A simple reading of Margaret Macdonald's statement (found on pages 245-248 in *The Rapture* by LaHaye) reveals that she promoted the *post-trib* position, NOT the pre-trib one! Take note:

---

[1] MacPherson, Dave., *The Incredible Cover-Up* (Medford: Omega Publications, 1975) 93.
[2] *Ibid.*, 85.

> I saw the people of God in an awfully dangerous situation, surrounded by nets and entanglements, about to be tried, and many about to be deceived and fall. . . . This is the fiery trial which is to try us. It will be for the purging and purifying of the real members of the body of Jesus; but Oh, it will be a firey trial. . . . The trial of the church is from Antichrist. It is by being filled with the Spirit that we shall be kept.[3]

The "Scottish lassie" did not catapult the pre-trib doctrine! That is *not* what she taught! MacPherson even admits that "Margaret saw a series of raptures (and she was actually a partial rapturist, with or without the label).[4]

PRE-TRIB *BEFORE* 1830

MacPherson is also not a very good "researcher" and "journalist." Notice how his comments are contrary to the *evidence*:

> . . . all Christians before 1830 who held to an imminent coming really held to an imminent post-trib coming . . . No one before 1830 ever believed in an imminent pre-trib coming. Nor did they differentiate the return of Christ and the rapture of the church.[5]

Below are the following facts that prove otherwise, some of which we have noted previously:

1. The pretribulation rapture is discussed by a Baptist pastor named Morgan Edwards called *Millennium, Last Days Novelities*, written in 1788.[6]

---

[3] LaHaye, Tim, *The Rapture* (Eugene, Oregon: Harvest House Publishers, 2002) 247.
[4] MacPherson, *The Incredible Cover-Up*, 85.
[5] *Ibid.*, 110.
[6] LaHaye, Tim, *The Rapture* (Eugene, Oregon: Harvest House Publishers, 2002) 42.

2. A martyr named *Hugh Latimer* burned in 1555 believed in the rapture:

> Peradventure it may come in my days, old as I am, or in my children's days . . . the sants 'shall be taken up to meet Christ in the air' and so shall come down with Him again.[7]

3. The statement of a sermon on the last days written possibly by Ephrem of Nisibis (306-373). He was a Syrian church father. The latest date suggested is between 565 and 627.[8] Note:

> Why therefore do we not reject every care of earthly actions and prepare ourselves for the meeting of the Lord Christ, so that he may draw us from the confusion, which overwhelms all the world? . . . All the saints and elect of God are gathered together before the tribulation, which is to come, and are taken to the Lord, in order that they may not see at any time the confusion which overwhelms the world because of our sins.[9]

4. A quote by St. Victorinus, Bishop of Petau in A.D. 270 in a commentary on Revelation:

> And I saw another great and wonderful sign, seven angels having the seven last plagues; for in them is completed the indignation of God. For the wrath of God always strikes the obstinate people with seven plagues, that is, perfectly, as it is said in Leviticus; and these shall be in the last time, when the church shall have gone out of the midst.[10]

---

[7] *Ibid.*, 29 [LaHaye quoting Ryrie, Charles, *The Basis of the Premillennial Faith* (New York: Loizeaux Brothers, 1953), 29.]

[8] *Ibid.*, 43.

[9] *Ibid.*, 43-44. [LaHaye quoting Grant, Jeffrey, *Apocalypse* (Toronto, ON: Frontier Research Publications, 1992), 85-94.]

[10] *Ibid.*, 156. [LaHaye quoting St. Victorinus, Bishop of Petau, "The Writings of Tertullianus," trans. R.E. Wallis, *Commentary on the Apocalypse of the Blessed John*, vol. III, published by

1 THESSALONIANS 5

MacPherson endeavors to use 1 Thessalonians 5 to prove a post-trib rapture:

> It's unfortunate that there is a chapter division right after I Thessalonians 4:18. I Thessalonians 5:1 begins with the word "But" (a connecting word). Anyone reading both chapters without interruption can easily see that chapter five continues to describe I Thessalonians 4:13-18 as the "day of the Lord" - the time when "sudden destruction" comes on the ungodly world. This ties in with the coming of Christ in judgment. All of which means that the church's "catching up" will be post-trib; if sudden destruction were to take place *before* or *during* the tribulation, how could there be a tribulation?[11]

Just because chapter five is a continuation of chapter four does not dictate that it is describing 1 Thess. 4:13-18. Rather, it is moving *forward* in the storyline of events. The "rundown" is as follows:

1. The **"day of the Lord"** is the physical, literal second advent of Jesus Christ. We call this the "revelation." See the following verses: Isa. 13:6; 13:9; Jer. 46:10; Ezek. 13:5; Joel 1:15; 2:1; 2:11; 2:31; 3:14; Amos 5:18,29; Obadiah 1:15; Zeph. 1:7,14; Zech 14:1; Acts 2:20.

2. Since we are **"the children of light"** we are NOT **"appointed"** to this **"wrath"** of Rev. 6:16,17.

T. Clark, 1870, 428.]
[11] MacPherson, *The Incredible Cover-Up*, 107.

3. The whole passage is one of contrast. The **"children of light"** are distinguished between those of **"the night."** Our salvation from destruction is contrasted with the false **"safety"** of the lost; and our "catching up" with their **"not escap[ing]."**

2 PETER 3 – "LOOKING"

> Pre-tribs tell us that we can't look for Christ's imminent return because certain things have to happen *first*. Thus the rapture is imminent, but the second coming is not.
> II Peter 3:12-13 reminds us to be looking for the time when "elements shall melt with fervent heat" and looking for "new heavens and a new earth" – all of which is at least a thousand years away, according to many pre-tribs. Why, then, can't we watch for a post-trib coming that might be just a few years away?[12]

The second advent is *not* "imminent" according to the Lord Jesus Himself! The first twenty-six verses of Matthew 24 tell any *sane* "researcher" of the signs *prior* to the second advent!

Additionally, MacPherson cares *nothing* about the context of 2 Peter 3, which is **"the last days"** (verse 3), and *anti-covetousness* (verse 11). Peter is telling someone (who is capable of taking a **"spot"** - verse 14 with Rev. 13:1-3, 18) not to **"fall"** (verse 17 with Heb. 6) into the trap of Satan. This **"error of the wicked"** (verse 17) is connected to the *god* of this **"heavens and earth, which are now"** (verse 7 with Gen. 1:8 and Eph. 6:12)! MacPherson puts the church in this Tribulation section of 2 Peter, not even realizing he has consigned a possibility of saved people losing their salvation. [He, along with all others who reject the AV 1611, fail to

---
[12] *Ibid.*, 108.

comprehend Tribulation application in Matthew, Hebrews, James and Peter's epistles.]

OLD TESTAMENT SAINTS "BORN AGAIN?"

We will conclude our rebuttal of MacPherson's errors with one more quote: "The Old Testament saints were also born again and indwelt by the Holy Spirit (Ezek. 36:26-7)..."[13]

The passage he quotes in Ezekiel is written in the *future tense,* as a promise of restoration to the nation of Israel *corporately.* This takes place when "**all Israel shall be saved**" (Rom. 11:26), and is contingent upon them "**dwell[ing] in the land**" (Ezek. 36:28).

MacPherson perverts Old Testament soteriology in order to make Israel and the Church synonomous. He then equates Church Age saints with Tribulation saints, stating, "both are saved by grace and the blood of Christ (Eph. 1:7, Revelation 7:14)."[14]

Dave MacPherson is following the serpents tactics – telling ¾ of the truth in order to push a lie! The saints in the Tribulation MUST "**keep the commandments of God**" (Rev. 12:17; 14:12; 22:14) *and* believe in the blood! No Old Testament saint was ever "born again" even if they had the Spirit of God! Was Saul "born again?" He *lost* the Spirit of God, and received an evil spirit (see 1 Sam. 16:14)! Can that happen to you? Not if you are saved and born again in this Age (Eph. 1:13; 4:30; John 7:37,38).

MacPherson's fanatic and faulty accusations, along with his defective Bible exegesis classifies his book for *file thirteen.*

---

[13] *Ibid.,* 113.
[14] *Ibid.*

BOOK TWO: *THE LAST DAYS ACCORDING TO JESUS*
(*When Did Jesus Say He Would Return?*)
BY: R.C. SPROUL

PRETERIST PSYCHOSIS!

Calvinist R.C. Sproul (featured on a popular radio program "Renewing Your Mind") proliferates his prejudicial preterist "**private interpretations**" (2 Peter 1:20) in his book, *The Last Days According To Jesus*.

OLIVET DISCOURSE FULFILLMENT

> The preterist view includes the tribulation and the abomination of desolation with signs that take place prior to the destruction of Jerusalem.[15]

Sproul by quoting Russell, Albright and Mann says that the abomination of desolation was the placing of the "idolatrous images"[16] of the Roman soldiers (ie. Roman imperial eagle) in the temple area in A.D. 70.

Not only does this preterist nonsense rebuff the *future* cross-reference to 2 Thessalonians 2, its logic, when applied consistently is incongruous! They claim that "the abomination of desolation" had to be fulfilled 37 years after Christ foretold it, but allow Daniel's prophecy (of the same event) over 600 years of leeway. Notice their faulty assumption:

> We can interpret the time-frame references literally and the events surrounding the parousia figuratively. In this view, all of Jesus' prophecies in the Olivet Discourse

---

[15] Sproul, R.C., *The Last Days According to Jesus* (Grand Rapids: Baker Books, 1998) 39.
[16] *Ibid.*

were fulfilled during the period between the discourse itself and the destruction of Jerusalem in A.D. 70.[17]
[*"Parousia" refers to the second advent.*]

Preterist contend that Matthew 24 had to be fulfilled in A.D. 70 or Jesus' prophecy would have failed:

> If both "this generation" and "all these things" are taken at face value, then neither all the content of Jesus' Olivet Discourse, including the parousia he describes here, have already take place (in some sense), or at least some of Jesus' prophecy failed to take place within the time-frame assigned to it. [18]

Well, if the events of Matthew 24 were fulfilled what about the "**wars and rumors of wars?**"

Sproul quotes a few sources listing these "wars" as follows:

> . . . there were violent tumults between the Jews and the Greeks, the Jews and the Syrians, inhabiting the same cities . . . great apprehensions were entertained in Judea of war with the Romans . . . [19]

The Jews fighting suppression hardly qualifies for worldwide wars, nor depicts a fulfillment of the text. Dr. Ruckman:

> "**Wars and rumours of wars**" cannot be applied too well to the immediate time, nor to the apostles who lived before 70 A.D. There is no mention of either "wars" or "rumours of wars" in the Book of Acts, which runs right up to 62 A.D . . . Again, it is impossible to force the passage into the 33-70 A.D. setting. *Nation does not rise against nation* until there are some *nations* to do the "rising," and this cannot be said to be really true until

---
[17] *Ibid.*, 66.
[18] *Ibid.*, 65.
[19] *Ibid.*, 36.

after the invasion of Rome by the Goths, Visigoths, Vandals, and Huns. The passage, then, undoubtedly begins with discussing the events of the END time (Dan. 7,9,11), and only by desperate mishandling and misapplication can the chapter be applied to 70 A.D.[20]

To further construct an A.D. 70 fulfillment, Sproul follows his mentor (J. Stuart Russell) thoughtlessly declaring that

> the carcass where the eagles will be gathered refers to the guilty and devoted children of Israel who will be destroyed by the Roman legions. The carcass is Israel, and the eagles are Rome.[21]

"DAY OF THE LORD" = A.D. 70?

Sproul correctly conveys the preterist ideology regarding the "day of the Lord." He states that they (preterists) "see the fulfillment occurring much closer to Pentecost, namely in the destruction of Jerusalem."[22]

His reasoning is bolstered by scholars (dispensational and preterist) who think as he does: that "part of Joel's prophecy was fulfilled at Pentecost."[23] This disreputable logic presumes that the phrase "**but this is that**" (Acts 2:16) refers to the speaking in tongues. Who (but a *trustworthy* scholar) would miss the cross-references that explain the phraseology? "**But this is that**" refers to the text of scripture that Peter was getting ready to preach out of! Observe the verses:

> *Matt 9:13* **But go ye and learn <u>what that meaneth</u>, I will have mercy, and not sacrifice: for I am not**

---

[20] Ruckman, Peter S., *Matthew* (Pensacola: Bible Believers Press, 1970) 520-521.
[21] Sproul, *The Last Days According to Jesus*, 41.
[22] *Ibid.*, 76.
[23] *Ibid.*, 77.

come to call the righteous, but sinners to repentance.

Matt 12:7 **But if ye had known what** <u>this meaneth</u>**, I will have mercy, and not sacrifice, ye would not have condemned the guiltless.**

Matt 16:18 **And I say also unto thee,** <u>That thou art Peter</u>**, and upon this rock I will build my church; and the gates of hell shall not prevail against it.**

Lev 10:3 **Then Moses said unto Aaron,** <u>This is it that</u> **the LORD spake, saying, I will be sanctified in them that come nigh me, and before all the people I will be glorified. And Aaron held his peace.**

Ex 16:23 **And he said unto them,** <u>This is that which</u> **the LORD hath said, To morrow is the rest of the holy sabbath unto the LORD: bake that which ye will bake to day, and seethe that ye will seethe; and that which remaineth over lay up for you to be kept until the morning.**

Peter does not refer to the speaking in tongues as "**this**" until verse 33! None of Joel's prophecy was fulfilled at Pentecost. Peter is simply preaching a "future kingdom awaiting, Messianic message" to the Jewish people who killed their King.

THE 2ND COMING OF ELIJAH

Since Elijah is prophesied to come *prior* to the day of the Lord, Sproul (as all preterists) must revert to John's coming as a fulfillment. Sproul quoting Russell:

The explicit declaration of our Lord that the predicted Elijah was no other than His own forerunner, John the Baptist (Matt. 11:14) enables us to determine the time and the event referred to as "the great and terrible day of the Lord."[24]

Did Russell (Sproul's "maharishi") not remember that Jesus taught that John's fulfillment of Elijah was conditioned upon someone "receiving" it?

Matt 11:14 **And if ye will receive it, this is Elias, which was for to come.**

Moreover, Elijah's "cry in the wilderness" (see Rev. 12) is not rejected as John's. There are countless conversions among the "house of Israel" in the Great Tribulation (see Rev. 7 and 14).

THE "LAST DAYS" ARE GONE

Preterists are almost as bad as hyper-dispensationalists. They eliminate much scriptural application by forcing verses into diminutive time brackets. "According to the preterists 'the last days' refers to the time between the advent of John the Baptist and the destruction of Jerusalem."[25] By this statement all preterism should be considered "radical," or "full." Full preterists (also called "consistent") believe 1 Cor. 15 "refers to a spiritual resurrection, not a bodily resurrection; and this resurrection has already taken place."[26] This logic, if consistently "squeezed out" teaches that the rapture and resurrection are past, the Tribulation is past, the second advent

---

[24] *Ibid.*, 79.
[25] *Ibid.*, 85.
[26] *Ibid.*, 160.

is past, and all events of the book of Revelation are over. To *that* Paul aptly wrote:

> *2 Tim 2:17-18*
> **17 And their word will eat as doth a canker: of whom is Hymenaeus and Philetus;**
> **18 Who concerning the truth have erred, saying that the resurrection is past already; and overthrow the faith of some.**

Sproul (attempting to be "moderate" instead of "radical") announces:

> I am convinced that the substance of the Olivet Discourse was fulfilled in A.D. 70 and that the bulk of Revelation was likewise fulfilled in that time-frame. . . Jesus really did come in judgment at this time, fulfilling his prophecy in the Olivet Discourse. But this was not the final or ultimate coming of Christ. The parousia, in its fullness, will extend far beyond the Jewish nation and will be universal in its scope and significance. . . . It will be, not merely a day of the Lord, but the final and ultimate day of the Lord.[27]

There you have it. An anti-dispensational, anti-rapture, postmillennial Reformed ordained member of the Presbyterian church, stating that the second coming of Jesus Christ will be in two stages! The first one was a secret (no one saw Him in A.D. 70!) and the second one visible. The very scheme they wrestle with (the second coming in two stages: ie. rapture then revelation), they admit to. It reminds one of the blunders of Calvinism, and is a classic example of typical un-biblical scholarship.

---

[27] *Ibid.*, 158.

The "*partial* preterists" have invented TWO "days of the Lord," TWO "last hours" (1 John 2:18-20) and TWO second advents. The "*full* preterists" believe that the Antichrist was Nero,[28] the rapture occurred around A.D. 70 or "that the rapture adapts a Roman ceremony of victory and is therefore symbolic."[29] They (both avenues "full" and "partial") expect to see "the virtual Christianization of the nations,"[30] and "the success of the great commission in this age of the church."[31] In other words, they are living in a dream world.

BOOK THREE: *A CASE FOR AMILLENNIALISM*
Understanding the End Times
BY: KIM RIDDLEBARGER

AMILLENNIAL ABSURDITY!

Kim Riddlebarger (pastor of Christ Reformed Church in Anaheim California) reawakens the dead amillennial perspective in his book *A Case for Amillennialism.*

Claiming to have converted from dispensationalism, Riddlebarger thinks he can point out the "errors" of premillennial dispensationalism.[32] He contends that amillennialism "is a more biblical way to understand the Bible's teaching on the coming of the Lord and the millennial age."[33]

IN A NUTSHELL

---

[28] *Ibid.*, 186.
[29] *Ibid.*, 169.
[30] *Ibid.*, 200.
[31] *Ibid.*
[32] Riddlebarger, Kim, *A Case for Amillennialism* (Grand Rapids: Baker, 2003) 11.
[33] *Ibid.*

Below is a lengthy quote stating the Reformed amillennial position, and summarizes the entire 271 pages of this book:

> Amillennialists hold that the promises made to Israel, David, and Abraham in the Old Testament are fulfilled by Jesus Christ and his church during this present age. The millennium is the period of time between the two advents of our Lord with the thousand years of Revelation 20 being symbolic of the entire interadvental age. At the first advent of Jesus Christ, Satan was bound by Christ's victory over him at Calvary and the empty tomb. The effects of this victory continued because of the presence of the kingdom of God via the preaching of the gospel and as evidenced by Jesus' miracles. Through the spread of the gospel, Satan is no longer free to deceive the nations. Christ is presently reigning in heaven during the entire period between Christ's first and second coming. At the end of the millennial age, Satan is released, a great apostasy breaks out, the general resurrection occurs, Jesus Christ returns in final judgment for all people, and he establishes a new heaven and earth.[34]

PROMISES TO ISRAEL, DAVID AND ABRAHAM

Riddlebarger states that "the promises . . . are fulfilled by Jesus Christ and his church during this present age." He embraces the typical "present" or "realized" millennialism and restricts many promises of God Almighty. The following verses cannot possibly have application to Jesus Christ or the church:

Deut 30:1-6
1 And it shall come to pass, when all these things are come upon thee, the blessing and the curse, which I have set before thee, and thou shalt call them to mind among all the nations, whither the LORD thy God hath driven thee,

---
[34] *Ibid.*, 31, 32.

2 And shalt return unto the LORD thy God, and shalt obey his voice according to all that I command thee this day, thou and thy children, with all thine heart, and with all thy soul;
3 That then the LORD thy God will turn thy captivity, and have compassion upon thee, and will return and <u>gather thee from all the nations</u>, whither the LORD thy God hath scattered thee.
4 If any of thine be driven out unto the outmost parts of heaven, from thence will the LORD thy God gather thee, and from thence will he fetch thee:
5 And the LORD thy God will <u>bring thee into the land which thy fathers possessed</u>, and thou shalt possess it; and he will do thee good, and multiply thee above thy fathers.
6 And the LORD thy God will circumcise thine heart, and the heart of thy seed, to love the LORD thy God with all thine heart, and with all thy soul, that thou mayest live.

Notice in the above passage, the gathering is physical, and *international.* It cannot refer to the return under Ezra and Nehemiah, or a spiritual gathering of "spiritual Jews."

Jer 16:14-15
14 Therefore, behold, the days come, saith the LORD, that it shall no more be said, The LORD liveth, that brought up the children of Israel out of the land of Egypt;
15 But, The LORD liveth, that brought up the children of Israel from the land of the north, and from all the lands whither he had driven them: and I will bring them again into their land that I gave unto their fathers.

As the first gathering was of the literal seed of Abraham, Isaac, and Jacob "**out of the land of Egypt**" (vs. 14), so the second gathering is of the literal Jewish seed from "**all the lands**" (vs. 15).

> *Ezek 36:24* **For I will take you from among the heathen, and gather you out of all countries, and will bring you into your own land.**

The context is NOT the church, or the Lord Jesus Christ, but rather, "**the house of Israel**" (see verse 22).

Notice that the *unconditional promise* of a land grant is not to a "spiritual seed," or just "any" of Abraham's seed. It is directly give to Abraham, Isaac, Jacob, and *their* "seed!"

Abraham

> *Gen 12:7* **And the LORD appeared unto Abram, and said, Unto thy seed will I give this land: and there builded he an altar unto the LORD, who appeared unto him.**

> *Gen 15:7* **And he said unto him, I am the LORD that brought thee out of Ur of the Chaldees, to give thee this land to inherit it.**

> *Gen 15:18* **In the same day the LORD made a covenant with Abram, saying, Unto thy seed have I given this land, from the river of Egypt unto the great river, the river Euphrates:**

Isaac

> *Gen 26:3* **Sojourn in this land, and I will be with thee, and will bless thee; for unto thee, and unto thy seed, I**

will give all these countries, and I will perform the oath which I sware unto Abraham thy father;

Jacob and his "seed"

Gen 48:3-4
3 And Jacob said unto Joseph, God Almighty appeared unto me at Luz in the land of Canaan, and blessed me,
4 And said unto me, Behold, I will make thee fruitful, and multiply thee, and I will make of thee a multitude of people; and will give this land to thy seed after thee for an everlasting possession.

ROMANS CHAPTER 11

What does Kim Riddlebarger do with Romans chapter 11? He sure does not believe it as it is written. For, if he did he would have to concede to Israel's restoration as a national entity. Instead he offers various "interpretations" to get around the sense of the passage.

He claims that the question found in verse one, **"Hath God cast away his people?"**

> is not to be understood as, Has God cast off ethnic Israel with respect to his special plan for the future? But rather, has God cast off ethnic Israel altogether? . . . The question is, therefore, not to be understood in the sense of does Israel have any future, but has God already cast Israel off?[35]

If God has not "cast Israel off" then it follows that there is a plan (detailed in Romans 11:26-27) for them in the future! Riddlebarger substitutes a physical salvation of a physical seed

---
[35] *Ibid.*, 186.

with a spiritual salvation (John 3:5) of a spiritual seed (Galatians 3:26-29). Notice his exposition:

> It is clear, however, that Israel's salvation must come to pass in the same way in which salvation has come to Gentiles. . . . ethnic Jews will be saved in the same way in which the members of the present believing remnant are saved, only in such great numbers that Paul could say 'all Israel' will be saved.[36]

So, "all" really does not mean "all." I guess that is the norm for the misshaped thinking of Reformed Calvinists. "Salvation . . . the same way." Have we not heard this familiar tune before? Riddlebarger arrived at this conclusion because he disregarded the context – the second advent of Jesus Christ!

> *Rom 11:26* **And so all Israel shall be saved: as it is written, There shall <u>come out of Sion the Deliverer</u>, and shall turn away ungodliness from Jacob:**

The entire chapter is dealing with corporate groups (Jews and Gentiles) not individual salvation! Israel will be saved (all of them) when Jesus comes to rescue the remnant at the close of the Tribulation.

THE AMILLENNIAL "MILLENNIUM"

Riddlebarger insists that "the millennium is the period of time between the two advents of our Lord."[37] He does not take Revelation 20 literally in any sense of the imagination. Note:

> It was at the cross that Christ defeated Satan. Therefore, with the coming of the kingdom, Jesus Christ has progressively

---
[36] *Ibid.*, 182, 193.
[37] *Ibid.*, 31.

bound Satan through the worldwide preaching of the gospel and the expansion of Christ's church.[38]

Jesus Christ did not bind Satan at Calvary! Does Riddlebarger think the world we are living in is one in which Satan is "bound?" Notice how he invents his own terminology to cover up his heterodoxy. He says that Christ has "progressively bound Satan." What is *that*? According to amillennialists it is "God's restraint of satanic deception of the nations."[39] Riddlebarger does address the question, "how can Satan be 'bound' when there is obviously so much evil in the world?"[40] He explains away the valid contradiction by a plea to the "meaning" of the verse, instead of what it actually says:

> What this "binding of Satan" means is that after the coming of the long-expected Messiah, Satan lost certain authority which he possessed prior to the life, death, burial, resurrection and ascension of the Savior. It does not mean that all Satanic operations cease during the millennial age as many opponents of amillennialism mistakenly assume. The binding of Satan simply means that Satan cannot deceive the nations until he is released at the end of the millennial age."[41] *[emphasis added]*

"Satan cannot deceive the nations?" Tell that to the missionaries in India, Paua New Guinea, China, and *fifty* other "nations." He is deceiving them (2 Cor. 4:4) enough whereby MOST of them are going to hell (Matt. 7:13)! The "amillennialists millennium" is inconsistent, ironic and illogical. The Millennium is *not* "a present reality!" The Bible teaches that in the Kingdom Age the "**unclean spirit**" will "**pass out of the land**" (Zech. 13:2); while Paul affirms the presence of these spirits during the Church Age (1 Tim. 4:1; 1 Cor. 10:20). Even in the

---

[38] *Ibid.*, 197.
[39] *Ibid.*, 204.
[40] *Ibid.*, 210.
[41] *Ibid.*

book of Acts (after the supposed "binding of Satan at Calvary") demonic spirits are actively working. See: Acts 5:16; 8:7; 10:38; 13:10.

Riddlebarger's defective assumptions lead to teaching that "Christ is presently reigning in heaven"[42] during this *spiritual* Millennium. While the scriptures teach Christ "**sat down on the right hand of God**" (Heb. 10:12), they *never say* that Christ is seated on a throne in heaven and ruling!

Covenant theologians and progressive dispensationalists assume Revelation 3:21 defends their position. They are in error. Jesus is NOT seated on *his* "throne" in Rev. 3:21! That is understood as a future event based on the grammatical structure of the verse. Notice, "**overcometh will**" (future tense). Observe also that Christ is seated "**with**" God the "**Father in his throne**." A statement relating the deity of Jesus Christ with regards to the resurrection is hardly a proof text for a Davidic throne in heaven and a "spiritual millennium" during this age!

TRIBULATION AND MILLENNIUM TOGETHER?

The "case for amillennialism" finds itself in *double jeopardy*. Kim Riddlebarger aptly represents the ominous amillennial arrangement, parading its fallacies. First, he claims that "the tribulation period . . . is the entire church age,"[43] then, he says "the millennium is the period of time between the two advents of our Lord . . ."[44] So, the Tribulation and Millennium are simultaneous occurring *now?* That is the extremity of the amillennial covenant theology "perspective."

---

[42] *Ibid.*, 32.
[43] *Ibid.*, 21.
[44] *Ibid.*, 31.

Two Questions Answered

Kim Riddlebarger thinks the "premillennialist interpretation creates more serious theological problems than it solves."[45] He asks a few questions that premillennial dispensationalists are not supposed to have the answers to. [Some dispensational authors may not, but Bible believer's do!]

His first difficulty concerns the revolt at the end of the Millennium. He asks: "Who are these people who are deceived by Satan, who then revolt against God, only to be consumed by fire from heaven?"[46] Why, that is an easy question. They are the nations that are deceived by Satan (Rev. 20:8). Riddlebarger has a problem with "resurrected bodies coexist[ing] with people who have not been raised from the dead and who remain in the flesh."[47]

Riddlebarger dismisses the numerous examples *in scripture* of "resurrected bodies coexisting" with others (see: 1 Ki. 17:17-23; 2 Ki. 4:32-37; 2 Ki. 13:21; Luke 7:12-15; Luke 8:49-55; John 11:43-44; Acts 9:37-40; Acts 20:9-1). In other words, *his teaching is NOT based on scripture, but private interpretation.*

Furthermore, Riddlebarger is ignorant that the "sheep" of Matthew 25 have offspring. When Jesus returns and sets up His kingdom, He will judge the nations (Matthew 25). Those "nations" (Matt. 25:42) who treated the Jews right are the sheep that are allowed into the kingdom. They are *not resurrected,* they are present at the advent! They have flesh and blood bodies that can reproduce. [Remember this is the kingdom of heaven. Compare 1 Cor. 15:50 where "**flesh and blood cannot inherit the kingdom of God.**"] We know this because there are "children" in the kingdom age (see Isa. 65:20).

---

[45] *Ibid.*, 231.
[46] *Ibid.*
[47] *Ibid.*

Riddlebarger (as all amillennialists) "spiritualizes" the first resurrection: "the first resurrection is the believers' regeneration."[48] He REJECTS the plain verses that teach that the "**first resurrection**" is in three parts (1 Cor. 15:22-25 with Deut. 16:16).

1. **THE FIRSTFRUITS**: Christ and those Old Testament saints that rose at that time (Matt. 27:52,53). [Note that the 144,000 Jewish men *may* be part of this group (see Rev. 7:1-8; 14:1-5).]

2. **THE HARVEST**: Church Age saints who have died, and living saints raptured.

3. **THE GLEANINGS**: Tribulation Jews raptured at the end of the Tribulation, and the resurrection of martyrs (Rev. 14:14,15; Rev. 20:3,4).

To those who accuse us of inventing three resurrections, we answer in one word – "trinity."

Deut 6:4 **Hear, O Israel: The LORD our God is one LORD**:

If God Almighty chooses to operate in "threes" who are we to question Him? There are *two* resurrections, and the first one is in *three parts*.

The second question Riddlebarger raises, concerns the Millennial sacrifices. The answer to this question from our dispensational friends (LaHaye, Ice, Walvoord, Pentecost, Ryrie et. al.) is wanting as usual. They refuse to believe the scriptures when they speak contrary to their preconceived notions. Since we have already covered this material under our section on the

---

[48] *Ibid.*, 222.

Millennium, and proven *why* these sacrifices are reinstated, we will not be redundant. Suffice it to say that they are for the national atonement of Israel as a communal *nation*. They are *not* for individual salvation. Individual salvation is by *works* in the Millennium, NOT FAITH.

The fact that no major dispensationalists could answer Riddlebarger's questions was primarily what led him from premillennial dispensationalism to covenantal amillennialism:

> These things bothered me for some time, and the more questions I asked of my pastors and teachers, the more troubling the answers became.[49]

The unreasonable answers from the majority of "qualified dispensational scholars" should have bothered him. What Riddlebarger needed was a Bible believing dispensationalist to **"expoun[d] unto him the way of God more perfectly"** (Acts 18:26).

We thus conclude our rebuttal to this amillennial proponent. His position is unfounded and unbiblical.

---

[49] *Ibid.*, 245.

THE BIBLE BELIEVER'S GUIDE TO DISPENSATIONALISM

Epilogue

The superlative characteristic about the Bible is it's *holiness*. Consigning it to the level of other writings is cynical at best, and blasphemous at worst. Assuming to understand its contents *fully*, is nearly as unscrupulous as the former, and being a dispensationalist does not warranty against deception.

With this in mind (plus the fact that we have only "scratched the surface"), the Bible believing dispensationalist must approach the Bible as one that "trembles at his word" (Isa. 66:5), understanding He has entrusted the **"rightly dividing"** to *us*.

To those who refuse to be **"a workman that needeth not to be ashamed;"** they have sealed their fate. Future revelation (from the canonical scriptures) will be withheld from them, surrounded by "discrepancies" and "contradictions." They have disobeyed the one, solitary, commandment in the scriptures to "**study**," and therefore to them the Bible is "**a book that is sealed**" (Isa. 29:11).

May our prayer be as David's, one of unreserved dependence upon God for revelation and illumination:

> Open thou mine eyes, that I may behold wondrous things out of thy law.
> Psalm 119:18

The Bible Believer's Guide To Dispensationalism

Bibliography

BIBLES:

Companion Bible. Grand Rapids: Kregel, 1990

Defenders Study Bible. Grand Rapids: Word, 1995

New Scofield Reference Bible. New York: Oxford, 1967

Ryrie Study Bible. Chicago: Moody Press, 1976

Scofield Reference Bible. New York: Oxford, 1909

Tim LaHaye Prophecy Study Bible: AMG, 2000

BOOKS:

Baker, Charles F. *A Dispensational Synopsis of the New Testament.* Grand Rapids: Grace Publications, 1989

Bass, Clarence B. *Backgrounds to Dispensationalism.* Grand Rapids: Baker Book House, 1960

Cooper, David L., *The God of Israel.* Los Angeles: Biblical Research Society, 1945

Cox, William E. *An Examination of Dispensationalism.* New Jersey: P&R Publishing, 1980

Evans, Herbert F. *Dear Dr. John: Where is my Bible?* Harlingen, TX: Wonderful Word Publishers, 1976

Gerstner, John H., *Wrongly Dividing the Word of Truth.* Morgan: Soli Deo Gloria Publications, 2000

Greene, Oliver B., *Revelation.* Greenville: The Gospel Hour, 1963

Henzel Ronald M. *Darby, Dualism and the Decline of Dispensationalism.* Tucson, Arizona: Fenestra Books, 2003

Ironside, H.A., *Revelation.* New Jersey: Loizeaux Brothers, 1920

———. *Wrongly Dividing the Word of Truth.* New York: Loizeaux Brothers, 1938

Jamieson, Fausset, Brown, *Commentary on the Whole Bible.* Grand Rapids: Zondervan, 1961

LaHaye, Tim; Ice, Thomas, *Charting the End Times.* Eugene, Oregon: Harvest House Publishers, 2001

———. *The End Times Controversy.* Oregon: Harvest House, 2003

———. *The Rapture.* Eugene, Oregon: Harvest House Publishers, 2002

Larkin, Clarence, *Daniel.* Glenside: Rev. Clarence Larkin Est., 1929

———. *Dispensational Truth.* Glenside: Rev. Clarence Larkin Est., 1920

———. *Rightly Dividing the Word of Truth.* Glenside: Rev. Clarence Larkin Est., 1920

———. *The Second Coming of Christ.* Glenside: Rev. Clarence Larkin Est., 1918

———. *The Spirit World.* Glenside: Rev. Clarence Larkin Est., 1921

Lindsey, Hal, *The Late Great Planet Earth.* Grand Rapids: Zondervan, 1970

Bibliography

MacPherson, Dave, *The Incredible Cover-Up.* Medford: Omega, 1975

Marcussen Jan A. *National Sunday Law.* Thompsonville, Il: Amazing Truth Publications, 1996

Mathison, Keith A., *Dispensationalism.* New Jersey: P&R Publishing, 1995

McGee, J. Vernon, *He is Coming Again.* Pasadena: Thru the Bible Books, 1980

———. *Thru the Bible with J. Vernon McGee Volumes 1, 3, 4, 5.* Pasadena: Thru the Bible Radio, 1983

Modlish, James, *Mystery of the Ages.* Port Orchard: Local Church Publishing, 1997

Pember, G.H. *Earth's Earliest Ages.* Grand Rapids: Kregel, 1975

Pentecost, J. Dwight, *Things to Come.* Grand Rapids: Zondervan, 1958

———. *Thy Kingdom Come.* Grand Rapids: Kregel, 1995

Poythress, Vern S., *Understanding Dispensationalists.* New Jersey: P&R Publishing, 1987

Riddlebarger, Kim, *A Case for Amillennialism.* Grand Rapids: Baker, 2003

Rose, Timothy P., *Bible Believing Dispensationalism.* Auckland: PRAE Books, 2004

Ruckman, Peter S., *Acts.* Pensacola: Bible Believers Press, 1974

———. *Charts and Outlines.* Pensacola: Bible Believers Press, 1997

———. *Galatians, Ephesians, Philippians, Colossians.* Pensacola: Bible Believers Press, 1973

———. *Genesis.* Pensacola: Bible Believers Press, 1969

———. *Hebrews.* Pensacola: Bible Baptist Bookstore, 1986

———. *The History of the New Testament Church, Volumes 1, 2* Pensacola: Bible Believers Press, 1984

―――. *How to teach Dispensational Truth.* Pensacola: Bible Believers Press, 1992

―――. *Hyper-Dispensationalism.* Pensacola: Bible Baptist Bookstore, 1985

―――. *Matthew.* Pensacola: Bible Believers Press, 1970

―――. *Ruckman's Bible References.* Pensacola: Bible Baptist Bookstore, 1997

―――. *The Sure Word of Prophecy.* Pensacola: Bible Believers Press, 1969

―――. *Twenty-Two Years of the Bible Believer's Bulletin Vol. 3.* Pensacola: Bible Baptist Bookstore, 2000

―――. *The Two Raptures.* Pensacola: Bible Baptist Bookstore, 1996

Ryrie, Charles C., *Dispensationalism.* Chicago: Moody Press, 1995

Scofield, C.I., *Rightly Dividing the Word of Truth.* New Jersey: Loizeaux Brothers, 1896

Sadler, Paul M., *The Historical Beginning of the Church.* Germantown, WI: Berean Bible Society, 1996

Sproul, R.C., *The Last Days According To Jesus.* Grand Rapids: Baker Books, 1998

Stam, C.R. *Acts Dispensationally Considered Volumes I, II.* Germantown Wisconsin: Berean Bible Society, 1954

―――. *Water Baptism.* Germantown Wisconsin: Berean Bible Society, 1998

Stauffer, Douglas D., *One Book Rightly Divided.* Millbrok: McCowen Mills Publishers, 1999

Tabb, M.H. *Dispensational Salvation.* Ft. Walton Beach, Fl: Foundation Ministries, 1991

Tibbetts, Jeffrey A. *Genesis 1:1-3.* Pensacola Fl: Tibbetts Publications, 1997

Vance, Laurence M., *The Other Side of Calvinism.* Pensacola: Vance Publications, 1991

Van Impe, Jack, *Revelation Revealed.* Royal Oak: Jack Van Impe Ministries, 1982

Walvoord, John F., *The Final Drama.* Grand Rapids: Kregel, 1993

Whitcomb, John C. *The Early Earth.* Grand Rapids: Baker, 1972

DICTIONARIES:

Ayto, John *Dictionary of Word Origins.* New York: Arcade Publishing, 1990

The Random House College Dictionary. New York: Random House, 1973

Dictionary of Premillennial Theology. Grand Rapids: Kregel, 1996

Gesenius, William *A Hebrew and English Lexicon of the Old Testament including the Biblical Chaldee.* Boston: The Riverside Press, Cambridge 1880.

ELECTRONIC:

"Dispensation," Nelson's Illustrated Bible Dictionary, (Thomas Nelson Publishers; PC Study Bible)

"Dispensation," The New Unger's Bible Dictionary, (Moody   Press, PC Study Bible)

Barnes, Albert, Notes on the Old Testament (from Barnes' Notes, Electronic Database. Copyright (c) 1997 by Biblesoft)

Hovind, Kent Are there billions of years between Genesis 1:1 & 1:2? (http://www.drdino.com)

Morton, Timothy S. The Difference is in the Dispensations (http://members.citynet/morton/)

NEWSPAPERS AND PERIODICALS:

Smith, Shelton., "*One Book Rightly Divided* Reflects Ultra-dispensationalism," The Sword of the Lord 07/05/02:

Sadler, Paul M. "From the Editor," The Berean Searchlight 0303:

Hunt, Dave, "Q&A," The Berean Call 02/2005:

The Bible Believer's Guide To Dispensationalism

Subject Index

A

A.D. 70: 19, 275, 349, 350, 351, 354, 355
Abomination of desolation: 349
Abraham's bosom: 83, 128, 138, 146, 258, 286
Abrahamic Covenant: 9, 11,12, 13, 217, 267
Adamic Covenant: 9, 217, 249
Advanced revelation: 60, 124
Age:
  Definition of: 14-18,
  Different ages: 18 11, 14, 15, 16, 18, 100, 144, 147-148, 150, 153, 158, 169, 181, 195-200, 214, 215, 218, 242, 250, 266, 285, 318, 329, 348
Alexandreanus: 166
Alexandria Egypt: 35
Alexandrian manuscripts: 23, 37, 71
Alexandrian school: 36
Amillennialism: 6, 22, 27, 28-29, 30, 38, 355, 361, 362

Angels: 150, 254-255, 267, 288, 300, 306 *see also sons of God*
Animal sacrifices: 83, 199, 205, 309
Antichrist: 39, 65, 69, 104, 115, 119, 194, 232, 254-255, 266, 288-297, 343, 344, 354 *see also Man of Sin*
Apocrypha: 166
Apostolic signs: 150, 186
Armageddon: 106, 300-301
Assembly of God · 198

B

Babylon: 83, 266, 275, 301, 312
Balfour Declaration: 275
Baptist: 12, 29, 31, 38, 46, 60-61, 70-72, 104, 107, 114, 132, 147, 149, 156, 158-159, 164, 169, 188, 205, 209, 223, 281, 295, 307, 318, 320, 344, 353
Baptist brider: 149, 209

Bible believers: 8, 23, 33, 40, 44, 47, 58, 78, 80, 82, 87, 118, 148, 171, 183, 216, 232, 237, 290
Blood atonement: 59, 132, 201, 206, 208, 210, 282, 283
Body of Christ: 34, 51, 58, 63, 75, 76, 81, 85, 98, 109, 149-153, 157, 164, 169, 172-173, 178, 181, 184, 189, 196, 281-282, 303, 307, 311, 317-325, 328, 340
Bohairic: 166
Born again: 41, 89, 98, 115, 122, 127, 177, 189, 198, 248, 256, 281, 288, 348
Bride: 168, 245, 307, 319
Bruising the serpent: 43, 106

C

Calvinism: 5, 6, 13, 31, 57, 73, 75, 127, 170, 281, 285, 354
Calvinist: 24, 101, 121, 170, 171, 176, 193, 210, 239, 346, 356
Campbellite: 45, 79, 210
Capitol punishment: 259, 263
Celestial bodies: 300
Christian bookstore · 340
Christians: 36, 54, 57, 83, 88, 113, 117-118, 153, 156, 171, 175-177, 190, 193, 295, 296, 303, 339, 343-344
Chronology: 48, 265, 299
Church:
  Beginning of: 318, 322
  Body of Christ: 4, 13, 22-23, 45, 58, 85-88, 113, 114, 122, 158, 181, 281-286
  Local assembly: 149-152, 286
Church Age: 10, 14, 18, 22, 28, 51, 80, 98, 144-145, 147-150, 153-158, 167-168, 181, 184, 186, 190-191, 194, 196, 198-201, 210, 214-215, 251, 273, 277-278, 281-282, 285-286, 288, 297, 304, 318-319, 329, 332, 334, 348, 361
Church Age doctrine: 147-150, 153, 168, 328
Church fathers: 57, 59, 102, 166, 343
Church history: 2, 19, 59, 83, 150, 155, 341
Church of England: 63
Church of God: 75, 85, 159
Circumcision: 204, 250, 268, 325, 326
Commissions: 107, 209, 230, 232, 244, 248, 257, 310, 326, 355
Companion Bible: 43, 74-75
Confession of sin: 13, 160, 166, 329-332, 337-340
Conscience: 10, 214, 217
Continental drift theory: 47, 264
Covenant:
  Defined: 11-12,
  Misc: 5-6, 24, 31, 74-75, 79, 87, 101, 122, 134, 213, 216, 223, 224, 246-249, 251, 254, 258-263, 267-268, 272, 274-283, 307, 331, 343, 358, 362
Covenant theologians: 6, 123, 358
Covenant theology: 5-6, 31, 359
Creation: 70, 219, 232-233, 236-237, 240-243, 246
Creation evangelists: 220, 222
Creation scholarship: 237

D

Daniel's Seventieth Week: 64, 114, 151, 167, 286-287, 295, 298, 349

Darkness: 30, 92, 94, 202, 224-225, 227-228, 234, 239, 242, 266, 287, 335-336
Davidic Covenant: 9, 101, 217, 275
Davidic throne: 13, 101, 308, 362
Day of Christ: 112, 289-290, 292-294, 296
Day of the Lord: 111, 290, 294, 296, 346-352
Dead Sea: 196, 241
Death: 6, 10, 59, 72, 83, 89, 103, 106, 110, 116, 118-119, 121-123, 129, 132-133, 140, 142, 145-146, 154-155, 159, 162, 177, 195, 206, 210, 227, 241-242, 247-248, 253, 255, 259, 263, 272, 285, 312-313, 324, 361
Devil: 239, 255, 317 *see also Satan and Lucifer*
Devotional application: 52, 90, 149
Disciples: 5, 46, 83, 103, 106, 114, 185, 199, 201, 208-209
Dispensationalism:
  Camps of: 12-14
  Definition of: 6-11
  History of: 54-72
  Hyper: 13, 63, 74, 76, 98, 153, 168, 201, 316-339
  Overview: 3-5
  Scholars: 125, 133, 195, 305, 365
  Scofieldian: 14
Dispensations:
  of the Church: 218
  of Conscience: 10, 217, 249
  of the fullness of times: 214
  of God: 8
  of Grace: 9-10, 105, 281, 286
  of Human Gov.: 10, 217, 263
  of Innocence: 216, 246, 248
  of the Kingdom: 217
  of the Law: 79, 217, 275
  of the mystery: 331
  of the Patriarchs: 269
  of Promise: 217, 269
Dispensational Truth: 38, 68, 70, 71, 74, 213
Dispensationalist:
  Anti: 5, 57, 58, 85, 121, 124
  Bible believing: 19, 39, 219, 363
  Moderate: 14
  Nominal: 168
  Normative: 14, 72, 130
  Progressive: 13, 91, 101, 276

E

Eden: 8-9, 246-247, 259, 312-313
Edenic Covenant: 216, 220
Edom: 196
English: 8-9, 11, 15-16, 18, 60, 64, 69, 80, 147, 166, 183, 230-232
Ephesus: 150-152, 155
Ephraem Syrus: 60
Eschatology: 18-19, 164, 235, 298
Eternal Covenant: 12, 218, 311-313
Eternal salvation: 118, 135, 137-138, 147, 156, 159, 174-175, 177, 181-182, 307
Evangelicals: 66, 73, 147, 175

F

Faith and works: 129, 147, 154, 164, 285
Fall of man: 11, 97, 240, 248-249
Falling away: 112, 176, 181, 186, 289, 290
Fellowship: 45, 47, 63, 65, 97, 329-339

Final authority: 14, 33, 39, 57, 232, 341
First advent: 89, 100, 105-108, 110, 352
Firstfruits: 115, 360
Forbidden fruit: 232, 248, 261
Forgiveness: 202, 209, 280-281, 309, 329-334, 340

G

Gap theory: 71-72, 220-223, 227, 235, 247
Garden of Eden: 114, 237, 239, 258, 312
Gentile: 4, 7, 10, 42, 45, 59, 65, 81, 85, 87-89, 130-131, 169, 201, 204-205, 207-208, 210, 250, 266, 274, 282-284, 292, 313, 320, 325-327, 334, 360
Geology: 220, 241
Giants: 256-257
Godhead: 297, 325
Gospel:
  Four gospels: 120, 203, 318
  of the Kingdom: 185, 194, 201, 250, 288, 338
  of Grace of God: 10, 122, 194, 204, 208
Grace: 9-10, 120, 143-144, 153, 214, 278, 281, 286, 317, 320, 329, 339, 348
Great white throne: 301
Greek: 9, 16, 18, 33, 36, 48, 60, 71, 80-81, 89, 147, 161, 165, 173, 183, 207, 283-284, 288, 290, 316, 327

H

Ham: 89, 221, 227
Harclean Syriac: 166

Hebrew: 11, 16, 60, 71, 81, 89, 147, 153, 170, 224, 226, 230-232, 237, 254
Hell: 26, 31, 33, 69, 79, 122-123, 128, 131-133, 138, 140-141, 143, 152, 156, 164, 186, 197, 228, 240, 241-242, 274, 309, 352, 361
Heresies: 42, 307, 339
Holiness: 138, 144, 186, 190-191, 304, 329, 367
Holiness Church: 159, 334
Holy Ghost: 32, 46, 79, 80, 92, 128, 129, 174, 177-178, 185, 204-209, 281, 286, 296, 320-322, 327
Holy Spirit: 12, 21, 38, 43, 60, 61, 83, 101, 104, 115, 145, 194, 198, 205-206, 209, 283, 285, 295-297, 324, 348

I

Image of God: 100, 226, 245, 256
Imminence: 288
Inheritance: 97, 134, 161, 162, 171, 178, 264
Interpretation:
  Allegorical: 33-38, 40, 44
  Biblical: 34, 38-39, 50, 287
  Grammatical-historical: 23, 35, 102
  Literal: 19, 29, 36-39, 40-41, 50
  Private: 32-33, 80, 142, 183, 224, 349, 359, 363
Israel
  Captivity of: 253, 275, 282, 353
  National atonement: 282, 309, 364
  People of God: 78, 172-173, 329, 344

J

Promises to: 29, 206, 280-283, 320, 352-353, 355
Restoration of: 22, 282, 308

Jehovah's Witnesses: 42, 79, 263
Jerusalem: 21, 36, 45, 47, 69, 104, 107, 117, 136, 146, 160, 163, 168, 185-186, 189, 194, 209, 250, 276-279, 308-309, 312, 321-322, 333, 349-353
Jesus Christ:
  Ascension of: 203
  Appearance of: 300, 303
  Earthly ministry: 64, 98, 105-106, 131, 215, 250, 275, 320, 327
  Deity of: 277, 296, 358
  Resurrection of: 10, 89, 103, 206, 258, 285
  Revelation of: see Second Advent
Jewish: 42, 45-46, 86, 113, 115, 146, 164, 173, 176-177, 189-190, 194, 203, 209, 218, 268, 274, 280-281, 283, 302, 313, 318-319, 325-326, 352, 354, 357, 364
Joel's prophecy: 348, 349
Judgment Seat of Christ: 190, 337
Justification: 36, 51, 58, 123, 133, 136, 145, 269

K

King James Version:
  Apocrypha: 166
  Authorized Version: iii, 11, 14, 16-18, 42, 60-61, 69, 74, 147, 165, 222, 231-232, 247, 296
  Author's position: iii, 14,
  Dictionary: 42
  Dispensationally: 165-166, 216, 224, 230, 231, 232
  King James Only: 72, 73, 108, 147
  KJV: 49, 61, 164, 166, 168, 183, 230, 231
  Modern debate: 69
  Ousted by scholars: 34, 39, 57
  and Revival: 58
  Scofield's view: 16, 69
Kingdom Age: 12, 126, 145, 158, 196, 200, 277, 307, 361, 363
Kingdom of God: 28, 87, 90-102, 201, 240, 356, 363
Kingdom of heaven: 25, 87, 90-102, 217, 244, 275, 363
Koran: 337

L

Lake of fire: 156, 196, 240, 241-242, 309, 312-313
Laodicean: 69, 151, 152, 266
Last Supper: 199
Law: 8-10, 31, 127, 129-132, 137, 140, 145-146, 214, 217, 250, 253, 271-272, 274-278, 368
  Commandments: 79, 149, 163-166, 190, 194, 200, 215, 274, 348
  Moral law: 272, 273
  of Moses: 129, 273
Laying on of hands: 206
Left Behind books: 193
Looking forward to the cross: 14, 117, 127
Lordship salvation: 163
Lucifer: 236-238, 243 *see also Devil and Satan*

M

Man child: 301, 302
Man of sin: 112, 289, 297 *see also Antichrist*
Mark of the beast: 87, 118, 159, 186-189, 194, 215, 292, 304, 340
Mennonite: 263
Methodist: 31, 182
Millennial Age: 9-18, 23, 30-31, 60, 65, 115, 126, 153, 186, 195-197, 215, 241, 263, 268, 306-312, 340, 355, 361, 364
Miracles: 35, 38, 157, 185, 265, 325, 352
Monarchy: 307
Mosaic Covenant: 12, 217
Muslim: 268

N

National atonement: 282, 309, 360
Nestle's critical apparatus: 166
New birth: 87, 93, 98, 100, 122, 268
New Covenant: 9, 11-12, 153, 218, 280-282, 309
New Scofield Reference Bible: 8, 16, 119-120, 124, 154, 176-179, 181, 247, 257
New Testament saint: 142, 146, 336
Noahic Covenant: 217
  Noah's day: 233, 234
  Noah's flood: 220, 227, 233-236, 254, 260

O

Oikonomia: 9

Old Testament saints: 83, 115, 121-122, 128, 136-138, 143-144, 270, 348, 364
Old Testament salvation: 128, 132, 140, 278
Omniscience of God: 10
Overcoming: 152-162, 362
Oxford: 68

P

Palestine: 209, 295
Palestinian Covenant: 12, 134, 275
Paradise Lost: 238
Parenthetical Age: 106, 286
Partial rapturist: 342
Paul the apostle: 208, 325
  Pauline mystery: 334
  Paul's revelation: 98, 200-201, 283, 316
People of God: 78, 172, 173, 328, 341 *see also Israel*
Pergamos: 150, 152
Personal righteousness: 79, 128, 134, 136, 217
Physical prosperity: 201
Plymouth Brethren: 54-56, 63, 65
Postmillennialism: 22, 27, 30-31, 85, 90, 351
Power of God: 121, 185, 207
Prayer: 13, 49, 133, 174, 184, 209, 331, 333
Preaching: 8, 30-31, 52, 59, 67, 91, 122-123, 129, 204, 250, 322, 331-332, 353, 356, 360
Presbyterian: 26, 29, 31, 66, 175, 307, 354
Preterist: 10, 18-19, 349-355
Prison epistles: 76, 318, 328
Protestant: 29, 58, 307
Pyramids: 71, 238

R

Rapture:
  Pre-tribulation: 59-60, 64, 115, 149, 287-288, 297, 342
  Post-tribulation: 302, 304-305, 307, 310, 341-345
Re-creation: 225, 233, 239, 243, 246
Redemption: 5, 114, 120-122, 126, 145, 189
Reformed: 4-5, 13, 24, 29, 31, 57-58, 91, 101, 121, 124, 176, 281, 354, 355, 360
Regeneration: 359
Remission of sins: 107, 205
Repentance: 175-179, 183, 191, 205-206, 330-351
Replenish: 217, 230-232, 244-248, 312
Restoration: 22, 268, 282, 308, 337, 348, 359 *see also Israel*
Resurrection:
  First: 30, 115, 359
  Misc: 10, 19, 30-31, 89, 101, 103, 114-115, 120, 137, 142, 145, 185, 203, 206, 258, 285, 288, 305- 306, 311, 337, 353, 356, 362, 363
  of Old Testament saints: 114
Rewards: 97, 137, 151, 155, 157-158, 161, 179, 180-182
Righteous: 112, 121, 128, 130-143, 211, 252, 261-262, 274, 314, 351
Roman Catholicism: 22, 29, 36, 44, 58, 65, 71, 87, 302
Roman imperial eagle: 349
Russia: 295

S

Sabbath: 82-83, 173, 204, 272-273, 286, 309, 340, 352
Sacrifices: 11, 64, 127, 146, 189, 196, 272, 364
Salvation:
  Dispensational: 117, 125
  Physical salvation: 118, 122, 262, 359
  Plan of salvation: 45, 74, 78, 123, 127, 129, 195, 208, 210, 215, 247, 320
  Saved by faith: 10, 117, 126-127, 195, 215, 285
  Saved by grace: 103, 150, 247, 278, 348
  Saved the same: 3, 121, 124, 137, 142, 157, 172, 181, 197, 209, 269, 285, 317
Satan: 3, 30, 33, 44, 89, 105, 157, 193, 196, 216, 220, 227, 235-246, 251- 253, 255, 258, 269, 290, 293, 296, 338, 347, 356, 360, 361, 363 *see also Devil and Lucifer*
Scholars: 33, 38, 57, 71-73, 101, 117, 121, 124-125, 133, 164, 195, 197, 205, 222, 251, 305, 351, 365
Southern Baptist: 29, 68, 102
Science: 37, 48, 220, 260
Scofield Reference Bible: 38, 65, 68 *see also New Scofield Reference Bible*
Second advent: 89, 105-106, 108, 110-113, 158, 189, 203, 291, 300, 302, 306, 346, 347, 350, 353, 360
Seed: 25, 86, 98, 106, 163, 217, 236-238, 244-245, 247, 251-253, 267-269, 270, 275-277, 308, 312, 357-359
Serpent: 106, 236, 245, 252 *see also Devil, Lucifer, and Satan*
Signs: 80, 86, 109, 146, 173, 186, 207, 210, 268, 288, 290, 293, 325, 347, 349

Sin: 13, 87, 117, 121, 138-139, 141, 146, 176, 179, 181, 188-189, 206, 217, 227, 235, 239, 241-242, 263, 278, 279, 285, 298, 304, 312-313, 329-340
Sin unto death: 186
Sin wilfully: 188, 189
Sinless: 59, 137, 189, 235, 237, 239, 248, 279, 329, 336
Sinner: 10, 33, 74, 108, 117, 132, 167, 195, 283
Sinner's prayer: 193, 198
Siniaticus: 166
Smyrna: 150, 152
Son of God: 42, 97, 243, 257
Sons of God: 71-72, 98, 100, 170, 216, 232, 233, 236, 238-239, 242-246, 251-260, 268, 295, 340 *see also Angels*
Son of man: 100, 103, 110-111, 303, 305, 309
Son of Perdition: *see Antichrist*
Soul: 2, 41, 57, 68, 75, 83, 100, 118, 122-123, 130, 136, 138-141, 202, 273, 278, 317, 356
Substitutionary: 59, 126, 132, 206, 210, 317, 339
Sure mercies: 143, 278

T

Temple: 42, 61, 64, 82-83, 146, 160, 194, 209, 272, 275, 286, 289, 295, 306, 309, 349
Tertullian: 166
Textus Receptus: 61, 290
Theonomist: 31
Throne of David: 101, 196, 249, 276
Tongues: 8, 111, 198, 206, 207-208, 210, 292, 326, 351, 352
Transitional periods: 145, 197, 198, 200, 204

Tree of life: 113, 117, 149, 154-155, 163-168, 241-242, 244, 248, 258, 311- 313
Tribulation:
Great Tribulation: 161, 171, 192, 215-216, 251, 298, 301,
Tribulation period: 80, 144, 145, 151, 192, 298, 339
Tribulation saints: 115, 153, 155, 301-302, 305-306, 311
Tribulation salvation: 143, 147-148, 156-161, 169, 174, 191, 202
Trumpet: 111, 293, 304, 307
Two advents: 105, 108, 356, 360, 362

U

U.N.: 268
Unclean spirits: 185, 196, 327
Unconditional promises: 11, 87, 267, 308, 358
Universe: 94, 196, 235, 237, 239, 241, 257
Unsaved: 26, 33, 44, 130, 256, 286, 324

W

Warfare: 92, 107, 263
Water baptism: 13-14, 45, 74-75, 80, 205-206, 268, 318-320, 325-340
Wicked: 25, 31, 128, 134-135, 138-143, 252, 276, 310, 347
World to come: 17, 194, 306
Worldwide Church of God: 75

Y

Young earth: 222, 226, 235

THE BIBLE BELIEVER'S GUIDE TO DISPENSATIONALISM

Name Index

A

Ankerberg, John: 195
Armstrong: 75
Asbury, Francis: 176
Augustine: 28, 29, 62

B

Baker, Charles: 13, 75, 316, 319, 324,
Ball, Alwyn: 68
Bengel, Johann A.: 37
Berean Bible Society: 75, 316
Blue, Ken: 14
Bogue, David: 62
Breese, David: 195
Brookes, James Hall: 54-55, 60, 65-66
Bruno, Giordano: 37
Bullinger, Ethelbert: 7, 13, 44, 72, 74-75, 124, 134, 142, 158, 224, 252, 256, 316, 318, 319

C

Cartwright, Peter: 176
Cary, William: 63
Chafer, Lewis Sperry: 13, 39, 55, 56, 71-73, 121, 280
Chalmers, Thomas: 221-222
Clarke, Adam: 62
Clement of Alexandria: 35, 62
Cooper, David: 40
Copernicus: 37
Couch, Mal: 91, 195
Crutchfield, Larry: 23, 35
Culbertson, William: 16

D

Darby, John Nelson: 7, 13, 38, 54-65, 181, 280, 341
Dean, Robert: 126, 127
DeHaan, M.R.: 179, 183
Des-cartes: 37

E

Edwards, Morgan: 60, 344
Erasmus, Desiderius: 36
English, E. Schuyler: 16

F

Faber, George · 62
Feinberg, Charles L.: 16
Flechiere, John: 62

G

Gaebelein, Arno: 68, 165, 181
Gaebelien, Frank E.: 16
Galileo: 37
Gerstner, John: 23, 24, 56, 121-126
Gipp, Samuel: 14
Gouge, William: 62
Grady, William: 33, 219
Greene, Oliver: 155, 157, 165, 179
Gromacki, Robert: 195

H

Ham, Ken: 221
Hindson, Edward: 195
Hobbes: 37
Hodges, Zane: 195
Hovind, Kent: 221-222, 227-231, 235-237
Hume: 38
Hunt, Dave: 114-115, 147, 195,

I

Ice, Thomas: 11, 35, 147, 150, 195, 235-236, 281, 364

Irenaeus: 62
Ironside, Harry: 7, 13, 71-75, 147, 149, 164-166, 214, 318

J

Jamieson, Robert: 132, 133
Jeremiah, David: 195
Jones, Sam: 176

K

Kant, Immanuel: 38
Kepler, Johann: 37

L

LaHaye, Tim: 3, 11, 18, 23, 48, 59, 64, 73, 126, 128-129, 147, 149-150, 155, 195, 235-236, 281, 297, 299, 310, 343, 364
Larkin, Clarence: 7, 15, 21, 38, 64, 68, 70-73, 86, 104, 110, 147, 149, 177, 181, 213, 214, 230, 234-235, 239, 255-256, 286, 296, 299
Lee, Robert E.: 65
Leontine, Cerre: 65
Lightner, Robert: 35
Lindsey, Hal: 18, 112-113, 147
Locke: 37
Luther, Martin: 37
Lutzer, Erwin: 195

M

Mackintosh, Charles Henry: 54
MacPherson, Dave: 289, 342-348
Martyr, Justin: 62
Mason, Clarence E.: 16
McClain, Alva J.: 16

McGee, J. Vernon: 7, 110, 132, 142, 171, 173, 192, 195, 256-257
McPheeters, Tom: 66
Milton: 238
Morris, Henry: 168, 226-246, 265
Morrison, Henry C.: 176
Moody, D.L.: 4, 7, 54, 56, 61, 65-69, 73, 116, 134, 198, 214, 267, 281
Muller, George: 65

N

Norris, J. Frank: 38

O

O'Hair, J.C.: 13, 75, 316, 318
Origen, Adamantius: 23, 28, 35, 37, 57

P

Pember, G.H.: 181, 225-226
Pentecost, Dwight: 6, 13, 18, 23, 24, 28, 29, 55, 73, 88, 97, 122, 127, 129, 130, 147, 151, 152, 161, 181, 195, 203, 235, 262, 287, 296, 297, 299, 364
Pirie, John: 68
Priestly, John: 62
Poiret, Pierre: 62

R

Rice, John: 133, 148, 166-167
Riddlebarger, Kim: 28, 355-365
Rogers, Adrian: 195
Ruckman, Peter: 14, 73-74
Russell, David: 62

Ryrie, Charles: 4, 8-9, 13-14, 23, 34-35, 39, 55-56, 61-62, 73, 75, 116-117, 119-121, 123-127, 131, 134, 137, 147, 181, 195, 205, 214-215, 267, 280-281, 284, 318, 364
Rosenthal, Marvin: 295

S

Sadler, Paul: 318, 320, 322
Schuler, Bob: 176
Scofield, C.I.: 13-16, 54-56, 60, 63, 65-74, 80-81, 85, 93-94, 102, 105, 119-120, 123-127, 134, 149, 154, 165, 176-177, 179, 181, 188, 214, 223, 225, 247, 249, 254-255, 257, 269, 283, 286, 290, 296, 337
Smith, Shelton: 316, 317
Smith, Wilbur M.: 16
Spinoza: 37
Sproul, R.C.: 19, 349-354
Stam, C.R.: 13, 72, 75, 316, 318, 319, 322
Stauffer, Douglas: 11, 14, 33, 100, 140, 144-145, 148, 153, 195, 198-199, 215, 219, 296

T

Tabb, M.H.: 125-127, 137-138, 141, 151, 155, 158, 161-168, 182-183, 269
Tan, Paul: 35
Taylor, John: 62
Towns, Elmer: 195
Tregelles, Samuel P.: 54

V

Van Impe, Jack: 147, 154-155, 165, 195, 299

W

Walvoord, John: 13, 16, 18, 23, 28, 30, 35, 55, 73, 121, 147, 181, 195, 299, 360
Watts, Isaac: 62
Welch, Charles: 13
Wesley, John: 69, 176
Whitby, Daniel: 30
Wettstein, Johann: 37
Whitcomb, John: 222, 224, 227-228, 230, 235, 240

THE BIBLE BELIEVER'S GUIDE TO DISPENSATIONALISM

Verse Index

GENESIS

Gen. 1:1 - 20, 221, 225-226, 233-235, 237, 239, 242
Gen. 1:2 - 20, 216, 220-224, 229, 232-236, 239-243, 246-247, 257
Gen. 1:3 - 225, 243
Gen. 1:4 - 5, 228-229, 266
Gen. 1:5 - 229
Gen. 1:6 - 225
Gen. 1:7 - 5, 225
Gen. 1:8 - 233, 347
Gen. 1:9 - 239, 264
Gen. 1:11,12 - 234
Gen. 1:16 - 225, 263
Gen. 1:18 - 229
Gen. 1:22 - 231
Gen. 1:26 - 100, 226, 243
Gen. 1:27 - 100, 226
Gen. 1:28 - 20, 120, 227, 230-231, 247
Gen. 1:31 - 227, 246
Gen. 2:3-4 - 226

Gen. 2:7 - 141, 224
Gen. 2:25 - 224
Gen. 2:6 - 237, 259
Gen. 2:9 - 240, 311
Gen. 2:17 - 248
Gen. 2:25 - 249
Gen. 3:1-13 - 257
Gen. 3:3 - 101
Gen. 3:5 - 20
Gen. 3:8 - 259
Gen. 3:15 - 43, 106, 237, 245
Gen. 3:17 - 308
Gen. 3:19 - 248
Gen. 3:21 - 339
Gen. 3:22 - 168, 241, 313
Gen. 3:24 - 258, 259
Gen. 4:11,12 - 259
Gen. 4:11-13 - 50
Gen. 4:16 - 259
Gen. 4:16,17 - 259
Gen. 4:26 - 254
Gen. 5:1 - 226
Gen. 5:2 - 244
Gen. 5:3 - 245, 256
Gen. 5:5 - 248

Gen. 6-9 - 265
Gen. 6:1-4 - 20, 232
Gen. 6:2 - 255
Gen. 6:3 - 266
Gen. 6:4 - 255
Gen. 6:7 - 234
Gen. 6:13 - 234, 260
Gen. 6:17 - 234
Gen. 7:1 - 261
Gen. 9:1 - 230-231
Gen. 9:3 - 263
Gen. 9:5 - 50, 263
Gen. 9:6 - 226, 256
Gen. 9:11 - 260
Gen. 9:28 - 20
Gen. 10:5 - 5
Gen. 10:9 - 266
Gen. 10:10 - 266
Gen. 10:25 - 5, 264
Gen. 10:32 - 47
Gen. 10:35 - 47
Gen. 11:1 - 265
Gen. 11:6 - 266
Gen. 12:1-4 - 35
Gen. 12:3 - 86
Gen. 12:6 - 252
Gen. 12:7 - 268, 358
Gen. 13:15, 16 - 87, 268
Gen. 15:6 - 120, 269
Gen. 15:7 - 355
Gen. 15:12 - 229
Gen. 15:9,10 - 11
Gen. 15:17 - 267
Gen. 15:18 - 358
Gen. 16:1-3 - 252
Gen. 17:7-8 - 267
Gen. 17:9-14 - 302
Gen. 18:1,2 - 255
Gen. 18:23 - 135
Gen. 20:2-5 - 87
Gen. 21:22 - 201
Gen. 22:1-19 - 269
Gen. 26:3 - 358
Gen. 26:5 - 271
Gen. 38:3-5 - 259

Gen. 40:8 - ii, 12, 33, 50
Gen. 41:5 - 100
Gen. 44:31 - 146
Gen. 48:3-4 - 359
Gen. 49:9 - 44
Gen. 49:11 - 106
Gen. 49:24 - 108
Gen. 50:20 - 252
Gen. 50:24 - 268

EXODUS

Ex. 1:10 - 252
Ex. 1:15 - 252
Ex. 2:5 - 252
Ex. 3:1 - 237
Ex. 3:5 - 237
Ex. 7:3 - 86
Ex. 10:21 - 229
Ex. 11:10 - 35
Ex. 14:20 - 229
Ex. 16:23 - 352
Ex. 19:8 - 145
Ex. 20:8 - 82
Ex. 20:11 - 226, 235
Ex. 20:21 - 229
Ex. 20:21 - 228
Ex. 31:16,17 - 82
Ex. 32:1 - 224
Ex. 32:32-33 - 160
Ex. 34:7 - 79

LEVITICUS

Lev. 5:5 - 330
Lev. 10:3 - 352
Lev. 10:11 - 81
Lev. 18:5 - 142
Lev. 19:3 - 273
Lev. 19 - 273
Lev. 19:9 - 306
Lev. 26:14-39 - 275
Lev. 26:40 - 330

NUMBERS

Num. 5:3 - 145
Num. 5:7 - 330
Num. 10:4 - 111
Num. 14:22 - 35
Num. 15:33-35 - 272
Num. 16:33 - 240
Num. 25:7 - 270

DEUTERONOMY

Deut. 4:11 - 228, 229
Deut. 4:29-31 - 268
Deut. 4:34 - 86
Deut. 5:22, 23 - 229
Deut. 6:4 - 364
Deut. 6:25 - 74, 79, 124, 128, 134, 145
Deut. 7:9 - 79
Deut. 7:10 - 117
Deut. 9:14 - 160
Deut. 15:20 - 146
Deut. 16:16 - 115, 363
Deut. 17:11 - 81
Deut. 18:18 - 327
Deut. 24:1 - 253
Deut. 25:1 - 135
Deut. 27:2 - 224
Deut. 28:14 - 143
Deut. 28:29 - 229
Deut. 30:1-6 - 356
Deut. 30:3 - 105
Deut. 32:7-8 - 264, 312
Deut. 32:7 - 266
Deut. 32:20 - 128
Deut. 33:27 - 137

JOSHUAH

Josh. 6:5 - 111
Josh. 7:19 - 331
Josh. 22:2
Josh. 24:7 - 229

JUDGES

Judg. 2:1 - 267
Judg. 2:1 - 87
Judg. 2:17 - 79

1 SAMUEL

1 Sam. 1:11
1 Sam. 2:9 - 229
1 Sam. 3:9 - 118
1 Sam. 10:5,6 - 145
1 Sam. 15:28 - 89
1 Sam. 16:14 - 115, 145, 348
1 Sam. 18:10 - 145
1 Sam. 19:9 - 145

2 SAMUEL

2 Sam. 4:11 - 135
2 Sam. 7:12 - 275
2 Sam. 7:14,15 - 276
2 Sam. 7:24 - 224
2 Sam. 12:13 - 143, 278, 332
2 Sam. 22:12 - 229
2 Sam. 22:21 - 126, 146
2 Sam. 22:22 - 146
2 Sam. 22:29 - 229
2 Sam. 23:4 - 187
2 Sam. 23:6-7 - 180

1 KINGS

1 Ki. 2:12 - 101
1 Ki. 2:24 - 101
1 Ki. 3:3 - 79
1 Ki. 8:32 - 135
1 Ki. 11:34 - 79
1 Ki. 17:15 - 43

1 Ki. 17:17-23 - 363
1 Ki. 18:1 - 43
1 Ki. 18:45 - 187
1 Ki. 19:8-11 - 237
1 Ki. 21:7 - 89

2 KINGS

2 Ki. 2:13,14 - 73
2 Ki. 4:32-37 - 363
2 Ki. 8:6 - 79
2 Ki. 13:21 - 363
2 Ki. 17 - 95
2 Ki. 19:15 - 90

1 CHRONICLES

1 Chron. 1:19 - 47, 264

2 CHRONICLES

2 Chron. 6:1 - 228-229
2 Chron. 7:12 - 146
2 Chron. 9:4 - 201
2 Chron. 15:3 - 81
2 Chron. 17:1 - 253
2 Chron. 17:7 - 146
2 Chron. 17:9 - 122
2 Chron. 21:4 - 253
2 Chron. 21:17 - 253
2 Chron. 22:1 - 253
2 Chron. 22:10 - 253
2 Chron. 30:22 - 146
2 Chron. 34:2 - 79
2 Chron. 35:3 - 81, 146
2 Chron. 32:27 - 201

EZRA

Ezra 1:1 - 89
Ezra 6:15 - 299
Ezra 7:10 - 81
Ezra 7:17 - 299
Ezra 7:25 - 146
Ezra 9:12 - 87
Ezra 10:2-44 - 87

NEHEMIAH

Neh. 1:6 - 331
Neh. 8:8 - 146
Neh. 8:9 - 122
Neh. 9:29 - 142
Neh. 10:30 - 87
Neh. 11:1 - 36

ESTHER

Est. 1:2 - 89
Est. 3:6,12,13 - 253

JOB

Job 1,2 - 239
Job 1:6 - 20, 255
Job 2:1 - 20, 255
Job 3:3 - 302
Job 3:4-6 - 229
Job 5:14 - 229
Job 3:17,18 - 146
Job 4:7 - 201
Job 8:6 - 201
Job 9:4 - 201
Job 10:21-22 - 229
Job 11:14-20
Job 12:22 - 229
Job 15:22-23 - 229
Job 15:30 - 229
Job 17:12 - 229
Job 17:13 - 146
Job 18:18 - 229
Job 19:8 - 229
Job 20:26 - 229

Job 22:11 - 229
Job 23:17 - 229
Job 26:7 - 233
Job 28:3 - 229
Job 28:5 - 240
Job 29:3 - 229
Job 30:26 - 229
Job 34:22 - 229
Job 36:11 - 201
Job 37:4 - 307
Job 37:19 - 229
Job 38 - 225
Job 38:4-7 - 236
Job 38:6,7 - 236
Job 38:7 - 232, 238, 255
Job 38:9 - 229
Job 38:19 - 229
Job 38:22,23 - 157
Job 41 - 228, 247
Job 42:3 - 219

PSALMS

Ps. 1:6 - 135
Ps. 2:7 - 115
Ps. 3:7,8 - 122
Ps. 5:5 - 117
Ps. 5:10 - 79
Ps. 7:8 - 126, 136
Ps. 9:7 - 90
Ps. 9:17 - 84, 128, 142
Ps. 11:4 - 90
Ps. 11:5 - 117
Ps. 13:1 - 46
Ps. 14:1 - 33
Ps. 16 - 101
Ps. 18:8-11 - 228
Ps. 18:9 - 229
Ps. 18:11 - 229
Ps. 18:20 - 136, 146
Ps. 18:24 - 146
Ps. 18:28 - 229
Ps. 18:40 - 79
Ps. 19 - 50

Ps. 21:4 - 135, 276
Ps. 22 - 110
Ps. 22:1 - 52
Ps. 23 - 46
Ps. 24:1-7 - 197
Ps. 31:16 - 122
Ps. 32:5 - 331
Ps. 33:4 - 80
Ps. 35:24 - 136
Ps. 37:3 - 201
Ps. 38:18 - 331
Ps. 47:2 - 90
Ps. 48:2 - 117
Ps. 51:11 - 115, 143, 145, 278, 285
Ps. 51:13 - 330
Ps. 55:15 - 142
Ps. 63:9 - 240
Ps. 68:9 - 187
Ps. 68:21 - 43, 106
Ps. 69:28 - 160
Ps. 74:13 - 228, 247
Ps. 74:14 - 157
Ps. 82:5 - 229
Ps. 82:6-7 - 257
Ps. 86:2 - 136, 144
Ps. 88:6 - 229
Ps. 88:18 - 229
Ps. 89:20, 24 - 278
Ps. 89:39 - 20, 223
Ps. 91:6 - 229
Ps. 91:14-16 - 14, 143
Ps. 93:1-2 - 314
Ps. 97:2 - 228, 229
Ps. 103:17-18 - 262
Ps. 103:19-22 - 90, 228
Ps. 104:6-9 - 265
Ps. 104:20 - 228-229
Ps. 105:28 - 229
Ps. 106:30,31 - 270
Ps. 107:10 - 229
Ps. 107:14 - 229
Ps. 109:13 - 160
Ps. 109:14 - 244
Ps. 110 - 101

Ps. 110:1 - 109
Ps. 110:6 - 106
Ps. 112:1-3 - 201
Ps. 112:4 - 229
Ps. 118:11 - 79
Ps. 118:12 - 180
Ps. 119 - 101
Ps. 119:18 - 368
Ps. 119:160 - 80
Ps. 128 - 201
Ps. 130 - 282
Ps. 132:11,12 - 101
Ps. 138:2 - 61
Ps. 139:6 - 220
Ps. 139:7 - 297
Ps. 139:11, 12- 229
Ps. 139:21 - 117
Ps. 143:3 - 229
Ps. 143:12 - 79

PROVERBS

Prov. 2:13 - 229
Prov. 3:9,10 - 201
Prov. 4:19 - 229
Prov. 7:13 - 45
Prov. 8:8,9 - 34
Prov. 8:23 - 242
Prov. 9:18 - 142
Prov. 10:3 - 201
Prov. 10:11 - 135
Prov. 15:11 - 142
Prov. 15:24 - 142
Prov. 20:20 - 229
Prov. 28:13 - 330
Prov. 28:18 - 146
Prov. 30:5-6 - 102

ECCLESIASTES

Eccl. 1:3,9,14 - 44
Eccl. 2:13-14 - 229
Eccl. 3:17 - 135
Eccl. 5:17 - 229
Eccl. 6:4 - 229
Eccl. 7:20 - 137
Eccl. 8:14 - 137
Eccl. 9:1,2 - 137
Eccl. 11:8 - 229
Eccl. 12:12 - 279

ISAIAH

Isa. 2:3 - 196
Isa. 2:6 - 231
Isa. 4:4 - 282
Isa. 5:8 - 266
Isa. 5:11-14 - 142
Isa. 5:20 - 229
Isa. 5:24 - 189
Isa. 5:30 - 229
Isa. 6:5 - 332
Isa. 7:14 - 35
Isa. 8:22 - 229
Isa. 9:2 - 229
Isa. 9:7 - 101, 249
Isa. 9:18-19 - 180
Isa. 11 - 17
Isa. 11-12 - 268
Isa. 11:1-9 - 196
Isa. 11:7 - 308
Isa. 11:11 - 100
Isa. 13:6 - 346
Isa. 13:9 - 346
Isa. 14 - 236
Isa. 14:9 - 240
Isa. 14:11 - 146
Isa. 14:12 - 238
Isa. 14:13-14 - 236
Isa. 14:16 - 238
Isa. 19:2 - 89
Isa. 23:2 - 231
Isa. 24:1 - 223
Isa. 24:21 - 228, 247
Isa. 26:11 - 189
Isa. 27:12-13 - 268
Isa. 27:13 - 237

Isa. 29:11 - 33, 368
Isa. 29:18 - 229
Isa. 30:27 - 189
Isa. 30:30-33 - 241
Isa. 33:12 - 189
Isa. 33:24 - 282
Isa. 34:5-10 - 196
Isa. 34:9 - 241
Isa. 36:1 - 253
Isa. 38:1 - 253
Isa. 38:10 - 146
Isa. 40:1-5 - 107
Isa. 40:9 - 209
Isa. 42:7 - 229
Isa. 42:16 - 229
Isa. 43:5-7 - 268
Isa. 43:6 - 254
Isa. 43:23-28 - 282
Isa. 44:22 - 196, 282
Isa. 45:3 - 229
Isa. 45:7 - 229
Isa. 45:12 - 226
Isa. 45:18 - 222-223
Isa. 49:9 - 229
Isa. 50:10 - 229
Isa. 53 - 283, 317
Isa. 53:1 - 33
Isa. 53:3 - 103
Isa. 53:3-5 - 283
Isa. 54 - 302
Isa. 55:3 - 278
Isa. 58:10 - 229
Isa. 59:9 - 229
Isa. 60:1-3 - 303
Isa. 60:2 - 229
Isa. 60:15 - 137
Isa. 61:1,2 - 105
Isa. 63:1-6 - 106
Isa. 64:5 - 136
Isa. 64:6 - 136-137
Isa. 64:6-7 - 330
Isa. 65:17 - 314
Isa. 65:20 - 363
Isa. 65:17-20 - 279
Isa. 66:1 - 90

Isa. 66:2 - 41
Isa. 66:5 - 367
Isa. 66:7 - 302
Isa. 66:23-24 - 241, 309

JEREMIAH

Jer. 1:6 - 302
Jer. 2:31 - 229
Jer. 4:23 - 20, 223
Jer. 13:13 - 101
Jer. 13:16 - 229
Jer. 16:14-15 - 268, 357
Jer. 17:25 - 101
Jer. 18:7 - 89
Jer. 18:18 - 81
Jer. 22:19 - 276
Jer. 22:29,30 - 217, 276
Jer. 27:8 - 89
Jer. 30:7 - 100, 113, 298
Jer. 31 - 153, 280-281
Jer. 31:7-10 - 268
Jer. 31:25 - 231
Jer. 31:31 - 281
Jer. 36:23 - 276
Jer. 46:10 - 346
Jer. 50:20 - 196
Jer. 50:32 - 189
Jer. 51:58 - 189

LAMENTATIONS

Lam. 3:2 - 229
Lam. 4:20 - 302
Lam. 5:19 - 90

EZEKIEL

Ezek. 3 - 138, 141
Ezek. 3:20 - 132, 138, 145
Ezek. 11:14-18 - 268
Ezek. 13:5 - 346

Ezek. 13:21 - 142
Ezek. 14:14 - 138, 262
Ezek. 18 - 132-133, 142-143, 262
Ezek. 18:5, 9 - 138
Ezek. 18:12 - 133
Ezek. 18:19 - 138
Ezek. 18:20 - 128
Ezek. 18:20-28 - 139
Ezek. 18:21-29 - 143
Ezek. 18:24 - 132
Ezek. 20:8-11 - 271
Ezek. 20:11 - 142
Ezek. 20:12 - 82
Ezek. 20:20 - 173
Ezek. 20:33-38 - 268
Ezek. 22:17-22 - 268
Ezek. 26:2 - 231
Ezek. 27:25 - 231
Ezek. 28 - 238, 243
Ezek. 28:14 - 20, 237
Ezek. 31:14 - 240
Ezek. 31:18 - 259
Ezek. 32:8 - 229
Ezek. 34:23 - 200, 302
Ezek. 36:22-24 - 268
Ezek. 36:26-27 - 347
Ezek. 36:24 - 358
Ezek. 36:28 - 348
Ezek. 37,38 - 115, 311
Ezek. 37:12 - 311
Ezek. 37:24, 25 - 302
Ezek. 37:25 - 308
Ezek. 38:22 - 189
Ezek. 40-48 - 196
Ezek. 43:18 - 146, 309
Ezek. 45:15 - 309
Ezek. 46-48 - 268
Ezek. 48:35 - 20, 308

DANIEL

Dan. 2 - 89, 255, 266
Dan. 2:22 - 229
Dan. 2:43 - 251
Dan. 2:44 - 93, 313
Dan. 4:3,25 - 90
Dan. 4:17 - 89
Dan. 5-7 - 90
Dan. 5:16 - 12
Dan. 6:27 - 86
Dan. 7 - 90, 348
Dan. 7:13-14 - 21
Dan. 7:24 - 90
Dan. 7:26 - 158, 170
Dan. 8:17 - 158, 170
Dan. 8:19 - 158
Dan. 9 - 292, 348
Dan. 9:4 - 331
Dan. 9:7 - 45, 292
Dan. 9:26 - 158
Dan. 9:27 - 64
Dan. 11 - 348
Dan. 11:4 - 90
Dan. 11:21 - 298
Dan. 11:27 - 158
Dan. 11:35 - 158
Dan. 11:40 - 158
Dan. 12:3 - 137
Dan. 12:4-13 - 158, 170

HOSEA

Hos. 1:10, 11 - 282
Hos. 5:15 - 332
Hos. 8:14 - 189
Hos. 12:10 - 25
Hos. 13:13 - 302

JOEL

Joel 1:15 - 346
Joel 2:1 - 346
Joel 2:2 - 229
Joel 2:11 - 346
Joel 2:23 - 187
Joel 2:31 - 229, 344

Verse Index

Joel 2:32 - 281
Joel 3:14 - 346
Joel 3:16 - 303

AMOS

Amos 4:13 - 229
Amos 5:18,29 - 346
Amos 8:11 - 46
Amos 9:13 - 308
Amos 9:14-15 - 268

OBADIAH

Obadiah 1:15 - 346

MICAH

Micah 5:2 - 110
Micah 7:8 - 229
Micah 7:14 - 157
Micah 7:18 - 282

NAHUM

Nah. 1:8 - 229
Nah. 2:10 - 20, 224

HABAKKUK

Hab. 2:4 - 126, 128, 142, 144, 281
Hab. 3:13 - 43, 106

ZEPHANIAH

Zeph. 1:7 - 346
Zeph. 1:14 - 346
Zeph. 1:18 - 190
Zeph. 2:1,2 - 268
Zeph. 3:8 - 190

HAGGAI

Hag. 2:11,12 - 81

ZECHARIAH

Zech. 3:1-3 - 224
Zech. 3:9 - 282
Zech. 10:8-12 - 268
Zech. 12:10 - 126, 196
Zech. 13:2 - 20, 196, 361
Zech. 14:1 - 346
Zech. 14:16 - 117, 196

MALACHI

Mal. 2:7 - 81
Mal. 2:12 - 101
Mal. 4 - 50
Mal. 4:1 - 180
Mal. 4:4 - 190

MATTHEW

Matt. 1 - 100
Matt. 1:18-20 - 253
Matt. 1:21 - 203
Matt. 3:1-3 - 107
Matt. 3:2 - 93, 96
Matt. 3:6 - 332
Matt. 3:10 - 180
Matt. 3:10-12 - 190
Matt. 3:11 - 328
Matt. 3:12 - 181
Matt. 4:1-11 - 157
Matt. 4:16 - 229
Matt. 4:17 - 93, 96
Matt. 5-7 - 197, 307
Matt. 5:3 - 88, 93, 96

Matt. 5:8 - 192, 304, 306
Matt. 5:10 - 88, 93
Matt. 5:16 - 36
Matt. 5:17 - 275
Matt. 5:19 - 93
Matt. 5:20 - 93
Matt. 5:22 - 241
Matt. 5:30 - 196, 241
Matt. 5:35 - 308
Matt. 5:44 - 79
Matt. 6:13 - 184
Matt. 6:20 - 8
Matt. 6:23 - 229
Matt. 6:27 28 - 281
Matt. 7:13 - 361
Matt. 7:21 - 93
Matt. 8:11 - 93, 96, 282
Matt. 8:12 - 30, 88, 93, 229
Matt. 9:6-8 - 184
Matt. 9:13 - 351
Matt. 9:17 - 79, 200, 275
Matt. 10 - 150
Matt. 10:1 - 185
Matt. 10:7 - 93, 96
Matt. 10:22 - 118, 158, 170, 178, 192
Matt. 10:27 - 229
Matt. 10:28 - 241
Matt. 10:30 - 154
Matt. 10:32,33 - 160, 192
Matt. 11:1 - 96
Matt. 11:3 - 107
Matt. 11:11 - 93, 96
Matt. 11:12 - 93, 96
Matt. 11:14 - 349, 353
Matt. 12:5 - 272
Matt. 12:7 - 352
Matt. 12:10 - 282
Matt. 12:18 - 250, 282
Matt. 12:26 - 89
Matt. 12:32 - 17, 186
Matt. 12:40 - 84, 240, 282
Matt. 13 - 283, 306
Matt. 13:3 - 88, 93
Matt. 13:11 - 93

Matt. 13:24 - 93
Matt. 13:25 - 25
Matt. 13:30 - 26, 190
Matt. 13:31 - 93, 96
Matt. 13:33 - 25, 93, 96
Matt. 13:38 - 25
Matt. 13:39 - 158, 306
Matt. 13:40 - 26, 158, 187
Matt. 13:42 - 26
Matt. 13:43 - 314
Matt. 13:44 - 93
Matt. 13:45 - 93
Matt. 13:47 - 93
Matt. 13:49 - 158
Matt. 13:50 - 241
Matt. 13:52 - 93
Matt. 14:15-21 -157
Matt. 15 - 201
Matt. 15:22-28 - 250
Matt. 16:14 - 302
Matt. 16:18 - 50, 286, 352
Matt. 16:19 - 93
Matt. 17:1 - 237
Matt. 17:2 - 303
Matt. 18:1 - 93
Matt. 18:3 - 93, 96
Matt. 18:4 - 93
Matt. 18:8 - 241
Matt. 18:9 - 131
Matt. 18:17 - 151, 286
Matt. 18:18 - 241
Matt. 18:23 - 93
Matt. 19 - 17, 129, 201
Matt. 19:14 - 88, 93, 96
Matt. 19:17 - 79, 131, 200
Matt. 19:18 - 263
Matt. 19:23 - 93, 96
Matt. 19:24 - 96, 201
Matt. 19:25 - 178, 201
Matt. 19:28 - 277
Matt. 19:29 - 154, 161, 193
Matt. 20:1 - 93
Matt. 21:2-5 - 104
Matt. 21:44 - 108
Matt. 22:2 - 93

Matt. 22:11,12 - 159
Matt. 22:29-30 - 185, 254-255
Matt. 22:36-40 - 273
Matt. 22:44 - 109
Matt. 23:3 - 47
Matt. 23:13 - 93
Matt. 24 - 80, 113, 215, 345, 350
Matt. 24:3 - 158, 170
Matt. 24:6 - 158
Matt. 24:7 - 20, 300
Matt. 24:13 - 79, 109, 118, 149, 158, 164, 170, 178, 194, 292, 306
Matt. 24:14 - 158, 194
Matt. 24:15 - 189
Matt. 24:22 - 178
Matt. 24:29 - 300
Matt. 24:30 - 21
Matt. 24:31 - 268, 304, 306-307
Matt. 24:36 - 110-111
Matt. 24:40 - 305
Matt. 24:42 - 110, 194, 305
Matt. 24:44 - 100, 110, 305
Matt. 25 - 196, 215, 306, 311, 363
Matt. 25:1 - 93
Matt. 25:14 - 93
Matt. 25:21 - 277
Matt. 25:30 - 229
Matt. 25:31 - 21, 196
Matt. 25:32 - 307
Matt. 25:41 - 240, 310
Matt. 25:42 - 363
Matt. 26 - 12
Matt. 26:28 - 107
Matt. 27:5 - 42
Matt. 27:22 - 33
Matt. 27:42 - 118, 178
Matt. 27:45 - 229, 234
Matt. 27:52, 53 - 364
Matt. 27:53 - 84, 115
Matt. 28 - 208, 286, 326
Matt. 28:1 - 83
Matt. 28:18 - 90
Matt. 28:19,20 - 57

MARK

Mark 1:4 - 107
Mark 1:14, 15 - 96
Mark 3:11 - 328
Mark 4:30 - 96
Mark 6:23 - 90
Mark 9:31-32 - 103
Mark 9:43 - 309
Mark 9:47-48 - 240-241
Mark 10:14,15 - 96
Mark 10:23 - 96
Mark 11:10 - 90
Mark 12:4 - 43
Mark 13:13 - 202
Mark 13:20 - 118
Mark 13:26 - 21
Mark 13:32-33 - 111
Mark 14:42 - 98
Mark 15:31 - 202
Mark 15:33 - 229
Mark 16:16 - 79, 205, 209, 326

LUKE

Luke 1 - 196, 202, 338
Luke 1:5,6 - 274
Luke 1:32 - 27, 89, 101, 277
Luke 1:33 - 249, 277
Luke 1:71 - 118, 178, 202
Luke 1:79 - 229
Luke 2:26 - 237
Luke 3:1,2 - 48
Luke 3:3 - 107
Luke 3:38 - 20, 97, 243
Luke 4:4 - 220
Luke 4:5 - 238
Luke 4:18,19 - 105
Luke 4:23-27 - 282
Luke 6:20 -96
Luke 5:17 - 184
Luke 7:12-15 - 363
Luke 7:28 - 96, 97
Luke 7:48-50 - 201

Luke 7:50 - 178
Luke 8:12 - 178
Luke 8:49-55 - 363
Luke 10:9 - 96
Luke 10:21 - 59
Luke 10:25 - 162
Luke 10:28 - 131, 142
Luke 10:37 - 42
Luke 11:34, 35 - 229
Luke 12:3 - 229
Luke 12:51 - 5, 266
Luke 13:18 - 96
Luke 13:23 - 178
Luke 13:20,21 - 97
Luke 13:28, 29 - 96
Luke 16 - 75, 84, 128, 133, 146, 286
Luke 16:16 - 97
Luke 17:20 -93
Luke 17:21 - 92
Luke 18:16-17 - 96
Luke 18:18,20 - 200
Luke 18:24 - 96
Luke 18:26 - 178
Luke 18:30 - 186
Luke 18:42 - 118, 178, 202
Luke 19 - 17
Luke 20 - 311
Luke 20:35,36 - 310
Luke 21:20-24 - 46, 275
Luke 21:25 - 20
Luke 21:27 - 21
Luke 21:34 - 189
Luke 22:20 - 281
Luke 22:53 - 229
Luke 23:34 - 209
Luke 23:35 - 178
Luke 23:43 - 258
Luke 23:44 - 229
Luke 24:4 - 255
Luke 24:11 - 103
Luke 24:23 - 255
Luke 24:45 - iii
Luke 24:49 - 186, 322, 324
Luke 24:51,52 - 30

JOHN

John 1:4 - 142
John 1:5 - 229
John 1:11, 12 - 245
John 1:12 - 98, 100
John 1:17 - 74, 119-120, 124, 127
John 1:25 - 327
John 1:29 - 283
John 1:42 - 50
John 1:51 - 196
John 3:3 - 88, 97, 248
John 3:5 - 88, 97, 359
John 3:6 - 248
John 3:8 - 283
John 3:16 - 88, 137, 153
John 3:36 - 137, 154, 200
John 4:9 - 86
John 4:19 - 327
John 4:20 - 209
John 4:24 - 82, 97
John 4:48 - 86
John 5:24 - 115, 154, 193
John 5:39 - ii, 80, 148
John 6:14 - 327
John 6:57 - 25
John 6:63 - 25
John 7:37 - 348
John 7:38,39 - 122, 135, 322, 348
John 7:40 - 327
John 7:43 - 5
John 8:12 - 37
John 8:21 - 132
John 8:24 - 132, 141
John 9:16 - 5
John 10:16-18 - 282
John 11:43-44 - 363
John 12:20-22 - 250
John 12:24 - 98
John 12:29 - 307
John 13:15 - 46-47
John 14:3 - 293

Verse Index **399**

John 14:16 - 145
John 14:17 - 199
John 14:20 - 199
John 14:26 - 98, 145
John 15:4 - 199
John 15:7 - 199
John 15:26 - 145
John 16:7 - 145
John 17:21 - 322, 324
John 18:36 - 29, 277-278
John 20:1 - 146
John 20:19 - 83, 146
John 20:31 - 200
John 21 - 330

ACTS

Acts 1:4-5 - 324
Acts 1:6 - 106
Acts 1:8 - 203
Acts 1:10 - 255
Acts 1:11 - 21, 105, 293
Acts 2 - 45, 59, 80, 99, 185, 199, 204, 206, 208, 292, 320, 323, 325-326
Acts 2:16 - 351
Acts 2:20 - 229, 318, 346
Acts 2:22 - 86
Acts 2:27-31 - 84, 240
Acts 2:29,30 - 277
Acts 2:36 - 200
Acts 2:38 - 45, 79-80, 107, 204-205, 208, 210, 320, 326
Acts 2:39 - 282
Acts 2:42 - 53
Acts 2:47 - 322
Acts 3:12 - 88, 186, 284
Acts 3:19 - 196, 200, 210, 282, 309
Acts 4:8 - 88, 284
Acts 4:10 - 284
Acts 4:29,31 - 81
Acts 4:30 - 86
Acts 5:14 - 322

Acts 5:16 - 361
Acts 5:21 - 284
Acts 5:30 - 154
Acts 5:31 - 284
Acts 5:35 - 284
Acts 5:39 - 44
Acts 6:2 - 81
Acts 6:7 - 81, 205
Acts 6:8 - 185
Acts 7 - 99, 204
Acts 7:13 - 100, 173
Acts 7:38 - 149, 286
Acts 8 - 204, 206, 209, 283, 320, 323
Acts 8:3 - 284
Acts 8:7 - 361
Acts 8:14 - 81
Acts 8:17-18 - 207, 209
Acts 8:20 - 194
Acts 8:26-35 - 317
Acts 8:30 - ii
Acts 8:31-35 - 16
Acts 8:32 - 282
Acts 8:35 - 283
Acts 8:35-37 - 208
Acts 8:37,38 - 210
Acts 9 - 318-319, 324, 328
Acts 9:1-5 - 303
Acts 9:5 - 323
Acts 9:37-40 - 363
Acts 10 - 204-205, 325
Acts 10:38 - 185, 361
Acts 10:39 - 154
Acts 10:44-46 - 210
Acts 10:48 - 326
Acts 11 - 204
Acts 11:1
Acts 11:26 - 36
Acts 12:5 - 284
Acts 12:24 - 81
Acts 13 - 99, 204, 319
Acts 13:10 - 361
Acts 13:11 - 229
Acts 13:34 - 143
Acts 13:38, 39 - 146

Acts 13:40,41 - 282
Acts 13:44,46 - 81
Acts 13:46 - 204
Acts 15 - 45, 204
Acts 15:11 - 204, 250
Acts 15:18 - 244
Acts 16 - 320
Acts 16:31 - 202
Acts 17:13 - 81
Acts 17:26 - 264
Acts 18 - 99, 204, 318-319, 323
Acts 18:11 - 81
Acts 18:25 - 209
Acts 18:26 - 365
Acts 19 - 210, 320, 332, 334
Acts 19:1-6 - 209
Acts 19:1-9 - 206
Acts 19:2 - 207
Acts 19:6 - 208, 320
Acts 19:18 - 332
Acts 19:20 - 81
Acts 19:37 - 286
Acts 20 - 204
Acts 20:7 - 83, 146, 205
Acts 20:9-1 - 363
Acts 20:18 - 146
Acts 20:21 - 334
Acts 20:24 - 10, 194
Acts 20:27 - 6, 40, 134
Acts 20:32 - 97
Acts 21 - 296
Acts 21:11 - 296
Acts 21:28 - 88, 284
Acts 22:6 - 303
Acts 26:7-8 - 203
Acts 26:18 - 229
Acts 26:20 - 334
Acts 27:20 - 118
Acts 27:23 - 255
Acts 27:31 - 118
Acts 28 - 75, 99, 203-204, 318-319, 325
Acts 28:28 - 207

ROMANS

Rom. 1:3 - 277
Rom. 1:5 - 123
Rom. 1:16 - 204, 207
Rom. 1:17 - 126, 128, 142, 281
Rom. 1:25 - 39, 78
Rom. 2 - 87, 131, 250, 274
Rom. 2:5 - 112
Rom. 2:12-15 - 130, 274
Rom. 2:13 - 251, 274
Rom. 2:14-15 - 250
Rom. 2:19 - 229
Rom. 2:26 - 128
Rom. 3:4 - 80, 148
Rom. 3:5 - 128
Rom. 3:10 - 136
Rom. 3:18 - 172
Rom. 3:21 - 128, 145
Rom. 3:22 - 128, 145
Rom. 3:23 - 136
Rom. 3:25 - 107
Rom. 4 - 269, 270
Rom. 4:3 - 57, 120, 133
Rom. 4:5 - 165
Rom. 5:12 - 241, 256, 312, 241
Rom. 6:3 - 328
Rom. 6:4 - 142
Rom. 6:14 - 285
Rom. 6:23 - 79, 154, 191
Rom. 7:4 - 98, 245
Rom. 8 - 17, 141
Rom. 8:4 - 128
Rom. 8:15 - 172, 308
Rom. 8:17 - 97, 158
Rom. 8:19 - 245
Rom. 8:29 - 100, 102, 115
Rom. 8:34 - 276
Rom. 9:24,25 - 282
Rom. 9:32 - 144, 143
Rom. 10 - 118, 123, 162, 262
Rom. 10:1 - 88
Rom. 10:3 - 128
Rom. 10:4,5 - 134

Rom. 10:5 - 142-144
Rom. 10:9-13 - 202
Rom. 10:10-13 - 154
Rom. 10:12 - 87, 283
Rom. 10:13 - 281
Rom. 10:16,17 - 123
Rom. 11 - 35, 282, 320, 359
Rom. 11:1-25 - 88
Rom. 11:1,2 - 190
Rom. 11:2 - 22
Rom. 11:6 - 143, 144
Rom. 11:13 - 45
Rom. 11:20 - 172
Rom. 11:26 - 113, 119, 203, 347, 360
Rom. 11:27-31 - 196
Rom. 11:33 - 220
Rom. 12:5 - 284, 325
Rom. 13:11 - 295
Rom. 13:12 - 229
Rom. 13:11-13 - 335
Rom. 14:17 - 88, 92, 93, 97
Rom. 15:10 - 190
Rom. 15:19 - 86, 186
Rom. 16:7 - 323
Rom. 16:17 - 53
Rom. 16:20 - 43, 106
Rom. 16:25 - 286
Rom. 16:26 - 123

1 CORINTHIANS

1 Cor. 1 - 320
1 Cor. 1:7 - 110, 290, 295
1 Cor. 1:8 - 290
1 Cor. 1:9 - 337
1 Cor. 1:10-13 - 336
1 Cor. 1:17 - 328
1 Cor. 1:27 - 262
1 Cor. 1:28 - 336
1 Cor. 1:30 - 323
1 Cor. 2:5 - 336
1 Cor. 2:8 - 105
1 Cor. 2:13 - 50
1 Cor. 2:14 - 40
1 Cor. 3 - 190
1 Cor. 3:1-4 - 337
1 Cor. 3:17 - 335
1 Cor. 3:11-15 - 290
1 Cor. 3:16 - 146, 286
1 Cor. 3:17 - 286, 337
1 Cor. 3:18-23 - 336
1 Cor. 4:1-5 - 337
1 Cor. 4:2 - 337
1 Cor. 4:6 - 337
1 Cor. 4:14 - 337
1 Cor. 4:18-20 - 337
1 Cor. 5:1,2 - 338
1 Cor. 5:4,5 - 290
1 Cor. 5:6 - 338
1 Cor. 5:13 - 338
1 Cor. 6:1-12 - 337
1 Cor. 6:5 - 338
1 Cor. 6:11 - 167
1 Cor. 6:13-20 - 337
1 Cor. 6:18 - 338
1 Cor. 6:19 - 146, 286
1 Cor. 7 - 248
1 Cor. 8 - 337
1 Cor. 8:5-6 - 328
1 Cor. 8:13 - 16
1 Cor. 9:1-6 - 337
1 Cor. 9:17 - 8
1 Cor. 9:27 - 176, 179
1 Cor. 10 - 337
1 Cor. 10:20 - 361
1 Cor. 10:32 - 4, 81, 85, 88
1 Cor. 11 - 318, 337
1 Cor. 11:31 - 332
1 Cor. 12 - 286, 337
1 Cor. 12:13 - 87, 284, 322, 324, 328
1 Cor. 12:27-31 - 286, 323
1 Cor. 13:8 - 111
1 Cor. 14 - 337
1 Cor. 15 - 146, 288, 353
1 Cor. 15:1-4 - 145, 194, 197, 270
1 Cor. 15:3,4 - 317

1 Cor. 15:8 - 303
1 Cor. 15:12-19 - 337
1 Cor. 15:22 - 248
1 Cor. 15:22-25 - 115, 363
1 Cor. 15:24-28 - 94
1 Cor. 15:28 - 266, 311
1 Cor. 15:45 - 226, 230
1 Cor. 15:50 - 92, 363
1 Cor. 15:51-52 -293
1 Cor. 16:2 - 83, 146

2 Corinthians

2 Cor. 1:14 - 290
2 Cor. 2:17 - ii, 35, 333
2 Cor. 3 - 283
2 Cor. 3:6 - 281
2 Cor. 4:4 - 27, 238, 245, 256, 361
2 Cor. 4:6 - 229
2 Cor. 4:16 - 175
2 Cor. 5:1 - 171
2 Cor. 5:1-8 - 146
2 Cor. 5:6 - 83, 84
2 Cor. 5:11 - 190
2 Cor. 5:14-17 - 266
2 Cor. 5:19-21 - 74
2 Cor. 5:21 - 128
2 Cor. 6:4 - 229
2 Cor. 7:1 - 172, 333, 339
2 Cor. 7:9 - 338
2 Cor. 7:11 - 338
2 Cor. 8:1 - 83
2 Cor. 8:9 - 337
2 Cor. 10:4 - 92
2 Cor. 11:2 - 307
2 Cor. 11:3 - 244, 252
2 Cor. 12:2 - 94, 258
2 Cor. 12:4 - 258
2 Cor. 12:21 - 338
2 Cor. 13:10 - 48

Galatians

Gal. 1:8 - 288
Gal. 1:13 - 323
Gal. 2 - 45
Gal. 2:7 - 204
Gal. 2:9 - 204
Gal. 2:14,15 - 205
Gal. 2:16 - 79
Gal. 2:20 - 126, 128, 144
Gal. 3 - 162
Gal. 3:10 - 10
Gal. 3:11 - 126, 143, 274, 281
Gal. 3:12 - 134, 142-143, 145
Gal. 3:13 - 145, 154
Gal. 3:19 - 271
Gal. 3:23-24 - 146
Gal. 3:26-29 - 359
Gal. 3:27 - 328
Gal. 3:28 - 87, 284, 288
Gal. 4:14 - 255
Gal. 5:21 - 97

Ephesians

Eph. 1:3 - 87, 149
Eph. 1:13 - 348
Eph. 1:7 - 348
Eph. 1:10 - 8, 312
Eph. 1:13 - 145, 285
Eph. 1:18 - 178
Eph. 1:20 - 276
Eph. 1:21-22 - 90
Eph. 1:22,23 - 158
Eph. 1:22 - 286
Eph. 2 - 247, 254
Eph. 2:1,2 - 30
Eph. 2:7 - 15
Eph. 2:8 - 118
Eph. 2:8,9 - 10, 14, 79, 145-146, 191, 206, 285
Eph. 2:13 - 292
Eph. 2:14-16 - 321
Eph. 2:15 - 273

Eph. 2:19 - 87
Eph. 3:2 - 8
Eph. 3:3 - 286, 324
Eph. 3:4 - 324
Eph. 3:5 - 15
Eph. 3:9 - 9
Eph. 3:21 - 15, 16, 20
Eph. 4 - 128, 146, 319
Eph. 4:4,5 - 326
Eph. 4:8,9 - 84
Eph. 4:14 - 53
Eph. 4:15 - 286
Eph. 4:30 - 145, 348
Eph. 5 - 248
Eph. 5:5 - 90, 97
Eph. 5:8 - 229, 335
Eph. 5:11 - 229, 333
Eph. 5:11-14 - 334
Eph. 5:14 - 335
Eph. 5:21 - 172
Eph. 5:23 - 286
Eph. 5:30 - 284
Eph. 6 - 233, 247
Eph. 6:12 - 92, 228-229, 347

Philippians

Phil. 1 - 286
Phil. 1:6 - 290
Phil. 1:10 - 290
Phil. 1:21 - 83, 84
Phil. 1:23 - 146
Phil. 2:6 - 245
Phil. 3:12 - 339
Phil. 3:20 - 293
Phil. 4 - 294
Phil. 4:5 - 294

Colossians

Col. 1:5 - 32
Col. 1:12 - 171
Col. 1:13 - 90, 97, 229
Col. 1:14 - 283
Col. 1:15 - 245
Col. 1:18 - 286
Col. 1:25 - 8
Col. 1:26 - 9, 15
Col. 2 - 247
Col. 2:10-23 - 146
Col. 2:12 - 328
Col. 2:14 - 274
Col. 2:15 - 205
Col. 2:16 - 285
Col. 2:17 - 196, 285
Col. 3:1 - 276
Col. 3:4 - 294
Col. 3:23,24 - 97

1 Thessalonians

1 Thess. 1:10 - 115, 294
1 Thess. 2:2 - 81
1 Thess. 2:13 - 41, 81, 333
1 Thess. 2:19 - 290
1 Thess. 3:13 - 114
1 Thess. 4 - 115
1 Thess. 4:13-18 - 115, 346
1 Thess. 4:16 - 307
1 Thess. 4:18 - 112, 346
1 Thess. 4:15-17 - 114
1 Thess. 4:17 - 291
1 Thess. 5 - 343
1 Thess. 5:1 - 111, 346
1 Thess. 5:4-8 - 336
1 Thess. 5:6 - 294
1 Thess. 5:9 - 115
1 Thess. 5:17 - 333

2 Thessalonians

2 Thess. 1:7 - 291
2 Thess. 2 - 20, 237, 288-289, 292, 294, 296, 349
2 Thess. 2:2-3 - 112
2 Thess. 2:3-8 - 189

2 Thess. 2:7 - 161
2 Thess. 2:8 - 291
2 Thess. 2:8,9 - 190
2 Thess. 2:8-12 - 310
2 Thess. 3:5 - 294

1 TIMOTHY

1 Tim. 1:3 - 53
1 Tim. 1:6 - 1, 358
1 Tim. 1:9 - 336
1 Tim. 1:10 - 53, 336
1 Tim. 1:16 - 320
1 Tim. 2:15 - 119
1 Tim. 3:2 - 66, 67
1 Tim. 3:15 - 286
1 Tim. 4 - 109
1 Tim. 4:1 - 361
1 Tim. 4:6 - 53
1 Tim. 4:10 - 174
1 Tim. 4:13 - 53
1 Tim. 4:16 - 53
1 Tim. 6 - 263
1 Tim. 6:4 - 51
1 Tim. 6:14 - 294

2 TIMOTHY

2 Tim. 1:7 - 172, 190
2 Tim. 1:12 - 290
2 Tim. 1:18 - 290
2 Tim. 2:11-13 - 97
2 Tim. 2:12 - 158
2 Tim. 2:15 - ii, 3, 6, 12, 27, 54, 78, 82, 129, 134, 153, 184,
2 Tim. 2:17-18 - 350, 354
2 Tim. 3 - 109
2 Tim. 3:13 - 27
2 Tim. 3:15 - iii
2 Tim. 3:16 - iii, 44, 49, 51, 80-81
2 Tim. 4:2 - 53
2 Tim. 4:3 - 54, 179

2 Tim. 4:18 - 90

TITUS

Titus 1:2 - 135, 276
Titus 1:15-16 - 178
Titus 2:13 - 294
Titus 2:14 - 173
Titus 3:5 - 165, 167

PHILEMON

Philemon - 199

HEBREWS

Heb. 1:2 - 170, 303, 306
Heb. 1:3 - 245, 256
Heb. 1:13 - 29
Heb. 1:14 - 161, 162
Heb. 2 - 194, 245
Heb. 2:1 - 162, 169
Heb. 2:1-4 - 169
Heb. 2:3 - 162, 169, 189
Heb. 2:5 - 186
Heb. 2:9 - 177
Heb. 2:10 - 173
Heb. 2:11 - 100
Heb. 2:17 - 327
Heb. 3 - 215
Heb. 3:1 - 327
Heb. 3:6 - 154, 159, 170-171, 195
Heb. 3:11 - 172
Heb. 3:12 - 33, 169
Heb. 3:13 - 169
Heb. 3:14 - 159, 170, 189
Heb. 3:18 - 172
Heb. 4:1 - 169, 171-172
Heb. 4:3 - 172
Heb. 4:5 - 172
Heb. 4:8-11 - 172

Heb. 4:9-11 - 172
Heb. 4:11 - 189
Heb. 4:12,13 - i
Heb. 4:14 - 159, 178, 195, 276, 327
Heb. 5:9 - 174
Heb. 5:12,14 - iii, 213
Heb. 6 - 80, 176, 178, 184, 194, 215, 304, 345
Heb. 6:3 - 189
Heb. 6:4 - 175, 191
Heb. 6:4-6 - 79
Heb. 6:4-12 - 174
Heb. 6:8 - 170
Heb. 6:11 - 170
Heb. 6:15 - 267
Heb. 6:18 - 159
Heb. 7:25 - 277
Heb. 8 - 12, 281
Heb. 8:1 - 276
Heb. 8:8 - 281
Heb. 8:10-12 - 153, 281
Heb. 8:13 - 274
Heb. 9:1 - 272
Heb. 9:9-10 - 272
Heb. 9:14 - 334
Heb. 9:16-17 - 10
Heb. 9:17 - 199
Heb. 9:19 - 272
Heb. 9:26 - 170
Heb. 9:27 - 123
Heb. 9:28 - 304, 306
Heb. 10 - 215, 281
Heb. 10:4 - 116, 132
Heb. 10:10-12 - 146
Heb. 10:12 - 276, 361
Heb. 10:12-14 - 176, 179
Heb. 10:14 - 153, 339
Heb. 10:14-17 - 281
Heb. 10:23 - 159, 179, 188, 195
Heb. 10:23-27 - 188
Heb. 10:26 - 189
Heb. 10:29 - 33
Heb. 10:36 -172
Heb. 10:38 - 142

Heb. 11 - 130
Heb. 11:1 - 117, 126, 195
Heb. 11:2 - 252
Heb. 11:5 - 305
Heb. 11:7 - 262
Heb. 11: 9 - 267, 268
Heb. 11:25 - 173
Heb. 11:28 - 169
Heb. 11:39,40 - 143
Heb. 12 - 332
Heb. 12:2 - 276
Heb. 12:3 - 169
Heb. 12:13 - 169
Heb. 12:14 - 174, 194, 304, 306
Heb. 12:14-15 - 190-192
Heb. 12:15 - 169
Heb. 12:16 - 169
Heb. 12:25-26 - 303
Heb. 12:28 - 172
Heb. 13:4 - 248
Heb. 13:7 - 170

JAMES

James 1:1 - 51
James 1:12 - 191
James 1:27 - 191
James 2 - 123, 126, 269
James 2:21 - 143
James 2:24 - 191
James 4:4 - 117, 191
James 5:7,8 - 187
James 5:7-9 - 191
James 5:12 - 191
James 5:14 - 51
James 5:15 - 51
James 5:17 - 43
James 5:19-20 - 191

1 PETER

1 Peter 1:5 - 191
1 Peter 1:7 - 191

1 Peter 1:9 - 191
1 Peter 1:10-11 - 103
1 Peter 1:13 - 191
1 Peter 1:18,19 - 167
1 Peter 1:20 - 191
1 Peter 1:23 - i, 98, 245
1 Peter 2 - 146
1 Peter 2:3 - 191
1 Peter 2:5,9 - 81
1 Peter 2:8 - 191
1 Peter 2:9 - 229
1 Peter 2:10 - 173
1 Peter 2:12 - 191
1 Peter 2:21 - 47
1 Peter 2:24 - 154
1 Peter 3:15 - 342
1 Peter 3:16 - 324, 329
1 Peter 3:19 - 84
1 Peter 3:20 - 118, 122
1 Peter 3:22 - 90, 276
1 Peter 4:5 - 191
1 Peter 4:7 - 191
1 Peter 4:12 - 191
1 Peter 4:13 - 191
1 Peter 4:16 - 191
1 Peter 4:17 - 191
1 Peter 4:19 - 191
1 Peter 5:1 - 191
1 Peter 5:4 - 191
1 Peter 5:8 - 3
1 Peter 5:10 - 191
1 Peter 5:14 - 324, 329

2 Peter

2 Peter 1:11 - 90
2 Peter 1:18 - 237
2 Peter 1:20 - ii, 12, 349
2 Peter 1:20-21 - 32
2 Peter 1:21 - 33
2 Peter 2 - 234
2 Peter 2:4 - 229
2 Peter 2:5 - 262
2 Peter 2:17 - 229
2 Peter 2:5 - 118, 123
2 Peter 2:20 - 191
2 Peter 3 - 233, 238, 240, 347
2 Peter 3:1-7 - 232
2 Peter 3:6 - 227, 234
2 Peter 3:7 - 243
2 Peter 3:12 - 111, 347
2 Peter 3:13 - 347

1 John

1 John 1 - 76, 329, 340
1 John 1:7 - 167
1 John 1:7-9 - 153, 333
1 John 1:9 - 329, 340
1 John 2:3-9 - 191
1 John 2:8 - 191
1 John 2:13,14 - 154, 191
1 John 2:17, 18 - 191
1 John 2:18-20 - 354
1 John 2:24 - 191
1 John 2:28 - 191
1 John 3 - 340
1 John 3:1-3 - 245
1 John 3:2-3 - 295
1 John 3:8 - 43, 245
1 John 3:9 - 188
1 John 3:12 - 244, 252
1 John 4:4 - 154, 159
1 John 5:4 - 154, 159

Jude

Jude 3 - ii, 26, 47
Jude 5 - 119
Jude 6 - 229, 254
Jude 13 - 229

Revelation

Rev. 1:1 - 291
Rev. 1-3 - 150

Verse Index

Rev. 1:3 - 148, 149, 158, 292, 297
Rev. 1:5 - 153, 167, 245
Rev. 1:7 - 21, 108, 114
Rev. 1:14 - 191
Rev. 1:19 - 302
Rev. 2:1 - 150
Rev. 2:5 - 152
Rev. 2:7 - 149, 154, 155, 297, 311
Rev. 2:8 - 150
Rev. 2:10 - 152
Rev. 2:11 - 149, 154, 155, 297
Rev. 2:12 - 150
Rev. 2:13 - 195
Rev. 2:16 - 152
Rev. 2:17 - 149, 154, 156, 297
Rev. 2:22 - 299
Rev. 2:25 - 195
Rev. 2:26 - 155, 157
Rev. 2:29 - 149, 297
Rev. 3 - 153
Rev. 3:1 - 151
Rev. 3:3 - 158, 195
Rev. 3:4 - 159
Rev. 3:5 - 152, 156, 159
Rev. 3:6 - 149, 297
Rev. 3:7 - 151
Rev. 3:8 - 160
Rev. 3:10 - 151, 152, 299
Rev. 3:11 - 195
Rev. 3:11-12 -160
Rev. 3:13 - 149, 297
Rev. 3:14 - 151
Rev. 3:21 - 159, 161, 277, 362
Rev. 3:22 - 149, 152, 297
Rev. 4 - 149
Rev. 4:1 - 307, 319
Rev. 5:10-24 - 158
Rev. 5:12 - 109
Rev. 6:4 - 298
Rev. 6:9 - 158, 189, 310
Rev. 6:12 - 300
Rev. 6:12-14 - 300
Rev. 6:16 - 300, 303, 306, 346

Rev. 6:17 - 346
Rev. 7 - 305, 306, 353
Rev. 7:1-8 - 364
Rev. 7:13 - 167
Rev. 7:14 - 167, 300, 348
Rev. 8:7 - 20
Rev. 8:8 - 20, 301
Rev. 8:12 - 300
Rev. 9 - 300
Rev. 9:14 - 300
Rev. 10:6 - 306
Rev. 10:6,7 - 300
Rev. 11 - 301, 305
Rev. 11:3 - 301
Rev. 11:6 - 187
Rev. 11:11 - 297
Rev. 11:13 - 300
Rev. 11:15 - 89, 238, 245, 307
Rev. 11:15-19 - 300
Rev. 11:19 - 20
Rev. 12 - 215, 238, 353
Rev. 12:4 - 300
Rev. 12:6 - 157, 301
Rev. 12:10 - 90
Rev. 12:11 - 159
Rev. 12:12 - 292
Rev. 12:14 - 11, 292
Rev. 12:17 - 118, 163, 167, 194, 304, 348
Rev. 13 - 193
Rev. 13:1-3 - 345
Rev. 13:8 - 10
Rev. 13:8 - 128
Rev. 13:10 - 341
Rev. 13:18 - 345
Rev. 14 - 215, 250, 288, 305, 306, 353
Rev. 14:1-5 - 302, 364
Rev. 14:6 - 120
Rev. 14:8 - 301
Rev. 14:11 - 186, 292, 304, 340
Rev. 14:12 - 118, 163, 167, 194, 302, 341, 348
Rev. 14:13 - 34, 149
Rev. 14:14 - 301, 302, 305-306,

364

Rev. 14:15 - 305, 360
Rev. 14:18 - 305
Rev. 14:20 - 106, 301
Rev. 15:3 - 190
Rev. 16:3 - 301
Rev. 16:10 - 90, 229
Rev. 16:12 - 300
Rev. 16:15 - 149
Rev. 16:18 - 300
Rev. 17 - 71, 301
Rev. 17:12,17 - 90
Rev. 18 - 301
Rev. 19 - 199, 307
Rev. 19:6 - 314
Rev. 19:9 - 149
Rev. 19:14 - 27
Rev. 19:16 - 89
Rev. 19:19-20 - 241
Rev. 20 - 199, 288, 301, 360
Rev. 20:1,2 - 20
Rev. 20:1-6 - 196
Rev. 20:3,4 - 364
Rev. 20:4 - 158
Rev. 20:5,6 - 115
Rev. 20:6 - 149, 158, 306
Rev. 20:8 - 363
Rev. 20:10 - 240, 241
Rev. 20:11 - 234
Rev. 20:11-15 - 84, 191, 195, 197, 240-241, 312-313
Rev. 20:15 - 111, 156
Rev. 21 - 12, 19, 199, 248
Rev. 21:2 - 286
Rev. 21:9-10 - 167-168, 286
Rev. 21:17 - 255
Rev. 21:24 - 119
Rev. 22 - 12, 19, 113, 199, 215
Rev. 22:2 - 155, 242, 311
Rev. 22:3-5 - 314
Rev. 22:7 - 149
Rev. 22:14 - 39, 117-118, 133, 148, 140, 155, 163-164, 166-168, 194, 242, 248, 302, 311, 348

Rev. 22:16 - 150